Intimacy and the Anxieties of Cinematic Flesh

Intimacy and the Anxieties of Cinematic Flesh

Between Phenomenology and Psychoanalysis

Patrick Fuery

BLOOMSBURY ACADEMIC
NEW YORK · LONDON · OXFORD · NEW DELHI · SYDNEY

BLOOMSBURY ACADEMIC
Bloomsbury Publishing Inc
1385 Broadway, New York, NY 10018, USA
50 Bedford Square, London, WC1B 3DP, UK
29 Earlsfort Terrace, Dublin 2, Ireland

BLOOMSBURY, BLOOMSBURY ACADEMIC and the Diana logo are trademarks of Bloomsbury Publishing Plc

First published in the United States of America 2023
Paperback edition published 2024

Copyright © Patrick Fuery, 2023, 2024

For legal purposes the Acknowledgments on p. xiv constitute an extension of this copyright page.

Cover design: Eleanor Rose
Cover image: Rachel Wiesz in The Favourite, 2018, Dir. Yorgos Lanthimos © Alamy

All rights reserved. No part of this publication may be reproduced or transmitted in any form or by any means, electronic or mechanical, including photocopying, recording, or any information storage or retrieval system, without prior permission in writing from the publishers.

Bloomsbury Publishing Inc does not have any control over, or responsibility for, any third-party websites referred to or in this book. All internet addresses given in this book were correct at the time of going to press. The author and publisher regret any inconvenience caused if addresses have changed or sites have ceased to exist, but can accept no responsibility for any such changes.

Library of Congress Cataloging-in-Publication Data

Names: Fuery, Patrick, 1957-author.
Title: Intimacy and the anxieties of cinematic flesh: between phenomenology and psychoanalysis/Patrick Fuery.
Description: New York: Bloomsbury Academic, 2023. | Includes bibliographical references and index. | Summary: "Combining two distinct philosophical fields to the study of cinema, Patrick Fuery proposes the first study showing how phenomenology and psychoanalysis are explored through their commonalities rather than differences"– Provided by publisher.
Identifiers: LCCN 2022028556 (print) | LCCN 2022028557 (ebook) | ISBN 9781501376351 (hardback) | ISBN 9781501376320 (paperback) | ISBN 9781501376344 (epub) | ISBN 9781501376337 (pdf) | ISBN 9781501376313 (ebook other)
Subjects: LCSH: Psychoanalysis and motion pictures. | Motion pictures–Philosophy. | Motion pictures–Psychological aspects.
Classification: LCC PN1995.9.P783 F835 2023 (print) | LCC PN1995.9.P783 (ebook) | DDC 791.4301/9–dc23/eng/20220929
LC record available at https://lccn.loc.gov/2022028556
LC ebook record available at https://lccn.loc.gov/2022028557

ISBN: HB: 978-1-5013-7635-1
PB: 978-1-5013-7632-0
ePDF: 978-1-5013-7633-7
eBook: 978-1-5013-7634-4

Typeset by Deanta Global Publishing Services, Chennai, India

To find out more about our authors and books visit www.bloomsbury.com and sign up for our newsletters.

*This one is for my family, who are all that really matter. Joshua, Noah, and Morgan who give me more joy, more happiness, and more delight than they know.
For Kelli, the love of my life. You really are a gift from the Universe. Once more but even more so, I am grateful for you.*

CONTENTS

List of Illustrations ix
Preface xi
Acknowledgments xiv

Where Intimacy-Anxiety Was, There (Cinematic) Flesh Shall Become: Toward an Introduction 1

1 The Intimate Spectator, the Cinematic Ego, and the Nothing (To Be Anxious About) 19

   The Spectator's Othered Consciousness 20
   The Spectator and the Cinematic Ego 30
   The Enthymematic 45
   a) The *Ego* and Narcissism 47
   b) Enthymematic *Lacunae* and/as Consciousness Modifications 54

2 Cinema's Enduring Object and Time 57

   Two Models of Time and the Now in Freud and Husserl 59
   Cinema's Enduring Object; the Enduring Object of Cinema 73
   Flesh in Time—Condensing Presentification and the Struggle for the Now: *Don't Look Now* 93

3 Four Modalities of Intimate and Anxious (Cinematic) Space 103

   A Psychoanalytic Secret 111
   A Phenomenological Paradox 112
   The Internal as Intimacy Projected into the External Space which Creates Anxiety (Projected Forfeiture) 113
   The Internal as Intimacy Projected into the External Space which Produces Intimacy (the Projected Familiar) 119

The External as Intimacy Introjected into the Internal, Producing Intimacy (Introjected Familiarity); And the Inversion (External Intimacy Producing Anxiety) (Introjected Defamiliarization) 125

The External as Anxiety Introjected into the Internal, Producing Anxiety (Introjected Crisis); And Its Inversion, External Anxiety Producing Intimacy (Introjected Masochism) 130

4 Shading the Real: Cinema's Sensual Phantasms 135

Lacan's Real 137
Husserl's Irreal 141
Phantasy of the Intimate ir-Real 150
On Semblance 159

5 Passionate Abnormalities and the Disturbances of Wildness 167

Wild Meaning and the Wolves 170
Owness, Nature, and the Sensually Seen Body 178
Wildness and the Corporeal Sublime 182
Passionate Abnormalities 184

6 The Desire to Not Be Protected: Breathless Desires of the Nightmare 199

Nightmares' Aporiastic Howness 200
Nullity: Nightmare As the Deceptive Object 206
Belief (At the Point of Collapse) 209
Phallocentric and Racist Nightmares at the Level of the Repressed 212
Liquification of Flesh at the Level of the Double Ego 218
The Mirroring Effect of the Nightmare at the Level of Desire 226
Feminine Sexuality and Daughter-Mother Conflict 228
Hysteria as Resistance; Flight as Sexual Act and Surplus Jouissance 230

Bibliography 235
Index 239

ILLUSTRATIONS

Figures

1. Freud's model in *The Interpretation of Dreams* 64
2. The Wolf Man's drawing of the wolves 172

Diagrams

1. Freud's model in *Project for a Scientific Psychology* 60
2. Freud's model in *The Interpretation of Dreams* 62
3 and 4. Husserl's models of time in *PICT* 67
5. Husserl's time-consciousness model and Hitchcock's *Rear Window* scene 79
6. From "*Seminar on 'The Purloined Letter'*" 140
7. From *Seminar XX, On Feminine Sexuality, the Limits of Love and Knowledge: Encore* 160

Images

1. Rear Window 76
2. Rear Window 77
3. Rear Window 77
4. "I wanted to be loved because I was great . . ." from *Tree of Life* 84
5. "I'm nothing" from *Tree of Life* 87
6. "Look at the glory around us . . . the trees . . . the birds" from *Tree of Life* 87

7 From *Tree of Life* 88
8 From *Tree of Life* 88
9 "I lived in shame; I was disloyal to it all. A foolish man." From *Tree of Life* 89
10 From *Tree of Life* 89
11 "Father . . . Father . . . Father, always you wrestle inside me; always you will" from *Tree of Life* 90
12 From *Tree of Life* 92
13 From *Tree of Life* 92
14 From *Don't Look Now* 98
15 From *Gravity* 116
16 From *Roma* 123
17 From *Roma* 124
18 From *Dogtooth* 134
19 From *The Wicker Man* 148
20 From *The Wicker Man* 148
21 From *The Favourite* 154
22 From *The Favourite* 155
23 From *The Favourite* 155
24 From *Trouble Every Day* 191
25 From *Trouble Every Day* 191

PREFACE

In *Phantasy, Image Consciousness, and Memory* (HUA XXIII) Edmund Husserl asks, "What is it *to leave a thing undecided?*".[1] If the "thing" here is a film and how we approach it, one might say that it has never been left, just attended to in innumerable ways. Yet many of these "ways" are contested, divergent, and apparently incompatible to the point that to focus on one seems to compel a leaving of others. Perhaps the key to Husserl's seemingly disarming question is *undecided*; to "leave" a critical approach for another, divorcing oneself from alternative positions, is to take up with another so all else is undecided. Contained within such an annulment is the possibility that what is left is not dismissed but can instead be rendered as *undecided*. This is to suggest, as Freud once did, that we are condemned to exist in the shadow of the unfinished business (of "childhood").

Furthermore, Husserl's question invites us to regard the status of the thing as existing in indecision. In doing so the very *nature* of the thing becomes the focus of attention—and of course this is phenomenology in all its pleasurable complexities. We have, to continue in the Husserlian spirit, shifted our attentive glance toward something else. If we do not leave the thing undecided, then we have taken up the critical attitude; we have decided to try and understand the essence of the thing itself. If we "become" a Deleuzian, a Lacanian, a Foucauldian, a semiotician, an investigator of ideology, gender analysis, or race, a film historian, a researcher in LGBTQI+ ... each approach leaves the cinematic thing undecided as it tries to decide what the cinematic thing is from its own critical perspective. Indeed, the trajectories of film analysis are all paths to leaving things unresolved so as to give order to the thing itself. Husserl's question has another dimension, for it also foregrounds the intentionality of "what is it to leave." That is, what happens to us when we make this decision, take up the intent to investigate from a certain position knowing that so much will be left undecided? Sometimes we do this with awareness, sometimes through tradition, sometimes in innocence, and sometimes with resigned pragmatism. No

---

[1] *Phantasie, Bildbewusstsein, Erinnerung (1898–1925)*. The quote appears in the Appendix 'The Modifications of Believing: Belief (Certainty), Inclination, Doubt, and so on, in the Sphere of Simple Intuition' p. 338.

matter which, the end result is that the thing itself will always remain undecided.

I have teased apart, perhaps overly so, this question of Husserl's to acknowledge that this book is just as tormented as any with the choices to be made regarding its theoretical approaches and the absences to be worked around in terms of scholarship and examples. However, it was precisely these issues that formed the embryonic ideas and questions. Always haunting the form and content of the argument was this awareness that so much is left undecided. Rather than try to cover everything in an attempt to address all that is left aside, these absences underpinned a fundamental aspect of the investigation. More is said in the Introduction on the strategies adopted to engage phenomenology, psychoanalysis, and cinema; suffice to say for the moment that the opening gambit was to ask if such a conversation between the three is at all possible, and to address the vexatious issue of how to not leave either phenomenology or psychoanalysis when one of these systems of thinking is adopted. What perhaps does require one additional comment here is what *types* of phenomenological and psychoanalytic approaches are taken up, and how they are played out in the cinematic examples.

Given the extensive work (cinematic and otherwise) that has been done over the last 120 years or so since Freud and Husserl produced their disruptive, era-defining systems of thought, it may seem counter-intuitive to focus on these two almost entirely. Both film philosophy and film psychoanalysis have created extraordinarily rich traditions, flowing out from their core agendas to influence, by way of example, the critical approaches of feminism, gender studies, race (including post-colonialism), Continental philosophy (in particular), aesthetics, ideology, and historicism. In their own traditions there have been divergences (each leaving certain things undecided), notably, Maurice Merleau-Ponty has strongly shaped a great deal of the phenomenological approaches to film and Jacques Lacan for psychoanalysis and cinema. In some ways it seems that Husserl, in particular, had been left undecided, as well as certain aspects of both Freud and Lacan, in understanding film as a mode of thinking in itself. This became the starting point, quickly reframed by the question *is it possible to bring (Husserlian) phenomenology and (Freudian) psychoanalysis into conversation to devise a new way of approaching film?* Here the thing(s) left undecided were many: what of Heidegger, Merleau-Ponty, Bergson, and even Deleuze? What of Object Relations, Melanie Klein, Wilfred Bion, or Christopher Bollas? And what of the scholarship that has emerged within these fields? This is an issue that I have attempted to address in the Introduction. Finally, two concepts were adopted to explore the relationship between phenomenology, psychoanalysis, and film: intimacy and anxiety. These were chosen not because they are necessarily shared or dominant themes in these fields (although it is easy to see some overlaps), but because they offered a way to explore how viable it is to bring these complex systems of thought together. The strategy here was to see if a relationship between intimacy and anxiety can be articulated in terms of collocating phenomenology and psychoanalysis in terms of cinema's material (including form, socio-cultural domains, and spectatorship).

ACKNOWLEDGMENTS

Without anxiety, I freely acknowledge the many who, with great intellect, humor, and friendship, contributed to whatever good parts exist here. As always, it goes without saying that the convolutions, errors, and misjudgments are all entirely my own.

An author could not want for a more enjoyable experience working with a publisher than Bloomsbury and I thank everyone there for the efforts they gave this work. I doubt anyone could wish for a better editor than Katie Gallof. In equal parts she gave excellent advice, support, and good humor. Katie's willingness to take on this project was a considerable part of its story. I also wish to thank Stephanie Grace-Petinos who gave such wonderful guidance—clearly a very generous person! I am grateful to Daniele Struppa and his enthusiastic engagement with ideas; he is a valued colleague and friend and I continue to appreciate his support both professionally and personally. Horst Ruthrof is a researcher I have long admired. His intellectual rigor and love of ideas are quite simply inspirational. His work has provided me with the fertile ground of phenomenology and patiently tested my psychoanalytic proclivities. I also thank Christopher Bollas and Whitney Davis for their expansive minds and the works they have produced for us all. I also thank my students in the Creative and Cultural Industries program at Chapman University. I "guinea-pigged" them with ideas as I was writing. Although they had no choice, they engaged with the concepts in the enthusiastic manner that youth and American life allows. My mother, who passed away as the final edits were taking place, taught me the value of not taking life too seriously. No doubt she would have put a copy of this on the shelf with my other books and not read a page of it; but her pride was worth far, far more. For Joshua, Noah, and Morgan—well, no one could ask for three better sons. Each one has given me more than they will ever know. I am grateful to each of them. And of course, Kelli. Beyond words, Kelli is the center of everything for me. As my best friend she was always there, as a reader she was perfect for not only is she eminently qualified to read such material but also did so with a balance of encouragement and critique, and as a partner, she gave all with such a generous spirit. She encapsulated my attitude towards this project when she told others that I was like a dog, oblivious to the world, happily rolling in the long grass. To her, I express my eternal gratitude and love.

Where Intimacy-Anxiety Was, There (Cinematic) Flesh Shall Become

Toward an Introduction

There is no avoiding the consequential issues, with all their enticing potential as well as entrapments, that shadow any and all explorations that lay before us. Notably, how does one achieve an effective integration and balance between cinema and the critical approaches of phenomenology and psychoanalysis when: (a) the philosophical concepts, ideas, histories, and challenges are immense, complex, and long-standing?; (b) there is a need to work through some tightly woven concepts and allow them to enter into a dialogue with equally tightly woven concepts from a different field?; (c) in doing so these vast analytic systems need to be re-imagined, all the while locating the ideas alongside and within the cinematic implications?; and (d) there is a constant requirement to legitimize a "usefulness" of such material for cinema? It is not enough, for example, to say that when dealing with cinema, this book positions it as a type of philosophical discourse in itself, hoping that will ensure a tighter connection between the films and concepts. Just as it is quite inadequate to seek out fundamental ideas and concepts from phenomenology and psychoanalysis, hoping that if they look similar and sound similar that they will end up being similar. We should all proceed with caution in alignments that have such silkiness to their appearance and ease to their connectivity.

If phenomenology and psychoanalysis are two "languages" seeming to share certain purposes, lineages, and issues, then cinema may prove to be our Rosetta Stone, enabling us to explore and understand them through a dialogue. Of course, the inversion is also the case: "cinema" becomes something different precisely because of this phenomenologico-psychoanalytic critical intervention. At the heart of this issue is one of the key motivations for this book. That is, rather than solely (simply?) being an examination of potential combinations of phenomenology and psychoanalysis as critical methodologies, the discussions *need* cinema to make such an examination possible, as well as acknowledging cinema's potential to be an iteration of critical analysis in itself. Hence the concepts of anxiety, intimacy, and flesh are not simply illustrations and examples of representation (i.e., how films represent them or construct them as part of their "language" and narratives). Instead, cinematic anxiety, for example, is seen here as a concept along the same lines as we find in phenomenology or psychoanalysis. In these terms, anxiety is positioned as an essential part of cinema, and intimacy as an essential process of becoming a spectator and sustaining that role. That said, there is not a purity here, and it is sometimes the case that when cinema is dealing (philosophically speaking) with something like intimacy we can see a comparable narrative or formal version (an intimate scene, a film's evocation of intimacy, a moment of anxiety-inducing apprehension, and so on). These complex and somewhat unstable terms of intimacy and anxiety are used here precisely to allow the exploration of combining and interchanging phenomenological and psychoanalytic ideas to take place. This is the foundation of the relationship between cinema and critical thinking in this book.

If we can speak of layers of a book there are, essentially, three here:

First, how Husserlian phenomenology and Freudian/Lacanian psychoanalysis, so often seen as contradistinctive, might be explored through their potential commonalities rather than differences. The aim here is not to force some syncretic model, but rather to allow a much-needed conversation to take place.

Second, to postulate an approach to film through this phenomenological/ psychoanalytic reconceptualization. Within the limitations of a single book this is a gesture toward devising a new type of theorizing, moving away from the established models found in film theory based in the two distinct approaches of phenomenology and psychoanalysis. Somewhat ironically this will involve, on the one hand, returning to the classical/foundational ideas in Edmund Husserl's phenomenology to move beyond recent phenomenological approaches to film; and diverging from the classical/ foundations of psychoanalytic approaches to film to offer a fresh perspective on this important theory in cinema. To this end, the discussions focus almost entirely on the foundational thinkers, notably: Husserl, Sigmund Freud, and Jacques Lacan, and some of the "followers," Edith Stein, Roman Ingarden, Maurice Merleau-Ponty, Mikel Dufrenne in phenomenology, Melanie Klein, Ernest Jones, Julia Kristeva, and Rosine Lefort in psychoanalysis. The deliberate strategy to focus on these original thinkers (Husserl, Freud, and Lacan) is because is through their works that we might develop a new and distinctive approach. This proved to be a truly substantive amount of work, and an immense amount of ideas and concepts to deal with. The absence of the rich scholarly material that has become phenomenological film theory and psychoanalytic film theory is not meant in any way to dismiss the work of many fine and significant scholars.¹ The aim here is to return to the origins of phenomenology and psychoanalysis, and to remain true to this required an approach which directly engages with these formative thinkers and their work. The "return" to Husserl, Freud, and Lacan is a necessary strategy given the aim of the book is to explore phenomenology and psychoanalysis as combinable and combined. For this reason alone it is essential to address the ideas in their unmediated (as "pure" as possible) versions. The other motivation is to address the lack of a sustained engagement with Husserl in film philosophy. Other than Alan Casebier's *Film and Phenomenology* (1991),² film phenomenology has been dominated by Maurice Merleau-Ponty's ideas and works.³ This is, of course, a legitimate turn, but it has left a significant gap in the scholarship.

Third, to work through and test the viability of these first two layers, three interconnected "concepts" are proposed—intimacy, anxiety, and flesh. Anxiety is situated as a driving process of the cinematic in both its materiality and the experiential. Anxiety is posited as the agitational connection for the cinematic relational experience. For this relationship to take place there must be a type of intimacy.

These intimate anxieties and anxious intimacies will be examined as they construct, and are played out, in "flesh."⁴ The book will posit that it is by forming an intimate relationship of attachment with the film that we become spectators.⁵ Let us recall that Old English gives us *flæsc*—flesh; and from *Beowulf* we gain the wonderfully descriptive *flæschama*—flesh-covering, as in a garment (i.e., the body as dressing for the soul; *hama* is also womb), *flæsclic*—carnal, and *flæschord*—the body (flesh and hord, treasure or hoard). Hence, flesh is variously a covering for the soul, carnality, related to the womb, and valued. It simultaneously is seen as absolutely distinct from the soul and carnal yet valued and bearing life. "Flesh," here, is what is formed in cinema through intimacy and anxiety; "flesh" is the body, and

---

¹Rather than list these here, when appropriate I have noted key scholars throughout the discussions.
²Casebier's book focuses on ideas of representation and cinema; he also deliberately argues this against Lacanian psychoanalysis. As noted, here the emphasis is how these issues can be brought into conversation.
³One specific example may illustrate the difficulties and limitations of this turn. Without addressing Husserl's as yet not examined *Nachlass*, this bias has also led to a certain distortion of Husserl's actual position. (cf. e.g., Ruthrof 2021).
⁴Flesh has become a well-worked term in film phenomenology via the influential work of Vivian Sobchack (1992, 2004), however this has been overwhelmingly based on Merleau-Ponty's work. The use of flesh here rests very much on Husserl, and the combinatory ideas with psychoanalysis. This is the difference of the term here.
⁵Film is our exemplar, but it is possible to imagine this also works when we look at a painting, read a novel, and so on. What shifts is the materiality of the text; but they all invite and require intimacy. That said, it is worth recalling Lessing's *Laocoon* which has set up runnels of thought on the affects of image vs. word.

the attendant aspects, that results from, and is a residual of, film's *eidetic* moments; flesh is not the nothingness of being (the denial and refutation of subjectivity), nor is it a corporeal assertion of the "body," even though both of these are understandable summations. Flesh is the more exposed, more vulnerable, the less mediated (raw), the more intimate, and therefore more anxious. In these ways, flesh is a curious combination of both subject and body as they are played out through intimacy and anxiety. It is through the linking of flesh with intimacy and anxiety that the term is explored in a different way than existing (Merleau-Ponty based) film scholarship, along with the emphasis on Husserl, Freud, and Lacan. Each chapter explores how concepts and critical processes can be worked through in terms of this complex and somewhat slippery term "flesh." In this sense, flesh combines with, for example, time, space, wildness, the nightmare, and so on, in each dedicated chapter. Thus, flesh is used throughout to mark an instability and simultaneously interconnection between intimacy and anxiety. This is to acknowledge that flesh is an agitational word, problematizing, and often confronting. It also acknowledges that flesh connects with body and subject in quite unique ways, based on anxiety (the loss of subjectivity, the reduction of the body) and intimacy (carnality and soul-covering). Finally, flesh is employed to mark the intimate spectator and their anxious relations.

I wish to eschew the more apparent relationship between anxiety, intimacy and cinema (i.e., films that represent anxiety and intimacy or have them as their principal narrative theme), although some films of this type will certainly be discussed. Instead, the book proposes that intimacy and anxiety are deeply recurring processes and fundamental to cinema's existence; they are an essential part of film's capacity to engage us. Rather than being a theme or representational mode, intimacy and anxiety are seen here as core defining attributes of cinema as both an individual and shared/cultural process. Understanding these attributes, in turn, allows us to explore the combinations of phenomenology and psychoanalysis. Similarly, the cinematic re-imagining of anxiety and intimacy means that we can begin to think of these as analytic concepts, and processes of analysis, rather than themes.

The binding of anxiety and intimacy in this sense "leads" to flesh (and its cinematic presences), with all its carnality, life-giving, embodiment, and valued qualities. To this end, a key part of the ensuing work will consider how and why this binding takes place. Here we can parallel Freud's *Wo Es war, soll Ich werden* (where id was, there ego shall be); or, as Lacan translated it *La où était ça, le je doit être* (417; 425: 2006) (where it was, there I shall become).[6] This is re-imagined here and can be rendered as "where

---

[6] Lacan is forcefully adamant on this. His analysis in (and the title is telling) "The Freudian Thing: or the Meaning of the Return to Freud in Psychoanalysis" of Freud's German includes a word-by-word breakdown of why the English translation is flawed.

intimacy was, there anxiety shall be" or "where intimacy was, there anxious being shall become." In cinematic terms this can be further reconfigured as "where intimacy-anxiety was, there (cinematic) flesh shall become." There is something altogether apt in linking intimacy to psychoanalysis's great theme of the id, for there is an uneasy, compelling, and excessive aspect to both; just as anxiety as an egocentrism returns us to ideas in both psychoanalysis and phenomenology. Both of these complex couplings will be taken up throughout the book.

Another issue that invariably arises when we engage with philosophically driven ideas and textual systems, in this case cinema, is striking a balance between the concepts and films. The approach here is based very much on the idea that film is not simply a textual exemplar or a way to illustrate the ideas, but a way of thinking through the concepts. I ultimately decided the most appropriate way of handling the material was to establish the key concepts from phenomenology and psychoanalysis, working through the issues of how best to combine them, and then bring the films in as a way to address the combinatory aspects. This did mean that the discussions of the films tend to come in later in the chapters. Hopefully this has enabled a more integrated film-to-concept approach.

So far these terms of anxiety, intimacy, and flesh have been spoken of in terms of this binding, and how we might deliberate on each in terms of the others. At this point the reader may well be saying "well, ok, but what is meant by each of these?" This is the work of the following chapters, and to locate this, and the overall project of this book, a short summation of each chapter follows.

Chapter 1 explores how three interconnected, foundational ideas from Husserl, Freud, and Lacan can be re-imagined in terms of cinema, and the forming of an understanding of intimacy, anxiety, and flesh within such contexts: first, to be a film spectator is to take up an othered conscious; second, the spectator is formed within and alongside what is called here the cinematic ego; and third, the cinematic ego and attendant othered conscious are enthymemic in the active processes of spectating, which is seen as based on lack, and the missing object born from the Nothing. The chapter commences with a discussion of "Nothing," initially from a Kierkegaardian perspective. This is Kierkegaard's "profound secret of innocence", which is the relationship of Nothing to anxiety. The point we are aiming for is to expand and explore the core issue, that is, how Nothing, anxiety, and intimacy "develop" the cinematic spectator, and how this can be devised within, and even be formational in, the analytic experience. There will be reason to return to this conceptualization of the Nothing, in part because it is one of the most crucial aspects of phenomenology and psychoanalysis; and its cinematic turns are full of possibilities. The term "analytic experience" is coined here to refer to those moments where phenomenology, psychoanalysis, and cinema come together to form an interpretative moment. In other words, the analytic experience recognizes cinema's critical capacities (rather than something "solely" to be analyzed), and the possibilities gained in bringing psychoanalysis and phenomenology together within such a determining context.

The chapter then proposes the idea of the spectator's othered consciousness, first by contrasting it to the "innocent" spectator of a single conscious, and then to the othered consciousness of critical awareness and activity. "Single" and "othered" are linked directly to both phenomenological and psychoanalytic concepts in terms of a "composing Nothing." "Composing" is a strongly based phenomenological term of action and intentionality, while "Nothing" takes us to psychoanalysis. Perhaps the simplest way of thinking about this Nothing in terms of psychoanalysis is through the dream. Our dreams are often unremembered by us, that is, they remain a nothing to the conscious mind. When they are recalled, they can appear meaningless (meaning has the status of no-thing), however for psychoanalysis what appears contains a Nothing to meaning. That is, their meanings are disguised and buried, requiring work to become a meaningful something. Of course, this Nothing is not not-something; it always has the capacity to mean, always exists in the meaningful possibilities. This idea is extended to cinema via phenomenology to become the composing Nothings. In all film experiencings there are almost endless nothings that go unnoticed, unseen, and unheard; and even when many are noticed they can still retain the status of nothing. Cinematic composing Nothings are the intimate moments when the spectator (which can operate at the cultural level—there are cultural intimacies in constant operation) translate through these Nothings into the meaningful somethings. Composing Nothings is the work performed to gain and enact meaning through the formations of intimacy. These composing Nothings are possible through, and are a requirement of, othered conscious, which emerges through the intimacies formed in the act of spectating, and necessarily includes acts of what Husserl calls *Gewahren* ("be" and/or become aware (of)). This "becoming aware" is the birth of the intimate othered conscious spectator.

The othered conscious spectator is thus committed to the work, in both senses of the phrase: committed to the film as (aesthetic, pleasurable, loved, traumatic, and so on) work; and committed to working with the film in the formations of meaning. This means that all versions of interpretation (including intimacies and anxieties) emerge from the othered consciousness precisely because of this entwining of spectator and film. In this sense, the othered consciousness takes place when the spectator formulates meaning, experiences an affective relationship, in some way locates the sense of self in a relational context with the film, or, at the most critically and reflexive moments, engages with the (phenomenological) experience of the experience. Through this, the othered conscious spectator and the film exist in potentia as what Husserl calls a "universal apodictically experienceable structure" (1950: §12). Although the caveat here must be that this is only possible within the larger critical apparatus of the analytic experience, such a structure could emerge as the spectator reflexively engages with her self's relationship(s) with the film.

The next section of the chapter engages with the issue of the ego, proposing that we can speak of a cinematic ego. I take this moment to apologize to the reader (and do so once more in the chapter itself) for the unwieldy, yet necessary, distinctions made for the term "ego" between the phenomenology (Ego), psychoanalytic (ego), and the proposed combinatory version (*ego*). This is one of those moments where the term is shared but used in quite distinctive ways; the aim here is not to distill the word to a common point, but rather to pursue the possibilities of a version of *ego* which accommodates the various iterations and produces a sense emerging from the analytic experience. (Even within each of the analytic approaches there are variations—e.g., Lacan's use of ego is Freudian, but not entirely Freud's; Husserl's use shifts over time.) It is through this strategy that we can speak of a film's *ego*. It does not refer to the *ego* of a film, rather it is cinema's capacity (and necessity) to devise a relational context with the spectator which operates *as if there were* an ego involved. In order to develop this concept of the cinematic *ego* a number of ideas are taken up, including: the *ego* as coherency and the apodictic; Ego/*ego* and the flesh; and the sensuously seen "living" body as erotic object-choice. This leads us to the idea that the intimate spectator operates through the *ego*'s unstable, polymorphic relationships to the internal and external worlds. Intimacy is formed in part through *Gewahren*, that growing awareness or readiness to be attentive toward the other, be it the othered parts of our self (internal) or the others in the world (external). The instability of this is derived in part from intimacy's bond to anxiety, and the creative shifts that take place between the internal and external.

The next section takes up the idea that cinema operates with, and as, a "system" of enthymemic structures which are part of the devisements to negotiate relations of intimacy, anxiety, and indifference. These enthymemes, the missing components in versions of syllogisms which are "filled out" (cognitively, aesthetically, personally, perhaps even empathetically, and so on), provide further opportunity to consider another side to the Nothing in its anxious-ridden moments; that is, anxieties that surround meaning and its contestations, absences, and abandonments. This key enthymemic quality is explored in terms of the othered *ego* and its function in the intimate spectating acts. The doubled *ego* and the spectator are constructed from a comparison between Lacan's "two narcissisms" and Husserl's double Ego. This is integral to an understanding of the intimate spectator, particularly in terms of the anxieties of missing meanings. The chapter concludes by considering how enthymemic *lacunae* can act in terms of consciousness modifications and the cinematic variants.

Chapter 2 explores certain ideas on time, largely through two models from Freud and Husserl. The aim is not to arrive at an overview of time in phenomenology and psychoanalysis (an impossible project it would seem; and many a reader might reasonably ask "what, no Bergson?"[7]); rather it is to propose a combinatory model of time that enables us to also consider cinema's capacity to act as part of the analytic processes. Central to this is the following key idea: that cinematic now-points are formed in and through intimacy and thus form cinema's "enduring objects." The conceptual frame of enduring objects is taken to refer to temporality; its etymological gift is in its original meaning "to harden." The fluidity of time and cinema thus becomes entwined in this lasting fixity, this hardening of interpretative values and direction. In some ways this fixity in time is linked to the earlier discussion on enthymemic *lacunae* given that both are dealing with the negotiations of intimacy through the missing. Now-points, which are a central concept in Husserl's time discussions, are defined as the meaning-making moments in cinema, and as such they are interpretative points constructed and devised through time. This is intimacy as the meaningful moments in cinema, derived in this instance from temporality. The discussion aims to locate this sense of intimacy and time as part of the formation of the reflexive subject/spectator, which necessarily comes to include anxiety. This leads to the following proposal: that intimate now-points create the reflexive modality that allows the cinematic enduring objects to form, and in doing so time is recognized as part of the meaning-formation processes. This returns us to a core theme of this book, where intimacy is, there anxiety will follow, and in this instance foregrounding the temporal structure. Once we enter into an intimacy, in this case with time (i.e., temporal intimacies and the intimate formed in and through time), we are also entering into temporal anxieties, which means we need to account for anxiety in the enduring objects. More simply put, we can happily live most of our days "outside" of an awareness of time. Most certainly we need to keep dates, arrive on time, have schedules . . . but these are rarely intimate moments of time. Those moments of temporal intimacy (such as falling in love, experiencing passion, encountering death, and living in terror) reveal this sense of entering into an intimacy with time that necessarily envelopes anxiety across a vast range of guises.

To better understand the construction of the enduring cinematic object the chapter engages with a number of examples, beginning with a distinction between a type of functional/practical now-point in cinema and those that construct the enduring object; this is also the distinction

---

[7]Other readers may also ask "what, no Heidegger?" To remain true to the strategy of dealing with the foundational thinkers there is not enough space to deal with the important work of Bergson. Heidegger is omitted on the grounds that his philosophy of Being and his hermeneutics are a major deviation from the fundamentals of Husserlian phenomenology; nor is Heidegger's politics relevant to the topic of this book.

between time passing (the unintimate temporality) and temporal intimacy. The chapter then presents a different interpretation of these issues through two sub-sections premised on this idea of the intimacy and anxiety of the now: intimacy and anxiety of/as the past and future, using a scene from Terrence Malick's *Tree of Life* (2011); Bodies in time—presentification and the struggle for the now, using a scene from Nicolas Roeg's *Don't Look Now* (1973). These scenes are employed to explore Freud's model in *The Interpretation of Dreams* (and the related versions in *Project for a Scientific Psychology*) and Husserl's model in *The Phenomenology of Internal Time Consciousness*. In particular, the discussion centers around the concept of now-points (fixing moments in time to "gain" meanings) and Husserl's idea of presentifications to work through issues of nowness and its relationship to newness. Once more, the framing of the analysis is through intimacy and anxiety as producers of flesh.

The idea of presentification is heavily linked to Husserl's theories of representation and representational processes. Presentify and presentification are the generally accepted neologisms for *vergegenwärtigenden*. (*Vergegenwärtigungen* (to visualize) and *vergegenwärtigen* (to recall) suggest that presentification can also be seen as holding multiple meanings.) Presentification is an integral part of internal time-consciousness, devised within the context of reflection and critically utilized to define temporality within this intentionality. Simply put, presentification is in many ways premised on the now-points, which are the moments, phenomenologically speaking, when we are engaged with an intentionality to time. This is time as a meaning-producing construct, as well as a moment of (fixed, hardened) time as meaningful. At the most literal of levels, the entire length of a film is a now-point, distinguished from the temporality of the external world. In itself, a film is made up of a seemingly endless series of now-points. The reveal in a murder mystery, the outburst of laughter in a comedy when the joke is realized and acknowledged, the affirming first or last kiss in a romance are all obvious and heavily signaled now-points because they declare meaningfulness and interpretative resolution. What are less apparent (and therefore potentially more interesting) now-points are those that are not declared; these are composing Nothings based on time. From here the discussion links back to Freud's model of the dream, notably condensation, leading to the idea that presentification might be read through certain aspects of condensation. From this we can examine film as an example of what is termed here "condensing presentifications." That is, the acts of condensing and compressing to yield a register where things stand ontologically and even, potentially, hermeneutically equal. Cinema is a system of condensing presentifications; that is, our perception and inner consciousness apprehend such Objects as unities of time, as well as how they extend beyond themselves in time (memory, recollection, etc.). Condensing presentifications, then, are premised on the fluidity of meaning, the transitional nature of all interpretations so that they operate as "truth," but just for the moment. What this suggests is that cinematic condensing presentifications form newness in the now; this can be seen as their primary function.

Chapter 3 considers how phenomenology's construction of *epoché* can be utilized to understand the intimacies and anxieties of/for the othered flesh in spatiality. Space is seen as a dynamic, with the internal-external divide constantly being challenged and redrawn. Within this dynamic spatiality we encounter the distinctions and their blurring of the inside and outside, which includes the further division of internal-as-self and the externality of things. Any internalized thing (i.e., formed in a relation) becomes, potentially, part of the self, or redefined in this relationship as the "not external." The inversion is also possible, meaning that the externalized self becomes less self and more thing. "Space" is to be interpreted within the context of "thing," and "self"; these in turn link to the related concepts of "object" and "subject." Spatiality, then, is the field where these relationships and identities are formed and experienced; and cinematic spatiality is the place where the re-imagining of things and others are experienced. It is perhaps self-evident that this discussion of thingness relates back to the issues raised in terms of the Nothing (i.e., no-thing) and composing Nothings.

The chapter focuses on space as a phenomenological and psychoanalytic issue, commencing with the internal, external, and the idea of the thing. As with so much of the material at hand, figuring the "thing" is complicated because it is necessary to recognize that both phenomenology and psychoanalysis have versions of it. With phenomenology we are confronted with the issue of Kant's "thing-in-itself" and Husserl's digressive path of *cogitationes*, which can be thought of as "the experience (of things) to know." Psychoanalysis also engages with the "thing," most notably in Lacan's discussions (via Freud) of *das Ding*. Clearly the (phenomenological) Thing and the (psychoanalytic) *das Ding* are of different analytic orders. This leads to what may seem like an absurd question "why does cinema have things?" and the companion questions of "what is a cinematic thing? what is cinema's thingness?" These are the issues that are utilized to bring the analysis together, for the discussion engages with versions of the Husserlian Thing, the Lacanian *das Ding*, and cinematic thing(ness).

This leads to one of the key analytic issues in the distinction between the Thing and *das Ding*: that the former is exploring the negotiations of reality, and its things, by consciousness (in a sense, intentionality as well as the phenomenological Ego); while the latter is the analysis of the removal from reality because of its impossibilities. To work through this the chapter takes up, via Lacan, a psychoanalytic secret (based on the reality principle and the unconscious) and the solution to a phenomenological paradox (which involves the consequences to object-things once *epoché* is enacted). The final aspect of the Thing-*das Ding* configuration involves three attributes of Thingness: Thing as/in time (*res temporalis*); Thing as enduring (*res extensa*); Thing as/in space (*res materialis*). From this point it is possible to propose a relationship between Thingness-*das Ding* and flesh, which forms a core aspect of the cinematic thing as well as cinematic things (and why they exist).

To work through these ideas four cinematic modalities of things are proposed, each explored in combination with a film:

a. *The Internal as Intimacy Projected into the External Space Which Creates Anxiety (Projected Forfeiture).*

   This is the idea that something intimate to the self is projected out and creates anxiety; "forfeiture" is used to suggest that this process requires the giving up of something, that is, there is a "cost" involved which is attached to the anxiety. The film discussed is Alfonso Cuarón's *Gravity* (2013).

b. *The Internal as Intimacy Projected into the External Space Which Produces Intimacy (The Projected Familiar)*

   As distinct from the first modality, this iteration engages with intimacy rather than anxiety; or rather, the projecting of the internal into the external creates a relationship of intimacy because of this sense of the familiar. What is sustained in such projections is a familiarization of the external through the intimate. The two examples worked through offer differing exemplars of this type of projected intimacy. They are Claire Denis's *High Life* (2018) and Alfonso Cuarón's *Roma* (2018).

c. *The External as Intimacy Introjected into the Internal, Producing Intimacy (Introjected Familiarity); And the Inversion (External Intimacy Producing Anxiety) (Introjected Defamiliarization)*

   The first two modalities are primarily concerned with projective acts; the next two take up the idea of the equivalent introjections. Because both introjection modes have a parallel inversion, it felt expedient to discuss the two iterations at the same time. In this first case, this means introjected familiarity and introjected defamiliarization are read through notions of intimacy, even though the affective objects produced are distinguished by their relationship to intimacy and anxiety. The example used here to elaborate further on introjection and the *a priori* as corporeal and the *Umwelt* (the outside world/environment) and *Innenwelt* (the inner world) is Ingmar Bergman's *Persona* (1966).

d. *The External as Anxiety Introjected into the Internal, Producing Anxiety (Introjected Crisis); And Its Inversion, External Anxiety Producing Intimacy (Introjected Masochism)*

The first iteration of this modality is that of the external world as one of such anxious anarchy and threat that when it manages to bypass all defense mechanisms, it is introjected as anxiety. The anxious thing is made intimate in this introjection. The example of *Persona* (1966) is seen as a variation on this, only the introjection was based around intimacy's mirroring of anxiety; here only crisis ensues. However, in keeping with the overall argument, there is a need to recognize the role of intimacy within this introjected crisis. The chapter explores Yorgos Lanthimos's *Dogtooth* (2009) as a version of introjected masochism.

Chapter 4 tackles one of the most complex, and most likely unresolvable, issues between phenomenology and psychoanalysis—that of the unconscious. The approach here is to foreground the very nature of this question/issue in terms of analytic reflexivity and marginalia. That is, the unconscious is such a fundamental aspect of psychoanalysis, how can we speak of a critical bringing together if phenomenology does not have an equivalent? This sets up the reflexive attitude; this is a reflection on the performance of analysis. The strategy is to approach the whole issue in terms of the "real,", commencing with the idea that Husserl's concept of *Geltungsfundierungen*—the processes around the founding, or statements, of validity—can be seen as a tactic for recognizing the unconscious from a phenomenological position. For this to have any chance of analytic success these phenomenological validity formations will need to accommodate and modify all acts depending on the intentionality of consciousness. "Value" (or pleasure formations, the formations of the good, anxiety formations, and so on—the core driver is formations in a phenomenological sense) becomes uncertain at times, and what was held to be "as such" shifts in the modalities of consciousness. It is precisely these shifts that bear witness to the role of the conscious (and, it will be argued, the unconscious) in validity formations.

The chapter then tackles the fundamental issue of the unconscious in terms of the real, that is Lacan's concept of the Real and Husserl's investigation of the *irreal*. It can be noted here that the chapter sets up three iterations to distinguish between these critical articulations and the "real" (i.e., "reality," mostly in the sense of external reality, or how we might use in it a casual sense): Lacan's Real (capitalized), Husserl's *irreal*, and a synthesizing version (where possible) to form the concept of the *ir-Real*. If Lacan's Real is deeply embedded in the conceptualization of the unconscious (distinguished as it is from the socializing, discourse-based exchange system of the Symbolic and the self/ego-based Imaginary), and Husserl's *irreal* is the non-real as the fundamental material of phenomenological investigation, then the *ir-Real*, it is proposed, is the common ground and new material for the unconscious in the analytic experience (i.e., the two theoretical approaches and cinema as theoretical apparatus). Thus, the aim is to explore how cinema as phantasy, and as analytic marginalia, devises and promulgates the intimate *ir-Real*.

The discussion then turns to an exploration of another way of conceiving the *ir-Real* (in the real and phantasy)—that of *semblance*. Both Husserl and Lacan employ this term at various times in their works, to different ends and reasonings. By looking at semblance as a unifying concept, the *ir-Real* should become clearer in both the cinematic and analytic contexts. This opens up the path to a reading of *ir-Real* as an unpicking of the binarism of "real" (and therefore significant) and "not real" (and therefore less valued), which in turn leads to the idea of it as something not excluded from reality. For phenomenology, this is because the act of consciousness, in its processes of apprehensions, encounters and experiences: a real object; a memory of that object; a phantasy of that object; a filmed version of that object, and so on. The distinguishing of them is not primarily through their ontology, but their presentation and reference to consciousness. For psychoanalysis, the need to treat memories, phantasies, hallucinations, and dreams as if they are absolutely filled with meanings (perhaps more real than reality for the person) is crucial to the analysis. One of the most profound offerings made by psychoanalysis is this sense of reality in all those versions that seem antithetical to that term.

The ontological challenge provided by the *ir-Real* (notably in this positioning of cinema as phenomenologically re-presentational) is explored through Lanthimos's *The Favorite* and one particular technical device, that of the fish-eye lens. This is read through Lacan's idea of the anamorphic stain, his work on mimicry, and deception and what he calls the sexual aim. From this point it is possible to explore in more depth the idea of semblance, phantasy, and the *ir-Real*, particularly in terms of both Husserl's and Lacan's analytic versions of truth and knowledge. Semblance sets up relational contexts between phantasy and reality, experiencing consciousness (in this context, being/subject), and representational systems. Furthermore, this is why semblance helps resolve a difficulty, that is: how are we to negotiate the ways in which psychoanalysis holds the material of the analytic experience (conversion hysteria and the corporeal signifiers of psychical issues; our dreams; the forgetting of names, and so on) as apprehensions of the true and real; and how phenomenology requires a differentiation between real and phantasy as consequential. Husserl provides us with the distinction of phantasy, notably with the idea of sensuous phantasms, which are the distinctive apprehensions of phantasy—it is what enables a phantasy to be experienced as such, and not as the perception of something "real." In other words, they do not exist as such in the phantasy but are part of the apprehension of that phantasy as phantasy.

Chapter 5 takes up the idea of wildness as disruption and resistance, particularly in terms of flesh as the most disturbing yet attracting version of the corporeal. These disturbances encapsulate anxiety, attracting through intimacy, and attaching both to the moment. The initial impetus comes from Merleau-Ponty's final, incomplete work, *The Visible and the Invisible* with its conceptual frames, the agitational interpretative possibilities, of flesh and the wild, particularly the ideas of wild meaning, the intertwining, and the chiasm as they related to the body. In such terms *wild* is located in terms of consciousness and reality (following on from the previous chapter), as a relational context of body-to-idea as a Nothing or implicit, and the issue of language and silence and the body as Being in the world.

The psychoanalytic parallel (of this anxious disturbance of proper Being in the world as it is invigilated as wild) constructed in the chapter comes from a number of case studies, notably Freud's Wolf Man and Rosine Lefort's case study of the wolf boy. These case studies are exemplars of wildness and disturbance through the body, not just within the sense of the "transposed" wolf-human, but also in/as the maternal body. This is where we may find rich potential of wildness and flesh. These are discussed in terms of *No Country for Old Men* (Coen Bros. 2007). This is further explored through Merleau-Ponty's employment of the idea of *praktognosia* ("practical knowledge" and the body in movement). The analysis then considers these ideas in terms of the film and the two wolf case studies.

Following this, the chapter looks at Husserl's ideas on nature (largely from *Cartesian Meditations*) and the sensuously seen body in its determination through apperception and the formation of identifications. Of particular significance is Husserl's identification-forming appresentations as co-perceptions, that is, the fusion between actual perceptions and appresentations so that they function simultaneously. This opens up the discussion to the possibility of appresentation in terms of identification (particularly to be read in terms of Klein's projective identification) and transference. Cinema invites such projective identificatory appresentations, for it is an integral part of the spectator's engagement with the narrative and its characters.

The next part of the chapter turns to the idea of wild flesh, read here in terms of intentionality colliding with a certain resistance to positions and states of being that operate as deterministic and unifying. One of the ways this takes place is through the intimacy of intentionality merging with the anxious moment. This is worked through with some cinematic examples, beginning with the idea of passionate abnormalities. "Abnormalities" refers here to a rather ambiguous set of discussions by Husserl related to appearances and slippage and our relational attachments to things and others. What is central to these abnormalities and the relations formed is what Husserl terms their quality of "over-thereness." This over-there positionality is a fundamental aspect of cinema for it is where we find both intimacy, that is, a film's capacity to enable us to see from over-there, as well as form relations in and for things and others that are over-there; and anxiety, that is, the disruptive potential of seeing from over-there. The chapter explores this idea of cinema and over-thereness, including cinema's capacity to embed anxiety (as distance) and intimacy (as closeness). From this it is suggested that cinema can be seen in these terms as a phenomenological apparatus, which forms the intimate and anxious work in their entirety for every film.

The implications of this, including how we might engage with this as a cinematic process, are discussed in terms of flesh and Claire Denis's *Trouble Every Day* (2001). The primary concern is how flesh evokes the recasting of apperceptions, of how the sensuously extreme seen body simultaneously provides an attraction and radical challenge to the Other (as body, subject, difference, and so on). One of the ways in which such distinctions can be made is through Lacan's conceptualization of the site of anxiety and desire and the relationship to *jouissance*. All of which brings us to the complex question of what constitutes wild flesh? This is investigated through Denis's film, and reference to some foundational aspects of the sublime in Kant and Burke, as well as Husserl's transcendental theory of experiencing (the "thereness-for-me") someone else and, consequently, of the Objective world. Cinema, as a cultural object, is particularly invested in these issues of thereness-for-me, and this is positioned alongside the other, interconnected sense of for-everyone. What is at hand here, then, is how wild flesh functions at the level of performative intimacy as a cultural object while "simultaneously" appearing as something for the individual; this links to the "over-thereness" derived from an interplay of intimacy and anxiety. What this suggests is that the impossibility of a cultural intimacy becomes possible because of the "thereness-for-me," which is actually a contradiction only capable of being sustained through ideology.

At this point the chapter introduces the relational context of wild flesh, intimacy, and empathy. The latter of these is taken up in terms of Edith Stein's important work on empathy, recognizing the external, foreign, otherness which we initially experience through the body. Of particular note is her conceptualization of givenness, or "con-primordiality." Con-primordiality (the other's scope and range of sensations as they are given to us, phenomenologically speaking) must take on unique attributes when the seen living body of the other is rendered as wild flesh, in this case as it is determined and produced in cinema's intimacies. It is thus suggested that the nature of cinema is premised somewhat on these affective negotiations and its history is constituted of such experiences. What is being proposed here is that cinema itself is formed through iterations of con-primordialities which are necessarily bound up with the "abnormal" the discordant, the negotiations of over-thereness, and otherness.

Chapter 6 takes up the nightmare in terms of its cinematic manifestations and how we might develop an understanding in terms of phenomenology and psychoanalysis. To this end the chapter commences by considering the "how" of the nightmare (i.e., how do we experience the nightmare?

How do we have nightmares and know them as such?) followed by the "what" of the nightmare, notably within its cinematic iterations. Between these two we can observe the function of the nightmare (why do we have them? what is the individual's nightmare? why do we culturally construct them? what constitutes a nightmare? and so on). The underlying premise here is that the status of "nightmare" is unstable, even given its recurring register of forms, tropes, and styles. Central to these discussions is the concept of desire which is used to provide a link between psychoanalysis and phenomenology. The underlying strategy for this is to read desire as an ego-centric positionality that can incorporate a psychoanalytic hermeneutic (i.e., desire as interpretative) and phenomenological intentionality (i.e., desire as consciousness determining); this is the othered consciousness of the *ego*. This aspect of the desire of the nightmare provides us with another issue, namely that in these experiences we adopt a certain type of desire which is both unique and seemingly contradictory. This is the desire to not be protected, which can be traced back to the "how" and "why" of the nightmare.

To devise a phenomenological approach to the nightmare the chapter engages with Husserl's ideas on phantasy, working toward an aporiastic howness, that is, the internal contradiction of the nightmare as a form of desire. This issue of phantasy is deeply embedded in Husserl's distinctions of the two orders of *Gegenwärtigung* (presentation/perception) and *Vergegenwärtigung* (re-presentation), thus allowing us a return to these concepts discussed in the first section of the book. The nightmare's aporiastic nature, its internal and represented defining attributes, is derived from the disturbance of presentation/actuality and re-representation/acting as if having actuality. This is significant in terms of defining the howness of the nightmare precisely because there needs to be a blurring of this sense of being before us. This concept of the aporiastic nature, akin to Husserlian phantasy, is employed to consider how the nightmare comes to be (in its materiality and experience), which in turn leads to the issues of why the nightmare is part of the cinematic discourse.

The chapter then turns to a consideration of the nightmare's capacity to act as if it is real. At the core of the nightmare's aporiastics is the contesting of the quasi, the "as if," and "as it were." This contesting originates from the (phenomenological idea of) positing of consciousness and its modifications. It is suggested that this operates in a number of ways, focusing on two in particular: the disputation of the quasi-reality of the nightmare because of an exaggerated affective force (the qualifying status of "this is a phantasy" is lost to overwhelming belief and affective responses so that the nightmare is experienced as "real"); and the experiencing (which necessarily includes the revelatory moment of terror) of the nightmare as a possessive phantasy. "Possessiveness," it is proposed, is a type of intimacy. That is, just as the nightmare possesses us, we similarly and actively possess our nightmares so that they are one's own, particular, and ego-centric in design and intent. In this possessional process we find the desire to not be protected.

This idea of the intimate possessiveness of the nightmare is explored through two aspects, both invested in cinema's role as a cultural apparatus. The first of these, nullity, is the space that nightmares are experienced in; the second, belief, is the collapse of the capacity to distinguish reality and phantasy. Nullity comes from Husserl's work on phantasy and reality, notably the indistinguishing of the real and the imagined, remembered, or thought-of object (or feeling, emotion, and so on). The nightmare, read within such a context, would appear to be this deceptive object, a nullity which challenges the status of, and distinctions between real and imagined. However, it is suggested here that the aporiastic basis means that before the nightmare becomes the deceptive object, this nullity process is particularly powerful, binding it through possessiveness.

The chapter then turns to aspects of psychoanalysis to explore these ideas of intimacy further, pushing them toward the role of anxiety, and the function of the "signal." This sets up the discussion of "who's nightmare?" for one person's nightmare can also be another's realized ideal. Similarly, we find in this the question of "who's anxiety?" and even "who's intimacy?" In one sense the veracity of the anxious signal is precisely what we have seen in cinema's requirement to take up a spectating position which may not be a "usual" or comfortable one. That is, the role of anxiety, via intimacy, to challenge comfort when that very comfort is filled with complex negativity. By combining the phenomenological with the psychoanalytic, the chapter returns to the *ego*, exploring Husserl's idea of the double Ego of the actual ego and what he calls the reproductional Ego. The phantasy Ego lives in phantasy and performs acts of consciousness within that realm as if they are real. It will judge, perceive, enjoy with an intentionality that these are felt as actually taking place. Hence, the desire is the desire to not be cared for, to relinquish the sense of being protected.

Three variants of this idea of the nightmare are then considered: first, phallocentric and racist nightmares at the level of the repressed; second, liquification of flesh at the level of the double Ego; third, the mirroring effect of the nightmare at the level of desire. Phallocentric nightmares are discussed within a counter reading of certain fairy-tale tropes; racist nightmares and their anxieties are explored in examples which include a contrast between D.W. Griffith's *Birth of a Nation* (1915) (white anxiety about the black body as nightmare) and Jordan Peele's *Get Out* (2017) and Spike Lee's *BlacKkKlansman* (2018) as the resistant black body. In these terms we can identify certain films where phantasy modifies subjectivity (i.e., the spectating space and its cultural resonances) so that the spectator is required to see the anxious signals (as defined by Lacan) that are developed both within and external to the text.

This previous section can be described as the nightmare and its politically contextualizing processes; the next section, called "Liquification of flesh at the level of the double Ego" takes up a different political approach, that of gender. The focus of the film is Agnieszka Smoczyńska's *The Lure* (2015). The analysis commences with a recalling of Lacan's alignment of anxiety to surplus *jouissance* and the issue of surplus value in such a configuration, and how cinema constructs such objects. The discussion considers how we might locate these ideas of surplus *jouissance* and the nightmare's aporiastic component in terms of the "surplus" as the space where the contradiction between the phantasy (nightmare, film, memory) experienced as needed/required and desired, and the fears and anxieties being played out. The aporia of the nightmare and these variants of the surplus are seen as crucial to understanding why the nightmare (in its cinematic forms in particular) is seen as pleasurable, which necessarily includes the reconfiguring of the anxieties of the nightmare as intimacy. These ideas are worked through in terms of *The Lure* and the flesh of the two mermaids as the liquefaction of the body.

The final section of the chapter looks at an inversion of the nightmare, exploring Robert Eggers's film *The VVitch* (2015). The strategy here is to work through some psychoanalytic concepts on anxiety and how these might be read in terms of the phenomenological *leibhaftlig* ("in person"). This is done through a number of aspects of the film, notably feminine sexuality and the daughter-mother conflict; hysteria as resistance; and flight as the sexual act and surplus *jouissance* leading to a reinscribing of certain political agendas based on gender and power.

1

The Intimate Spectator, the Cinematic Ego, and the Nothing (To Be Anxious About)

The rich and disturbing vein of thought that originates (if such a volatile word can be evoked in this context) with Kierkegaard, deterministically proceeds with and through the concepts of the negative and the Nothing. Kierkegaard configures this in a particular way (it is, after all, part of his larger agenda): "there is something that is not dissension and strife, for there is nothing against which to strive. What, then, is it? Nothing. But what effect does nothing have? It begets anxiety. This is the profound secret of innocence, that at the same time it is anxiety" (Kierkegaard 2015: 50). The supposed calming and reassuring utterance (cliché?) "there is nothing to be anxious about" thus becomes a statement on the very nature of anxiety; it is the Nothing that produces anxiety. That is, "there is (a) Nothing to be anxious about." This "profound secret" that binds innocence and anxiety together is played out in the domain of the Nothing. This binding is disguised (its surreptitious nature) not just in the aligning of innocence and anxiety, but also in the forming of doublings. It is to double business bound.[1] This reflexivity, where innocence and anxiety are the other's self, mirrored in Nothing, is the reference point for the following discussions.

The first point of clarification must be this term of "innocence," for Kierkegaard's fervent Christian inflection is eschewed here. Instead, the

---

[1] There is something altogether apt in referencing Claudius's guilt-ridden soliloquy in *Hamlet*. The self-reflexive turn, where he acknowledges his murderous act and the lack of any forgiveness, plays out Kierkegaard's anxieties and innocence. That, and of course the Danish connection!

focus is the philosophical underpinning of this word, aligning it with the sense of unformed knowledge, subject-formation, and power.[2] This allows us to engage further with the material of this investigation: of the analytic experience; of the relationship between intimacy and anxiety; and of cinema's role in this situation. The idea that is being worked toward here is the formulation of the innocent spectator (the uncritical, innocent bystander), is bound to the cinematic through these entwined doublings of innocence and anxiety. In this way it is possible to collocate "innocence" as a version of phenomenology's natural attitude or pre-phenomenological analytic position; or the analysand's pre-analytic status in psychoanalysis; or even the pre-psychoanalytic moment where both analyst and analysand attempt to establish the unconscious motivations and signals at hand. How we move from these positions into the reflexive, critical, and transcendental (in the Husserlian sense) positions is through the agitational forces of anxiety and the closeness of the bindings of intimacy. Innocence thus becomes the foil of the *epoché*. From this emerges further key ideas, including the internal and external, the frame and the barrier, the residual, and the relationship between the Nothing and the something.

This chapter explores three interconnected, foundational ideas for the ensuing discussions: (1) to be a film spectator is to take up an othered conscious; (2) the spectator is formed within and alongside the cinematic ego (which is defined as follows); (3) the cinematic ego and attendant othered conscious are enthymematic in the active processes of spectating, lack, and the missing object born from the Nothing. By working through these issues, it will be possible to expand and explore the core concerns at hand, how Nothing, anxiety, and intimacy "develop" the cinematic spectator, and how this can be devised within the analytic experience.

The Spectator's Othered Consciousness

To be able to work through the notion of an othered consciousness (in potentia an indeterminate multiplicity) when we watch a film, we need to articulate how such a concept might be addressed from a psychoanalytic and phenomenological perspective so as to arrive at the analytic experience. Let us begin with a disconcertingly brief definitional statement: spectating

---

[2]One example of Kierkegaard's use of innocence in this manner is in "Problema III," *Fear and Trembling*. See his reimagining of the fairy tale of Agnes and the merman. Despite her status (personification) of innocence, she is "not a quiet, tranquil girl; she enjoyed the roar of the sea, and the sad sighing of the waves gave her pleasure only because the internal storm raged more violently" (1983: 96). Innocence, for Kierkegaard, is fundamentally attached to guilt, and both are part of formations of seduction.

sites of single consciousness hold us in innocence; othered consciousness is the movement toward intimacy bound to anxiety. To work through this first some notes will be made on the two analytic approaches, commencing with psychoanalysis and then phenomenology. This will provide some common ground for a discussion on how othered consciousness is determined in and by the Nothing, leading to the idea of the spectator's othered consciousness. Central to the following is the idea that the analytic experience's counter (its dialectic other) to Nothing is the "something"; in both psychoanalysis and phenomenology this is determined as "ego," its role and function as the othered identity, as well as the acts of filling in the absences. In cinema, this "something" is of this order of the interplay between the spectator and cinema, but work needs to be done to establish it as such.

In the analytic field, the Nothing of psychoanalysis is the hermeneutic force and pressure of analysis, it is the *lacuna* that sets the scene for all subsequent analytic statements. Exactly how this psychical Nothing is discovered, made manifest, and analyzed beyond its inveigled presentations is, of course, the essence of psychoanalysis itself. The assertion of the Nothing as a "no thing," something to be ignored, overlooked, or something that is missed, or is misleading, is precisely what psychoanalytic techniques (its meta-discourses) are designed to uncover. The strongest assertions of Nothing are to be found in the base materiality of psychoanalysis—repression, overdetermination, condensation and displacement, disguise, negation, conversion (in the body), deferral, denial, and so on. When Freud corrects himself regarding anxiety, righting a previously held proposition, he shows this veiling process at the levels of both manifestation (how we see or experience anxiety) and critical analysis (what anxiety is and where it originates): "It was anxiety which produced repression and not, as I had formerly believed, repression which produced anxiety" (Freud *SE XX*: 32). Crucially, this illustrates that the Nothing is also found in the analytic process. This exploration of the Nothing is the fundamental work of psychoanalysis and informs its entire field in one way or another. However, it would be a misstep to think of the Nothing as a uniform phenomenon, and its inflections will shift according to analytic contexts, directions, and even the experience of it. For example, consider the following as illustrations of how the Nothing is manifested in terms of spectating acts (which are fundamental aspects to a theorizing of the othered spectator), immobility/impediments, and spaces in some of Freud's case studies. Had different terms been chosen, the Nothing would appear altogether differently:

    a.   as a normalizing process so that the crucial divergent aims are missed—from the "Rat Man" case study: "The current sexual life of an obsessional neurotic may often appear perfectly normal to a superficial observer; indeed, it frequently *offers to the eye*[3] far fewer pathogenic elements" (*SE* X: 161). Hence, we read "superficial observer" as site of innocence, and "far fewer" as an indicator of the Nothing. From this same case study, the missing Nothing as obsessional material: "After this I was left with a *burning and tormenting curiosity to see* the female body" (*SE* X: 157–8).[4] Here the Nothing (as an absence) is the female body as determined in the Rat Man's obsession, fixed through his gaze. "Fixed" is employed here with its double meaning of "to correct" and, in the photographic sense, of making stable and inhibiting change.

b. as the signifier that comes to define a subjectivity as determined in the absent, the Nothing. One example is Judge Schreber's assertion of the "Order of Things" and his need to be transformed into (i.e., *to be seen as*) a woman (see *SE XII* "Psychoanalytic Notes on an Autobiographical Account of a Case of Paranoia"). His anxious Nothing is the body he craves to be; he fills this Nothing with sustained and detailed memoirs, and in doing so attempts to create a something in his descriptions. Immobility here is shown by the lack of body change, and perhaps more literally as Schreber as prisoner.

c. as a reinscribed primary event, leading to a heavily disguised version, for example, the wolves dream in the "Wolf Man" case study which presents the primal scene as a Nothing. In this example we see a double Nothing: the primal scene as repressed (rendered as nothing in the conscious, except as a highly disguised form) and the missing aspect that allows Freud to develop his theory of the primal scene. *Immobility and being watched as well as watching* are two highly relevant aspects for the issues at hand.[5] Freud's *Inhibitions, Symptoms and Anxiety* (*SE XX*) commences with a discussion on inhibitions and impediments,[6] and this is the Nothing of movement. This further illustrates how the Nothing is presented in disguised forms; in this example the lack of mobility becomes a trace of

---

[3]Here, and throughout the following list, I have placed in italics markers of the gaze and to be gazed at to foreground the issue of looking.

[4]In the "Rat Man" case study, Freud discusses the relationship between obsession, repression, and scopophilia and epistemophilia—a detailing that could be compared to that most committed of cinema's spectators.

[5]This case study is discussed further in Chapter 5.

[6]Lacan subsequently examines Freud's use of inhibition, questioning why he doesn't use the word "impede": "Why not use the word 'impede'? This is precisely what's at issue. Our subjects are inhibited when they speak to us . . . To be impeded is a symptom." Lacan goes on to show how the etymology of the word fits in to his investigation: "*Impedicare* means to be ensnared" (2017: 10). This ensnaring is important for the discussion at hand and certainly links back to Lacan's idea of *Invidia* and *dompte-regard* developed in *The Four Fundamental Concepts of Psychoanalysis*.

the Nothing. This is also a key aspect of Jones's discussion of the nightmare (see Chapter 6), rendered as the inescapable weight on the body (most often described as on the chest).

d. as self-determining analytic technique. In "Psychogenesis of a Case of Homosexuality in a Woman" (*SE XVIII*), Freud describes the two phases of analysis—the presentation of psychoanalytic techniques and gathering of information from the patient; the patient's working through and re-living of the material (see 145–72, particularly 149). Freud also notes (as behaviorally significant and therefore analytically important) that the woman is happy and confident *to be seen in "the most frequented streets"* and she "distained no means of deception, no excuses and no lies that would make meetings with her [the loved other woman] possible and cover them" (146). In other words, she wants to be seen, wants to be recognized with the woman she loves.[7] The Nothing here is a *culture's incapacity to "see" or acknowledge otherness* (in this example a challenge to heteronormativity); that the woman wants to be seen is a corporeal act of defying the Nothing (sexually, analytically, politically, and so on). Immobility in this example is the woman's body to be seen in public, a corporeal declaration of a politized love.[8]

e. as the all-important, determining, clarifying, and enigma-resolving signifier and/or space. This is all the dream analyzes, all the disturbed acts and utterances, all the everyday psychopathologies, and so on that psychoanalysis undertakes to examine and interpret. In keeping with this list of indicatives, a specific example here is Dora's *obsessional contemplation* of the Madonna painting, which Freud subsequently reads as the missing state of motherhood and the child (*SE VII*: 96; 104). The Nothing is thus bound up with the maternal (for Freud's reading of Dora), the painting itself (which captures Dora's gaze), and Dora's stillness as she sits for many hours looking at the painting in the art gallery.

---

[7] It is, of course, indicative of Freud's times that this seems so surprising, shocking even. As Freud says, the woman "is quite neglectful of her own reputation" (146). Interestingly, Freud's tone overall is not condemning (as might have been expected for his time and social conditioning), and his analysis of this perceived neglectful attitude is to understand why, rather than necessarily change it. Of course, Freud was locked into his contemporary culture, and some of his comments toward women are disturbing. However, there is consistency in his work that focuses on the psychoanalytic, and even when he is frustratingly dated, conservative and even problematic in his attitudes toward women, there is still analytic insights to be gained. But all of this is beyond the direct issues here.

[8] Beyond the scope of this book, this aspect has potential connections with W.E.B. Du Bois' concept of othered consciousness. See *The Souls of Black Folk*.

This list could be extended, perhaps beyond limits, but even such a restricted set illustrates some of the aspects of the Nothing, the gaze, and the movement from the single frame of innocent consciousness. In all these examples, the Nothing begins as an interpretative *lacuna*, something that needs to be resolved. Before that can even take place, however, the Nothing itself, its status as such, must be recognized. In all these examples, what is missing (what defines the situation as containing a Nothing) must be acknowledged. This is why the act of looking (a proactive gaze that seeks) is important and is why it can be aligned to the innocent spectator. In the analytic experience, before we attempt to resolve the Nothing, we need to know that something is not there. This sounds self-evident, but the incapacity to recognize, or to misrecognize, the Nothing is a fundamental attribute of innocence (and the formation of the innocent spectator). It is also why anxiety lies at its heart.

Psychoanalysis forms the othered conscious by moving from the innocent analyst and analysand, first by recognizing the Nothing, and then working through what is held in this nothingness. Consider, for example, the dream you had the other night. Its first status of Nothing is this qualifier of "dream." In phenomenology it is the re-presented value ascribed to all phantasy and is therefore, necessarily, distinct from "actuality." The status of "dream as Nothing" is its best disguise, psychoanalytically speaking—it was, after all, just a dream. Second, there are the Nothings within the dream which, because of repression, are disguised to distract us from interpretations. These Nothings declare themselves as not worthy of attention (which is precisely what psychoanalysis focuses on). Third, there are the Nothings that align with Freud's "navel" of the dream (see *The Interpretation of Dreams*)—the unending, uninterpretable, and unresolvable depths of the dream. Fourth, there are the Nothings that act as resistances to seeing the dream as something of the self. This is the anxiety of reflexivity, for it involves articulating the underlying material presented in the inhibitions and symptoms, which once seemed of the other, as part of the self. This is an othered conscious because the status of innocence (the misrecognized or unrecognized) is not subsequently negated; it is not abandoned. Just as when the innocent spectator adjusts their interpretative gaze, the "original" gaze is retained (even if it is solely in the space of the negative). This is an idea that will be returned to shortly, for this is crucial to understanding how a film provides a site of "consciousness."

In phenomenology we can articulate this idea of othered conscious in a number of interconnected ways. Our focus will be on two that are well suited for an exploration of the intimate spectator: as a component of the phenomenological method (shifting from the natural attitude); and as a variant of intentionality. A brief comment on these two will now be made before turning to the film spectator.

Husserl's well-known formulation of the natural attitude (or standpoint) as we experience the world is not simply a passive one, constituted as it is of complex acts of perception,[9] judgments, feelings, emotions, and so on. It can be reinterpreted in terms of a holding of the Nothing. In that Husserl acknowledges the reality of objects, things, and others as being "present as realities in my field of intuition," they are mostly not present in one's attention (see 1931: §27). Even at this most fundamental of levels, Nothingness forms in the inattentiveness and/or wandering intuitions. This is the Nothingness held in abeyance, located as it is in a "dimly apprehended depth or fringe of indeterminate reality," with this infinite indeterminacy held in a "misty horizon that can never be completely outlined [that] remains necessarily there" (1931: §27). Furthermore, this natural attitude contains within it acts of processing that allows us to perceive things as goods, values, and utility. It ascribes the beautiful and ugly, the pleasant and unpleasant, usefulness, and to people the status of friend or enemy, liked or disliked, regardless of the attention paid (1931: §27). Beyond this, however, we can shift this reading of Nothing to produce a second order of Nothingness that acts in an interpretative manner. If the first of these Nothings is found in the lacks of the natural attitude (the unseen and unacknowledged in a world full of things and people), this second order is what takes place in the phenomenological bracketing. In this sense, the first Nothings are "no things" because they lack the status of the perceived; they are the things that exist around us, that could be seen, touched, enjoyed, produce excitement or disgust, could be the most extraordinary and sensuous or the most banal, but exist as Nothing because our attention has yet to turn to them (and perhaps never will). We note in Husserl's *Dingvorlesung* (Thing and Space Lectures) a key analysis of thing and perception. For example, "What is immanent to perception is not the same as that which is posited transcendently as a thing. If these were completely the same, then we would have two things, one immanent and one transcendent" (1998: §14). Husserl goes on to assert that the thing " . . . is not a givenness which can be given immanently in straightforward perception" (1998: §14). The second order of Nothingness, however, is devised out of *epoché*, bracketed off in the phenomenological method. This is Husserl's radical alteration, producing a unique form of consciousness (see *Ideas*: §31).

It is important to note that Husserl consistently articulates that the natural world's "there for us" status remains. It is within such a context that, broadly speaking, phenomenology divides experiences into the "natural" and "eidetic." This absolute insistence that bracketing does not

---

[9]Husserl tends to employ two different words for perception: *Wahrnehmung*—perception within a context of empirical reality; *Perzeption*—perception within a sense of the image (and so more often part of phantasy). By way of illustration, consider the following: "Hence by eliminating all symbolization and, on the other side, by cutting off every unification with the positing perception [*Wahrnehmung*] of the "image's surroundings, we obtain a pure positionless perception[*Perzeption*]" (2005: 536).

deny the existence of all that is excluded is read here as the same order of the production of a Nothingness that we noted in psychoanalysis. There is an active, insistent aspect to bracketing and the shifting from the natural attitude; it is *Gewahren* (see 1931: §34), a growing awareness, and explicit incitement of perception that shifts from the infinite horizon to a sense of presence that is both temporally and spatially defined. In this way it can also be seen, in addition, as corporeally determined.[10] (This will also be read, later, in terms of the spectator's experience of the film.) Later, Husserl will describe this idea of an interconnected All as "a universal unthematic horizon" and the natural attitude as the site of the world as pregiven (see *The Crisis of European Sciences and Transcendental Phenomenology*, hereafter *The Crisis*, notably Part IIIA, §38). This produces, via a transcendental *epoché*, a frame of consciousness that is "above the pregivenness of the validity of the world, above the infinite complex whereby, in concealment, the world's validities are always founded on other validities, above the whole manifold but synthetically unified flow . . . " (1997: §40). Here this bracketing aspect of above is the processing of the Nothing; note also here, and elsewhere[11] that the phenomenological method requires the status of Nothingness in order to perform bracketing, but there is a continual insistence on this Nothingness as holding a presence. This is the othered conscious from a phenomenological perspective; the psychoanalytic equivalent, as noted earlier, is the materiality, as well as immateriality, of the unconscious. This is, somewhat crucially for the overall theme of this project, how we might reconcile the difficult issue of the unconscious in the analytic experience.

Before turning to the cinematic implications let us make a few notes on intentionality within this context. Intentionality is heavily constituted in the shift from the natural attitude toward the formation of transcendental-phenomenological reflection, as Husserl puts it in *Cartesian Meditations*. This requires (has an insistence of) a surrendering of a previously held subjective position, where each such position is given up for the next because "reflection alters the original subjective process" (1950: §15). The Nothingness of intentionality is thus formed out of two sources. First, this surrendering of a subject type, that is, the transition to a subjective process that was Nothing (nonexistent in the natural attitude), and subsequently rendering the previous occupied subjective processes as Nothing, or at least a version of *Aufhebung*. This is a Nothing based almost entirely on a distinction between being phenomenologically active/directed or not.

---

[10]This aligns with Merleau-Ponty's reading of motility and intentionality (see 1962: 137–8). This also connects to the earlier discussion of Freud's case studies and immobility.

[11]For example, §38 and the pregivenness of the world; §39 and the idea of denial as a formation of the Nothing; §41 and abstention as a freeing of truth; Appendix III "The Attitude of Natural Science and the Attitude of Humanistic Science," where a nascent version of the idea of a "naturalistic attitude" is proposed.

Second, the Nothing of things, objects, people, and processes that were in the world and subsequently become part of the non-being of the world. This is the shift from the already-existing world ("I watch this film," "I enjoy the voice of this loved one," "I feel this anxiety") to one of reflexive experiencing which is "an experiencing experiencing... with all its moments... including the moments of perceiving itself, as a flowing subjective process" (1950: §15). It is here that we can also insert the idea of the innocent person (in the natural attitude) which in turn yields the innocent spectator.

Husserl describes the splitting of the Ego, that is the "disinterested onlooker" of the phenomenological Ego located earlier what he calls the "naïvely interested Ego" (1950: §15). This is transformative in other ways, including the rendering of a previously held (i.e., naïve) subject position as an object, and yet not a site of objectivity. This is the force of the reflexive moment. This phenomenologically defined naïve position is not the same as "innocence," but it does contribute significant critical insights into how we might understand it. Just as psychoanalysis' working through a dream (which necessarily includes recalling and describing as well as actual analysis) can be described as an experiencing experiencing (i.e., the experience of experiencing the dream in and through analytic processes), so phenomenology's shift out of the natural attitude allows for critical reflection of what is being experienced.[12] The analytic experience thus produces not a negation of the previously held frame of consciousness (the dreamer dreaming, the looking out the window to the street and trees, the smell of sea air), but a shifted position of reflexive, interpretative gesture(s). The naïve and innocent position becomes an object to be reflected upon, and so is included in the act of intentionality. The experience of smelling the briny, cool, sea air becomes the experiencing of that experiencing, so that not only is the experience different but also is the sea air itself. This is Husserl's transcendental-phenomenological self-experience (by the sea).

It is important to recall that Husserl insists on parallelism of experience in the formation of knowledge from experience. This is the idea that for every experience of actuality, there is a corresponding pure phantasy, an "as-if experience with parallel modes (as-if perception, as-if retention, as-if recollection" (1950: §12). This is a particularly psychoanalytic conceptualization, for it requires a binding of actuality and phantasy in all experiencing. As is noted in Chapter 6, there is the intentionality of consciousness as each of us as the spectator intuits the phantasy that is a film. There is also a version of intentionality (directionality of consciousness)

---

[12] A completely different philosophical iteration of this issue can be traced from the Wittgensteinian position of Norman Malcolm's work (notably *Dreaming*). Malcolm's theories on a branch of philosophical thinking about dream experience was impactful for a while. It lacks relevancy here in part because of its limitations on what the dream experience is.

that takes place within the film itself, operating as an as-if perception, layered onto the actual perception. This also relates to Husserl's notion of the double Ego, but different inasmuch as the film spectator's othered Ego (the Ego in phantasy consciousness) is not the same as the filmic constructions of it. Let us hold in reserve this issue and turn to cinema to explore these ideas of othered conscious and the innocent spectator in this transition from innocence.

By way of summary and for clarification, the following are somewhat provocative agencies to build from:

1. the innocent spectator commences from the site of a "single" conscious. "Single" here is employed in the sense of a homogeneous position, holding the unanalyzed, highly filtered gaze where the disguised is unrecognized or yet to be recognized, and the natural attitude is the formulating order. Of course, in itself such a position as "single consciousness" is an impossibility. The qualification of "single" is made in part through a sense of change; we move into and out of such singularities precisely through the intimate connections that are made;

2. in this position any composing Nothings are largely invisible; "a composing Nothing" is employed here to denote those elements of the film that have significance (come to evolve in meaning and interpretative values) as it is formed by the spectator, as distinct from the Nothings that will retain that status;

3. the othered conscious emerges through the intimacies formed in the act of spectating, which includes (phenomenologically speaking) protension and retention (particularly of textual material in its *lacunal* state), as well as the equivalences of considerations of representability and secondary revisions (from psychoanalysis);

4. the othered conscious (from the spectator's interactions with the film) necessarily includes acts of *Gewahren*, which is not in itself a fully formed phenomenological reduction but can be seen as at the very least an iteration of it. This is the shaping of perception/cognition in the interplay between spectator and film and the incitement to experience;

5. how this othered conscious plays out (i.e., how we experience the experience of the film) is bound up with the spectator's relationship with the actual film at that moment of watching. It is also formulated in the phenomenological as-ifs created in this spectating act as well as psychoanalysis' (Lacan is prominent here) versions of the gaze and narcissism (see as follows). The greater the intimacy, the greater the othered conscious;

6. there is a multiplicity of functions of the Nothing in this active (non-innocent) spectator, including intimacy (one's unsatisfiable desire

for the film and all its elements), and anxiety (including the fear of not knowing, the fear of the Nothing persisting and therefore being excluded);

7. the othered conscious spectator is thus committed to the work, which includes appresentational efforts (e.g., the interpretative negotiations of Nothings);
8. from this work and these efforts, the undone innocent spectator formulates intimacies of intentionality;
9. all versions of interpretation (including intimacies and anxieties) emerge from the othered conscious precisely because of this entwining of spectator and film. In this sense, the othered conscious takes place when the spectator formulates meaning, experiences an affective relationship, in some way locates the sense of self in a relational context with the film, or, at the most critically and reflexive moments, becomes the experience of the experience;
10. through this, the othered conscious spectator and the film exists in potentia as what Husserl calls a "universal apodictically experienceable structure" (1950: §12). Although the caveat here must be that this is only possible within the larger critical apparatus of the analytic situation, such a structure could emerge as the spectator reflexively engages with her self's relationship(s) with the film;
11. this site would also involve the recognition of the film and act of spectating as formulated through the actual and phantasy (as-if) experiences.

The transition from the innocent spectator (essentially, the bystander who does not get involved) to the state of othered conscious is more than simply a movement from passivity to activity, or even proactive constructions of meaning(s). As indicated earlier, othered conscious is a commitment to intimacy (and the attendant anxieties) because it involves phenomenological pairing (see later in this chapter), the formation of a relationship (which can include "community" and Husserl's monadistic actions, or even a version of transference), the recognition of the self in the experience, and the capacity to be affected. Indeed, such a transitional process is not automatic, and it is quite common to watch a film without taking up the othered conscious position. There are always sites (of resistance or failings or simply incapacities) from spectator and/or film that makes the othered conscious unlikely or even largely impossible. However, this should not be misread as a version of being alienated from the film. Gender, class, race, ethnicity, time, and or temporal distance, cultural distance, political agendas, ideology, boredom, cinematic stylistics, aesthetics, deeply embedded complexities, desires and concupiscent motivations (and their lacks), masochistic (economic) relations, or the need for evasions—all of these, and the countless others, could be cited as reasons for the persistence of the innocent, ambivalent, spectator. Indeed, it is the case that such conditions do produce a certain predisposition, but the root cause of the lack of othered conscious is to be found in intimacy (and its absence) and the specific conditions determined in the analytic experience. That is to say, either a version of phenomenological or psychoanalytic analytic processes, or, as is posited here, a combination of the two approaches. To work through this issue further let us turn to a companion topic in the form of the ego.

The Spectator and the Cinematic Ego

The talismanic word "ego" features prominently in both psychoanalysis and phenomenology. It predates both Freud and Husserl and would certainly have been a term that both thinkers were used to hearing. It is necessary, for sake of clarity and because there are differences, to distinguish usage here, so "Ego" will be used to refer to the Husserlian/phenomenological sense (because Husserl consistently capitalized the word), and "ego" the Freudian/psychoanalytic version. When the word is used outside of these two analytic contexts (e.g., as a combination, or independent, of both versions) it will be italicized. This will also signal that their uses of the term differ from the Cartesian ego as the source of *cogitare* as they do from Kant's species subject as sharply distinct from any form of subjectivism.[13] In different ways phenomenology and psychoanalysis present us with a deeply complex version of what *ego* means and the task of summation, as well as comparison, can only take place here with some restrictions and caveats or the risk of a wild and unending discussion may become a reality. In phenomenology, for example, Ego is entangled in every part of its analytic existence, underpinning all forms of technique and method, commencing the phenomenological project, and is used as a centralizing point of reference for all investigations, as well as an issue of complexity that needs to be explored in itself. Let us spend a few moments considering the tenor of *ego* in both systems.

The Ego is so profoundly fundamental to phenomenology because of this status of absoluteness, derived not the least from Husserl's linking of it to "pure consciousness" and the transcendental subjectivity of the Ego *cogito*, which in turn forms the method of transcendental-phenomenological reduction. Without this devising of the Ego, it would not be possible for phenomenology to distinguish between the natural attitude and the consciousness formed through eidetic reduction. It is the concept (and

---

[13] I am grateful to Horst Ruthrof's insight on this clarifying aspect of Kant and the Cartesian ego.

acts) of Ego that, for example, re-orientates the life-world as existing in itself, to become a "phenomenon of being instead of something that is" (Husserl 1950: §8). Furthermore, Husserl allows for different "types" or status of Ego in the processes of exchange between the self and life-world, the experiencing of such exchanges, and the actions involved, including: the natural human Ego and the Ego of transcendental-phenomenological self-experience (see, e.g., 1950: §11); the Ego of self as a "peculiar owness" as distinct from others[14]; the human Ego as different from the non-human; and the psychophysical Ego's relationship to externality and its objects (1950: §44). There is also a contiguous version found in how the Ego is determined and determines through apperception, which Husserl speaks of in terms of the Ego and other/alter *ego*. By way of further example, Merleau-Ponty configures the *cogito* along these lines, but aligns it with the body (see *Phenomenology of Perception* Part Three: The *Cogito*). So, if the Ego is both a component of, and constituted by, this method it is little wonder that *ego* is invested with such intricacies. In the examples cited here, we see distinctions based on the Ego and the life-world (self and externalities), Ego as determined by phenomenological attitude/position and acts (natural vs reduction), and Ego as self as distinct from the other/others.[15]

This centrality and subsequent critical working through, although designed for different means and purposes, is also found in psychoanalysis, where the ego is a complex configuration of agency (of self) and activities (of other). By way of cursory summation, regard how Freud describes the ego within a range of processes which are formed in and by the relationships that the ego has with the unconscious and id. All these relationships engage with the internal (psychical, self)/external (world) divide, permitting exchanges, and shaping meanings. As we proceed with this summary, where possible parallels will be drawn with phenomenology's sense of Ego. Of course, there will be times when such connections will be impossible, but unless this becomes overwhelmingly the case, there should be some capacity for if not exactitude, then at least a sense of syncretism. In this spirit, the following will also note when the divergences are a step too far. Finally, whenever viable, each of the following sub-sections will include some discussion of the spectator and the cinematic *ego*, with the aim of building up such an idea gradually.

a) The Ego as Coherency and the Apodictic

In *The Ego and the Id*, Freud begins by stating that the ego is "a coherent organization of mental processes" (*SE XIX*: 8); similarly, in *Inhibition*,

---

[14]See Chapter 5 for further discussion on owness.
[15]See Chapter 5 for further discussion on ego and the other.

Symptoms and Anxiety (*SE XX*) the ego is described as an "organization" that "is based on the maintenance of free intercourse and the possibility of reciprocal influence between all its parts" (19). "Coherency" is important here for, just as with phenomenology, ego is seen as a centralizing entity.[16] It is possible to determine this attribute of coherency as a version of phenomenology's Ego as apodictic; thus, the *ego* is the site and agency of certainty, the organization of the "something" against the Nothing. However, there is also a part of the ego that forms, or is subsequently located, in the unconscious. This presents a seemingly potential difficulty, for how can an apodictically ascribed entity (phenomenologically speaking) operate as part of the unconscious? For psychoanalysis, the certainty of the unconscious is unquestioned (indeed insisted on), but its mechanisms, processional acts, and even manifestations are ongoing conundrums and mysteries. The ego is psychoanalysis' basis for the subject of certainty. How might we read this situation within a frame of absolute surety? The answer to this lies somewhat in Lacan's rendering of the unconscious and the Real. The Real can thus be read as the apodicticity of the unconscious for the ego. (On a side note to this issue, it is well-known that Husserl's Cartesian Ego is not altogether Cartesian, just as Lacan distinguishes the Freudian (and hence Lacanian) ego while acknowledging the overlap of the Real: "what the [Cartesian] I think is directed towards, in so far as it lurches into the I am, is a Real" (1986: 36))—although, note how Lacan describes this as "a" Real as distinct from a more universalizing "the" Real.[17]

The strategy here is to layer definitional aspects of the *ego* to slowly construct the concept of the cinematic *ego*. Clearly it would be nonsense to speak of a film's *ego*—at the very least it would render the term unrecoverable in an analytic sense. This is why "cinematic *ego*" does not refer to the *ego* of a film; rather it is cinema's capacity (and necessity) to devise a relational context with the spectator which operates *as if there were* an ego involved. Herein lies the intimacy of the spectating act; the anxiety that follows is twofold: the relinquishing of the *ego* as a coherent organization ("letting the right one in"); the transition from the innocent spectator and the confrontation with the Nothing, and its subsequent constructions and negotiations.

It is possible to add a further dimension to this idea of intimacy here, notably in terms of empathy, noting in advance the importance of Husserl's empathetic apperception.[18] Edith Stein presents us with a compelling

---

[16]Freud further distinguishes the ego's coherency in a comparison to actions of repression and pleasure. See *Beyond the Pleasure Principle SE XVIII*.

[17]Lacan goes further than this. In *The Instance of the Letter in the Unconscious*, for example, he describes the *cogito* as the cause of contemporary uncertainties and anxieties.

[18]The three *Nachlass* volumes on intersubjectivity (Hua XIII, XIV, XV) are particularly relevant to this aspect. For a summary statement of the relevant sections, see Ruthrof (2021) *Husserl's Phenomenology of Natural Language* (73–5).

phenomenological approach to empathy that offers possibilities to this sense of the cinematic *ego* and the intimacy of spectating. Stein rejects the idea that empathy is simply the adoption of the other's perspective, and that to be empathetic is to live the world of another as a distinct version of experience. Her argument is subtle and complex and rests to a large degree on her use of the term "primordiality." Stein employs primordiality to distinguish the "act side" of experiencing something and experiencing as *cogito* as "being-turned-towards" (see Stein 1989: 120–1). In other words, primordiality is the distinction of experiencing as it comes to be determined by and through a reflexive position. One example Stein gives is that of joy: "The memory of a joy is primordial as a representational act now being carried out, though its content of joy is non-primordial" (1989: 8). Similarly, there is the distinction in fantasizing: "The 'I' producing the fantasized world is primordial; the 'I' living in it is non-primordial" (9); and temporality: "The present non-primordiality points back to the past primordiality" (8). What Stein is aiming to achieve is an understanding of empathy as "the experience of foreign consciousness" (14), but she always wants to dismiss the idea that just because we become aware of, or feel, such an external position do we necessarily experience it in a reflexive mode. This is a classical phenomenological approach, emphasizing the layers of consciousness involved, the reflexive modality required, the differentiation of experiences, and so on. Our interests here are how we might adapt this Steinian version of empathy to intimacy and its cinematic variants. Happily, Stein gives us an example that should work well, for she speaks about watching an acrobat. To watch the acrobat (feel fear, anxiety, elation, relief as they somersault through the air into the hands of a catcher) is not to live the experience, corporeally and emotionally. As Stein puts it: "I am not one with the acrobat but only 'at' him. I do not actually go through the motions but *quasi*" (17). This "not one with" is the key here, for it leads on to Stein's assertion that empathy is not about being at one with the other, foreign experience. This is cinematic intimacy as it is understood here. The cinematic *ego* is invested with these same attributes of being "at" and *quasi*; and this is precisely why we can speak of a cinematic *ego* and our intimate connection with it.

The film spectator goes in search of the cinematic *ego*, even if they enter into this pursuit largely from a site of unawareness (a form of innocence). This "unawareness" is complex but works within a psychoanalytic version of the ego as repression and disguise, and in a phenomenological version in terms of appresentation (see the text that follows). In this way, the cinematic *ego* is the orientating and originating position; this is its coherency and organizational force. All that we experience in the experiencing of a film, how we encounter the presentifications, how we handle the as-if modes of phantasy (from passionate involvement to alienated disregarding), how we appresent (a concept we are required to return at a later point in the discussion) the sensuous other body, and so on . . . these are the necessary (apodictic) conditions of the cinematic *ego* and its intimate engagements.

b) Ego and the Body/Flesh

If coherency and the apodictic constitute one aspect of the *ego*, a second one is the *ego*, in terms of the analytic experience, in its function as a "go-between" of the internal, inner world, and the external world of otherness. Both Freud and Husserl, and a great many of those who follow, speak of this in terms of the body. For example, Freud, in theorizing the formation of the ego (and its distinction from the Id) locates the body as primary to both external and internal perceptions, notably with touch producing a type of internal perception. The ego is "first and foremost a bodily ego; it is not merely a surface entity, but is itself the projection of a surface" (*SE XX*: 19; 20). Lacan develops a sophisticated reading of the ego's link to the body and narcissism, starting as early as the 1936 paper on the mirror stage. There appears to be another conceptual stumbling block when we read in this paper: "It should be noted that this experience [the 'I' in psychoanalysis] sets us at odds with any philosophy directly stemming from the *cogito*" (2006: 75). However, it would be erroneous to link this "any philosophy" to phenomenology; Lacan is far closer to Husserl's divergent path from Descartes's *cogito*. (In *The Four Fundamental Concepts of Psychoanalysis* Lacan goes so far as to declare "that idiot Descartes!"; a parallel declaration in Husserl who, in *The Crisis*, states that it is "ludicrous" to see transcendental phenomenology as "Cartesianism".) Indeed, Lacan's exclusions of *cogito* philosophies strengthens this line of comparison of the ego. One of the crucial distinguishing aspects of Husserl's Ego *cogito* from the Cartesian method is derived precisely from this issue of the internal and external (and the "failure" of Descartes to effectively employ *epoché*). This is why Husserl states: "It remained hidden from Descartes that all such distinctions as 'I' and 'you'. 'inside' and 'outside,' first constitute themselves in the absolute Ego" (1997: §19).[19] It is from this analytic position, of the differentiating of the *ego* from various *cogito* frames, that permits us to follow Merleau-Ponty's reading of Freud in terms of flesh: "Hence the philosophy of Freud is not a philosophy of the body but of the flesh—The Id, the unconscious—and the Ego (correlative) to be understood on the basis of the flesh" (1968: 270).[20] The enfolding thus becomes: the *ego's* negotiating function of the interior/exterior, which includes the active enabling

---

[19]Later Husserl talks of the synthesis between Ego and other Ego, that is, of the "I-you-synthesis," noting that the "I-we-synthesis" is even more complicated. See *The Crisis*, especially sections 49, 50, and 51.
[20]The focus on, and hence usage of, "flesh" here continues the bringing of Husserl, Freud, and Lacan into conversation. For this reason the work on film and Merleau-Ponty's phenomenological take on "flesh" is not directly addressed, which I see as an important

(its coherency) of exchanges and flows, is performed at the level of the body (as narcissistic site), and in doing so becomes flesh; it becomes the *ego-as-flesh*. This is a crucial aspect of the spectator's relationship to the cinematic *ego*, to which we shall return shortly.

Before moving to the third aspect of the *ego* it is worth recalling Husserl's description of the Ego, the body, and what he calls the "over there" as distinct from the "from here". This is the other's body, appresented by the Ego and formed in and through the processes of pairing (see 1950: §51–4). Simply put, when we experience the other, we do so initially through the body. Our Ego and body, as "here," experience the other's Ego through their body (the sensuously seen) as "there." We appresent (their body and Ego) and in doing so form a connection (a pairing); this is what Husserl calls the assimilative apperception (1950: §54). This status of "here" and "over there" is significant because it determines all subsequent (inter)relations between Ego and other, underlining differences despite seeming to operate or establish versions of sameness. That is, the appresented other Ego will always be the body over there, no matter how the appresentational system proceeds.

The cinematic *ego* would appear to have an othered version of overthereness; there is the first order that each Ego-experiences in and with the body of the other (the "other's appresented primordial Nature" as Husserl puts it (1950: §55); there is the phantasy as-if rendering of the body when we experience re-presentations. In some ways the "as-if" status negates the first iteration (this is the "a film cannot have an *ego*" line of thinking), which suggests that we are actually dealing, phenomenologically speaking, with a re-presented Ego in cinematic terms. The spectator's appresentation of the film body commences from an over-over-there positionality. This is the body overthere that takes place in all forms of perception (our encounter with the other body) and the further "over" as we appresent (through the unique cinematic presentifications) the body of/in the film. Cinema compensates for this othered over-there through its materiality (i.e., the cinematic techniques to create "closeness"), its inherent narcissistic drive (in the Lacanian Mirror sense, see the text that follows), and the disguising of pairings as a normalizing aspect of perception (i.e., cinema's compelling invite to look and be looked at). Together, these processes work to create the cinematic *ego*-as-flesh rather than body.

c) The Sensuously Seen "Living" Body as Erotic Object-Choice

When Husserl distinguishes between *körperlich/körper* (bodily/body) as physical and *Leiblich/Leib* (bodily/body) as "living body" (1997: §9; §28)

---

parallel yet distinctive trajectory. Of particular note on this other trajectory is Vivian Sobchak's influential work on Merleau-Ponty, cinema, and body.

he is doing so in terms of the Ego and the world as bodily processes and actualizations. The first is the actuality of the life-world, the second is how we live in it as intuiting subjects. *Körper*, the physical body, has a sense of thingness for it is an object (presence) in the world of space and time; *Leib*, on the other hand, is one's own living body. They are, of course, closely connected, and Husserl describes it almost as a transitional process, as we move from the physical body to the lived one in the experiencing (i.e., Ego formation and Ego as body) of the self and the other (bodies) as Ego. This is not a sequential process, rather it is a core aspect of the appresentation of the other's Ego in the body. One's own living body is simultaneously physical and living (it has what Husserl calls *walten*, it prevails over objects), however the other's body requires ontic work to be seen as a living body for the Ego. This is the "living bodies of 'alien' Ego-subjects" (1997: §28) as they come to exist in the perceptual field, forming the complicated I-we-synthesis. It is also embedded in the question of how connections can be made and sustained between consciousness and the other/world: "if over against all consciousness and the essential being proper to it, it is that which is 'foreign' and 'other', how can consciousness be interwoven with it, and consequently with the whole world that is alien to consciousness" (1931: §39). Thus, we read this appresentational process between the physical and living body as part of the sensuously seen body.

Acknowledging that the I-we-synthesis offers a level of complexity in and of itself, how might we read the body/flesh of cinema and the spectator? Even at the risk of over-simplifying this set of convoluted relationships and their formative contexts, let us consider three iterations: (1) all bodies on the screen occupy a space/time of the physical. They are perceived as such (i.e., physical and as objects) within the natural attitude, by the innocent spectator, and potentially remain as such as we watch the film.[21] As all bodies commence from, and exist in, this manner they are all equally capable of becoming appresented or continue to exist in the shadowy background and on the periphery; (2) the spectator's appresentational processes, which includes the *walten* status (of prevailing over the body as object), shifts some of these bodies into the I-you-synthesis. This is the intentionality of the perceptual act, the harmoniously held synthesizing stream (of consciousness). These film bodies begin to take on attributes of the living body, held in the conditional status of as-if (phantasy's re-presentational mode). This is the relationship of interwoven consciousness of the other's

---

[21]Theoretically, and somewhat in practice, the star system works to distinguish the known body of celebrity as living rather than just physical. Part of this process is the extra-textual, or inter-textual (in the Bakhtinian sense), as the spectator arrives to the film already with interest in some bodies over others. However, this is an artifice that can only really operate in the most basic of ways, and certainly could not be described within an appresentational method. It could be argued, however, that this can potentially takes place in the second iteration.

Ego in nascent realization; (3) the I-we-synthesis forms in the spectator's Ego body/flesh and the appresented other Ego body/flesh. The "we" of spectator and cinematic body comes to challenge the conditional status of as-if and even the cinematic quasi-empathy. The glaring questions that present themselves here include: "why do we, as spectators, 'choose' one filmic body over another? Where does this object-choice emerge from? Why that body, in all its physicality, standing in the doorway, and not this other one, equal in its physicality, walking around the room?" The most obvious answer is that the film itself constructs certain bodies to be selected, it demands the spectator see some as quasi-living bodies (*Leib*) and others as merely existing in the physical (*körperlich*), even within those conditional aspects of as-if. However, even in the acknowledgment that this is how the aesthetic object works, and how we become spectators/readers in the participatory sense, the analytic experience allows for a different interpretation. This is where the phenomenological sensuously seen living body/flesh operates as the psychoanalytic erotic object-choice of the ego.

One of the common points of the *ego* for Husserl and Freud is that it is a unifying agency. For Husserl, this is the unitary transcending experience, the harmonious synthesizing, and so on; it is also why the I-we-synthesis is so complicated, as the Ego-consciousness attempts to incorporate (interweave) the other Ego-subject into its body. Freud's configuration appears different for it also includes, and analytically requires, an internalized unifying action. Even with the differences (e.g., Husserl of course does not have any equivalence of Id) the act of unifying, and the negotiations of internal/external present us with some intriguing conceptual overlapping. Let us consider a few of the ways Freud speaks of this unifying aspect of the ego, for in this lies the possibility to consider the erotic object-choice in phenomenological terms. In broad terms, this is the analytic issue of the internal and external as they are negotiated by the *ego*. The proposal here is that psychoanalysis' engagement with the internal-external has comparable gestures in phenomenology.

If we are to position the shift in *ego*-as-body from physical to living (*Leib*) (all the while acknowledging these can be simultaneously held states of being) within this context of the spectator's erotic object-choice, the first consideration must involve a reimagining of this as eidetic reduction.[22] Thus the proposition becomes: cinematic flesh is formed through ascribing the status of the "living body" to certain, chosen bodies on screen (the I-we-synthesis—i.e., made intimate) by the spectator's sublimated (erotic) object-cathexes. This requires some unpicking. Phenomenology's I-we-synthesis is

---

[22]It is important to note that "choice" of the object (*Objektwahl*) sounds proactive, that is, has intentionality—a version of choosing to choose. This is problematized by the act of object-choice happening at the infantile stage and therefore cannot have the usual sense of phenomenological intentionality ascribed to it at the conscious level. A potential reading would be to see this as unconscious intentionality. This is taken up in a later section of this chapter.

the renegotiated status of the Ego, as the appresenting subject (here the spectator) encounters the Ego of the other(s). As noted earlier, of all the possible bodies on screen, the spectator appresents but a few (perhaps even none if the film cannot or does not provide such an entity or capacity to do so). Because the *ego* is bodily (determined as well as "born from") this takes place initially, and continuously, in terms of corporeality. This spectating *ego* arrives at the screened body with pre-established object-cathexes; our capacity to become other than the innocent watcher, to be the attentive anxious spectator, is based on such a preparatory state. (Which is not to say that further object-formations cannot take place; indeed, this is part of the intimate spectator and cinema's capacity to engage us.) However, in as much as we might enact a version of eidetic reduction in this movement of the screened body to be one of *Leiblich*, with its bindings to the world and physicality, such a reduction will invariably commence from a site of the libidinally charged, yet there is not necessarily an ongoing attachment to the erotic (i.e., the object of the "loved one") nor does the living screened body retain that status (at least at the conscious level). The erotic object-cathexis enables the loss of innocence (the devisement of intimacy) but does not always hold or retain this affective power. This is why, eidetically speaking, the status of a living screened body does not have to look erotic to be libidinally driven; and vice versa—the libidinally driven does not always look erotic. The screened living body must also accommodate sublimation. Freud argues that the desexualization of the object-choice is a transformation of erotic libido into ego libido, transforming the drive into an oppositional one (*SE XIX*: 44–5). Hence, the body that functions as object-choice can do so beyond the libidinal as a version of transformed ego. This is how the I-we-synthesis can form and operate, for without it the *ego* could not allow for the other's *ego*, the otherness would remain, impermeable, defining that *ego* as that which is not (of) the self.

To push this idea further let us recall how the *ego* negotiates the id, for it is only through such negotiations that the I-we-synthesis is possible in the subject's relationship to both the self and the other, and how such relationships can be formed and sustained. The foreignness, its "abnormality" as Husserl describes it, of the other's *ego* is the preventative quality that needs to be overcome in order for there to be relation-formations. The other's *ego* exists as *ego* (as distinct from object), but unknown and perhaps unknowable. Phenomenology deals with this as the apperception of the other's body as we turn toward the other with intentionality; psychoanalysis speaks in similar terms but has the additional issue of a foreignness within the self. At the very least this is Lacan's version of extimacy—that which is so intimate and yet unknown (unconscious desires at the very least) that it becomes more intimate and more strange. To the ego, the id and super-ego are these agencies of the other, with the ego performing "reality-testing," as well as designating processes of time and motility. In these latter two processes we witness a strengthening of the ego as bodily based. Of course, these are also manifested in external versions; the super-ego becomes the socializing force, with the production and maintenance of the Law, the Good, the Beautiful, Discourse (and so the Symbolic) and so on, with each of these having its antagonistic, resistant others. The ego continually works to transform the id's disruptive and anarchic enactments into versions of ego, while the super-ego performs the function of transmuting both ego and id into "safe" socialized versions.[23]

An important clarification is required before continuing. Husserl speaks of the Ego's "glancing-towards" the object once the act of intentionality begins. This is a directed engagement with the object; it has *Achtsamkeit*, which carries the sense of attentiveness as well as care. Thus, the glancing Ego pays attention and cares about this object of consciousness; two attributes which would appear to lay the foundation for the Ego's accommodation of the other's Ego. These are also connotative of intimacy and, it is argued throughout here, an attendant anxiety. However, Husserl wants us to distinguish between this glancing Ego's attentive care, its *Achtsamkeit*, which is a version of recognition, and rendering of it in intentionality. There is a crucial difference between intentionality and apprehension of the object by consciousness: " . . . [the] intentional object of consciousness . . . is by no means to be identified with apprehended object" (Husserl 1931: §37). Instead we take on an evaluating act which is both part of the glance-toward and *Achtsamkeit*. These acts of valuation, the shaping of the glance-toward, yield an interpretative and affective engagement, they are: "in acts of joy to be enjoyed, in acts of love to the beloved, in acting to the action" (Husserl 1931: §37). (Here we add the acts of intimacy to be intimate, and the acts of anxiety to be anxious.) Significantly, however, they are not apprehended until there is an "objectifying turn of thought." The turning toward something can produce appreciation, but not apprehension (in the phenomenological sense). This, for Husserl, produces what he calls a "double *intentio*, a

---

[23]In section V ('The Dependent Relationships of the Ego') of *The Ego and the Id* there is a sustained discussion on guilt, some of which parallels Kierkegaard's approach to anxiety. This is seen, perhaps appropriately, when Freud deals with melancholia describing the powerful hold the super-ego has so that the ego: " . . . ventures no objection; it admits its guilt and submits to punishment" (*SE XIX*: 52); and later how the "excessively strong super-ego . . . rages against the ego with merciless violence" (54). It is not at all difficult to see Kierkegaard's religious-driven anxiety emerging from the externalized super-ego. This line would take us too far from the issues at hand, but it is noteworthy that Freud speaks of the categorical imperative of the super-ego, and the role of the ego in keeping this guilt unconscious. The opposite of the innocent spectator is not necessarily the guilty one, however in these terms, there is potential to read a distinct category of the guilty spectator and his/her (guilty) pleasures as the melancholic spectator. In some ways this is cinema's capacity toward devising what might be termed the traumatic spectator.

twofold directedness" (1931: §37). This can be compared to the physical or lived body, distinguished in part through this othered directedness.

So far all of this works within the current set of issues and interpretations: the Ego's glance-toward works nicely in terms of the screened body and the idea of the intimate spectator (our attentiveness and care for the screened body is formed through this intimacy); the spectator can experience some or all bodies in appreciation, but not necessarily in apprehension—only when they become the lived body (as flesh) does this take place, which is the objectifying turn of thought; and the acts of valuation shape the spectator's relationship to the body. What is proposed here is that the valuative act commences with intimacy as a primary function (i.e., the act of spectating cannot exist without it), which in turn shapes all subsequent acts of valuation. Herein lies the production of anxiety out of intimacy, for if valuative acts (the attentive care directed toward the object on screen) commence from the intimate, all apprehensions will be shaded accordingly. Terror, pain, desire, pleasure, the sublime as well as the inane, the frivolous, and so on, are first directed from a site of intimacy and the devisements that follow are apprehended within that set of valuations.

However, before we become too comfortable, there is another aspect to this phenomenological line of apprehension and attention which needs to be addressed, for it requires interpretative work to configure it within the analytic experience and our cinematic concerns and inflections. As noted earlier, psychoanalysis determines the ego as a mediator between the id and the external world order; phenomenology may appear to lack the concept of the id,[24] but it certainly engages at length between the Ego and the internal/external in a fashion that can be effectively reimagined for the issues at hand. Husserl insists on abandoning the notions of the inner and outer in terms of perception, instead positing what he terms immanent and transcendental perceptions. Immanent perceptions or "intentional experiences immanently related" are defined as when Ego and object "belong to the same stream of experience . . . whenever an act is related to an act (a *cogitatio* to a *cogitatio*) of the same Ego" (1931: §38). With the transcendentally directed, on the other hand, all acts are "directed towards essences, or towards the intentional experiences of other Egos with other experience-streams" (1931: §38). It is easy to understand why Husserl would want to make such a distinction, for the insight yielded (and analytic strategies that are opened up) makes "inner" and "outer" feel altogether limited. In these terms, the psychoanalytic ego must be located as transcendentally directed. Psychoanalysis' ego, and its relationship to the id and super-ego, is infused with transcendental perception because all three are precisely defined as not belonging to the "same stream of experience," even if they perform

---

[24] See the chapter on the nightmare for further discussion of this.

within the meta-structure (indeed, metapsychology in the Freudian sense) of conscious/unconscious. It is possible to read each of these in terms of the transcendentally directed acts, even if this is one of those moments when the ego of psychoanalysis has difference to the Ego of phenomenology. This difference is not simply based on the *ego's* relationship to self and other (as may appear to be the case), rather it is because the *ego* appears to hold simultaneously an immanent and transcendentally directed mode. Whereas phenomenology locates the transcendentally directed toward other Egos, psychoanalysis has to allow for this to accommodate the ego's relationship to the id and super-ego. One of psychoanalysis' greatest (and most disruptive and disturbing) contributions to thought has been the split subject (the *Ichspaltung*) where parts of the psyche are seen as foreign and alien to the self. Lacan's idea of *extimacy*, for example, is precisely the id as the unrecognized foreign part of our desires. Perhaps something like a transitional "immanent-transcendental directed mode," a tertiary level, could be accommodated within such a discussion. In turn, there is also the issue of unity, for as we noted at the outset, *ego* is a unifying agency for both analytic approaches, bringing the *ego* and its others into relational contexts (which are not necessarily homogeneous or synthesized). Further to this, where do we locate the intimate spectator? How is this spectator's *ego* located within this intentional set of experiencing?

To posit the concept of the intimate spectator there is a need to address this issue of the *ego's* relationship to the internal and external (including the transcendental and immanent perceptual systems). Intimacy is formed in part through *Gewahren*, that growing awareness or readiness to be attentive toward the other. Both phenomenology and psychoanalysis declare (consistently and with insistence) that they are analytic systems which foreground, utilize, and expose acts of reflexivity. So, when the combinatory system engages with the *ego* there is a necessary analytic frame of reflexive thinking. This takes place in the directed analysis of the internal (the *ego's* reflexive mode toward the self) and external (the *ego's* reflexive mode toward the self and the world); in both cases, components are othered to produce the internal othered self and the external othered world. To articulate the intimate spectator, anxiety is the marker of these reflexive modes, both internal and external. However, and this reveals the complexity of the matter, this reflexivity is not a simple binarism, rather it operates as modes or even intensities. This is because, somewhat curiously and seemingly contradictory, it is possible to be reflexive without being aware of this process taking place. Let us consider this within the analytic experience.

The complex dimensions of the experiencing experience are to be explored elsewhere here; it happens temporally (formations of now-points, discussed in more detail in the following chapter on time), spatially (the awareness of the body's motility and in space(s)), the disruptive moments of the nightmare and the sublime, and so on. For Husserl, this is the *cogito's* capacity at any time to become reflexive, to form a new *cogitatio* directed toward inner perception, and form the evaluative act driven by reflexivity (see e.g., *Ideas* § 38; 39). Crucially, for the issues at hand, Husserl locates a version of this reflexivity as apprehending and experiencing others (*Ideas* § 38) (in memory and empathy, to which we add intimacy cf. also Fifth Meditation in *Cartesian Meditations*). This is the conditional requirement to be a spectator, and particularly the intimate spectator in their quasi-empathic (primordiality) situation. (For Husserl, it should be noted, that it is located within the domain of phantasy, and so is a re-presentational process.) This is also the solution to the seeming contradiction of a reflexive act happening unawares. The very formation of the intimate spectator often takes place in an unknowingly reflexive manner as the experiencing of the experience of spectating and happens either through, or in combination with (this list is not complete): (a) in time as afterward—"I remember that film, or that moment in a film; I remember how it felt to watch that film; I experience my remembering of the film so that it comes into my ego," and so on; (b) through analytic work—"I watch this film through the analytic concepts; this film is experienced through the engagement with ideas or from an intentionality of critical work" (e.g., phenomenological *epoché* or psychoanalytic interpretation, or feminism, or social realism, and so on); (c) by intentionally adopting the reflexive stance—"I watch this film as a spectator who is gendered or located culturally, or whose pleasures lie in such a fashion and such a direction;" (d) through the work of the film itself as reflexive object—"As I watch this film I am made aware of its closeness or distance, its familiarity or strangeness (or defamiliarizations), to me;" (e) as a foregrounding of the experience of spectating as an act of empathy, memory, pleasure, anxiety, and so on—"As I watch this film I experience pleasure, but why?; whose pleasure is this, on the screen, in the other's body, that appears to be mine, but is constructed outside of my self/ego? Whose memories, acting as if they are mine, are these?"; (f) the ego's reflection of the film and the experience as spectator—"How is this collection of objects (bodies, spaces, moments) which coalesces into a film related to me and how do I construct it as such?"

Through these, and the other possibilities not listed, we align the intimate spectator with a conception of consciousness and its "intimate attachment with the real world" (Husserl 1931: §39) as it negotiates the Ego, its relationships with the external, and the other in reflexive acts. These reflexively directed acts of consciousness commence from, and are determined in, the *ego* as self and corporeal within this context of the external other. This is in keeping with Freud's defining of the ego's role as continually negotiating the demands of the internal (id and super-ego) with the demands of the external world. This connection can be made even stronger through Lacan's reading of the ego as an object, rather than the "I." The ego is thus "something else—a particular object within the experience of the subject. Literally, the ego is an object—an object which fills a certain function which we here call the Imaginary function" (1988b: 44) (translation modified). The Imaginary function, to recall, is the reflexive domain of the imago, the psychical moments when the self is, or can become or is in the state of becoming, self-aware, reflexively engaged with its position in the world. Read in this way, the organizing, coherent, negotiating ego performs these tasks under the gaze of the mirror. In these terms, as an object, the cinematic domain (its films, spectators, cultural embeddedness and resistances, histories, and futures) also contains a version of the ego. The cinematic ego would thus align with the idea of a series of *egos*, appearing in the "spectral decomposition of the function of the ego" and "this spectral decomposition is evidently an Imaginary decomposition" (1988b: 165). (Cinematically appropriate, although Lacan has the dream in mind.) For in psychoanalysis there is not a singular "ego," but this multiplicity of an object, with its polyphonic voices, constantly striving to sound unified in the storm of conflicting demands both internal and external. This series of egos is what we see in Husserl's *leibhaftigen*—the embodied self-presence of an individual object, which is "the individual or some logico-categorical modification of the same" (1931: §39 see also §15). This "logico-categorical modification" is read here as the relationship(s) of the *ego* to the states of dependent and independent, with the important conditional status of not directly determined by (i.e., not depending on or being independent of), rather through relations such as "of being in," "contained in," "related to," and so on. In other words, the ego is seen as a series which is determined in and by its constant modifications through these relational contexts and conditions which are located beyond dependencies and independencies. Thus, for example, part of the series of *egos* is being in the id or super-ego and so needs to address their demands through compromise and negotiation; another part can be contained in the intimate attachment to the world; and yet another part may find itself conditioned by its "related to" status of directed consciousness (loving, enjoying, fearing, judging, moralizing, and so on). The series of *egos* is thus read as unified and organized as "*ego*" but is actually constituted in each iteration of "being in," "contained in/ by," "related to," and so on. Significantly, the movement through the series necessarily implies an *ego* of something, and all other possible *egos* in the series become located in the Nothing. This is taken up in terms of the ego and narcissism in the following, particularly in the formation of the intimate spectator.

This same idea of the series of *egos* and their modifications (and modifying practices) can be applied to the formation of the intimate spectator and their anxious moments and, more dynamically, how such a spectator exists and functions. The intimate spectator is active (perhaps even activated in some ways) in the spectral decomposition of the *ego* (as a series of *egos*) because in their experiencing of the film, the object/status of the *ego* is modified. The embodied self-presence of the intimate spectator becomes, effectively, a series of *egos* in the encounter with the film. Each shift in directed consciousness, every affective turn, all acts of interpretation and appresenting, and so on, are formulated in this spectral, Imaginary decomposition. In this manner, it is possible to read Husserl's notion of conflictual Ego positionalities when we engage with phantasy (in this case, film), or when phantasy and reality mix. Husserl determines this in a number of ways, but the consistent interpretation he offers is dependent on the idea that the status of the Ego changes when it is confronted by these ontic shifts and as a consequence, the acts themselves change, or new acts and positionalities are generated. Similarly, the Ego changes and shifts what it turns its attention toward, what its glance is directed at. Two examples in terms of apprehensions illustrate this: "But if the apprehensions are inhibited, if they are apprehensions inhibited by other apprehensions, then we have altered and complicated phenomena" (2005: 544); "Things are so complicated precisely because every step of spontaneity again generates new 'apprehension,' and that means that it constitutes new objectivity" (2005: 543). The first of these comments reveals the idea of an inhibiting quality to apprehensions; this aligns with the shift in the *ego* series with the encounter of the different or new. The second comment shows how such a series involves new objectivity formations (which must include both the new objectivity and the grasping of the object as a new object) within a (supposedly) settled apprehending Ego. What is perhaps of even greater significance is the way in which Husserl sees inhibition as a disguised process which acts in an altering fashion: "Every positional experience can undergo 'inhibition,' interruption by other experiences, even if they are obscure; it can undergo conflicting overlapping with them, annulment" (2005: 545). These are precisely the ways in which psychoanalysis addresses the idea of inhibition and symptom formations in anxiety. Obscurity (repression and disguise), interruption, conflict, and annulment are all attributes that psychoanalysis uses to describe and define anxiety.

This process of the shifting series of *egos* even takes place prior to the spectator beginning to watch the film. As we turn our attention, our evaluating attentive care, this *Achtsamkeit*, to the film experience we arrive with a range of knowledges, preconceptions, emotions, and even prejudices regarding the film and how we might experience (judge, feel, react to) it. Intimacy begins prior to the film. This is to locate the intimate spectator in the Imaginary, each (spectral) decomposition and modification in the series of *egos* performing a reflexive task as we accommodate the film into the *ego* and the *ego* into the film (and thus the negotiations of internal/external, dependency/independency, relevancy/irrelevancies, self/other).[25] The

---

[25]This sense of the doubled *ego* is taken up in the following. Husserl's analysis of shifting positionality and modifications is apposite here. It is only through such shifts, and how divergent

relinquishing or preservation of "*egos*" within the series can be interpreted as a moment of anxiety (which can be pleasurable as well as disturbing). The intimate spectator's series of *egos* in the encounter with the film (i.e., the spectral decomposition of film and *ego* in this exchange) moves through, or holds together simultaneously, modifications; film and spectator shift and change as the series of *egos* are appresentationally directed, belong (or are alienated from), are contained in (or exceed the containment) these processes. Such an interpretation allows for reimagined processes of spectatorship; for example, a film's polysemes are actually products of the series of *egos* and subsequent/contiguous consciousness modification(s). To better understand how this can be such a compelling process, it is time to turn to a related issue.

The Enthymematic

As is noted elsewhere here (in Chapter 6 on possessiveness and the nightmare), Husserl employs the concept of enthymematic to explore the relationship between phantasy and reality. Given that we shall return to this at a later point, it is sufficient to note that Husserl's focus in terms of phantasy and the enthymematic relates to the structure of the rhetorical syllogism in terms of the absenting. This ties in with the issues at hand, but there will be a different inflection here, considering how we might analyze this in two related contexts: narcissism; and the spectator's consciousness modification of the film (intimacy) as well as the modification of her consciousness by the film (anxiety). It is done in this way to address how the internal/external (with all the above-mentioned attendant issues of multiplicity, polyphony and dissonance, *ego* as series, and modifications) is not a binarism, but a fluid site of activity and creation, as well as negotiations of integration and/or dissidence of intimacy.

Husserl begins Appendix XLV of *HUA XI* by stating "An important theme for my analysis is the mixture of phantasy and actually experienced reality, as well as the distinction between the phantasy of what is purely immanent and the phantasy of natural events" (2005: 545). The key term here is, of course, "mixture." The series of *egos* (and spectral decomposition

---

sites are formed, that the mixing of phantasy and reality can take place, phenomenologically speaking: "Positionality, however, is an essential characteristic that conceals in itself the ideal possibility of a 'corresponding' belief, of a belief that actually posits. To positionality there corresponds its modification, apositionality. To all doxic acts, then, quasi-doxic acts correspond: the appositional modifications of positional doxic acts. Modal variants, which, of course, are new positionalities, belong to positionality" (2005: 544). It is important to note that positionality and apositionality are not binarisms, a kind of attached "opposites." That Husserl speaks of quasi-doxic acts and new positionalities in the plural sense is of significance to our cinematic concerns, as well as the comparisons to Lacan's ego series.

in the case at hand) can be aligned to this sense of in-mixing; and the heterogeneous status (in ontology, temporality, self and other, and so on) of each component (phantasy, reality, Ego, *ego*) means that fluidity and instability are the indeterminacies and inconsistencies to be worked through. Put another way, the ontological differences between phantasy (the re-presentational material of dreams, films, memories, stories, psychoses, hysteria, and so on) and reality is an instability in the operation of the *ego* (a shift in its series). Temporality is of the same order, as noted in now-points and condensing presentifications[26]; it makes a difference to the *ego* if this perception is happening in the now, or in the past or future, or in the spaces in which it takes place. This is a difference that causes a shift to and in the *ego* itself as it treats a memory, a moment of the now, or an imagined future moment with difference. Consider, for example, how a memory's status and relationship to the *ego* is enacted as a difference (to the now, or this now-point as distinct from another one, to the *ego's* relationship to that memory "then" and "now"—"I remember how different I was then"; "I feel different now to then"; and so on) and the deferring actions that take place when we remember ("That memory changes how I feel now"; "You remind me of someone . . . but I defer the meaning of what this means" . . .). The same is true of cinema. The spectator remembers previous events and adjusts their understanding and feelings accordingly, but in doing so they produce a different meaning (possibly) and defer other possible meanings. Even more convoluted is when the spectator's experience of the film evokes a personal memory (a doubled phantasy), so that they are experiencing (phenomenologically directed) an experience (a film) mediated through another experience (memory).[27] The *ego* itself becomes different, or a different aspect of the *ego* is foregrounded. The spectator's intimacy can only take place through the series of *egos* and the engagement with the film. However, not all the iterations of the *ego* are valid, drawn-into, are intimate with all aspects of the film. The *ego's* organizing and interconnecting (mediating) role means that intimacy is a resonating function; what "resonates" with the spectator is really the validating (experiencing in phenomenological terms) *ego* within a series of *egos*.

Indifference, in this regard, is the misaligned *ego* of the (anxious) spectator. However, this should not be seen merely as a pattern of orientation and equivalence. If we take the case of temporality and pose the idea of indifferent time (which produces an indifferent now-point), the experiencing and validating *ego* is only indifferent at that moment. Another time, another

---

[26] See Chapter 2 on time for a discussion on presentifications in terms of the phenomenological 'origins' and how we might reimagine a psychoanalytic equivalent.
[27] There is something to be done with this idea of difference in terms of Derrida's *différance*. The difference between the *ego* in the series and the deferral of relationally derived constructions are certainly to be found here.

moment of the now-point, and the series of *egos'* relationship to that film (or the moment in that film) may well produce a different affective relationship, perhaps even one of absolute intimacy. In these terms, the now-point holds both the indifferent and intimate in the moment, which is only possible precisely because the *ego* is a series. This suggests that the series can hold its opposites and antagonisms, which is certainly in keeping with the analytic experience's reading of the *ego*. The word "indifference" is a gift in this sense, for just as it can be read as a separate *ego* position to intimacy, it is also a determining status; thus, an indifferent now-point can also be seen as a now-point in difference. That is, an *ego* position that has become separated and "sees" differently—it is an *ego* in-difference.

Cinema's "system" of enthymematic structures is part of the devisements to negotiate relations of intimacy and indifference. "System" is employed with caution here because although it is possible to imagine a systemic order (in the sense of being part of cinema's logic and aesthetics), articulating such an order is a large task, and beyond the direct concerns here. The focus needs to be on the intimate spectator and the analytic experience (primarily the issue of the *ego*), and so cinema's constructions of enthymemes will be discussed accordingly, as well as the idea of cinematic enthymemes as a somewhat unique aspect of this aesthetic/rhetorical form. Therefore, two exemplars are raised here: the *ego* and narcissism; and enthymematic *lacunae* and/as consciousness modifications.

A defining, and therefore shared, attribute of enthymemes is of course their pivotal *lacunae*, for without the missing premise or conclusion these structures would be more straightforward syllogisms. In this manner enthymemes can perform as moments of *concretization* (particularly in the sense which Roman Ingarden (1973a, b) uses the term as a proactive reader who necessarily constructs the work), as sense-making processes, and as sites of protensions as the spectator constructs possible futures and ideas. Furthermore, the *lacunae* aspect gives us an opportunity to consider another side to the Nothing in its anxious-ridden moments; that is, anxieties that surround meaning and its contestations. In the following discussions, this key enthymematic quality will be explored in terms of the doubled *ego* and how modifications take place in and beyond the spectating acts.

a) The *Ego* and Narcissism

So far, we have been dealing with two broad conceptualizations of the intimate spectator in terms of the *ego*. The first is that the *ego* is the organizational site for the mixing of the inner world and the external, the formations of self and other through this in-mixing, and the transitional processes involved (i.e., the "movement" between the internal and external, dependence and independence). The second is that there is not a single *ego*, rather the *ego* operates as or in a series of *egos*, which may perform the same fundamental functions of organization and mediation but can also be heterogeneously sited. This heterogeneity, it was proposed, can be located in processes and actions such as temporality, the body in the world and for the self (as flesh, such as Merleau-Ponty's flesh as element of being 1968: 139), motility and the body in spaces, instigations of affect, and so on. Part of the intimate spectator, in these terms, is the phantasizing *ego(s)* and the negotiation of reality and phantasy. To work through this idea further, these issues of mediation and multiplicity are located within a doubled *ego* and a resulting double narcissism. The strategy here is to consider how Husserl develops the double Ego, compare this to Lacan's model of double narcissism, and explore how this critical apparatus might work in terms of the intimate spectator.

Within such a strategy there is a need to account for the *ego*'s position in and outside of Nothing. One way of reading this in phenomenological terms is the doxic and quasi-doxic states formed through positionality and apositionality. This would be to locate the *ego(s)* as forming doxic positions, with varying degrees of contestation or agreement; and quasi-doxic *ego* positions emerging from this in-mixing. For each doxic positionality there is necessarily a related position located in or as Nothing. This is why the spectator can move in and out of affective states, become more or less intimate with the film, or more or less indifferent to it and even moments within it. For example, the film spectator's *ego* directs their apprehending gaze and experiences fear, or joy, or indifference. At this moment, this now-point, the *ego* forms a quasi-doxic position and all that it encounters in the film is understood and experienced within such an environment. But the spectator's partner's *ego* takes up another position (a different quasi-doxic attitude) and for all of the first spectator's fears, they experience indifference (or humor, remembered trauma, disgust, masochistic delight . . .). But the first spectator's position can shift (it almost invariably will), and the now-point of that *ego* in the series passes. However, there must be some investment in the *ego*'s attachment to the quasi-doxic position and the meanings and feelings produced therein; this is the formation of intimacy. On some occasions this attachment is strong enough to create a resistance to other positions, while other moments can see a fragile and easily dissolved attachment. The spectator's intimate relationship actually depends on some slippage in the series of *egos*, because each one produces a reinvigorated attachment. The sources of such attachments are multiple, but broadly they work between the spectator's interest, the text's inventions, and the cultural designators (what is permitted or denied, what has gone before, and so on). Such attachments can become so powerful that the *ego* can become invested at a deeper level; psychoanalysis has a multiplicity of iterations of this, one particularly interesting version is Lacan's aphanisis, which is the fear of the loss of the signifier of subjectivity (see in particular 1986: 216–29). This aphanisistic fear is really an anxiety of the Nothing that haunts the subject through Otherness. In such terms it has a near Kierkegaardian quality to it. Our investment in certain signifiers gives them such a crucial status that to lose that signifier is to lose the sense of being, of subjectivity, and of existence. This partly explains why some signifiers carry so much psychical power for the individual and even at the broader historico-cultural level. The counter to these attachments is abandonment, as the *ego* within the series shifts and either rethinks the interpretative or affective relationship they had or adopts a different perspective. This happens at the very site-specific (a single moment or scene within the film), a larger textual level (the film itself is "revised"), or at a systemic level (a sense of the world and all it contains changes in the spectator's valuations and judgments). Phenomenology's analysis of consciousness and reality necessarily includes this sense of shifting, and Husserl's comment works equally well in terms of the spectator's experience of the film. Thus we can reimagine the following in terms of film: "It can always happen that the further course of experience [the watching of the film as it unfolds] will compel us to abandon [from the site of the *ego* and its series] what has already been set down and justified [what the spectator has established in intimacy] in the light of empirical canons of rightness [at the individual, group, social, and historical levels of reading the film]" (1931: §46).

This process takes place because the *ego* is not the unary entity it first appears to be. This is somewhat self-evident in psychoanalysis, so let us consider how phenomenology develops such a proposition. For Husserl, whenever we engage with a mixing of worlds (here the actual, real world and the phantasized world of cinema) there are (at least) two Egos. It is worth quoting Husserl at length here: "It is also true that I can have a world belonging to phantasy hover before me. Moreover, since this world presupposes a center of apprehension at which I continually place myself, I will have in general and perhaps even necessarily a place in the phantasy world as phantasied Ego, quasi-seeing the phantasy world from the phantasied Ego's standpoint. But then we have precisely two Egos, the Ego of the phantasy world and the actual Ego, to which the act of reproducing belongs. And likewise, we have the duality of Ego-experiences, those that belong to the phantasy Ego—now meagerly, now vitally, and in abundance—and those that belong to the phantasying Ego. Just as in the case of the perceptual quasi-positing belonging to perceptual [*perzeptiven*] intuition (image intuition)" (2005: 556). The two Egos, for the issues at hand, are the actual Ego and the cinematized Ego. The phantasized/cinematized Ego is what enables the intimate spectator to form; and just as this cinematized Ego will produce quasi-judgments from the cinematized Ego-experience, what takes place will act as if it is "real."[28] This reality is the presupposed center of apprehension—but does this create a problem?

---

[28] See Chapter 4 for further discussion on the Real and reality.

The presuppositional nature, this sense of being required to occupy, seems to suggest that the film creates the site from which to experience, that is, to apprehend, make sense of, enjoy, to find pleasure or distaste or fear in, and so on. However, even if this site exists (which clearly it does in some sense, film theory has spent close to a century picking over it, and art theory even longer if we consider perspective in art to be comparable) phenomenology's response must be that the phantasized Ego position is a construction from the spectator and the film, as stable and unstable, agreed and contested, and fixed and fluid as any *ego* position. It should be noted that this issue is not Husserl's; his focus is on the relationship of the Ego, the actual world, and phantasy. What that phantasy is—a film, a dream, memory, a painting—is somewhat irrelevant to his argument because this is the phenomenological re-presentational quality of phantasy. The crucial aspect is that there is the center of apprehension which is taken up by the actual Ego in order to form the phantasizing, cinematizing Ego. What we also observe in this confluence is that there are not simply two Ego positions (actual and phantasizing), but a further "splitting" into experiencing in/by the phantasy Ego and the phantasizing Ego. Similarly, Husserl also speaks of the thematizing Ego, which is "productive" and "accepting," as distinct from neutral acts (2005: 707). This is an opportune moment to bring Lacan's double narcissism to the discussion.

Lacan's analysis of narcissism commences from two primary sources: (1) Freud's work of narcissism and its separation of ego libido and sexual libido (see, e.g., Freud *SE XIV*). It is noteworthy in these terms that Freud speaks of the ego's role in converting object-libido (through object-choice) into narcissistic libido (*SE XIX*: 24–5; 44–5) and these processes' relationship to sublimation; (2) Lacan's own work on the mirror stage as part of the secondary process of narcissism formation, leading him to assert (on a number of occasions) that "the human ego is founded on the basis of the Imaginary relation" which is "the Imaginary origin of the ego-function" (1988b: 115) (translation modified).[29] Even though the sexual libido and the ego instincts/drives (*Ichtriebe*) are different, they are indistinguishable (see, e.g., Freud *SE XIV*: 76 and Lacan 1988b: 119). It is from this complex interweaving of issues surrounding the ego, its drives, and objects, that Lacan produces the idea of two narcissisms.

The most obvious interpretation of two narcissisms is the primary and secondary, but that is only part of the story.[30] There is also this doubling

---

[29]Freud's conceptualization of the ego and narcissism is somewhat convoluted and does shift over time; it has produced considerable discussion of the "great reservoir of the libido." For sake of clarity here, it is important to recall that he designates a primary narcissism and a secondary one, the latter involves withdrawal from the object: "The narcissism of the ego is thus a secondary one, which has been withdrawn from objects" (*SE XIX*: 45).

[30]The other obvious designation would be Freud's distinctions between narcissistic and anaclitic object-choices (*SE VII, XIV*). However, this is tangential to the issues at hand.

through the relationship of the libidinal drives toward the self and/or toward the object; this is the two narcissisms of ego and object-choice. There is also a third doubling, Lacan's accumulative two narcissisms, which is determined through an in-mixing of the constitution of reality and the body (Lacan 1988b: 124). This is derived from Lacan's Schema of the Two Mirrors which reappears in various guises throughout his works, beginning, of course, with the mirror stage itself. All of this material, these revisited examinations by Lacan, can be reduced to the single issue of the self's relationship to reality; an issue that returns us to some fundamental phenomenological issues and ideas. Indeed, in these discussions we find a Lacan operating very much "within" the phenomenological.

Just as Husserl articulates the idea of two Egos in terms of reality and phantasy, devising positionalities that inevitably lead to indistinguishable differences between the phantasy Ego and the phantasizing Ego, so Lacan's two narcissisms are engaged with the constitution of reality (its apprehension) and the body as ontologically validating. This conditional aspect of "validation" is a further common point; for phenomenology it is, at the very least, apodictically driven, and for psychoanalysis it is the reflective state of forming (through ongoing attempts of authentication as psychical process) subjectivity. Thus, the first of the two narcissisms becomes "the narcissism connected with the corporeal image. This image is identical for the entirety of the subject's mechanisms and gives his *Umwelt* its form . . . It makes the unity of the subject, and we see it projecting itself in a thousand different ways . . .) (Lacan 1988b: 125). The "corporeal image" is both the individual's relationship to self (via the ego) and the constant reproduction of such images in the world in the attempt to confirm and sustain a sense of unity and relationship. Although this is not in itself the phenomenological natural attitude, it is not difficult to see how such a narcissistic construction of the *Umwelt* comes to be an integral part of such an attitude. The unity of the subject, which in the analytic situation is constantly dismantled and recognized as an illusion, is reproduced to further this relational context of (unified) self and the world. Let us return to this as a cinematic function after considering the other narcissism.

Lacan describes the second narcissism in particularly phenomenological terms: "the reflection in the mirror [of the schema, but more broadly as a site of reflexivity] indicates an original noetic possibility and introduces a second narcissism. Its fundamental pattern is immediately the relation to the other" (1988b: 125). This "relation to the other" is the defining and distinguishing attribute of this second narcissism, and consequently it becomes the ways in which we, all subjects in their subjective negotiations, form the sense of the self (the Imaginary) and "libidinal relation[s] to the world" (1988b: 125), with all the attendant aspects of belonging (or being alienated), making meaning (or the loss of meaning), as well as all possible ruptures and resistances. For Lacan, the second narcissism forms the libidinal being, determined in the reflected intersubjectivities of the Other. The relations that emerge from this libidinal being determine intimacy (among other things) and this allows us to locate the intimate spectator as part of this second narcissism. Furthermore, Husserl's "presupposed center of apprehension," discussed earlier, can be enfolded into this Lacanian double narcissism. For Husserl this presupposed center (which the Ego puts itself in) is a reflexive relationship to reality and phantasy, with the distinctions playing out accordingly; for Lacan the function of the ego plays a "fundamental role in the structuration of reality" (1988b: 126), which is determined precisely through the narcissistic reflexive positions. (This "fundamental role" aligns with phenomenology's transcendental Egological position.) The libidinal being (of the second narcissism) negotiates reality and phantasy (the imaginary worlds as well as Imaginary relations) from these presupposed centers of apprehension, and in doing so takes up the double Ego. Of course, the two narcissisms are not the double Ego. However, what can be argued is that the two narcissisms function within each of the double Egos through this structuration of reality, the drives of the self (*Ichtriebe*), the libidinal glance-toward, the reflexive modality of *ego* to reality, and the negotiations of the inner/external worlds when such in-mixing takes place.

This situation of the two narcissisms and the double Ego is an integral part of the intimate spectator. Let us list some of the ways that this operates.

i) The phantasizing Ego is libidinally driven (the libidinal being) because relations form through self-interest. The taking up of the appresenting "glance towards" is Ego driven (at its arrival at the most critically developed this is the phenomenological act). In cinematic terms this is intimacy formed through (self) interest. We may not be conscious[31] of this, but the spectator forms cinematic relations by "becoming" the libidinal being. This is the spectator "in love" with a film or an element (actor, sound, color, setting, and even memory of). This is the film (or element within it) as the loved object: "The loved object [a film], when invested in love, is, through its captative effect [intimacy] on the subject [spectator] strictly equivalent to the ego-ideal [Freud's concept of the super-ego] . . . there is a genuine perversion of reality [the intimate spectator] through the fascination [the center of apprehension] with the loved object and its overestimation [phantasy and hence the phantasized Ego]" (Lacan 1988b: 126).

ii) The double narcissism exerts considerable power (it is reality forming after all, leading to the Husserlian abandoning of "empirical canons of rightness") and part of this entails the distinguishing between reality and phantasy that takes place at the level of the *ego*. Husserl requires the double

---

[31]That is, in the analytic experience, psychoanalytically the "conscious" as the mediatory of self to external world; and phenomenologically the "conscious" as the directed appresenting glance.

Ego (the real Ego and the phantasy Ego), and then a further explication of the phantasizing Ego, to explain this. The intimate spectator, however, plays out the lack of distinction for as long as possible (extending now-points) and in as much "depth" as possible (extended appresentations). This desire, compulsion even, to extend the blurred distinctions between reality and phantasy can be reinterpreted in terms of Freud's comments on the ego and perception, reality, hallucinations, and memory. No matter how strong the memory, it is always distinguishable from external perception and hallucination; but hallucinations can seem like perceptions. The intimacy of the spectator relies somewhat on mixing all these elements (the re-presentational modes of phantasy) and holding off the distinctions. This can be seen as a type of (Freudian) cathexis (*Besetzung*), the quantity of psychical energy located in a feeling, body (or part of), issue, and so on. The distinction between these elements (memory, hallucination) is partly derived from cathexis, which in turn is built on the *ego's* relationship to the external world. Because the blurring of hallucination with perception takes place when cathexis (from a memory-trace) is completely integrated into the acts of perception (see Freud *SE XIX*: 13), it is proposed here that a weakened version of this forms in the intimate spectator's engagement with the film. In other words, the phantasizing Ego operates within the passage of cathexis (of intimacy) so that perception operates in the as-if; this is heightened in those moments when the film seems most "real," at its most intimate.

iii) All versions of these alternative sites and positions of the *ego* (as series, as double, as twofold in the narcissistic domain, and as formulations of cathected impulses) must negotiate the complex meta-critical issue of division, distinction, and the inseparable. For in each of these interpretative gestures there is the common issue of wanting to see distinctions, but all the while acknowledging that ultimately not only is this not possible, it is also a requirement of the interpretation. This is because in the designation of, for example, the real Ego and the phantasy Ego, the distinction appears to be two Egos, or perhaps two types of Egos, but there is always the sense that the unifying aspect of *ego* means that this is also the Ego located in two ontic (or doxic) fields. The issue is really one of how the unifying attribute of the *ego* copes with fields that attempt to split it.[32] The intimate spectator

---

[32]Expressed in a different way, Husserl articulates the differences in a tertiary sense: "what distinguishes the phantasy consciousness of the Ego from the image consciousness of the Ego, and how are both distinguished from the actual, positing Ego consciousness? More clearly: We have a perceptual [*perzeptives*] Ego-consciousness and a productive Ego-consciousness; we have an actual (positing) Ego-consciousness and a nonpositing Ego-consciousness. The memorial consciousness, the Ego in the memory, is reproductively positing along with all of its experiences. When I take the image not as an illustration but as something imagined, the Ego in the image (I live entirely in the image . . . and am part of it) is a perceptual [*perzeptives*], though not a positing, Ego" (2005: 540)

finds herself in this same position, and this can be the source of delightful anxieties. These are delightful, engaging, and desirous anxieties because they are cinema's interventions on the spectator. They are the reasons why we become spectators, work to stay as such (recalling the film long after it has finished, re-watching it, engaging in conversations about it, theorize about it, and so on), and willingly form intimate bonds with the film and its internal world order. The status of intimacy in this regard is part (and this is a phantasizing part, much like the difference between a phantasy Ego and a phantasizing Ego) of the unifying work of the *ego*. This is the internal unificatory processes as well as those that allow for the in-mixing of the external, actual and the internal, psychical. This work is part of cinema's enthymemes, to which we can now turn.

b) Enthymematic *Lacunae* and/as Consciousness Modifications

Cinematic enthymemes form intimacy by requiring a type of commitment from the spectator. It is certainly possible for enthymemes to function in a passive, accepting-without-question, manner. These are the moments that sweep over us, operating as simple narrative functions for example. The more complex relations that form in the spectator are those encased in intimacy and, by obligation, anxiety. Enthymemes, for Husserl (within this context), emerge from an ambiguity between reality and fiction, or the doubt of what is real and our contemplation of it (see 2005: 535–7). This can be related to the above reading of phantasy in terms of the double *ego* and two narcissisms, namely that the doxic states and positions are challenged, to a large part because "pure phantasy neutralizes, modifies all belief (2005: 672). Thus, enthymematic attributes are part of these *ego* formations, object connections, and subsequent acts of consciousness because they challenge the unary illusion of the *ego*, they require an investment by the spectator, they formulate object-attachments, and sometimes reveal the multiplicity of the *ego* series. They are, therefore, one of admittedly many mechanisms that a film has to create intimacy through a lacunal invitation. It is precisely what is missing, and that something is missing (its Nothingness), that forms both intimacy and anxiety for the spectator. The status of intimacy for/in the spectator enables us to locate what Husserl calls the abiding *epoché* (of living in phantasy) (2005: 690), and what we saw earlier in terms of Lacan's (narcissistic) structuration of reality. The enthymematic abiding is the lacunal intimacy of the spectator.

Cinema's enthymematic apparatus is more than textual devices, or sociohistorical constructs. They are part of the series of *egos*, the double Ego, and the two narcissisms because they require a shift in the positionality of the *ego* to make sense of the phantasy, to locate the *ego* within the phantasy (and real, actual world), to locate the interpretative sense of the self in such phantasies, and so on. This positionality, founded on intimacy (the spectator is required to be a part of, and to be in, the film) and anxiety (from the pleasurable delights of taking up this position to the unpleasures of alienation to the fears of aphanisis and to the apprehensions of missing out) is that moment in the series of *egos* where the spectator's relationships to the film are formed. To paraphrase Husserl, "we are somehow always in the film as film-Ego" (Husserl's original reads: "Since the sensuous appearance *eo ipso* presupposes an Ego-standpoint, I am somehow always in the picture as picture-Ego" (2005: 556)); the "somehow" in this instance is enthymematic.

To align the enthymematic structures with the series of *egos*, and subsequent actions of moving into and beyond various *ego* sites, is to acknowledge the polysemic nature of film. The *point de capiton* is only fixed momentarily; the missing component of the enthymeme remains missing even when it has been "filled out," because it is a site of shifting *ego* positions and their attachments to the film. When Husserl speaks of a "picture-Ego," he is really speaking of the Ego position constructed from the relationship of the Ego to the picture which is such a unique relationship that it alters both (Ego and picture); our adaptation to the film (and cinema because it is both textually specific and systemic) Ego is of the same order. This is how the intimacy forms in the *lacuna* (the devising Nothings) so that the Ego can become the film (and cinema)-Ego.

Furthermore, the missing components, which is the primary quality of all cinematic enthymemes, have a particular relationship to the spectator, because when they do not remain hidden, inciting the construction (actually or attempted) of meaning and affect, they act as a signal. They announce their operation and their absence, and this is part of the compulsion to watch, and where enjoyment can originate. In this way cinematic enthymemes act much like the signal in anxiety: "anxiety [is] a signal given by the ego in order to affect the pleasure-unpleasure agency" (Freud: *SE XIX*: 70). The spectator, in their intimacy, gains pleasure and/or unpleasure from the signals of anxiety which is produced by the enthymeme. This can be as simple and direct as the missing bits of information in the narrative, and as complex and indirect as the unanswered, seemingly unappresentable elements that float before us with perplexing intensity. The doubled Ego is in operation here because the spectator is required (is necessarily located within) the film/cinema-Ego along with the actual Ego. This is the Ego that shifts in the positing of phantasy (the experiencing of the experience of the film, a dream, a memory, and so on). The two narcissisms are in operation because whatever realities are being devised, they are done so from the relationship of the self to the self via the cinematic object. These cinematic objects, as with all interventional moments of reflexivity, both connect and alienate; thus, the spectator's intimacy is connected by devices such as enthymemes and alienated by them as the self-as-other. Or, described otherwise, whatever intimacies are formed as the spectator takes up the film/cinema-Ego position, investing the interpretative, affective self within the moment so that it acts as the quasi-real, there is a reflexive moment that reminds us that we are spectators after all. Hence, the doubled Ego and two narcissisms allow for a series of egos (usually and often) without a sense of conflict and posited as "seamless." It is when conflicts arise that cinema performs certain acts of disruption, stirring us out of complacency. Such conflicts may well be sites of anxiety that are actually sought out as meaningful moments and utterances.

2

Cinema's Enduring Object and Time

Both phenomenology and psychoanalysis devise time as the state of consciousness in intimacy and anxiety. Husserl sees time as something that is experienced, and therefore can only be understood, as an intimacy; this is phenomenological intimacy at its most profound, reasserting its version of the *cogito* as the primary mode for all interpretative gestures and issues. Anxiety is woven into this intimacy by the constant attentiveness we give to time and the crisis tied to the "enigma of subjectivity" (1997: §2). On the other hand, psychoanalysis has its own versions of intimacy of/in time (the ones that stand apparent include the "evolution" of intimacy through the time taken for transference and counter-transference to unfold, the time taken in the talking cure itself in the recounting of dreams, narcissism, the time of dreams and nightmares . . .). The extended discussions in psychoanalysis regarding anxiety as modeled on birth (see, e.g., Freud *SE XIX*), which is after all the subject's commencement and counting of time, binds temporality to these anxious intimacies.[1] What emerges when these are entwined is the compulsion of memory, the enticement of possible futures (and their answers), and the construction of the *now* as a unique version of subjectivity. Indeed, it is this concept of nowness that should allow us to work through a potentially contentious knot; that is, how we might relate the *cogito*-driven idea of time-consciousness (i.e., the intimate relationship of "I" to time) to the seeming external experience of cinema.

---

[1] For an altogether original example of how psychoanalysis, notably from a clinical perspective, explores the relationship of time and intimacy, see Christopher Bollas, *Catch Them Before They Fall: The Psychoanalysis of Breakdown* (2013). Here Bollas demonstrates the necessity of temporal awareness to deal with mental breakdown.

Time is a particularly complex and important aspect of phenomenology because it represents a unique positionality for, and mode of, consciousness. Let us recall that Husserl describes the unity of immanent time-consciousness as "the all-enveloping unity of all the experiences of a stream of experience" and it is that which "binds consciousness with consciousness" (1931: §118); in short, time-consciousness is not simply consciousness of and in time, it is a synthesizing process across all experiencing and iterations of consciousness. *The Phenomenology of Internal Time-Consciousness* (hereafter *PITC*)[2] is one of the key texts in Husserl's recurring efforts to produce a phenomenological analysis of time and consciousness to reveal the transitions between his earlier foundational ideas and the later works that formulate as well as solidify the phenomenological method. It is in this collection that Husserl grapples with many of the truly difficult aspects of phenomenology; aspects that need to be addressed for his analytic method to be considered viable. At the core of this is the issue of the internal *contra* external, and of the individual outside the context of the social. At the most fundamental level, this is the question of how we experience time as an individual and as a shared phenomenon.[3] For Husserl, this is the "phenomenological content of lived experiences of time" and "the lived experience of the perception and representation of time itself" (1973: §1). The inclusion of "phenomenology" in this phrase is deeply significant because it signals Husserl's desire to analyze not time content as such, but the phenomenological content of time. As Husserl so emphatically states: "Our aim is a phenomenological analysis of time-consciousness. Involved in this, as in any other such analysis, is the complete exclusion of every assumption, stipulation, or conviction concerning Objective time" (1973: 22). Similarly, the distinction between a lived experience of both the perception and reception of time is fundamental to what Husserl goes on to develop. This is the formation of intimate time at a double level, both carved out of a negation of Objective time: a theoretical intimacy of time; and time itself as intimacy. Time in Freud's works is an underestimated, yet crucial, aspect of psychoanalysis. Although not often directly asserted,

---

[2] *The Phenomenology of Internal Time-Consciousness* is a collection of Husserl's lectures and notes. The role of Edith Stein seems to be sadly understated in its published form, and even existence. Her efforts deserve to be more fully acknowledged, rather than Heidegger who claims editorship and dismisses Stein as essentially a typist. To read Stein's work on empathy, or her perspicacious comments and exchanges with Roman Ingarden, demonstrates a sharp and insightful mind that clearly played a key role in Husserl's work. Some of Stein's work is taken up elsewhere here.

[3] It is a well-known aspect of Husserl's work that historicity occupies a strange position. It is an issue beyond the direct concerns here, but it is noted that among Husserl's final works we discover his point that phenomenology's concerns with historicity is to "make comprehensible the *teleology* in the historical becoming the philosophical . . . as well as achieve clarity about ourselves, who are the bearers of this teleology" (1997: §15).

time is a cornerstone to Freud's work, appearing in a number of guises and conceptual frameworks.

This chapter will look at how ideas from one of the earliest works (*Project for a Scientific Psychology* (1895) hereafter *The Project*), can be located as engagements with the temporal, and how they are reconceptualized in *The Interpretation of Dreams*, continuing on to become a core feature of many key concepts, including repression, memory, and *Trieb* (particularly if the death drive is reimagined as a temporal anxiety). Once we have a sense of how these complexities might be engaged with in a unified fashion the work can commence on cinematic implications. The idea of what is called cinema's enduring object will be explored through a number of examples, including Alfred Hitchcock's *Rear Window*, Terrance Malick's *Tree of Life*, and Nicholas Roeg's *Don't Look Now*.

However, and this is a considerable "however," the centrality of time to both thinkers is not enough to form a syncretic argument; nor are there enough elements in this centrality to suggest that Husserl and Freud wrestled with, and devised solutions for, the problem(s) of time in the same manner. In fact, we may well be on more secure ground to argue that time for the two of them served vastly different purposes and processes. Husserl needed to figure out the experience of time to strengthen phenomenology as a distinct and viable methodology, in part by addressing some of its potential blind spots; Freud needed to figure out time to tease out mechanisms of psychoanalytic processes (such as repression and the time-based return of the repressed, memory and acts of recollection, the dream-work's temporal systems, and so on). Yet again we appear to be witnessing the parallel lives of an idea. At the possibly quixotic heart of this comparison is the very real issue that time served different purposes for Husserl and Freud, and we must tread carefully so as not to dismiss their divergent end goals. That said, there are genuine and stirring gains to be had. The following discussion will require some work to find the interstitial moments as we cycle between the two approaches. We will need to determine how the function and uses of time are seen as analytic methods; we will also need to position time as a phenomenological and psychoanalytic construction; and of course, we will need to see how all of this fits into the cinematic fabrications of intimacy and anxiety. This, it will be posited, can be best understood through the idea of *nowness* and the enduring objects (of time).

Two Models of Time and the Now in Freud and Husserl

I would like to start by looking at versions of models that Husserl and Freud used to explicate formations of consciousness in relation to time, most

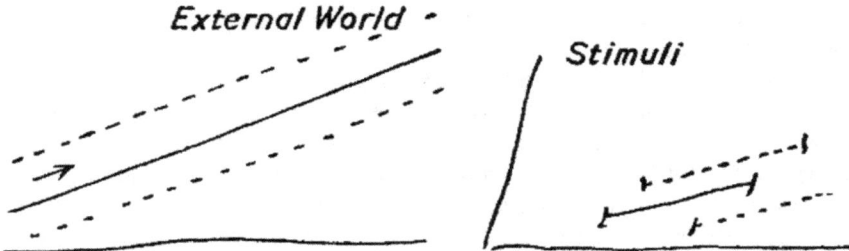

DIAGRAM 1 *Freud's model in* Project for a Scientific Psychology. *There is another model—found in Letter 52 in the Fliess Papers (SE I)—which appears to be the embryonic form of this and the model from* The Interpretation of Dreams *(as follows). Here Freud maps out the stages of perception (*Wahrnehmungen*), registering or fixing of perceptions (*Wahrnehmungszeichen*), the unconscious, and the preconscious. He declares: "If I could give a complete account of the psychological characteristics of perception and of the three registrations, I should have described a new psychology" (Freud SE Vol 1: 234–5). This newness is what we find in* The Interpretation of Dreams. *Husserl's use of* Wahrnehmungen *is noteworthy here, particularly in his differentiation from* Perzeption: *the first for perception and empirical reality, the second for perception of the image. This is taken up in other chapters, particularly in relation to reality and nothing.*

notably in the formation of "nowness," as well as its relationship to memory.[4] Husserl's models are the "running off phenomena" (*Ablaufsphänomene*) and the impressional context, which in turn lead to a variation demonstrating apprehending. Freud's first model appears in *The Project for a Scientific Psychology* and the second in *The Interpretation of Dreams*. The discussion shall begin with Freud's works.

Freud's model is not explicitly expressed in terms of time; however, it can be interpreted in this way as it works out the processes of memory formed through external stimuli.[5] In this model Freud distinguishes between quality and quantity of stimuli in the external world and their relationships to perception, sensation, and memory. That is, the relational movement of stimuli from the outside world into our own inner world of the psyche, which we can read as: processes of time, processes in time, and

---

[4]As has been already noted, the parallel lives of Husserl and Freud tempt us to look for connections. Their shared background knowledge and experience with Brentano is apposite here. For although it is readily apparent that Husserl responded to Brentano's ideas on time (*PICT* has numerous discussions and rejoinders), and Freud at the least knew of them, there is no real evidence that they engaged with them in any sense of commonality. Part of the following acknowledges that Brentano has varying historical significance in both Freud and Husserl.
[5]This is a good example of how we can reread Freud's idea in terms of time, even if the original intent was not focused on the temporal.

the confluence of these as processes formed over time. The distinguishing features of the model are all based around a shift from the seemingly endless stimuli of the external (the endless sweep of the arrow and lines in the left-hand graph) to the narrowed/selected, perceived, and remembered (the restricted and finite lines in the right-hand graph). It is noteworthy that Freud's terms repeatedly emphasize reduction, restriction, limiting, and excision; apposite terms to a type of phenomenological reduction, albeit without the same meta-apparatus that Husserl insists on. Put another way, in the Freudian model we find the nascent theorizing of how the external world and consciousness "exchange" stimuli, how these are embedded as sensations in the unconscious, and how they become part of our inner world order over and through time. It will be posited here that this distillation is an untheorized version of apprehension processes, not as nuanced as Husserl's "eidetic singularities" (Husserl 1931: §12) as he explicates movement from generalities to specifics, or independent to dependent (Husserl 1931: §15), but certainly within the same deliberations of actions of reduction. This requires further explication and will be later returned to via the discussion on "Consciousness and Natural Reality" in *Ideas*.

Freud utilizes this conceptualization of the systemic reduction of stimuli as he hypothesizes the movement of perception-sensation-memory (recalling that the premise of *The Project* is to explain, or at least suggest, a neurological basis of psychology) to explore how memory is formed and expressed. In an important passage (both within the context of *The Project* and the formulation of future ideas and concepts), Freud turns to issues of satisfaction, perception, and hallucination:

> Thus the experience of satisfaction leads to a facilitation between the two memory-images [of the object wished-for and of the reflex movement] and the nuclear neurones which had been cathected during the state of urgency . . . Now, when the state of urgency or wishing re-appears, the cathexis will pass also to the two memories and will activate them, and in all probability the memory image of the object will be the first to experience this wishful activation. I have no doubt that the wishful activation will in the first instance produce something similar to a perception-namely, a hallucination. And if this leads to the performance of the reflex action, disappointment will inevitably follow. (Freud *SE I*: 381)

This passage is a cumulative one, preceded by a number of key propositions, notably: there is a direct interplay between internal demand/desire and external satisfaction; that it is the internal (corporeally based) that is the most insistent for (emotional) change and satisfaction; for any sense of satisfaction to take place there must be some change and input from the external world; but the tensions addressed by such changes are only momentarily satisfied. It is here that we find one of Freud's core ideas (that will become a crucial aspect of primary and secondary processes, and object relations in the future, as well as Lacan's theories of desire): "This path of discharge thus acquires an extremely important secondary function viz., of bringing about an understanding with other people; and the original helplessness of human beings is thus the primal source of all moral motives" (Freud *SE I*: 379). For our concerns here, this lack of satisfaction, these obscured realities of recurring disappointments, this dependence on a negotiation of the external with the internal, are the foundations of anxiety. Furthermore, this is a model based on the deep embeddedness that forms *meaningful* memories and psychical connections, that is intimacies. Recall that this model is premised on reduction to significance—even if, at the conscious level, the reasons why are not always apparent. There is a particularly aesthetic potential here, for in this idea of meaningful memories and perceptual foci we encounter an aspect of the *intimate spectator*. This issue of why in the vastness of stimuli found in a film we select some over others as significant and worthy of recall, and thus establishing what is termed here a relationship of intimacy, will be discussed further with the specific film examples. It is sufficient to note here that this is the work of the composing Nothing and the temporal domain. Even more importantly, it can be seen as a model of time and anxiety, because the meaningfulness is formed through reduction as well as through connected memories; it is a "repetitive state of craving, in *expectation*" and "tension due to craving prevails in the ego, as a consequence of which the idea of the loved object (the *wishful* idea) is cathected" (Freud *SE I*: 369; 361). In some ways we are witnessing here an early version of what will become the compulsion to repeat. It is now time to turn to Freud's model in *The Interpretation of Dreams* to explore this idea further.

This diagram appears in section VII, The Psychology of the Dream-Process, of *The Interpretation of Dreams* (found late in the work), in the sub-section "Regression." This is the section that begins with the famous, and harrowing, "Father, don't you see I'm burning" dream—an example of external stimuli

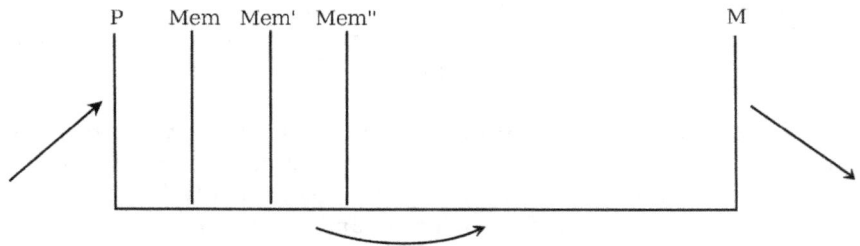

DIAGRAM 2 *Freud's model in* The Interpretation of Dreams.

(the light from a fallen candle), melded to probably memories of words spoken by the feverish child in traumatizing times, shaping a dream. In short, this parallels much of what we see in *The Project*. The decisive aspect of this dream, for Freud, is not the challenges of interpretation (which is the driving issue in most dream analyzes we see throughout *The Interpretation of Dreams*), but rather the opportunity to clarify the difference between dreams and waking life; that is, the blurring of the ontological distinctions and the dream-work's capacity to incorporate the external world into its created world order. When Freud expresses this as a necessary issue to address in the understanding of dreams (and thus psychoanalysis as a methodology), he parallels Husserl's interdiction for phenomenology overall, and as a function within certain ideas and concepts (phantasy being an excellent example here). By way of example, note Husserl's contextualizing statement in *Ideas*: "It [phenomenology] develops as a course of self-reflexion taking place in the region of the pure psychological intuition of the inner life, or, as we might also say, as a 'phenomenological' reflexion" (Husserl 1931: §7). This fundamental issue of self-reflection as it enables and sustains the meta-discourse (of phenomenology, of psychoanalysis, of cinema as critical thinking); of how it constantly locates all analysis within the context of the self and the inner life; and of how it insists on the necessity of interpreting the internal and external as having a relational context far beyond the apparent—this is the conceptual material at hand in both systems. As Freud commences this section of *The Interpretation of Dreams* it is striking how his deliberations on the ontological status and relationships of dreaming and waking life (the internal and external) resonate with Husserl's "phenomenological residuum" (Husserl 1931: §33)—the concept he introduces to set up the discussion on consciousness, natural reality, and their differences. The child's plea in the dream, "to see," has its echoes in Husserl's promise of insight for anyone taking up the phenomenological method, as well as the more specific concept of *Gewahren*, the glance attending to/becoming aware of in acts of consciousness.

For sake of brevity, and to hone and focus Freud's model for our concerns, the following are some summary aspects of the model:

i. A primary driver of the model is to articulate the difference(s) between the inner, psychic life and waking, ideational (Freud's term) life.
ii. The model is composed of "agencies" or systems that Freud metaphorically compares to a compound microscope; that is, a series of lenses.
iii. From this Freud articulates first a spatial and then a temporal set of psychical processes (the passing through a series of agencies/systems).

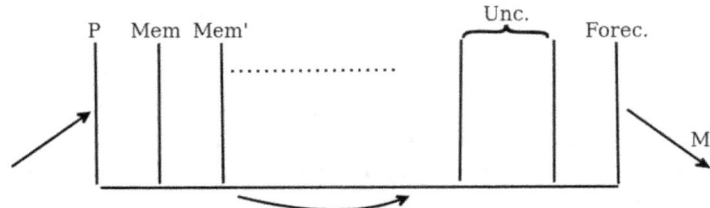

FIGURE 1 *Freud's model in* The Interpretation of Dreams.

iv. These psychical processes move from stimuli to "innervation," which can be seen as a type of discharging of energy.

v. Freud designates the components of the apparatus the "ψ-system"—which is precisely the designation he ascribed to formations of memory in *The Project*: " . . . which are the vehicles of memory and presumably, therefore, of psychical processes in general" (Freud *SE* I: 360).

vi. Thus, this is a model that sees perception enter one side (P), move through a series of agencies/systems before being innervated at the so-called motor end (M). (See Figure 1.)

vii. Freud closes the discussion of this first version of the model by describing it as a "reflex apparatus" and adds: "Reflex processes remain the model of every psychical function" (Freud *SE* V: 540).

From this basic model Freud builds a more complex picture of processes of perception, memory, and psychical layering. He describes the ways in which a perception creates traces in the psychical apparatus, that become what he terms memory-traces. Importantly, Freud specifies that these memory-traces are permanent and as such alter and shape the psychical apparatus. He distinguishes between the open-ended perceptual side (which has no memory) and the formations of memory-traces that are created.[6] This, in turn, yields associative combinations—simply put, the permanence of these traces means that they form subsequent associations, which in turn means

---

[6]Freud's organization of the model means that consciousness and perception cannot be equated—a position that aligns very much with Husserl's. As Lacan puts it: "When we speak of unconscious processes coming into consciousness we are indeed obliged to place consciousness at the exit, whereas perception, with which it is in fact closely bound up, is to be found at the entrance" (Lacan 1988a: 163). Further to this: "Hence, the way in which the diagram is constructed has the singular consequence of representing as disassociated, at the two terminal points of the directed circulation of psychic movement, two sides of one and the same function, namely perception and consciousness. This difficulty can in no way be attributed to some sort of illusion stemming from spatialization, it is internal to the very construction of the schema" (Lacan 1988a: 140).

that ensuing perceptions are selected within a pre-established context of meaningfulness. This distinguishing aspect of permanence and transitory is part of the psychical typology; the Pcpt system lacks memory and is part of consciousness whereas memories "are in themselves unconscious" (Freud *SE* V: 541). It is important to note that the model dictates a temporal simultaneity in the perceptual field (which is why we see the series Mnem, Mnem^i, Mnem^{ii} toward the left-hand side of the model), which is not to be found in the "later" stages.

In the final version of the model we see that the motor end is specified as the preconscious (which becomes the stage of discharge, indicated by the arrow on the right). Here, and later in the discussion on primary and secondary processes, we find the rather curious (re)introduction of "attention." It is a link back to *The Project* and, admittedly, is not pursued with any substance in Freud's subsequent works; but its interest lies here in phenomenological possibilities. This construction of attention, it will be argued later, resonates in potentia with phenomenology's concept of intentionality as well as its version of attention and becoming aware.

We are now at the point where regression becomes the interpretative turn. If the model is premised on a movement from left (perception) to right (motor system/preconscious), with memory-traces being formed along the way, then the regressive aspect is how dreams move from right (out of the unconscious and through the preconscious) to left (to become perceptible). Lacan points out that the logic of the diagram is, in part, a topographical one: "On the level of topographical regression, the hallucinatory nature of the dream led Freud, in accordance with his schema, to articulate it with a regredient process, to the extent that it would bring back certain psychic requirements to their most primitive mode of expression, which would be situated at the level of perception" (Lacan 1988a: 163). This does not negate the temporal aspects of the model; indeed, it rather reinforces them.[7] The regression concept that Freud is engaged with is precisely about transformations as they take place at both the topographical and temporal levels. This also helps explain Freud's tripartite designation of regression: topographical (as found in the model); temporal ("deep" psychical structures formed over time); and formal, where "primitive methods of expression and representation take the place of usual ones" (Freud *SE* V: 549). With the caveat that all three forms have at their heart issues of time, and usually recur together. It is noteworthy that Freud quotes Nietzsche (*SE* V: 550) to emphasize the temporal aspect; of the archaic past and our struggles

---

[7]In this same seminar Valabrega points out: "This apparatus is constituted of various systems which one doesn't have to, Freud tells us, give a spatial order, but rather an order of temporal succession. As a consequence, one mustn't believe in the spatiality of the schema. It is a temporal topography" (Lacan 1988a: 137).

to reach it. Regression means both the work of the unconscious and its manifestations, as well as the work of psychoanalysis as an interpretative process. In this way regression performs as part of the psychical system and as part of psychoanalysis' hermeneutic framework.

We are not that far removed in Freud's models from Husserl's assertion that: "One cannot discover the least trace of Objective time through phenomenological analysis" (Husserl 1973: §1). The psychoanalytic interpretation of regression is precisely not about objective time because regression is a psychical process. This is comparable to Husserl's distinction between "phenomenologically sensed" and "Objectively perceived" time; the notion of the "sensed" aligns with, for example, Freud's psychoanalytic defining of memory-traces, the regressive actions toward "the sensory ends" (Freud *SE V*: 545), and the dream-work's "transfer" (*Übertragung*) system. This does, however, raise an important issue as to how we can draw together these models when Husserl spends a great deal of time in *PICT* sectioning off what is not valid for a phenomenological study of time, notably in psychology. There are many examples, but here is one that would appear at first glance to create an impasse for the analytic experience: "Psychological apperception, which views lived experiences as psychical states of empirical persons, i.e., *psycho-physical subjects*, and uncovers relationships . . . and follows their developments . . . —this psychological apperception is something wholly other than the *phenomenological* (Husserl 1973: §2). A surface reading of this would seem to align, and so discount, it with the Freudian work considered earlier. However, this would be a misreading of Freud; indeed, Freud eschews this psychological apperception for the same reasons that Husserl does. For to hold this stance would be to negate psychoanalysis' primacy of the unconscious. (It is not without some irony that one of the most complex issues—the unconscious—in the phenomenological-psychoanalytic world order should come to our aid here.) Perhaps it is fitting that Husserl references Brentano's work on time in the context of past failures in blending subjective and objective time. This may well be a moment where we see Brentano's shadow also in Freud's early work. Once more, it is important to note that in Freud's models one of the driving aspects is how memory and the past are an inseparable element of the now. In both Husserl's and Freud's models one of the crucial aspects under investigation is how nowness is formed, and how the now slides down into "memory," and yet always remains connected, and somewhat projected. (As Freud pointedly notes, any theory of the mind worth reading has to offer an insight into memory.) This is an apposite moment to turn to Husserl's models.

These models appear approximately halfway through *PICT* in the section "The Continua of Running-Off Phenomena—The Diagram of Time." Prior to this, Husserl rigorously sets up the phenomenological method (particularly its distinctive features), and follows with a working through of the model

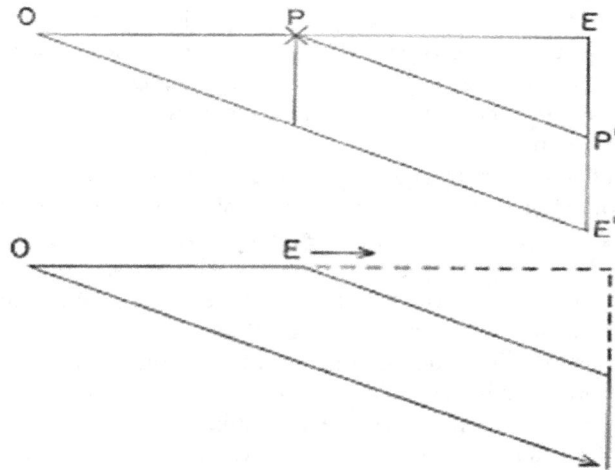

DIAGRAMS 3 AND 4 *Husserl's models of time in* PICT.

as an explication of this method. As with the discussion of Freud's model earlier, it may be useful to offer some explanatory and summary comments:

i. The letters within the model refer to the following: O-E is the series of now-points (see as follows); O-E' is the "sinking down"; E-E' is the relational context of the now-points to the horizontal past; E→ is the "series of nows which possibly will be filled with the other Objects" (Husserl 1973: §10).

ii. The running-off phenomena, or modes of temporal orientation, is a key aspect of the model. This is the phenomenological defining attribute of temporal Objects; this is what determines their idea. Temporal Objects are "Objects which not only are unities in time but also include temporal extensions of themselves" (Husserl 1973: §7)—they hold the past and future in the now, which is precisely how psychoanalysis determines temporality and the conscious-unconscious relational order. The idea of temporal extensions is foundational in this discussion with psychoanalysis and cinema.

iii. This attribute of extensionality means that every component and action is part of a dynamic continuity that cannot be divided into individual units. This idea of a complete and unified process is crucial to the model as it underpins the phenomenological reading of time. In turn, this continuum is continually being transformed.

iv. Within this continuum, every action of running-off can only take place once—therefore the transformation is continuous.

This is a beautiful model, strikingly simple in design but somewhat baroque in its folds and implications. Husserl's insistence on the connectivity of all the elements, that they have permanence and uniqueness at each iteration, makes dividing up the various attributes somewhat more difficult and certainly more constrained.

Husserl talks of the running-off process as a "continuous union" (Husserl 1973: §14) of the perception and retention, which is striking how it resonates with Freud's assertion that all the elements in the formation of memory-traces take place temporally simultaneously. This is key common ground, for just as Husserl insists on the idea of "time" being held synchronously as a defining aspect of phenomenological sensation, so Freud reiterates the timelessness of the unconscious (with the role of the preconscious to order through time) and of the id's lack of understanding of time (*SE XXII*: 66).[8] Here we witness the relationship of time to the Nothing as outlined in Chapter 1. Synchronism is a version of timelessness because time as duration is negated. Furthermore, this is the "lack" of objective time in phenomenology's investigations, focused as it is on internal time-consciousness. Similarly, Freud argues that dreams are optative—of a wishful nature and out of time, not past, present, or future—and embrace all the elements in continuous union, to employ Husserl's term. To test this potential comparison further we can turn to the concepts of presentification and secondary remembrances.

The idea of presentification is heavily linked to Husserl's interpretation of representation, and in particular the role of noesis and noema. (These are taken up elsewhere here, suffice to note for the issues at hand that our deliberations require such an acknowledgment.) Similarly, the concept of "phantasy" is crucial to the understanding of presentification because it is invested in the related modes of the real and reality; this is taken up in the chapters on wildness (Chapter 5) and nightmares (Chapter 6). Presentify and presentification are the generally accepted neologisms for *vergegenwärtigenden*. *Vergegenwärtigungen* (to visualize) and *vergegenwärtigen* (to recall) suggest that presentification should also be seen as holding these resonances. Husserl clearly wants us to think of this as unique and distinct from, say, representation or even presentation. This is because presentification is an integral part of internal time-consciousness, devised within the context of reflection and critically utilized to define temporality within this intentionality. It is also an aspect of Husserl's caveat to avoid employing the idea of appearance

---

[8]This would be an ideal moment to introduce Henri Bergson's ideas on succession and duration, comparing them to Husserl's discussions of these, and in turn looking to how Freud's idea on the experiential aspects of the dream-work might fit in. It must be confessed that time does not allow for it here and would take us too far afield.

when it comes to temporal Objects because they are immanent Objects (Husserl 1973: §10). Let us take a couple of the defining attributes to observe this, the first dealing with intentionality and consciousness: " . . . presentifications have the unique property that in themselves and according to all phases of lived experience they are presentifications in another sense, namely, that they have a second intentionality of another sort, one peculiar to them and not characteristic of all lived experiences. This new intentionality has the peculiarity that, as regards its form, it is a counter-image of the temporally constitutive intentionality, and, like this intentionality, reproduces in every element a moment of a flux of the present, and in totality a total flux of the present. Thus, it sets up a reproductive consciousness of a presentified immanent Object" (Husserl 1973: §23). Here we see Husserl introducing the idea of a different order of intentionality, premised on the temporal. To paraphrase Husserl, there are two "types" of presentification (in this context our relationship to the Object), one being temporal. This temporally based presentification disturbs the "present," creating a moment of fluidity as well as an impact on the whole process of time-consciousness. The thing that is present (experienced) is also part of the present (now moment), and it is this layering that renders time-consciousness and intentionality as part of the phenomenological moment. The idea of "reproductive consciousness" can be read as consciousness directed toward (or by) memory or phantasy (i.e., involving something that is in consciousness but absent—recalling something like the melody, to cite a recurring example by Husserl, or an image or experience). "Immanent" here is subjectivity as the source (of knowledge, experience . . .), and the immanent Object is the sensations and intentionalities of the subject. To understand this, we need to remind ourselves of the time model.

Recalling that the model is premised on union and continuity, the horizontal line is "movement" through time, while the vertical line is sinking into pastness of the retained as time advances; across these we find the retentional chain which exists "lengthwise along the flow of consciousness." So, O—E is the series of now-points; E—E' is the sinking down of now-points so that they *also* exist as a past. (The "'" mark indicates the status of memory, so E' is the memory of E as it has sunk down.) A significant issue here is the distinction between the perceived (present) and the remembered (past) as they operate within this sense of continuous now-points, which is the synchronistic aspect of time. Husserl makes this distinction in terms of presentification: "the temporal present in recollection is remembered, presentified. And the past is remembered in the same way, presentified but not perceived. It is not the primarily given and intuited past" (Husserl 1973: §10). Although this may sound self-evident, Husserl wants us to recognize that the temporal present and the past share the common aspect of presentification but experience it differently. Importantly, this difference is premised not on exclusion (the present does not exclude the past's status) but on this idea of the continuous union. In time-consciousness the past and the present are equally subject to presentification. This is very important in phenomenology; it is equally important in psychoanalysis, for the contemporaneity of past and present is one of its foundational premises. The recurrence of the actions of "return" (of the repressed, of the dream-work through considerations of representability, and so on) and "recall" (the talking cure) are some of the most obvious examples of this in psychoanalysis.

This dialectic produces an unusual version of nowness—a version that allows us to understand how nowness works because what normally passes within the frame of consciousness as unseen becomes foregrounded. This is the idea that nowness passes constantly, but every now and then it is held up to be examined. The nowness of the past is psychoanalysis's core business—bringing it to the fore and making the nowness that has passed into a nowness of the present. A significant issue here is the distinction between the perceived (present) and the remembered (past) as they operate within this sense of continuous, always connected now-points. By way of further example, consider how Lacan reads Freud's concept of repetition automatism (or compulsion) (notably in *Beyond the Pleasure Principle SE XVIII*) and *fort/da*: "the symbol of the object is precisely the object that is here [*l'objet là*]. When it is no longer here, we have the object incarnated in its duration, separated from itself, and which . . . can be in some sense always present for you, always here, always at your disposal" (Lacan 2013: 31). The absence of the object (its passing into the past as well as physically missing as the child rolls the spool away in the anxious playing out of the absent/present mother) is, in Husserl's terms, presentified but not perceived, that is incarnated in its duration. This raises yet another point of comparison, for Lacan distinguishes time's relationship to meaning (both how time is established in meaning and how meaning emerges from and through time) as two versions: times for understanding and moments of concluding (2006: 213). Lacan's agenda is (at least) twofold in that he locates time as a process of problem-solving (see "Logical Time and the Assertion of Anticipated Certainty"—which, as the title suggests, is the drive toward the psychoanalytic solution in time); and time's role in the distinguishing of versions of dialectical analysis.[9]

Later I wish to propose that this dual presentification is also a primary function in cinema, and these cinematic objects become incarnated in the durational presentifications. To understand this, it is necessary to

---

[9]Notably, even though Lacan positions this in terms of the process of psychoanalysis as training, its origins come from Freud's case study of the Wolf Man and the need to determine when the primal scene took place and the revisions that take place "after the fact."

acknowledge that presentifications have a unique relation to memory and perception because they create/carry a reproduction of the original experience. Husserl describes this as a hovering before us but unable to be grasped. Like Macbeth's dagger, we see and experience it, potentially with full psychical affect, but it carries far more (from the past) than what we perceive. This is Husserl's second intentionality, which is also part of his idea of quasi-judgements. At face value, it may seem that we can connect this to psychoanalytic ideas about, say, hallucination, dreams, and even hysteria—but really it has a home closer to Freud's idea of the preconscious, particularly as an agency of temporalizing and memory formations as defined in *The Interpretation of Dreams*. That Husserl links second intentionality to time (a temporally constitutive intentionality and a flux of the present) means that these presentifications are invested in things like memory and phantasy—that is, modes of consciousness that are not to do with the present and/or perception. In Freud's regression diagram we can read the preconscious as the locus of now-points that work between the present, past, and past-present.

Cinema's construction of time (and this should not be read as simply time in film, or even temporal structures such as "beginning" or "end," for this is part of the analytic experience) performs a phenomenological role precisely because it is entirely constituted of reflexive presentifications. To understand this, consider how cinema performs modifications of time as a phenomenological act; this can be illustrated by adapting Husserl's idea of how certain presentifications (for our interests, cinema) modify consciousness: "These [cinematic experiences] are presentifications, modifications of presentations, they make us conscious of the modality of time, e.g., not that which *is*-itself-there but that which *was*-itself-there or that which is in the future, that which *will-be*-itself-there" (1997: 105). In this way cinema performs time as a conscious modification through its constant (and necessary) proposing of "is," "was" and "will-be" there (although to the last of these we might want to qualify with "might-be" given cinema's capacity to set up multiple narrative possibilities). Simply put, a film's time system(s) performs this "conscious of the modalities of time" and in doing so has the capacity to extend beyond itself to reflect on temporality itself. This is an essential part of intimate time.

Another way in which presentification is linked to temporality is by what Husserl calls secondary remembrances: "Now, just as immediate presentifications are joined to perceptions, so also can autonomous presentifications appear without being joined to perceptions. Such are the secondary remembrances" (Husserl 1973: §14). Husserl gives the example of recalling a melody—and of how "the now-point of the perception corresponds [to] a now-point of the memory" (Husserl 1973: §14). This suggests that now-points are a multiplicity—formed, and held, both in the past (secondary remembrances) and the present (immediate presentifications) and are connected in the phenomenological process of remembering. For Husserl remembrance is a mode of consciousness and as such is measured in and against all the other modes. In the model we see this in terms of the running-off and sinking down processes: the now-point of E—E' is formed by the perception of E, the sinking down to form the memory (E'), and the two held in continuous union, so that E is a presentification constituted of perception and memory. (In the *fort/da* game we witness the same process as the child plays out "control" of this continuous union between "here/now" and "gone/past.") This union is, notably, part of a network, a continuity, of now-points, present and past.[10] The now-point of P—P' is also held in this continuous union, so the now-point of E connects to memories P' and E'. In this way, Husserl's continuum of the "enduring Object" (Husserl 1973: §10) bears striking similarities to the ways in which Freud speaks of the unconscious and Lacan speaks of the Real.[11] In a moment we can consider what cinema's enduring Object might be and look like.

A further point of connection here is with the psychoanalytic model of afterwardness (*Nachträglichkeit*). When we experience afterwardness we are placed in a moment of a flux of the present; the unique intentionality that Husserl speaks of is comparable to the layers and flux that evokes/provokes afterwardness. Thus, in psychoanalytic theory, just as with Husserl's description, we have (at the very least) a dual intentionality woven into the conscious manifestations and unconscious motivations. Remembering (i.e., presentification beyond perception) marks the point where these intentionalities come together, shaping one another and producing the sense of flow and continuity, as well as the flux that is the now-points. Our nowness is challenged or unhinged because it is made sense of (given intentionality) by past events that have, in psychoanalytic terms, been repressed. This idea can be pushed further—Husserl's idea of unique intentionality of secondary remembrances is comparable to the layers and contradictory flows that repression creates.

This allows us to consider the idea that (phenomenology's) now-points can be seen as the markers of the intervention of the unconscious in the processes of conscious actions and manifestations. The Freudian parallel here is condensation as a version of the sinking down process. Laying this onto Husserl's model, we arrive at: from perception, O, to now-points of P and E to form OE' (the process of condensing), EE', and EP'E'. These

---

[10] "This is the mode of running-off with which the immanent Object begin to be. It is characterized as now. In the continuous line of advance, we find something remarkable, namely, that every subsequent plane of running-off is itself a continuity, and one constantly expanding, a continuity of pasts" (Husserl 1973: §10).

[11] This relationship is discussed elsewhere, specifically Chapter 4 on the Real; and I reiterate the acknowledgment of the complex relationship that phenomenology has with the concept of the unconscious.

iterations of EP'E' are condensations. The difference being that for Husserl this is an analysis of time-consciousness, but for Freud it is an analysis of repression and disguise (in the dream-work). This difference cannot be ignored (it is a divergence of goals), and yet the comparison should not be abandoned either. Here we see the possibilities of bridging the gap in terms of the cinematic version of sinking down as condensation.

Further to this, in Lacanian terms this can be described as Symbolic markers determined in and by the Real and negotiated through the Imaginary. We are therefore adding another layer to Husserl's dualism of intentionality. Thus:

Symbolic presentifications = perceptions mediated through discourse (cinema being the exemplar here but other textual systems could work equally well).

Real presentifications = a disturbance of the now-point of "memory" but in the sense of Lacan's idea that in the Real "all words cease and all categories fail" in what is defined as "an anxiety-provoking apparition of an image" (Lacan 1988b: 164) and that it is the "vanished instant" (2013: 42). The concept of Real presentifications is challenging because it requires us to take Husserl's transcendental subjectivity, which he aligns so closely to Descartes's *cogito* Ego, and apply a reflexive turn. And yet this is precisely what Husserl requires of us, and defines as the phenomenological method, to gain "the self reflexion taking place in the region of the pure psychological intuition of the inner life" (Husserl 1931: 17); just as Lacan articulates the role of psychoanalysis to investigate (reflexively) the Real. This is the fundamental issue for Lacan in terms of the Real (and reality), that is, not in the subject's adapting to reality [*réel*] but "to get one's own reality—that is, one's own desires—recognized" (2013: 37). This is the reflexive relationship of one's desires to reality and the Real. To achieve this requires a version of the phenomenological act of bracketing. The unconscious has no time structure; so, the Real is beyond memory, which is why the now-points form a continuous union.

Imaginary presentifications = the continuity of now-points as determined by the transcendental Ego subject; the Imaginary presentifications are the Husserlian "reproductive consciousness of a presentified immanent Object"—it is the Imaginary that gives this the immanence. This links back to the Real presentification, locating the now-points and memory-traces as determined by the Ego.

Cinema's Enduring Object; the Enduring Object of Cinema

It is time now to embrace a *cinematic turn*, and the challenge we have before us is not simply to apply the concepts articulated so far to film examples; rather it is to see if cinema can provide the fervent and nurturing connections to bring the ideas closer together. In these terms, what follows is less a textual analysis, and more a locating of cinema as part of the theoretical issues; of cinema's capacity to act as an analytic process. Our concerns must lie with the issue of cinema performing analytic actions akin to phenomenology and psychoanalysis, and in this case how it enables us to understand the issues that these approaches are dealing with. The looming together, this action of weaving the warp and weft of phenomenology and psychoanalysis, is premised on the following key idea: that cinematic now-points are formed in and through intimacy and thus form cinema's "enduring objects." Enduring objects refers to Husserl's idea that there is a continuity of pasts, of which these are a primacy: "therefore, the continuity of running-off of an enduring Object is a continuum whose phases are the continua of the modes of running-off of the different temporal points of the duration of the Object" (Husserl 1973: §10). I wish to compare this to, among other things, the Freudian unconscious, and the cinematic possibilities of "experience" (*erlebenis*). This is why a film has a continuous moment of now-points, made up of the newness (both as inventive in the cinematic apparatus and, more pragmatically, within each film and the experiencing of it) of now-points that apparently mark transitional moments. These moments are crucial to the interpretation of cinema in this phenomenological and psychoanalytic theorizing because *now-points in cinema are interpretative points*; that is, they are the meaning-making moments, and thus the engagement with the composing Nothing. As such, these cinematic now-points are unique in that they are fashioned though intimacy and, simultaneously and with continuance, form intimacy. This is intimacy as the meaningful moments in cinema. Recalling that both models explored earlier are premised on refection (they have a reflexive compulsion), part of the aim is to locate this sense of intimacy and synchronistic time with the reflexive subject/spectator; this reflexive mode is also the site/sight of anxiety. Bringing all these disparate elements together looks something like this: intimate now-points create the reflexive modality that allows the cinematic enduring objects to form. This is why enduring cinematic objects endure as the now, and so are spectator, rather that purely textually, conceived and driven. Reiterating and inflecting a core theme of this book, where intimacy is, there anxiety will follow. Once we enter into an intimacy with time, we are also entering into temporal anxieties, which means we will also need to account for anxiety in the enduring objects. Furthermore, that these are enduring means that anxiety can originate from this conflation of the synchronistic and the never-ending. To work through this the following is divided into two sub-sections premised on this idea of the intimacy and anxiety of the now: intimacy and anxiety of/as the past and future, using a scene from Terrence Malick's *Tree of Life*; Bodies in time—presentification and the struggle for the now, using a scene from Nicolas Roeg's *Don't Look Now*.

Intimacy and anxiety of/as the past and future: Terrence Malick's Tree of Life

Let us begin by returning to one of the common points in the two models by Freud and Husserl, the continuity and unity of all the temporal elements. This means that succession, rather than duration, is the organizing principle of temporality; it means that time in both models is not a linearity, for if it was then neither the running-off phenomena (*Ablaufsphänomene*),[12] these "modes of temporal orientation," nor the formation of memory-traces outside of time, would be possible. This also means that the past, present, and (possible) futures are held together permanently and continuously. (To recall, in Husserl's time model the dotted line indicates the possible futures that will or could connect to the now-points; it is the formation and activation of protensions.) For phenomenology this is integral to internal time-consciousness and its investigation, and for psychoanalysis it is essential to the analytic process as the past is used to make sense of and interpret the present. (The dream-work is precisely the holding together of the past and present with equal presence, ontology, and importance.) This is because in both cases the past is actually read as, and sustains an impactfulness and relevance to, the present—hence the continuum. But how does this work in cinema? And how are we to use this to understand the construction of the enduring cinematic object? The distinction must be made between a type of functional/practical now-point in cinema and those that construct the enduring object; this is also the distinction between time passing and intimacy. For it is only when intimacy takes place, and anxiety is formed, that the now-points can be seen as forming the enduring object.

If we contrast two films that *appear* to be a reflexive form of intimate time and anxious spaces, we will be able to note that things are not always as they seem. Hitchcock's *Rear Window* (1954) and Fred Zinnemann's *High Noon* (1952) have all the overt trappings of films that are about anxious, intimate spaces (*Rear Window*) and intimate, anxious times (*High Noon*). Yet we gain little, perhaps nothing, for the purposes here in reading them this way. In fact, we gain more by inverting this reading and arguing that *Rear Window* creates, and requires, the running-off phenomena of now-points, and therefore intimacy, based on moments of time, more than is witnessed in *High Noon*. This is because *Rear Window* effectively buries

---

[12]*Ablauf* carries the meanings "sequence," "expiry" as well as "draining off" or "course." These iterations have interesting implications in temporal contexts.

and disguises its intimate, anxious time-based now-points by creating such a dominant spatial world order. The film obscures the spectator's capacity to see anything other than anxious spaces; *High Noon*, on the other hand, is unrelenting in its anxious time, largely disavowing any sense of spatial intimacy. So, where does *Rear Window*'s time intimacy originate and become part of the necessary continuity of running-off of the now-points? Perhaps there is an ironic aspect to commencing with this example, for the origins of intimate time takes place with Hitchcock himself—that overt reflexive moment when he appears briefly in one of the windows, winding a clock (see Image 1 as follows). Perhaps the further irony is that for all the psychoanalytic work done on Hitchcock's films and *auteurism*, perhaps they are better suited to be read in terms of the phenomenologically based *cogito*. Note Husserl's declaration in *Cartesian Meditations* as he articulates the phenomenological method and keep this image of Hitchcock, the controlling director governing space and time throughout all his films, in mind: "life in and by which the objective world in its entirety exists for me, precisely as it exists for me. All that the "world," all spatial and temporal being, exists for me; it is, so as to say, made for me" (Husserl 1950: §7).

Our momentary, passing (perhaps almost invisible, and so a good example of the Nothing) connection with this scene of time's manipulation sinks down—it transitions so quickly from E–E'—and the film returns to its spatial diegesis of small screens and the *mise en abyme* films within films. Yet it is a memory trace and now-point, and its affective force continues and unifies. If we dismiss, placing them to one side, the other more narratively

IMAGE 1 *Rear Window.*

IMAGE 2 *Rear Window*.

IMAGE 3 *Rear Window*.

charged references to passing time (Lisa's pressings for the relationship and marriage, the waiting for the removal of the cast and a return to mobility and therefore freedom, the anxious waiting for people to arrive to rescue the troubled), the now-points in this Husserlian continuum of phases occurs in the massage scene with the foregrounding of Jeff's watch; and when Jeff first begins to suspect Thorwald of murder, noting the times of his coming and goings (Images 2 and 3).

These are the three parts of the sinking down that creates the intimacy of the now-points through the signifiers of time. Within them we connect with the recurring issues of reflexivity (*Rear Window* is overtly a reflexive text on cinema,[13] covering the full range from spectator's scopophilia, spatiality of film as subject-matter, diegetic reminders of emotional actions, and so on), the body stripped to its most vulnerable (which aligns Jeff with Thorwald's murdered wife), and the need for proof of evil (in this moment it is time). This is why these three seemingly inconsequential references, these flickers and mere gestures, to time construct a now-point that forms a far more profound continuity. This can also be read in terms of Freud's models; let us revisit an earlier quotation: "Now, when the state of urgency or wishing re-appears, the cathexis will pass also to the two memories and will activate them, and in all probability the memory image of the object will be the first to experience this wishful activation. I have no doubt that the wishful activation will in the first instance produce something similar to a perception-namely, a hallucination" (Freud *SE I*: 381). Here we meld the notion of the now-point with this process of initiating the memory image; the wishful activation is the running-off because it requires a bonding of the presently experienced and the past. What stands out here, of course, is this complex word "hallucination" as a contiguity of perception. This is the intricate issue of phantasy, of which we will have further need to explore and return to with some frequency. This is also the point that the first Freud model can be reintroduced. For when we ask, how are now-points formed within the endless stimuli, evocations, and productions of a film? That is, how does the spectator "settle" on now-points when there appears to be a near infinite number of possibilities to draw from and focus on? These are the points where meanings are formed precisely because they act as "of the now" and worthy of sinking down. Just as Freud's model illustrates the delimiting actions, moving from the endless stimuli to the contained, which is really the construction of psychically significant perceptions, memories, and affects, so our engagement with a film is a narrowing down and restraining of all possibilities to those that resonate. This is a crucial aspect of what is being called "intimacy" here. For in this resonance we are experiencing the now-points and memory-traces that come to yield a film; without them we are left with dissatisfaction and disinterest.

If we take a fairly simple path and map the earlier to the models, we can produce:

Here O-X is the formation of now-points as we watch the film (three examples are given, derived from representations of time in the film; in this case the now-points are literally based on representations of time). With the conflation of elements (X-X1'-X2'-X3') in the bottom right part of

---

[13]This is nowhere more apparent than in the clock-winding scene as we see Hitchcock's reflection in the glass to the left. As with all gazes in the film, the corporeal Hitchcock twists and looks into the apartment space, the ethereal Hitchcock looks, oppositely, out into an unseen space, perhaps the space of another apartment. This is the split gazes of Jeff (old life gaze of adventure/new life gaze of marriage), Lisa (old life gaze of wealthy socialite/new life gaze of adventure), and so on.

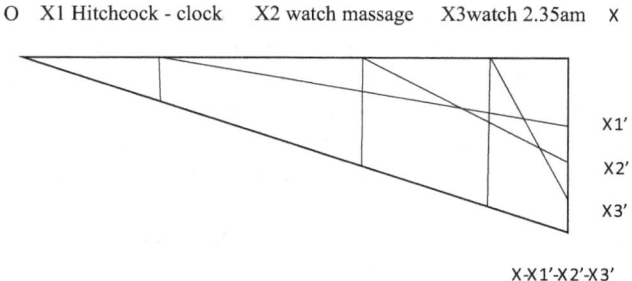

DIAGRAM 5 *Husserl's time-consciousness model and Hitchcock's* Rear Window *scene.*

the diagram representing the *Ablaufsphänomene* (the sinking down, the running-off, the expiration) as well as what might be called the provocation of hallucination as perception (positioned as diagonally opposite O, which stands as perception, the watching of the film as well as the focus on moments).[14] This is an unsatisfying rendering of the enduring object, but it does begin to open up some of the ways in which this is constructed. Yet it remains an unfulfilling model; more is to be gained if we push deeper into the potential weave.

Malick's *Tree of Life*[15] provides a lushly devised musing on time, typical of a director that embraces a philosophically driven interpretation of cinema. And even though the entirety of the film deserves analysis in these terms, the focus here is on a single scene. This will allow the introduction of the idea of *terza rima*[16] and the forgotten fourth time. *Terza rima* permits us to think about both Husserl's and Freud's deliberations on how the now-point shifts its ontological status between what is, what was, and how they transition. "Ontological status" is appropriate here because a great many of Husserl's struggles (he admits to questions, seeming impasses, and paradoxes) originate from this issue. It should also be noted that these questionings also emerge from a less acknowledged aspect—that is, even though Husserl excludes Objective

---

[14]*High Noon* lacks this because it continually, manifestly, asserts the passage of time.
[15]*Tree of Life* resists reduction to synopsis because it is so infused with complex ideas, daunting connections, and extraordinary visuals. The "story" of Mr. O'Brien (Brad Pitt) and Mrs. O'Brien (Jessica Chastain) and their son, Jack (Sean Penn) is presented as a near existential, Kierkegaardian domestic angst yet located within the immensity of the creation of the Universe and end of the world. Jack, a troubled and disillusioned architect, reflects on his early life, inviting the spectator to connect the contrasts in his stony, distant father and inviting mother. The scene explored here captures many of the recurring motifs and style of the film, positioning the everyday travails of the family within themes of spirituality, Nature, death, and the seeming meaninglessness of existence.
[16]*Terza rima* is the rhyming scheme created by Dante in *The Divine Comedy*. It consists of a rhyming structure of A-B-A; B-C-B; C-D-C, and so on.

time to reveal the phenomenological internal time-consciousness analysis, much of the latter part of his study in *PICT* is drawn back to measuring, perhaps even covertly comparing, the two orders. I wish to employ the idea of *terza rima* to illustrate a key aspect of this ontology of time. Husserl teases out the issue of now-points and their status within processes of modification, the issue essentially being a contradiction between flowing and fixing:

> The now-phases of perception constantly undergo modification. They are not preserved simply as they are. They flow. Constituted therein is what we have referred to as sinking back in time . . . In the flow of time, in the continuous sinking away into the past, there is constituted a non-flowing, absolutely fixed, identical Objective time. This is the problem . . . From the point of view of phenomenology, only the now-point is characterized as an actual now, that is, as new. The previous temporal point has undergone its modification, the one before that a continuing modification, etc. (Husserl 1973: §31)

It is important to note Husserl's qualifying "for phenomenology"—this is a reflexive utterance. Husserl is engaged in the eidetic reduction process and hence he needs to account for the shifting status of the now, how it is fixed and modified at the same time; how there is union and consistency as well as change and revision within the system. Psychoanalysis has to deal with precisely the same issue: how does one create interpretation in a system that continually modifies and fixes, offers seeming certainty and fluidity, at the same time? Compare, for example, how similar Freud's stated challenge is to Husserl's comment earlier: "there are obvious difficulties involved in supposing that one and the same system can accurately retain modifications of its elements and yet remain perpetually open to the reception of fresh occasions for modification" (Freud *SE* V: 540). Also, note how Husserl has defined the now-point as "something new" (its newness determines the implementation of the now-point) and how this is compatible with Freud's "reception of fresh occasions." *Terza rima*, in this context, is a system that holds flow and continual modification at the same time. Each rhyming line anticipates forward and links back, each middle line reaches forward in expectancy of the next linking rhyme. The task of reading cinematic constructions, in this case a scene from *Tree of Life*, as now-points in a *terza rima* structure underlines the complex nature of cinema as a medium of many attributes: image, sound (including music, voice, voiceover, background sounds, and so on), colors, narrative points, the bodies on screen . . . For *terza rima* to perform as is wished for here—as a model of now-points and memory-traces—we need to look for a repetition of elements, an embedding and layering that does more than simply link us back and forward in phenomenological retentions and protensions. This is the flow (past and possible futures) and fixing (the repeated rhyme) that we can explore more fully in the *Tree of Life* example.

The scene, "I am nothing," occurs toward the very end of the film and runs for approximately 2'.30", beginning with Mr. O'Brien (Brad Pitt) outside a factory and concludes with Mr. O'Brien and his son, Jack, in the yard outside their house. There are many elements in this sequence that illustrate the phenomenological and psychoanalytic aspects we have been dealing with.[17] At the very least we witness an excellent, and quite literal, example of the way Husserl discusses melody as an example of time-consciousness with the way Malick utilizes music and, even more importantly, the voice across the scene (acting as a meta-discursive sound bridge).[18]

To return to the issue Husserl deliberated on in the quotation cited earlier: From the point of view of phenomenology, only the now-point [*functioning deterministically in the sequence "I am nothing" as meaningfulness*] is characterized as an actual now [*our experienced, perceived presentness as we watch and listen*], that is, as new [*the excitations of the new in the film as it moves us "forward"*]. The previous temporal point [*each iteration of elements within the film as we have experienced it and been affected*] has undergone its modification [*within itself and within its location of other shots, sequences, mise-en-scène, montage etc.*], the one before that a continuing modification [*our work as phenomenologically derived and defined film spectator*].

Similarly, here is the process at work in psychoanalytic terms: the "I am nothing" scene is read as the directed circulation of psychic movement—perception and consciousness—distinguished through the formations of psychical resonating now-points. This resonance emerges from, for example, the delimiting stimuli and their "value" (Freud's model 1), the regressive processes moving from perception to the unconscious and from the unconscious, via the preconscious, "back" to the conscious as disguised forms (Freud's model 2 from *The Interpretation of Dreams*).

---

[17]One element beyond the direct issues at hand, but full of potential, is Malick's references to Fyodor Dostoevsky's *The Brothers Karamazov*. O'Brien's words resonate with Markel's anguish and realizations in his dying days. Markel, in seeking peace, states: " . . . there was so much of God's glory around me: birds, trees, meadows, sky and I alone lived in shame. I alone dishonored everything, and did not notice the beauty and glory of it all" (Dostoevsky 2009: 325).

[18]This "voice across scenes"—sound bridges—is a common device in Malick. Note its use in, for example, *The Thin Red Line* with Witt's soliloquies, in *Badlands* with Holly's alternate interpretations of what we are witnessing on screen, and in *Days of Heaven* with the voice of Linda working often external to, and cut adrift from, the images (due to a large part because of Malick's technique of allowing the actor, Linda Manz, to freely talk over the film during the final editing). Voices and sounds in Malick's cinema are a good example of now-points exceeding their textual domain; they move from film to film, linking through self-reflexive explication by character, narrative, and director.

A further, more nuanced, way to bring the theoretical approaches together is psychoanalysis'version of association. Association is a recurring concept with critical longevity in Freud's work.[19] It has considerable potential for the concerns at hand, because at its core is the idea that associations are formed when ideas, sensations, and suchlike are simultaneously held and woven together in time; the past and present are re-forged. Freud describes the process (within the context of condensation): "Associative paths lead from one element of the dream to several dream-thoughts, and from one dream-thought to several elements of the dream" (Freud *SE V*: 301).[20] Just as Husserl extensively details the interplay between the now as it forms and sinks down to allow/form a new now, all within the moment of simultaneity, so Freud works through association as systemic path formations which necessarily operate as an internal time-consciousness outside of objective time. Husserl's concept of Objective time, put to one side in his phenomenological investigation, must also be placed in abeyance because associative paths do not distinguish between the past and the present—everything is taking place as if it is the now. Associations, like the sinking down phenomena, operate in a simultaneity of time; this is the foundational structure in Freud's model 2, with the first "Mnem" point, as with Husserl's first sinking down point (in the *Rear Window* example this is O-X-X') being precisely this moment. Mnem traces produce associations;[21] after this first one, each association and now-point builds connections with subsequent ones. (This description needs to acknowledge the caveat of now and the new now are not necessarily sequential.) The moments where now-points and associations (associative value creates a simultaneity—the sinking down axis) operate is in the dialectical processes of resemblances. Lacan's take on this provides further grounds for linkage: "[Freud] shifts implicitly from associationism to what it is reducible to it, the category of resemblance being the first dialectical category" (Lacan 1988b: 139).[22] This dialectical approach offered by Lacan opens up Husserl's now-points and offers some solutions to the problem of

---

[19]For example, we find it as early as *The Project*, in the studies of hysteria with Breuer, in *The Interpretation of Dreams*, and later work on neurosis.

[20]Freud quotes Goethe's *Faust* to emphasize the myriad connections: "Unseen the threads are knit together/And an infinite combination grows."

[21]"The perception system has no memory whatever, it cannot retain any associative traces . . . the basis of association lies in the mnemic systems . . . mnemic elements leave a variety of permanent records. The first of these Mnem systems will naturally contain the record of association in respect to the simultaneity in time; while the same material will be arranged in a later system in . . . respect to kinds of coincidence, so that one of these later systems, for instance, will record relations of similarity" (Freud *SE V*: 541).

[22] A further level of Lacan's reading reflected in this comment is that he positions Freud's theory of association as having some historical connection to the socio-political theory of associationism, a popular theory in Europe in the late nineteenth and early twentieth century. This is the "shift" he is referring to here.

the now and the new. If we reread the now-point as dialectical we manage to preserve Husserl's flow and fixity—the new now-point sinks down, forms dialectical associations with other (avoiding the word "previous" here for obvious reasons) now-points as a version of dynamic exchange. (Note the structure in Husserl's time model; it is constructed of a series of interconnected dialectical substructures.) Freud somewhat avoids this issue by arguing that it is only at the first Mnem point that memory forms, but this is not so far from Husserl as first seems. And this is how it can be seen in the *terza rima* schema: the connections/links between elements (now-points/memory-traces) is associative, perceived in its now-points and then woven together as it sinks down. We need to be clear that these processes and actions are at the same time a hermeneutic system and not! It is because it is in the sense of interpretative, interdictive, and/or instructive—that is, fixity (the first by the spectator, the second by the organization of the film itself); it is not because of this movement of multitudinous associations and sinking downs—that is, fluidity.[23] *Terza rima* fixes, but only at a specified point; there should be constant reminders that the "rhyming" structure is selected and should never be held firm. This is similar to Lacan's *point de capiton*, discussed in *Seminar III, The Psychosis* and *Seminar V, Formations of the Unconscious*—in the endless fabric of flowing meaning we arrest moments to seem like truth; these are the fastening buttons to hold things down and proffer interpretative value. This is also the work of the composing Nothing, momentarily fixing a sense of significance within the vastness of possibilities. The seduction of all these iterations is the illusion of "understanding," of reaching a moment of "ah, I understand"—but tricked by the forgotten status of the now-point's ephemeral nature.

The first example of *terza rima* in this sequence is movement and motion. Malick's camera, like sound, is rarely still; it washes over images like waves, changing the impressions in the sand, but only momentarily. However, we can begin with an even more obvious example: the walking of characters. It looks something like this:

1. Mr. O'Brien walking along a metal bridge, away from the camera—*rima* A (Image 4)
2. Mr. O'Brien walking toward the house, toward the camera—*rima* B (Image 5)
3. Mrs. O'Brien (Jessica Chastain) walking along the street with Jack, her son, toward the camera—*rima* A (Image 6)

---

[23] I am grateful for Horst Ruthrof's insightfully pointing out that Kant's reflective-teleological reasoning or the hermeneutics of Gianni Vattimo avoid interpretive prescriptions. This does reshape this idea of hermeneutics as prescriptive process.

IMAGE 4 *"I wanted to be loved because I was great . . . " from* Tree of Life.

4. Mrs. O'Brien walking along the street, away from the camera—*rima* B (Image 7)
5. Mr. O'Brien walking across the room, inside the house—*rima* C (Image 8)

Crucial to this sequence is sound, or more particularly the combinations of music (the same piece plays over heterogeneous time and space) and voiceovers (first O'Brien and then Jack). These in themselves provide an overt associative value and connections as images sink down. However, there is more to the sound-image bridges, for the now-points and associations are forming dialectical relations for and with the spectator. These are the intimate moments. (It is fortuitous, but not necessarily a condition, that this sequence is heavily invested in intimacy and anxiety—we shall return to this in a moment.) What is "laid-over" this sequence is both O'Brien's soliloquy, confessional statement, stream of consciousness, and his son's revelatory comments on their relationship—all three work as they are traditional sound tropes that lay outside of time, that is non-diegetical.[24] This concept of "laid-over" is a cinematic version of the arrows found in both Husserl and Freud's models—they are more than the directional movement as they also provide the cogency of elements to fuse.

---

[24]This is also an interesting parallel to the spectator in cinema and Freud's description of hallucinations: "My explanation of hallucinations in hysteria and paranoia and of visions in mentally normal subjects is that they are in fact regressions—that is, thoughts transformed into images" (Freud *SE* V: 545).

Indeed, almost any cinematic process (from voice to movement to editing to narrative structures) can be aligned with these Husserlian and Freudian driving arrows; this is the conversion of such processes into formations of now-points and the devising of the new. The images as follows note some of the key phrases contained in O'Brien's reflections. There are disjunctions as the images show absolute ordinariness—the everydayness of life—contrasting to the deeply confessional and sensual words that come to interpret them. This is further intimacy because it makes associative values between the ordinary struggles and the profound questions of the ego *cogito*. What we are also witnessing is cinema's capacity to form now-points through its disparate elements. Thus, a cinematic now-point can form if a key element changes even when numerous other elements remain constant. This questioning of a life in the midst of the everyday allows both sides to propel us toward an anxiety. The known, every day is not often seen as the repository of intimacy, and yet it is precisely that because of its knownness; profundity can often seem removed from the intimate because we so often don't know how to handle it, and yet it can be one of the most intimate qualities of feelings.

These now-points are, thus, formed out of this dialectic of ordinary and astonishing, which really does show the cinematic potential of Husserl's astute analysis of the now-point.[25] To witness the ordinary man and woman (their existence of a now-point of mortality and the everyday) dusted with the phrases "I wanted to be loved because I was great . . ."; "I am nothing"; "I was disloyal. I lived in shame . . . "; "Look at the glory around us . . . the trees," and so on . . . this is the requirement of fixing and fluidity. Of course, this sequence holds together because of this layering of associations and interconnected now-points, so the *terza rima* illustrates just a fraction of how it operates. The example before us can be read as follows: (a) there is a flow of movement toward, away, and then across the camera. Each of them is a temporal now-point in as much as they operate as a "now." The cuts between O'Brien and Mrs. O'Brien in the opening sequence are parallel moments of the same time; the scenes in the house and garden take place in a different temporal now, most likely after this; (b) *rima* A (Images 4 and 6) are linked, tenuously, directionally. A far "stronger" link

---

[25]This may be an apposite moment to remind ourselves of Husserl's "distinction" between time as an actuality and the critical intent of the lectures found in *PICT*. Husserl begins with a disarmingly simple statement that "naturally, we all know what time is; it is that which is most familiar" (§1). To this, Husserl adds that once the analytic work to discover what time-consciousness is "we are involved in the most extraordinary difficulties, contradictions, and entanglements" (§1). This is the key to the arguments and analyses that follow—that we are dealing with a distinction between time as it is known as an actuality, and the phenomenological analysis of time. This addresses Derrida's subsequent argument of Husserl and the concept of presences. That is, Husserl's now-points are not simply the same as the now of time as it is "known" in the pre-phenomenological acts.

is in the manifestation of private emotions in public spaces; (c) this link is furthered through the words—O'Brien's need to be "loved because he is great" is unraveling (we learn that the factory is closing and he may lose his job). The image of his wife and son is associative to these emotions of love, loss, shame, and foolishness; (d) *rima* B (Images 5 and 7) are now-points that locate *rima* A in the past. We see O'Brien walking toward the house, where we see Mrs. O'Brien and Jack; (e) in this sense, *rima* B, located in (shot 2) and after (shot 4) *rima* A, illustrates a fundamental aspect of Husserl's time-consciousness: "The now as the actual now is the giveness of the actual present of the temporal position. As a phenomenon moves into the past, the now acquires the character of a past now. It remains the same now, however. Only in relation to the momentarily actual and temporally new now does it stand forth as past" (Husserl 1973: §31). This notion of a past now remaining as the same now underpins the phenomenological analysis, just as its equivalence is found in the psychoanalytic simultaneity of nowness devising associative networks; (f) this means that *rima* A and *rima* B do not just qualify one another (as would be the case for a type of Eisensteinian/Pudovkinesque montage sequence), rather they are essential in determining what Husserl, speaking of phenomenological consciousness, calls "true identity" (Husserl 1973: §31), which leads to essence. In this way we can speak of cinematic processes such as montage and *mise-en-scène* as part of the phenomenological processes of producing now-points, and consequently, as part of the analytic processes for eidetic reduction. The now-points in this sequence (no matter how they are determined) carry with them, via the now and past now processes, this revelation of true identity. Here we witness a version of the cinematic enduring object. The enduring now/object endures because of the past now, which is fundamental to the structure and meaning of the sequence (and the film overall); this is part of *cinemaness* as phenomenology would call it.

There is more work that can be done with this sub-sequence, at the very least the idea of how now-points and associative values are formed, how they are made stable and destabilized, how this sense of true identity passes into currency so that it comes to stand as what the images/narratives "mean." However, I would like to move to the second part of this sequence, and suggest that what we have been dealing with is a cumulative now-point and enduring object which can be positioned in its own right as such. In doing so, when we move to this next part of the film that becomes the past now, shaping the now through this sense of true identity. That is, the next now confirms (or denies) the true identity—enduring object—as it has been formed and then sinks down. This next sequence consists of the struggle with the news about O'Brien's job (Image 10) (which, in itself, has already sunk down as it becomes located in the new now of a much larger life crisis "I wanted to be loved"), and the complex relationship between O'Brien and Jack, his son.

IMAGE 5 *"I'm nothing" from* Tree of Life.

IMAGE 6 *"Look at the glory around us . . . the trees . . . the birds" from* Tree of Life.

If, as is being posited here, now-points in cinema (and in consciousness) form through and by intimacy, this sequence works as an illustrative case. To repeat, it is not a necessary condition that the intimate now-point is actually dealing with intimacy as a subject or has it as its raw narrative material, or indeed either and both of these as affective processes. Rather, that now-points and enduring objects are in themselves acts of intimacy.

IMAGE 7 *From* Tree of Life.

IMAGE 8 *From* Tree of Life.

That issues of, and struggles with, intimacy are found in this sequence is useful to discuss the process as an almost overdetermined example. In the first part of the sequence the now-points form through associative (in the psychoanalytic sense) intimacy. That is, the spatial and temporal separation of the characters has to be overcome to evoke this now-point of intimacy. This is done through the voiceovers of O'Brien and Jack, perhaps most

IMAGE 9 *"I lived in shame; I was disloyal to it all. A foolish man."* From Tree of Life.

IMAGE 10 *From* Tree of Life.

overtly when O'Brien achingly implores us, and importantly himself, through those Dostoevsky-inspired words to "Look at the glory around us." The *terza rima* sequence creates the associative intimacy because it moves through a series of now-points, each sinking down to what, in Husserl's model, would be located in the cumulative bottom, right point (the dialectic of intimacy as the now-points associate with and leave memory-traces), and

IMAGE 11 *"Father . . . Father . . . Father, always you wrestle inside me; always you will"* from Tree of Life.

in doing so become retentionally significant. This struggle with intimacy is confirmed as the spectator aligns with Jack as he watches (Images 9, 10, and 11) both internally and then externally his parents' travails (a visual metaphor constructed by the sequence to mirror the exterior and interior of consciousness, and the adult-child worlds). This growing intimacy—this true identity of intimacy as a sense-making process—determines the second part of the sequence in the newness of the now-point.

Jack's voiceover resonates with emotion, defining a need and desire for intimacy which seems to have been denied him. The awkward semi-apologetic words from his father underline a strained and distant relationship between father and son (contrasted with the closeness of the mother and son—the two paths of nature and grace which we hear, at the beginning of the film, in Mrs. O'Brien's stream of consciousness). For these words to work within the now-points, and to sink down in the dialectical process, there needs to take place what Husserl calls the formation of a new object. In this example, the new object is required to overcome the contradistinctions of intimacy (as forming the now-points) and the struggles with intimacy within the narrative. Two moments of (psychoanalytic) associative value can illustrate how this takes place, both linking us back to anxiety and intimacy.

Jack's words of "Father . . . Father . . . Father, always you wrestle inside me; always you will" (Image 11) carry that same insistence of the letter of the unconscious (to paraphrase Lacan) that was noted earlier in the dream analyzed by Freud; the burning son asking the father to see him, notice his pain, offer relief and comfort. (This imploring to be seen is also linked to the forming now-point of "seeing the glory" as both desire the unseen to be seen, the nothings to become composing Nothings.) The call for intimacy, profoundly noted in the shift from the father's voiceover to the son's, yields up in much the same way as the burning child dream does, this enduring object. It endures because it passes along the chains of "now," reinforced in the sinking down phenomena; or, psychoanalytically speaking, it passes along the regressive chain into consciousness, producing reinforcing associations and condensations. This is the intimacy of the scene, its *speculator* nature,[26] that requires us to hold on to each moment as a past now.

Between these two now-points, the shift from the adult-to-adult, to the adult-to-child, emerges the attempts to overcome the lack of intimacy and the burden of anxiety. This is the burden from the expected (lack of intimacy will often produce a type of anxiety that may appear the same as intimate anxieties, but functions differently) as well as the unexpected (a core theme in this book, that of intimacy's attachment to anxiety). The attempts are cinematically shown through the flesh (Images 12 and 13); this is the flesh produced through anxiety which is also seen in the burning child dream. This is an appropriate moment to refer to a passage from Lacan that deals with anxiety. In this we see the same issues at hand, the producing of flesh in the existential crisis of revelation and self-reflexivity: "There is a horrendous discovery here, that of the flesh one never sees, the foundation of things . . . the flesh from which everything exudes, at the very heart of the mystery, the flesh in as much as it is suffering, is formless, in as much as its form in itself is something which provokes anxiety. Spectre of anxiety, identification of anxiety, the final revelation of *you are this*" (Lacan 1988: 154–5). This works as an analytic comment on O'Brien, notably in the final sentence as we see in O'Brien his recoiling from his shame, the feeling of a lack of being loved (even though he actually is), of foolishness, and of disloyalty. It also works as a description of Jack's flesh as formless suffering (as both child and adult). As with the burning child in the dream, this is the Father's incapacity to provide succor, physically, emotionally, financially, and so on. This is also the now-point of a different conflation, where the father is revealed as being the burning child, both declaring that they need to be seen in this conflagratory state. This final affect is important because it is O'Brien's revelatory anxiety that he was loyal to the company (he states he never missed a day of work) but disloyal to himself and, mostly, his son. As Lacan puts it, this is the anxious, reflexive, awareness of "you are this." This is also why we can read these images (the embraces, of care from the mother and the strained one from the father) of

---

[26]from the Latin which gives us both to watch and examine, as well as to speculate.

IMAGE 12 *From* Tree of Life.

IMAGE 13 *From* Tree of Life.

bodies as flesh.[27] The act is an attempt to give form to the formless anxiety. The associative value of "you are this" is captured with the repetition of "I" in O'Brien's voiceover and mirrored in Jack's construction of "you"

---

[27]It should be noted that much of this scene is constructed, and therefore positional, as the male (in both flesh and voice) in desperation and anxiety, and the silent, corporeally defined (as mother) woman who offers consolation. There are gender politics waiting to be unpicked here, not the least because of this idea of formless anxiety and intimacy. This will be taken up in later chapters.

and "I" as his stream of consciousness implores his father to see him. Note also Lacan's description of anxiety as the flesh suffering and also being formless. Here we have a different type of psychoanalytic alignment with phenomenology, which is taken up in a later discussion.

Flesh in Time—Condensing Presentification and the Struggle for the *Now: Don't Look Now*

The chapter now turns to the idea of dual presentification as a primary function of cinema, referring to Nicolas Roeg's *Don't Look Now*.[28] Let us begin by underscoring a connection, considering how the idea of presentification might contain certain aspects of condensation. From this we can examine the film as an example of condensing presentifications. One clarification before we commence: presentification is inextricably tied to Husserl's construction of phantasy,[29] which is a topic taken up in greater detail later. The following discussion is limited to presentification and time, holding the rich complexities of phantasy in abeyance. As will be taken up later, phantasy is a key issue for both phenomenology and psychoanalysis extending beyond the issues of time discussed here.

Presentification and condensation may appear to be an unusual alignment given their critical origins and intent, but there is potential here to reimagine both terms and yield up a different reading of cinematic time through this idea of condensing presentifications. Furthermore, once this has been tackled the ground should be better prepared for the ensuing discussion on phantasy. I do not wish to argue that condensation and presentification are somehow the same, or even that they perform the same sorts of analytic procedures. Rather, the point here is how the two can be brought together in dialogue, and the possibilities and implications for understanding the cinematic dimensions. The foundational idea of condensation comes, of course, from *The Interpretation of Dreams*; it is a crucial aspect of the dream-work for Freud (Lacan describes it as a "formidable discovery"

---

[28] *Don't Look Now* begins with the death of John and Laura Baxter's young daughter and the subsequent trauma of the parents. They travel to Venice where Laura meets two sisters, one who claims to be a psychic who suggests she sees the daughter. The film utilizes the ambiguity of presence, the emotional disconnection between John and Laura, and the possibility of finding the lost to explore issues of reality and nightmare. Just as the parents lose their daughter, they also lose one another exemplified in a sex scene, which takes place shortly after meeting the sisters. The interchanging cuts across time and space between passionate intimacy and calm, slow acts of dressing is a synecdoche of the narrative itself. The spectator moves across times, spaces, intimacy, threat, distance, the occult, and the everyday so that the very ordinary is invested with the occult unknown.
[29] Hence, "'Phantasy' always includes here all presentifying acts and is not employed in contrast to acts of position" (Husserl 1973: §6).

(1988a: 266). The discussion contains a number of dream examples, most famously the "Dream of the Botanical Monograph," and links with the following section on displacement to form a substantive aspect of Freud's analytic method. It is also, significantly, a precursor discussion to the later works on the unconscious and *The Psychopathology of Everyday Life*.

Freud begins the section by pointing out that condensation in the dream is a "large-scale" operation, suggesting the rolling unendingness of the analysis. It is too large, too complex, too many tendrils and networks to ever be fully grasped or contained. This interpretative challenge is precisely what defines *The Interpretation of Dreams* as such an important work. Largeness is what makes the dream-work such an enticing, and impossible, object. There is a small passage midway through the section that resonates with the issues at hand—perhaps appropriately, this is the section that carries in embryonic form the later works on the unconscious and psychopathologies that take place in the everyday: "The work of condensation in dreams is seen at its clearest when it handles words and names. It is true that words are treated in dreams as though they were concrete things, and for that reason they are *apt to be combined in just the same way as presentations of concrete things*" (emphasis added) (Freud SE V: 313). Freud can be seen as articulating a quasi-phenomenological concept here, because the idea that words and names are, in dreams, presented and combined as if they are concrete things mirrors Husserl's phenomenological reduction. (It is noteworthy that this "as if they are" attribute is exactly what doesn't take place in dreams' presentifications; there is no qualifier of "as if they are," they simple "are," determined beyond ontologies in the transcendental moment. It does, however, configure the presentifications involved in the recalling and retelling of the dream.) Here, now, is Husserl:

> It is certainly generally true that in phenomenological reflection all appearances, imaginings, thoughts, etc., . . . lead us back to a flux of constitutive phases which undergo an immanent Objectivation, even the memories, expectations, wishes, etc., belonging to appearances of perception (external perceptions) as unities of internal consciousness. Therefore, presentifications of every kind such as the flow of lived experiences of the universal, temporally constitutive form also constitute an immanent Object. (Husserl 1973: §23)

Once more, with full acknowledgment that we are dealing with two uniquely introspective and directed sets of ideas, what we find here is part of the defining aspect of condensing presentifications. Freud's point that ontological origins and distinctions (words, names, concrete things) are negated in dreams can be blended with Husserl's flux of immanent Objectivation. This is the true substance of condensation; not the production of polysemes and tracing backs of origins of the dream material (which of course are deeply important to the psychoanalytic project and so should not be trivialized nor dismissed), but rather the condensing and compressing to yield a register where things stand ontologically and even, potentially, hermeneutically equal. By way of further example, when Freud states that whenever possible the dream-work converts temporal relations into spatial ones (*SE XXII*: 24) we are witnessing a variant on the dream's capacity to refuse distinctions and categories as they exist to the conscious mind. In this way condensation can be seen as part of the "unities of internal consciousness"; that is, condensation is a synthesizing process, taking place in, and formulating, internal consciousness.

There is a point where this amalgamation may seem on the point of collapse, and it centers around time. Presentifications, Husserl argues, do not simply conflate time so that past and present are held as the same. A perception and a memory are both presentified, but we need to distinguish between what Husserl calls reproduction[30] and forms of the present and past (see Husserl 1973: §24). This is a sort of "having one's cake and eating it" scenario because Husserl holds the past and present as equal in terms of presentification, but distinct in their internal time-consciousness. What saves us somewhat is condensation's status of process and analysis. That is, in the dream-work condensation operates to form the dream; in analysis, condensation is examined to interpret the dream. Presentification is part of the reproduction of consciousness (past) and how we can distinguish it from the now/present. It is the distinguishing of the analytic in psychoanalysis and reduction in phenomenology that represents the critical knot for us. To this end, the alignment of the phenomenological psychoanalyst/psychoanalytic phenomenologist is the one who does the distinguishing between process and analysis.

Cinema, itself, is a system of condensing presentifications. That is, at the apparatus level, what the spectator experiences is a presentification constructed out of, and presenting, condensation(s). However, this is not an adequate description, let alone definition, of what is at hand here. Recall that presentification is, substantively, Husserl's examination of time and the temporal Object.[31] Simply put, he wants to understand how our perception and inner consciousness apprehend such Objects as unities of time, as well as how they extend beyond themselves in time (memory, recollection, etc.). This is the relational aspect of experiencing the Object as a now-point and having it either linger on or be remembered at a later now-point. Husserl

---

[30]For Husserl, reproduction is perception, but is distinct because it is the presentation re-presented, that is of the past.
[31]The "Ver-" in Husserl's *Vergegenwärtigung* works as an active prefix indicating the process of "making present."

explores this idea, as noted earlier, of now-points being brought together (by our internal time-consciousness): "Is it possible to combine these successive, expiring [*ablaufenden*], representative data in one now-moment?" (Husserl 1973: §7).[32] The answer is, as we have seen, yes; the addition being made here to this is condensation, which is the *combining* of successive, expiring, representative data. As was noted in the *Tree of Life* example, now-points carry with them protension and retention, which the spectator constructs (often proactively) out of the images, sounds, narrative elements, and so on. The temporal aspects are part of the condensation process, just as the condensation forms part of what Husserl describes here as a combining of the representative data. What gets carried over, what is seen as having meaning and significance to be recalled, what is marked as a connection—these are the attributes of condensation as it yields up presentifications. It is this meaning-making aspect that is the second defining aspect of condensing presentifications. For what is presentified is determined as meaningful, and its combinations are what form the condensation with other meaningful, related signs (or data to link back to Husserl).

A further defining aspect of condensing presentifications relates to this combinatory action. As things run off (*Ablaufsphänomene*) how they are combined (condensation) into now-points is related to why they are combined. Cinema has its formal aspects to presentify what should or needs to be held in the running-off; the close-up is a prime example of Husserl's "Objectifying apprehension," establishing a now-point which needs to endure beyond its temporal state for the presented narrative to be shared. The word "Rosebud" is a flash, a mere duration of seconds, mouthed through a close-up of whiskered lips, but it is presentified in disguised form throughout the rest of *Citizen Kane*. However, there is also the antithesis of this process, where the spectator determines for herself the presentifications and their combinatory *Ablaufsphänomene*. This is the proactive aspect of condensing presentifications, produced during and after the watching of a film. This is a determining feature of condensation, denying a coding process in order to acknowledge a larger matrix. Consider Lacan's comment:

> You would be wrong to think that condensation simply means the term-by-term correspondence of a symbol with something. On the contrary, in a given dream, the whole of the dream-thoughts, that is to say the whole of those things signified, the meanings of the dream, is taken as a network, and is represented, not at all term by term, but through a set of interlacings. (Lacan 1988b: 266)

---

[32] Given *Ablaufenden* carries with it the connotations of "expiring," "running," and "draining"—all actions of moving away and leaving, we see here the interplay of what was—a presence—and what has left—an absence.

It is this aspect of interlacings, as opposed to the term-by-term registry, that distinguished condensing presentifications from the usual way of reading, for example, the close-up. The "traditional" term-by-term positioning of this cinematic device (like all others), gives way to interlacing condensations, with, through temporal Objectifying, meaning emerging out of presentifications. (How such an interlacing operates, i.e., forms meaningful combinations and becomes "readable," is a crucial question.)[33] In this way, a device such as the close-up cannot be seen to operate as a condensing presentification, unless it is positioned in the interlacings and combinatory *Ablaufsphänomene*. Let us turn to an example to explore this further.

I would like to suggest that Roeg's *Don't Look Now* can be read as a struggle for the now, played out in the body-made flesh. As such the condensing presentifications are formed through an intimacy with, and of, the struggle, rather than any sense of resolution. This unresolvedness is a consequence of the interlacings and combinations having an extensive indeterminacy. Herein lies the anxiety; the term-by-term correspondence yields to the interlacings, and in doing so produces unending (i.e., a different version of enduring) temporal Objects.[34] To suggest extensive indeterminacy of the film requires us to eschew how the film is usually interpreted—in the case of *Don't Look Now* this is of premonitions as explanatory gestures. It is certainly tempting to read the film as an example of presentification, where past, present, and future all stand outside of temporal definition and therefore are to be judged with a sense of uniformity (a technique common to Roeg's films, notably *Walkabout* and *Performance*).[35] This is an example of merging the successive, expiring representative data into yet to be fully formed now-points. In these terms it makes sense (i.e., it is a sense-making process) to read the film's intercutting technique of present and future as presentification (the sex scene and John Baxter's (Donald Sutherland) vision of his wife, Laura (Julie Christie), on the funeral boat are excellent examples). Similarly, it makes sense to read the recurring red color as merging to form, psychoanalytically speaking, overdetermined signification. These are set up by the film to entice the spectator to construct meaning by holding the combinatory *Ablaufsphänomene* to share

---

[33] The focus is on condensation, but the "companion" term of displacement cannot be ignored. It is the "mechanism" where the missing signified is recognized (see Lacan 1993: 124), and part of the "polyvalent, superimposed, overdetermined" (Lacan 2013: 17) acts of symptoms, dreams, to which we add cinema.

[34] The clear temptation here is to look at a David Lynch film, *Mulholland Drive* or even *Lost Highway*, for example. However, as much as such a film can permit our reading of indeterminacy for establishing meaning, it may be more apposite to choose a film less self-defining as open-ended.

[35] As Husserl points out in Appendix II of *PICT*: " . . . in the case of an intuitive presentification, that what is remembered hovers before us "in phantasy" . . . However we do not call the memory itself a phantasy" (Husserl 1973). This works perfectly for an analysis of both these films.

IMAGE 14 *From* Don't Look Now.

a preconceived interpretation. As with the device of the close-up, our intimacy with the film is established in a very deliberate fashion. All of this as a valid approach; indeed, the funeral boat scene works as an example of Husserl's perception, phantasy and memory as presentifications. When John sees Laura on the boat with the two sisters his confusion (shared by the spectator) stems from the belief that she is in England; the image sinks down, later becoming reread not as Laura in the present, but a premonition of his own future death. However, I want to suggest a further, differing aspect to illustrate the concept of condensing presentification.

We may begin this furthering of the concept by noting an important distinction made by Husserl in *Ideas*: "Between *perception* on the one hand and, on the other, *the presentation of a symbol in the form of an image or meaning* there is an unbridgeable and essential difference. With these types of presentation we intuit something, in the consciousness that it copies something else or indicates its meaning" (Husserl 1931: §31). This resonates with aspects of Freud's version of the dream-work: the copying, indicating, the intuiting of difference, the distinction of a "type" of presentation—these are all qualities of the dream-work and its analysis. Indeed, the "unbridgeable" is reminiscent of the way Freud speaks of the dream's navel and its impenetrable significations. It is also in keeping with Lacan's alignment of condensation with a metaphor when he speaks of the gap that requires the spark to bridge it: "Between the enigmatic signifier of sexual trauma and the term it comes to replace in a current signifying chain, a spark flies that fixes the symptom—a metaphor in which flesh or function is taken as a signifying element" (Lacan 2009: 431).[36] This "flying spark" across the

---

[36] It is somewhat fortunate that this quotation aligns so well with *Don't Look Now* in terms of sexual trauma and its (metaphoric) replacement signs; and that flesh is foregrounded by Lacan

gap to fix the symptom is core to Lacan's ensuing analysis. However, what is key to the Husserl passage is how it opens up a new way of approaching the issue raised in the preceding paragraph. The unbridgeable and essential difference is the divergent condensing presentification that exists outside of perception and presentation of a symbol—that is, the spectator and the filmic world order (image) and the horizon of interpretative values (meaning). A film's invitational construct (the binding of presentation of image/meaning to perception) closes the difference that Husserl speaks of here. But in doing so it delimits the interlacings; in short, we are given a pre-existing intuition (phenomenologically speaking) of perception to meaning. Yet, just as Husserl reminds us that every now-point must be new to be a now, the newness is closed down.[37] It is as if the film establishes the now-points so that newness is also predetermined and therefore anticipated. As such, the analytic judgements are restricted. If we are to take Lacan's point to heart, condensation is exactly about the openness (the immensity and largeness) of the connections. This aligns with Husserl's distinction between retention and reproduction (played out in primary and secondary remembrances) and the doubling of intentionality of memory and recall that produces a continuous and unending state of flux in memory (see, e.g., §25 *PICT*). In this way we are engaged in a version of not the fixing of meaning, but how such a meaning arises and appears to have fixity. Laura in the funeral boat makes recollective and retentive sense as a premonition; it has interpretative value in ordering and explaining other events and sequences within the film. That the spectator arrives at this afterward (i.e., as the film develops and fixes elements into this cohering narrative) is important because it means that we are required to revisit (i.e., representify and reconsider previous protensions and their retentive values) the moment in memory, comparing it to the original presentification. This is how we can understand the phenomenological aspect of this process as beyond mere perception and as forming now-moments.

Afterwardness (Freud's *Nachträglichkeit*) is the process of revelation—a moment when what has passed is seen for what it is, rather than what it could have been or might be. It is the arrival of interpretation where interpretation seems to work. There is a certain formation of power produced through this deferral of knowledge. What is at the heart of this is the idea that certain forms of textuality define themselves as existing in that moment when "knowledge" is seen. These are the texts that operate according to variants

---

as the signifying element. Another discussion could well engage with such a reading, but it is beyond the direct concerns here.

[37]Further to this: "The origin of the apprehension of time lies in the sphere of phantasy" and "That a great phenomenological difference exists between representifying memory and primary remembrance which extends the now-consciousness is revealed . . . " (Husserl 1973: §19).

of epistemological revelation. What the phenomenological, psychoanalytic idea and the textual rendering share is this layering of time-consciousness (the present "I think/believe I understand"; the past "I thought I understood but now revise"; and the past-present "I understand and I see the aftereffects") woven together. More than an issue of representation, however, these moments are revelatory in how knowing itself works. In this regard they challenge the relationship between noesis and noema; between the act/experience and the event/text. The act of watching cinema is a synecdoche of this larger process of how the past, present and potential futures are brought into a viable relationship. This is the conflation of all possible worlds into the nowness of knowing.

Condensing presentifications, then, are premised on the fluidity of meaning, the transitional nature of all interpretations so that they operate as "truth," but just for the moment. They hold the polysemic aspect in readiness, allowing what is presentified (perception, Object, memory, phantasy, cinema) to operate in this version of past-present time-consciousness as dynamic and flux-based veracity. Their status as enduring objects is held in a similar temporal vicissitudinal perspective. Laura in the funeral boat is such a presentification, for even if every aspect in the film works to confirm this interpretation (that it is a premonition of John's death) to allow it to pass as true, yet it must also hover before us as phantasy, as somehow questionable.

This may be clearer if we consider Husserl's comments on apophantic judgments. Via Aristotle, apophantic statements are made to establish the truth or falsity of a judgment. Section 134 in *Ideas* deals with Husserl's adaptation for his methodology. He phrases it as a defining aspect of what it is to be a phenomenologist: " . . . [the] great task is to follow up the phenomenological interlacings of essences *in all directions*. Every plain axiomatic exhibition of a basic logical concept becomes a new heading for phenomenological inquiries (Husserl 1931: §134). Husserl's emphasis "in all directions" is fundamental to this notion of cinematic condensing presentifications (just as is the term "interlacings"). Laura in the funeral boat is apophantically established as a premonition of John's death, and not the alternatives that first appear in the now-point: that she is somehow in two places at once (England and Venice); or that she didn't leave for England; or that it is an hallucination; or that it is a memory or dream; or that it is another moment in the film's recurring images of reflection and inversion; or it John's madness. All of these possibilities, these condensing variables of truth, are held in the now-point, sinking down in memory, only to be revived and revised once the narrative plays out. It is precisely these interlacings of possible meanings that create the intimacy of meaning through anxiety; and once there is the apophantic moment a different, less intimate, intimacy takes hold. This is the less intimate moment of shared understanding, as distinct from the (phenomenologically based) intuitive inner consciousness of meaning, or the psychoanalytic "solution" which speaks to the self.

The anxiety forms through the insistence of the apophantic, whereas the intimacy forms through its deferral.

In an altogether different way, the anxieties of the flesh in this scene reveal something other to this condensing presentification, its temporal flux, and the fragility of truth. Something other, and at the same time in alignment with this aspect of interlacings. The initial anxiety of the flesh is John's perception of Laura's body, dressed in black, gathered with the two sisters and gliding ethereally on the canal. This hovering flesh defines itself as an anxious condensation of Laura's death or madness. This interlacing condensation should include the idea of John's dead body or his madness, but this only comes at a later now-point and through the process of recollection and interpretative revisions. However, a more revealing approach, demonstrating how condensing presentifications operate in terms of flesh, is how the now-point of this scene connects (i.e., via *Ablaufsphänomene*) with the sex scene.[38] Whereas the sex scene utilizes cross-cuts to present temporal flux, moving between past, present, and future, the spectator is not given (presentified) the same cinematic devices in the funeral boat scene, even though this is precisely what is taking place in both scenes. The cinematic condensing is performed by the rendering of the body as flesh, presentified in death and the sexual, and this temporal flux which acts in an interlacing fashion. Without this condensing aspect of temporal flux the two scenes would not "merge" (i.e., form) in the now-point; there is too much distance between them (e.g., a scene of sexual intimacy that appears to mark a recovery in the relationship, with bodies entwined and moving as one; a scene where disentangled bodies are distant and distinctive from each other and moving in opposite directions, divided by a stylistic separation—John on a crowded, public boat, Laura with the sisters on their own). What this suggests is that cinematic condensing presentifications form newness in the now by taking the "essences in all directions" of the film text and produce interlacings (some of which carry the full weight of apophantic statements).

---

[38]Now-points are a multiplicity—formed both in the past (secondary remembrances) and the present (immediate presentifications) and are connected in the phenomenological process of remembering.

3

Four Modalities of Intimate and Anxious (Cinematic) Space

"I am aware of a world, spread out in space endlessly, and in time becoming and become, without end"—thus Husserl begins Section Two of *Ideas*; a description that continues with the commonplace and everyday (a writing table, the verandah, the garden, children in the summer-house) and flows to the edges of attention, the "dimly apprehended depth or fringe of indeterminate reality" (1931: §27). And now to Dora's first dream that reveals a house on fire, her mother's need to save her jewel case, her father's insistence on fleeing; and Dora's escape "We hurried downstairs, and as soon as I was outside I woke up" (Freud *SE VII*: 64). Thus, Husserl and Dora reveal in different yet relatable ways insights into space and self. Anxious and intimate spaces abound, but can we speak of types of spaces that are consistently positioned in these terms? If such spaces exist then is one of the consequences that all that is positioned in them can, and will, only be read in these terms of anxiety and intimacy? This is the construction of flesh as it is determined in and by the space it occupies and finds itself in, as well as the inversion of this—spaces transformed by the occupying anxious, intimate body. This suggests that there is a specific type of flesh produced in these spaces, and the spaces altered by these occupying bodies are yielded up in particular ways. When Husserl writes this opening section he occupies the intimate, inside area/space seated at his writing desk and his body becomes determined by this sense of the familiar; Dora occupies the intimate, inside space of her dream, which, like Husserl's space, is layered; the burning house, downstairs, outside, and then the spaces of the dream and waking life. In both cases we also witness the apperception of the outside fringes of an indeterminate (anxious) reality defined precisely as a space external to the internal world of the self.

To explore this idea of the spaces of intimacies and anxieties, two cinematically devised dynamic spatial sites will be posited: anxious "external" space made intimate, and intimate, "internal" space made anxious. In doing so the examination will consider how phenomenology's construction of *epoché* can be utilized to understand the intimacies and anxieties of/for the othered body and the implications of this for the body as flesh. Within this dynamic spatiality we encounter the distinctions and their blurring of the inside and outside. "Space" is to be interpreted within the context of "thing," and "self"; these in turn link to the related concepts of "object" and "subject." Spatiality, then, is the field where these relationships and identities are formed and experienced; and cinematic spatiality is the place where phantasms[1] of things and others are experienced (Husserl's *cogitationes*). This version of spatiality is described as "dynamic" to suggest that there is an encouragement to fluidity, and these are not spaces where things become fixed and relationships become settled.[2] Cinematic spatiality, in this sense, is agitational and changing; and all that is located in it, and experienced through it, carry this dynamic, catalytic, polyvalent, fluidity. Just as we witnessed (in the previous chapter) now-points as temporal (and temporary) fixity, space-points are the illusion that objects in the world are somehow constant and stable, and the interrelations between them something tangible and recognizable. It is precisely the interplay of the interstitial spaces between the thing and the space as holder/delineator of the elements that bears witness to this dynamic. Furthermore, this dynamic is a process of composing Nothings, for the interplay between space and flesh is the rendering of meaningful spaces through flesh as thing. This can include the idea of a film itself as cinematic spatiality as well as the spaces "within" the film, and the experiential (*cogitationes*) spaces we occupy when we watch a film. Cinematic spatiality thus contains: cinema in itself, occupying a cultural space; the texts themselves; the psychical, affective space we enter with intimacy to become a spectator; textual specific sites; as well as the larger environments (cultural, temporal, psychical, and phenomenological).[3] Some restraint is devised here by focusing on intimate and anxious flesh in these ever unfolding and enfolding/enfolded spaces.

One of the primary sites of space, intimacy, and anxiety is the liminal zone of the body and its internality, and the externality of the world, including other bodies. Julia Kristeva's *Powers of Horror* (1980), via Mary Douglas's

---

[1] See Chapter 4 for more on this concept of phantasms.
[2] A version that is beyond the scope of this project is the emergence of virtual social space. Of course, social media did not exist for Husserl, Freud, and Lacan, but the ideas raised here, such as projection and introjection's relationship to intimacy and anxiety, would be appropriate themes to take up.
[3] For a different reading of the body, post-coloniality, and space see Laura Marks's *The Skin of the Film*. Marks's approach draws particularly on Gilles Deleuze.

work on disgust (1966), provides keen insight into how the movement between the internal and external can be transgressive, anxious-ridden, terrifying as well as pleasurable, sustaining, and joyous. It is important to acknowledge that the internal/external divide of spaces must always be at play here; we cannot consider intimacy or anxiety without recognizing this divide and the subsequent formations and articulations of spaces. The focus here is on the cinematic spaces that contain both intimacy and anxiety at the same time, which relies on a series of modalities. These include the sense of:

a. the internal as intimacy projected into the external space which creates anxiety (projected[4] forfeiture)
b. the internal as intimacy projected into the external space which produces intimacy (the projected familiar)
c. the external as intimacy introjected into the internal, producing intimacy (introjected familiarity); and its inversion (external intimacy producing anxiety) (introjected defamiliarization)
d. the external as anxiety introjected into the internal, producing anxiety (introjected crisis); and its inversion (external anxiety producing intimacy) (introjected masochism).

There must always be a mediating position with any iteration of these modalities because we are engaging in *cogitationes* (i.e., Husserl's idea of experience, experienceability, as well as experiencing experience) that we access via created consciousness. This takes place at one level through the film's characters; we experience the film through their Husserlian lifeworld. But to do so we also must bracket off our own, which in turn creates an additional layer of affect and analysis. So, at the very least all the modalities of projection and introjection require four layers of eidetic reductions and the *epoché* in order to experience the film. These are: (1) our own natural attitude; (2) the negotiation and negotiated lifeworld of the film; (3) the character's natural attitude and lifeworld order as mediating process; (4) the mediated materiality (objects, time, space, and so on). These layers (particularly the second, third, and fourth) are mediated and negotiated in the

---

[4]Terms such as projection and introjection in this context immediately summon up Melanie Klein's concepts. This will be taken up as we progress, suffice to note here that there is a certain Kleinian feel to the use here, as well as divergence. Introjection is defined by Klein as: "the mental activity in the child, by which, in his phantasy, he takes into himself everything that he perceives in the outside world," whereas projection is the attributing of the self to an external object (Klein 1988: 291). Klein's theory of the "good" and "bad" object is thus an integral part of these activities. Later Klein will introduce the term "projective identification" which addresses what she calls the complimentary process of introjection and projection (see "The Emotional Life of the Infant" (1952) and "Notes on Some Schizoid Mechanisms" (1946) (Klein 1975).

Husserlian sense of *Abschattung ist Erlebenis*—the experience of shading as we work with and through the textual system. The projected and introjected processes are at the heart of this mediating and shading. The fourth one of these, mediated materiality, foregrounds the relational contexts of subject to objects as they interact in the melding cinematic spaces.

As we proceed each of these modalities will be explored through cinematic examples. It is self-evident that the permutations involved are considerable; these limitations are acknowledged in advance. It is also noteworthy that these modalities of projection and introjection are in themselves fluid, and one cinematic example might readily crossover into another. The requirement here is to locate the larger issue of how space, intimacy, and anxiety can be read through the two analytic models at hand, and the cinematic potential of such a reading. Before we turn to these cinematic illustrations there needs to be some further discussion on space as a phenomenological and psychoanalytic issue, commencing with the internal, external, and the idea of the thing. It is important to acknowledge at the outset that the "thing" is far from straightforward in these two analytic contexts. With phenomenology (Husserlian in particular) we are confronted with the issue of Kant's "thing-in-itself" and Husserl's digressive path of *cogitationes* (the experience (of things) to know).[5] That is, the knowable is only achieved through the experience of the thing; for Kant anything that isn't (and can't be) known is a "thing-in-itself." This comes down to how we can only know something through *cogitationes* and the contesting arguments of whether anything exists outside of this experience. To proceed, we can take up some of the fundamental ways that phenomenology and psychoanalysis have engaged with the idea of the thing, inflecting it to think about space as a cinematic thing.

The idea of space as a cinematic thing is important here, in part because it enables us to foreground a particular issue which, at first, seems nonsensical. This is the question: why does cinema have things?[6] The most obvious answer is that if cinema did not have things, it would not exist, the screen

---

[5]For an insightful and compelling analysis of the complexity of translating Kant's *Ding an sich* as "in-itself" see Ruthrof (2013). Ruthrof points out that the English translation attributes a quality absent in the German "thing on its own," the "thing without perspective," or the "thing-at-itself."

[6]Such a question ties directly into much of the analysis found in Husserl's *Thing and Space* (1998). Husserl articulates *dinglichkeit* (thinghood) to explore relationships between perception and the thing. This includes distinguishing between perception and perceived thinghood, including ". . . the thing in the stricter sense of physical thing, and . . . the spiritual thing, the be-souled being, and, further, the distinction between 'one's own Ego' and the 'alien Ego'" (p. 7). Later, in §38, Husserl admits the near impossibility of the task at hand in an almost resigned tone: ". . . we will not be able to designate it as a reasonable goal to determine any thing whatsoever" (111). Underpinning the question of cinematic thinghood is the same near impossibility!

would be blank, motionless, soundless—indeed, the screen itself would not be present. However, if we are to treat this question with any sense of seriousness then what is revealed is that the nature of the thing in cinema is far from a given, far from uniform, or universal. Cinema's thingness is its uniqueness; the thing in cinema has been transformed, just as cinema is transformed through its things. Further to this, how do these cinematic things force themselves onto the screen? And how do they move from the depth and fringe of indeterminate (cinematic and beyond) realities to acquire this sense of thingness?

To enable the question of why cinema has things to become anywhere near meaningful, and even worthy of contemplation, we need to distinguish between two "types" of the thing. The first is that which resonates around Freudian and Lacanian theory and the conception of *das Ding*—the Thing; the second is the Husserlian reading of the Thing[7] as a distinguishing between objects out in the world and our experience, through pure consciousness, of them—the "sensibly intuited world of objects" (1997: §25; 1998: §10, §24, §39). (Which, significantly, is located within a discussion of Kant's ideas on the experience of things.) At first glance these two approaches seem to share nothing except the use of the word "thing," and they do not even share that. Husserl uses *Sachen/Sache* and Lacan spends a considerable amount of time discussing the difference between *Sache* and *Ding* so he can work through the latter as a radically different concept. As he puts it: "*Sache* and *Wort* are, therefore, closely linked; they form a couple. *Das Ding* is found elsewhere" (Lacan 1992: 45). However, if we utilize Husserl's Thing to reposition Lacan's idea of *das Ding*, we can conceive of cinema things in a new fashion and go toward addressing why they exist and how they are part of cinematic spatiality. It is important to note that this does not involve an attempt to treat *das Ding* and the Thing as somehow the same; indeed, this is exactly what is not involved here.

Lacan's most concentrated discussions of *das Ding* take place in the seminar *The Ethics of Psychoanalysis*; noteworthy because this is where he takes up ethics for psychoanalysis, and the potential that psychoanalysis has for addressing ethics in a wider (philosophical) sense. How very typical of Lacan, then, to devote so much time on a concept that is so anarchic and disturbing in a seminar on ethics. We can grasp the fundamental characteristics of *das Ding* relatively quickly: it is "the most archaic of objects" (106); the "relations of the subject to something primordial" (106); "the mythic body of the mother" (106); "the inaccessible" (159); "the place . . . where the inaccessibility of the object of *jouissance* is organized" (203);

---

[7]Hereafter, in an attempt to distinguish and yet encourage alignment of the Thing, *das Ding* refers to Lacan's use (via Freud); Thing refers to Husserl; and cinema's things will simply be called that.

"the place where the battlefield of our experience is situated" (203); "[it introduces] an erotics that is above morality" (84); "something attached to whatever is open, lacking, or gaping at the center of our desire" (84); "some disgusting object" (253); "represented by an emptiness, precisely because it cannot be represented by anything else" (129); "it always presents itself as a veiled entity; represented by something else" (118); and "characterized by its absence, its strangeness" (63). It is important to note that Lacan aligns sublimation with *das Ding* operating at the cultural level. This material can be unpicked as we proceed, for the moment it gives a sense of what Lacan intends by *das Ding*.

If distilled further, the recurring motifs of *das Ding* reside in this inaccessible quality, unrepresentable within signifying practices, and disruptive through its otherness. However, and this is crucial for the issues at hand, there is an affective quality to *das Ding*. This is why it is a non-thing; there is no thing to *das Ding*, rather it is attached, embedded, and implanted in and as alterity. It is somewhat parergonal, framing and reordering our experiences and rasping against our perceptions. We experience *das Ding* as a transformative process. Hence in the example of the maternal body, the mother's body becomes something else (mythic) when it is transformed by, and thus becomes, *das Ding*. It is this aspect that holds potential for a discussion of the Husserlian Thing.[8]

As noted earlier, for phenomenology, our relationship to the world of objects is through the sensibly intuited. Our perceptual processes are, if we allow a metaphor, a series of veils, or layers that the phenomenological reduction works through. Thus, for example, the perception of an object alters through time-consciousness, locating it as present (and in the present) or remembered (and therefore absent as an object but presentified to our consciousness); or it alters if it is "real" (empirically speaking) or a phantasy, or indeed as a remembered phantasy, and so on. Now it is not possible, or even desirable, to simply align this intuiting process with *das Ding*; but we can explore how the Husserlian Thing helps us to better understand what happens when we encounter *das Ding*, and how this phenomenological process yields up a different type of thing—the cinematic thing.

To proceed, let us recall how Husserl locates the Thing in terms of the Kantian Idea (i.e., distinct from Essence). We need to take a further step back to position this somewhat. Our apprehension takes place as/in a stream of experience,[9] which is directed, or "unified." We do this within a

---

[8]The maternal body has another relational context to *das Ding*, that of psychoanalysis' theory of birth, trauma, and anxiety. This supposed originary "trigger" of anxiety and subsequent trauma is a contentious but significant issue in the field. See, for example, Freud *SE XX* and *XXII* and the discussion of Otto Rank's *The Trauma of Birth*.
[9]See, for example, Husserl 1931: §83 "Apprehension of the Unitary Stream of Experience as 'Idea'."

context of boundless, limitless possible immanent intuitions; that is, we have an unending set of possible experiences, but there is a unitary focus that becomes our experience. This takes place within a context of what Husserl calls the "experience-fringe" (1931: §83). He describes how the glance/gaze is directed at an experience, but always has the possibility of redirecting to other experiences (those on the fringe). These experience-fringes are determined primarily through two ways: temporality (they take place as past (e.g., as memories), present, and possible futures) and new ways of presentations. Husserl's description relies heavily on a sense of the gaze and optics, but his argument is far more sweeping in intent:

> Thus an experience that has become the object of a personally directed glance, and so has the modus of the *deliberately* looked at, has its own fringe of experiences that are not deliberately viewed; that's which is grasped in a mode of "attention," and grasped with increasing clearness as occasion arises, has a fringe of background inattention . . . Thence spring eidetic possibilities: the bringing of what is not the object of a personally directed look within the focus of pure mental vision, raising the unemphatic into relief, and making the obscure clear and ever clearer. (Husserl 1931: §83)

This idea of eidetic possibilities is a core one, for this is the phenomenological method in action; it is how we establish and then direct the critical apparatus of phenomenology. Husserl is saying that it is through the eidetic processes that we are able to shift our attention on fringe-experiences, bringing them into "focus" (to continue the metaphor), or indeed even to lift them out of the invisible.

This raises the possibility that the eidetic could be employed to make the obscure *das Ding* clear and ever clearer, which is of course what Lacan is hoping to achieve, via psychoanalysis, in the seminar *The Ethics of Psychoanalysis*. He wants to raise our awareness of it—with all its obscure, often invisible, murky, fringeness—so we may better grasp its affective nature, or indeed even become cognizant of it. Elsewhere, in speaking of the death drive (which *das Ding* somewhat naturally is attached to), Lacan echoes a phenomenological approach to such a study: "When the entire Symbolic component of psychoanalytic practice is bracketed, the death drive is excluded" (2013: 33) (translation modified). In this manner we can describe Lacan's project in *The Ethics* seminar as a push toward the appresentation of *das Ding*. This is a substantive project to undertake, given his desire to provide a new version of ethics. For both Husserl and Lacan, the critical effort is to be able to redirect the apprehending consciousness toward the fringe, to bring what is denied, repressed even, from our "perception," yet ever present in its force. (It may well be the dark matter equivalent to the analytic praxis.) Approached in such a manner, this is a critical line of thought that is deeply relevant to how we might engage with marginality in cinema, which will be returned to shortly.

The eidetic is part and parcel of intentionality, and it is to this that Husserl ascribes the main theme of phenomenology. This is the idea that to have consciousness, we must always have consciousness *of* something; this is Husserl's loving the beloved or doing having a deed. So, as our consciousness is redirected to the fringe-experience via the eidetic, our consciousness' intentionality is redirected to that and is transformed, becoming, and forming different relationships. For example, the glance (as Husserl puts it) of consciousness to the beloved has the intentionality of loving, at the fringe are all those other possibilities (passion, anger, jealousy, lust, friendship, indifference, memories of walks in the forest . . .) and once the consciousness is redirected, then so too is the intentionality of it. These intentionalities have a further, apposite quality of positionality and relations. There is also a "farness from or nearness to the Ego," where we find "stirrings of pleasure, the early shaping of judgments, incipient wishes," (Husserl 1931: §84); this is the recognition of the Ego (phenomenologically speaking—there are differences for psychoanalysis of course[10]) as the center, and all that is determined is done so within this centralizing context. The nearness to the Ego will locate the thing as central to the directed intentionality, the further away the more it exists as a fringe-experience. (In which we see Husserl's concept of *horizons* as an ordering principle.) That Husserl describes these as attachments to the directed intentionality (they are stirrings, "early shapings," embryonic) means that we should not read the fringe as somehow detached; in fact the opposite is the case and the fringe "shapes" the directed gaze in particular ways and within types of guidance. These are the tendrils that connect the far from the near, and experience to experience (and experienceability). It is here that we are not so far from Lacan's *das Ding*, which is perhaps the definitive and absolute fringe-experience, negotiated through one of the most complex of all ego relations. After all, to gaze at *das Ding* must be the riskiest of adventures, drawing the ego into a complexity without compare. It is of medusal intensities, at least from the phallocentric domain[11]; yet gaze we do, often with compulsive anxieties. Our relationship to *das Ding* is an intimate one, even if there is often a resistance to this. It is a connection of extimacy (Lacan's term for that which is more intimate than intimacy and yet foreign to our self). It is in these terms that we locate the cinematic thing, acknowledging cinema's role in allowing for the apprehension of *das Ding* (in a rendered and therefore

---

[10] See Chapter 1 for the distinctions on Ego (phenomenological) ego (psychoanalytic) and their potential combination as *ego*.

[11] I add this qualifier, acknowledging Cixous' (1976 and 1986) powerful rereading of the Medusa, in "The Laugh of the Medusa," as a subversive challenge to the phallocentric domain.

diluted form), shifting our gaze to the fringe. We need to address some further issues before this idea can be explored more tangibly.

One of the internal tensions in a discussion such as this—the Thing and *das Ding*—is that the former is exploring the negotiations of reality, and its things, by consciousness; while the latter is the analysis of the removal from reality because of its impossibilities. Such tensions can be unpicked through a psychoanalytic secret and the solution to a phenomenological paradox.

A Psychoanalytic Secret

Lacan describes the secret to the reality principle is that even though it seems it leads us to engage with reality, it in fact isolates and removes the subject from it (Lacan 1992: 46–50). It does so because of *das Ding*; the reality principle as an analytic process cannot and does not rely on reality to make sense. If it did so then the substances of psychoanalysis (the unconscious, parapraxis, conversion hysteria, and so on, leading to *das Ding*) are denied. The reality principle needs to, and indeed does, lead us back to these matters and not to reality. In this way the reality principle, just like the pleasure principle, is about the unconscious. For the psychoanalyst it is the recognition that the subject's relationship to reality is always denied (see, e.g., Lacan 2013: 5). This is the crux of a strand of psychoanalysis—what is our relationship to reality? How do we make and engage with, in an ongoing manner, reality? We witness this in stark fashion in Freud's essay on negation; this is an essay that can be read as proto-phenomenological, particularly within the context of Husserl's Thing analysis, as it deals with perception, judgment, and presentation. "Negation,"[12] in summary, is the articulation of disbelief or denial when confronted by a repressed feeling/wish/idea. Freud sees it as the "taking cognizance of what is repressed; indeed, it is already a lifting of the repression" (Freud *SE XIX*: 438) by rendering it, in language, as a particular type of judgment. Freud speaks of the presentation of the repressed into reality; it gains existence. It then acquires an attribute, often of moral caliber. It is seen as "good or bad, useful or harmful" (Freud *SE XIX*: 439; see also *SE XIV* "The Unconscious"). Ultimately, and this is deeply significant, this becomes an issue of the internal and external: "It is no longer a question of whether what has been perceived (a thing) shall be taken into the ego or not, but of whether something which is in the ego as a presentation can be rediscovered in perception (reality) as well" (Freud *SE XIX*: 439). The introjection and projection of the internal and external is a relationship based on reality and consciousness/the ego.

---

[12]There is considerable discussion of the translation of *Verneinen* and *Verneinung*—to negate rather than to deny or to disavow. In Lacan, following the French translation, it becomes *denegration*. The German holds both senses of negation and denial.

The thingness of a negation (its denial through the words chosen, the signifiers put into place) is the presentation in the external world of something internal; and the internalization of something from the outside world into the ego. This can be reread in terms of the fringe-experience as a negation of the intentionality of consciousness (perception). Of course, not all fringe-experiences are negations, but they do display this same attribute of presenting in reality, functions of usefulness, and the relationship of the ego to the world. It is once the negation/fringe is made manifest that we witness the further judgment of the affective, such as the good or bad attribute. As we continue it will be useful to consider how negation operates as a type of modifier of intentionality; that is, how (for psychoanalysis) the intentionality of the utterance is reversed as it is read as repression. Repression is an inverted intentionality, taking the presentation of object/word/thing in opposite or misleading directions.

A Phenomenological Paradox

This phenomenological paradox we find articulated in the later Husserl when he discusses the intentional object. The paradox relates to what happens to intentional objects once the *epoché* has taken place, that is, do they become excluded from consciousness? What happens to the objects that were once in existence and now are removed and denied? Husserl's answer is as surprising as it is clever, for it relies on the notion of freedom: "The very *epoché* itself frees our gaze not only for the intentions running their course within the purely intentional life (i.e., the 'intentional experience' *Erlebnisse*) but also for that which these intentions in themselves, with their own 'what'-content, posit as valid . . . it also frees our gaze for the way in which they do this, i.e., in what modalities of validity or of being" (Husserl 1997: §70). Husserl is dealing with the *epoché* as a meaning-producing process; that is, the bracketing process gives meaning by locating the intentional act and its objects a contained meaningful sense. This is how we can read Freud's negation as an intentionality formed through the *epoché*. Negation is a validating status for both psychoanalysis and phenomenology as it turns the intentionality into a meaning ("you say this, but it means the opposite because of repression" and the response "you tell me that what I say means this, but I deny that meaning"). The validity component of the *epoché* can be extended to the Freudian sense of judgment (the object as good/bad, helpful/harmful) as validating the intentional object. This also somewhat resolves the "opposite directions" of negation, yielding the "what"-content of the negation as a manifestation of the repressed and its denial. The *epoché* holds these together as a container of the two oppositional stances (the analyst seeing the presentation as a repressed thought, the one who utters it in denial, in negation) through this validation and freeing of the gaze. Such a reading is supported by the way in which Husserl speaks of the *epoché* as producing a new internal world and for an evincing experience and its relation to objects in the real world (1997: §70). This aligns, once more, with the internal/external spaces and projection and introjection, which can also be seen as acts of intentionality.

There is one final issue of relevance here before we turn to apply these ideas to cinematic things. Husserl articulates three attributes to Thingness in its ideal essence (1931: §149). As we experience time we encounter the form of the Thing as time as it presents itself *res temporalis*, which is the Thing as enduring; *res extensa*, the Thing of space, which is the infinitely changing spatial relations and unlimited movability; and the Thing as *res materialis*, which is causality and connectivity. All three aspects, it should be noted, share the quality of infinitude, enduring, and unendingness. The Thingness of time, space, and causal connections is without end, limits, and in constant states of change (a quality i.e., also found in cinematic spatiality). This is not simply because, as is readily apparent, these are boundless concepts, rather it is also because there is the difference between the appearance of such things and their underlying essence. For Lacan, this is the operation of the Symbolic and constructions of meaning and meaningfulness: "it is not merely because the phenomenon represents a displacement—in other words, is inscribed in Imaginary phenomena—that it is an analyzable phenomenon.... a phenomenon is analyzable only if it represents something other than itself" (2013: 15). To become the analyzable, then, is dependent on the reflexive modality (the Imaginary), and the displacement of this aligns to phenomenology's Thingness. The boundlessness of the Thing is tied to its *eidos* rather than its appearance. This is why Husserl describes the Thing as an empty X which becomes the bearer of determinations (see, e.g., 1931: §40), and is distinguished within defining contexts of "mere appearance" and "true thing." Here we find a further way of clarifying cinematic flesh. Husserl states: "The *'true Being'* would therefore be entirely and *fundamentally something that is defined otherwise than as that which is given in perception as corporeal reality*" (1931: §40). The "defined otherwise," it is argued here, is the intentionality of flesh as it is found in cinematic things, contradistinctive to the body in this context of "corporeal reality." This is an opportune moment to turn to some cinematic examples.

The Internal as Intimacy Projected into the External Space which Creates Anxiety (Projected Forfeiture)

This cinematic configuration occurs when the internal object is given, as intentionality, into external space (of the subject) which creates anxiety. This is termed *projected forfeiture* because the cost of this projection is a "giving up" of validated objects of the self. The broken heart of unrequited love is one of culture's most enduring motifs of this; even before the heart is broken, we experience the pangs of anxiety, giving our "heart" with all the attendant fears that come with such a gesture. However, I wish to keep with some of the issues raised, notably how the *epoché* is devised to create a space where this forfeiture is played out as a spatial issue in its own right, that is, space is an object-thing in itself. The *res extensa* in such a context is space as movement within what becomes a cinematic discourse of space. Cinematic spatiality is determined by, and determines, the central, defining idea of movement in these films.[13] The *res materialis* is thus determined by causality and connectivity as a spatial domain. This cinematic spatiality becomes a fundamental aspect of anxiety because of this. In other words, these films utilize space and spatiality as an anxiety; such anxiety has been determined by the projection of intimate objects, including the body (in its fleshified primacy) as self. Further to this, it is important to note that this is not the representational field of these projected forfeitures (their representations as part of the narrative); rather it is cinema itself (its cinemaness) that offers up to the spectator these spaces and their projections. Thus, the spectator's intimate relations with a film necessarily involves *projected forfeitures* of some sort.

Gravity (Alfonso Cuarón 2013) can be read in these terms of cinema spatiality and its *res materialis* of things. We can bypass many of the more obvious aspects of a reading of this film and space; simply put, this would be a reading of the anxieties of outer space (a sort of Kantian mathematical sublime) contrasted by the minutiae of intimacies. The Thing of *res extensa* confronts us through the surrounding depths of unending space, in part because there are no limitations defining it and in part because it hovers before us,[14] always determining the background with the threat of a drifting, silent death. This immensity is contrasted with the tight, confining, restrictive intimacies (of the various spacecraft), which act not as antidotes, but further anxious sites. All of this, as said, can stand in its obviousness; instead, we can turn to cinema thingness to examine projected forfeiture and fringe-experiences.

The first example we note of this is the recurring, threatening return of space debris, which is, to keep with Husserl's terminology, *in media res*. Are we to read these colliding fragments (the so-called Kessler Syndrome) as *das Ding*? Perhaps, as they sweep from the unseen with terrifying force, returning destruction each time. However, a more subtle reading of *das Ding* can be had with the film's conclusion—which we shall turn to in a moment. These fragments are a good example of things as cinematic things,

---

[13]Clearly there are possibilities here with Merleau-Ponty's ideas on space and movement. See in particular his analysis of space, movement, and relative positioning through perception (1962: 267–73). This will be taken up in Chapter 5.
[14]See Chapter 4 on Husserl's idea of this "hovers before us."

because they are not of the binary domains (space and earth, human and environment, human and technology, and so on); they are unrecognizable bits of a something that was once a functioning piece of technology and now have become signifiers of anxiety, fatality, and survival. Their status of *in media res* shifts them from "whole" to "parts" so that their cinematic thingness rests in such anxious moments and actions. Similarly, they are not of space nor in space, occupying a region between the two. They have rapid mobility that contrasts with the humans, as well as other objects (such as the space stations, the Earth, and the stars). Their dynamic, swift, and chaotic movement defines the cinematic spatiality as one of betweenness (*in media res*). It is not enough to simply see this thingness of the debris as movement expected in all films, for the intentionality of the debris *is movement*. That is how it is experienced (phenomenologically speaking), how it is sensibly intuited; and once it has this intentionality further attributes are given (chaos, threat, anxiety, and death). And it is in this thingness of movement that lies the projected forfeiture of anxiety derived from intimacy. In these terms we witness a quite literal version of fringe-experience, as the terror sweeps from the unseen edge to the center of the screen.

The projected forfeiture here is derived from two interconnected sources. The first of these can be taken from Kierkegaard's (re) reading of the negative: "In logic *the negative* is used as the quickening power that brings movement into everything. . . . The negative, then, is the immanence of movement, it is the vanishing factor, what is annulled" (Kierkegaard 2015: 17;18). Kierkegaard's concern here is with the Hegelian dialectic; the annulled being the *Aufhebung* of "movement" from the dialectical process. The reworking here is to align this notion of the immanence of movement (the thingness of cinematic spatiality) in a twice-folded fashion: how cinema itself utilizes the "quickening power of movement" via the negative; and how this quickening power of movement works as the negative as projected forfeiture of anxiety in *Gravity*. The first of these is cinema itself (cinemaness), with the negative driving narrative structures, characters' actions, structures of relationships, and so on. Films create the negative (absences, non-presences) to drive the things that occupy their spaces along, giving them significance. This is a further response to the question of why cinema has things, for this is the response to the negative. The second of these is a realigning of the negative in its other sense (from the negative as non-presence to the negative as adverse). The thingness of the debris (bordering on *das Ding* here) holds both these aspects: it drives the narrative; and at the same time is the (Kierkegaardian) annulling, vanishing factor.

The second source of the projected forfeiture is not the debris sui generis but comes from the intimacy of Ryan Stone[15] (Sandra Bullock). This will

---

[15] The apt, Freudian, play on words with the name Stone in a film titled *Gravity* (the gravitational force and direness of the situation) lends itself to a reading on motion.

IMAGE 15 *From* Gravity.

lead into how we can consider *das Ding* as part of this process. The idea of projected forfeiture is as follows: a thing of intimacy, internal to the subject, is projected into the external world and in doing so there is some, and potentially even complete, forfeiture of that intimacy, and so the self as well. This is akin to Lacan's notion of aphanisis (the fear of the loss of the signifier as it stands in for the self—see *The Four Fundamental Concepts of Psychoanalysis*), but there are some differences. We see a quite literal projection of the body into anxious space(s) as the astronauts move between crafts, and in doing so continually risk a corporeal forfeiture of the self/body. However, by way of an alternate example, let us consider first the hallucinatory scene where the seemingly defeated Stone slips into self-induced unconsciousness toward death, and then the film's concluding scene. In the first example we see Stone on the brink of giving up; in this state she imagines, or perhaps hallucinates is a better term, the return of Matt Kowalski (George Clooney), who chides her into action. (In this way the fringe-experience becomes a different psychical process as Stone's psyche constructs a version of itself as Kowalski.) Her breathlessness and incapacity to focus are in sharp contrast to Kowalski's ease of breath and speech and sharpness of mind (signifiers that should indicate to the spectator that this is an ontic dissonance). The sound in this sequence matches the stages of projected forfeiture: first, alarm sounds as Stone collapses into the crisis; followed by absolute (meditative, spiritual) silence as Kowalski enters the capsule; a return to calming sounds as he speaks; and finally, a return to the alarms as Stone recognizes the hallucination for what it is, which is a shift in sensible intuition and a shift in intentionalities through sound and its absences. Phenomenologically speaking, this scene works well as an illustration of fringe-experience and intentionality. The demonstration of the projected intimacy in a space already invested with anxiety is the hallucination itself, which is the cinematic thing defining all other elements within the scene. The forfeiture is, of course, this intimacy transposed onto death. This is the near-far attribute of the intentionality to the Ego ("the farness from or nearness to the Ego" as Husserl puts it), as one's death, no longer a fringe-experience, is the nearness intentionality of consciousness. Stone's hallucination of Kowalski even offers her an easy, peaceful death, turning this anguish of the moment into something alleviated through the "safe" aloneness of space.

Let us now turn to the final scene of *Gravity* to read projected intimacy in a different but connected way. Having survived reentry to Earth, we witness Stone emerge into an idyllic landscape. It seems (textually) self-evident that this ending is one of birth and survival. Stone's struggle and then emergence from the (amniotic fluids) of the water, her laborious efforts to stand, her awkward first steps, and her gaze of the surroundings filled with a sense of newness and wonder. But why do we feel compelled to read these things, this cinematic spatiality, as one of birth (possibly renewal)? It is a purposefully designed celebratory ending, affirming life and the defeat of the negative. We follow Stone's gaze as she lies in the water, looking to the sky and watching shards of debris burn up in the protective environment of the Earth's atmosphere; a symbolic, visual rendering of life's success against the negative. But what if we instead extend the dominating projected forfeiture, the anxiety induced from externalized intimacy (and of course psychoanalysis' reading of birth as trauma and anxiety), into this scene? To do so, and to illustrate the analytic situation at hand, three conceptual frames can be taken up. This is Lacan's *das Ding*, Kierkegaard's "sin-consciousness' nonappearance," and Klein's primal process and persecutory anxiety.

Toward the end of his seminar on anxiety Lacan mentions in passing *das Ding*, but it is a deeply significant mention: "[anxiety] designates the most, as it were, profound object, the ultimate object, *das Ding*" (Lacan 2017: 311). However, this needs to be read within the context of a comment Lacan makes in *The Ethics of Psychoanalysis* when he states that *das Ding* is, at the level of the unconscious, outside notions of good and bad. The anxious object of *das Ding* must be seen as an intentionality (phenomenologically speaking) which, through *cogitationes*, shapes the affective resonances and in doing so defines the spatiality (the *res extensa*). This is negation acting as a modifier of intentionality, the denial of what is being produced out of the acts of intentionality, and sometimes even the denial of intentionality (as hermeneutic process) itself. If we are to read the unending cold, darkness of space as *das Ding* in *Gravity*, then because it does exist *res extensa* (without spatial end or boundary) and *res temporalis* (continuous and enduring) it cannot be "out there" or "over there from the Ego" and not on Earth. This is true because of the forfeiture of the projected intimacy that Stone (and we, the spectator) experience and will continue to do so.[16] The anxious object of *das Ding* turns out not to be (in) the infinitude of lonely space, rather (in) the forfeited projected intimacy. This, it is argued here, is the very heart of the process.

Now to Klein: "The primal process of projection is a means of deflecting the death instinct outward. Projection also imbues the first object with libido. The other primal process is introjection, again largely at the service of the life instinct; it combats the death instinct because it leads to the ego taking in something life-giving (first of all food) and thus binding the death instinct working within" (Klein 1975: 238). By way of context, Klein comes to this statement after a discussion of (and some small disagreement with) Freud's theory of the death drive and its relationship to the ego, the unconscious, and moral masochism. Her interpretation of these entwined processes of projection and introjection is, it should be noted, that they are necessary to psychical development and survival. It would be possible to read this Kleinian line here with Stone's hallucination. This would be the libidinal imbuing of the hallucination as object (the hallucination as object aligns perfectly with Husserl's notion of phantasms). If we read the hallucination as the projection of the ego, then the introjection is the life-giving utterances to survive. However, the projected forfeiture of intimacy opens up the final scene to be one not of the life instinct, but the binding of the death instinct. In such a reading we can ask how sure are we that this is a closing scene of happy survival and not a hallucination of the dying or dead Stone? If we allow for such ambiguity there is the return of *das Ding* as the unrepresented/unrepresentable death (and her gaze of the debris, the ultimate object, becomes one of watching her own death). Klein's argument that the infant needs to "master persecutory anxiety" in the interplay of internal and external by splitting objects into "helpful and loved and . . . frightening and hated" (Klein 1975: 238) does not mean that they are cleaved entirely; an attachment between the two always remains, which is why the status of the good and bad in objects can change. We, as spectators, work through *Gravity*'s final scene in this attempt to master persecutory anxiety, but in doing so recognize that the projected forfeiture is a binding of the primal process and actually reinforces the interchangeable and embedded aspects of the life and death instincts. This is the point that Freud arrives at when he speaks of moral masochism.

---

[16] Here we see a version of the phenomenological paradox discussed earlier. This is a cinematic moment of Husserl's answer to the *epoché* and what happens to those things "outside" the intentionality.

And now to Kierkegaard: "Death's anxiety therefore corresponds to the anxiety of birth . . . at the moment of death the human being finds itself at the extreme point of the synthesis [of spirit and body]" (Kierkegaard 2015: 112–13). This description of synthesis certainly fits with the hallucination scene as we observe a manifestation of the "spirit" and the dying body to show the synthesis of crisis. Similarly, the opening line pairs with the *res materialis* of the cinematic thing in terms of the corresponding and connecting anxieties of death and birth.[17] It is through this connection that the final scene is read as the duality or, better yet, in-betweenness of birth and death. The signifiers poignantly indicate a birth, but the projected forfeiture shifts the reading to death (or at least this as a viable alternative reading). The Kierkegaardian synthesis here is what happens in the object of *das Ding* so that it is neither birth nor death (it is *in media res*), but the corresponding anxieties of the two in this moment of synthesis. When this synthesis takes place, we witness the production of a version of cinematic flesh. The extreme point of synthesis shifts the corporeal toward flesh precisely because of the ways in which the subject relates to, for want of a better word, the "spirit." This is how the projected intimacy operates as a revised and anxious burdened return to the internal.[18]

The Internal as Intimacy Projected into the External Space which Produces Intimacy (the Projected Familiar)

The next modality is not to be seen as an inversion of affect to the one previously discussed; rather, our concern here is with intimacy (re)producing intimacy within the external space. This has been designated as the "projected familiar" because what is sustained in such projections is a familiarization of the external through the intimate. (This relates to issues of the uncanny which is taken up in Chapter 6.) Some obvious, and literal, examples of this would include Norman Bates's bird-filled sitting room in *Psycho* (Alfred Hitchcock 1960) to represent his psychical intimacies of madness; the manipulation of the park space in *Blow-Up* (Michelangelo Antonioni 1966) as the photographic gaze rendering public space as intimate; or anxious-ridden wilderness space beyond the homestead holding the returning

---

[17]Freud's analysis of the relationship of anxiety and birth is discussed elsewhere here.
[18]A potential parallel reading of this projected forfeiture, but one that opens up a different version of the Kierkegaardian synthesis, could take place in *Interstellar* (Christopher Nolan 2014). With typical Nolan delinearization of time, the projected forfeiture becomes part of the *res temporalis* of the Thing; once more space is the negotiated object(s) within this projection.

family in *The Searchers* (John Ford 1956). It is notable that in all of these examples the intimacies all turn out to be problematizing: Bates's intimacy is a perversion of (the) Mother; the photographic act is an inauthentic and intrusive intimacy; Ethan's intimacy is a disturbed and violent one. However, the two examples to be worked through here have a less literal connection, and are selected in part because of this, and in part because they offer differing exemplars of this type of projected intimacy. They are *High Life* (Claire Denis 2018) and *Roma* (Alfonso Cuarón 2018).[19]

The projected familiar is a controlling intimacy, shaping the external to align it with the internal. This can produce positive created world orders (e.g., in romantic comedies and musicals[20]) where the external spaces permit and endorse the projected familiar, or negative versions where the familiar is of a darker nature.[21] What is shared is intimacy as an intentionality of spatial reimagining. This is a phenomenological intentionality because it is irrelevant if the reimagining aligns with "reality" or is fantastical; the determining sensibly driven intuition is the Ego and its compulsion to produce an intimacy with the external. Therefore, to understand the "type" of spatial reimagining that is taking place we need to understand the intentionality of the intimacy. It is in this way that spatial reimagining is ultimately a version of the *epoché*, delineating and refining through bracketing off aspects of the external spaces through bracketed aspects of the internal.

The first example is *High Life* as hysterical intimacy and its spatial manifestations. The aim here is to work through this idea of hysterical intimacy, but to commence there needs to be an acknowledgment of the pleasure principle and the death drive found in the film. As with Claire Denis's *Trouble Every Day* (discussed in Chapter 5), sexuality and its

---

[19]Set aboard a spacecraft full of prisoners, the film explores the often cruel sexual psychopathologies of Dr Dibs (Juliette Binoche). Dibs is driven in a seemingly futile quest to create a child through artificial insemination, merging acts that are destructive in their attempts to create. Dibs eventually succeeds and a child, Willow, is born. As each person on the ship dies (often violently), Monte (Robert Patterson) raises the child. Dibs reveals to Monte that he is the father before ejecting herself into space.

Roma is a semi-autobiographical story of director Alfonso Cuarón. It centers on live-in housemaid Cleodegaria "Cleo" Gutiérrez, weaving her attentive care for the family's children into the wider social narrative of 1970s Mexico, notably the anti-government protests.

[20]For example, *Singin' in the Rain* (Kelly and Donen 1952) plays continuously with the manipulations of "reality," devising texts within texts to reinforce the projected familiar (character, narrative, and genre); *La La Land* (Damian Chazelle 2016) holds two different versions of this: it utilizes the dream sequence at the end of the film to negate the generic expectations, which can be seen as the collapse of the projected familiar; the inverse is the opening scene with the long, highly mobile camera work reimagining LA traffic jams as somehow the space for exuberant dreams and convivial passions.

[21]For example, in *Taxi Driver* (Martin Scorsese 1976) Travis Bickle's projected familiar intimacies construct the external world as one full of collapse and violence, where time and space lose their stability.

libidinous extremes in *High Life* are reoriented toward the death drive within a context of human *contra* science. Dibs's (Juliette Binoche) obsession to create life is performed with fascistic intent, dehumanizing the process through abstracted science, regimented schedules, machine interventions, and rape. Passion is reduced to masturbatory alienation and procreation to a series of failed experiments. Monte's (Robert Patterson) refusal to participate in all forms of sexual activity is measured as a type of moral character so that on a spaceship of criminals he retains the status of the guilt-ridden "innocent." In these terms he becomes the cinematic version of the anxious, psychoanalytically speaking, ego: "The ego which, on the one hand, knows that it is innocent is obliged, on the other hand, to be aware of a sense of guilt and to carry a responsibility which it cannot account for" (Freud SE XIX: 43). These responsibilities are invested in Monte's (literal) role as a father, but they are also found in more disguised, and morally ambiguous, forms such as Dibs's experiments. Along these lines, consider Monte in terms of Kierkegaard's version of anxiety and guilt: "If we let evil desire, concupiscence, etc. be innate in the individual, we lose the ambiguity in which the individual becomes both guilty and innocent. In the faintness of anxiety, the individual swoons and is for that very reason both guilty and innocent" (Kierkegaard 2015: 89–90). This Kierkegaardian ambiguity (and its Freudian link to the ego) is a defining attribute of this character. The child (Willow) born from the rape of Monte by Dibs (and insemination of Boyce (Mia Goth)) continues this sensibility of innocence, guilt, and uncomprehending responsibility (a recurring Denis trope) as she is raised alone in the spaceship by Monte after the death of all the other characters. Dibs's Medeaesque backstory goes some way to locating her hysteria-defined projected familiarity of intimacy. (Except for Willow, all children suffer death at her hands.)

Before continuing with the issue of hysteria, lets us consider the pleasure principle's destructive capacities, for it is within that determination that the reality principle is usually evoked. As Lacan puts it: "The reality principle consists in making the game last, that is to say, in ensuring that pleasure is renewed, so the fight doesn't end for lack of combatants. . . . The reality principle consists in husbanding our pleasures, these pleasures whose aim is precisely to end is cessation" (Lacan 1988b: 84). In this way Monte becomes the fleshified version of the reality principle within the projected familiarity of Dibs's intimacies (as a destructive, compulsive, and unending pleasure principle). It is precisely this Medean intimate projected familiarity that shapes the space (cinematic spatiality, including the relationship of objects) as it takes place in the past. The other projected familiarity comes from Monte, and then Willow's, intimacies. We see this as Monte's struggle as a father (the intimacy of parental life and paternal support) and then as Willow's urging him to undertake the journey toward the black hole (standing, perhaps once more, as a configuration of death and rebirth).

This chapter began with an evoking of Dora—Freud's most famous case study of hysteria; the case study he handled so badly. Freud commences with a misreading of Dora's desires. He assumes Dora is in love with Herr K (and himself) and fails to recognize that she is actually in love with Frau K. From such a starting point it is impossible for Freud to arrive at any accurate analytic position. This is the danger of projected familiarity, particularly when the analytic situation is the external space being shaped by the action of an *epoché* of erroneous assumptions. Simply put, Freud places his (analytic) intimacy into the space which holds Dora's hysteria, shaping it not as her intimacy but as his own. We see this same process taking place in Dibs's destructive and misaligned actions in *High Life*. If we followed this line back, Freud's actions become versions of hysteria as well, with the loss of reality derived from this projected intimacy. This is of the same order as Freud's projected intimacy in the lecture on femininity when he articulates (worrisomely—one can only hope for an ironic tone, but there is little evidence of that) that "women are the problem" (*SE XXII*: 100). Monte stands in opposition to this, his celibacy counter to her *jouissance*, his passive resistance against her excessive force. That their pasts link them through a common criminal act (the killing of a child/children) drives this hysterical counterpoint. Dibs manifests this intimate act by trying to recreate life, Monte in his refusal to participate.

This reading of *High Life* has been predominately psychoanalytic, so let us turn to the second example, *Roma*, to explore some of the phenomenological dimensions. In doing so we can consider how the two approaches can also be connected through this idea of projected familiarity and the intimate. As noted earlier, there is always a series of mediating positions in the experiencing and shading of cinema; and these projection and introjection modalities are particular aspects and processes within the experiencing. We witness a different version of the projected familiar in *Roma* as it operates in the mediating experientiality because there is the "additional" layer of the semi-autobiographical. The projected intimacy can be read, therefore, though Cuarón's biographical representations or the character of Cleodegaria "Cleo" Gutiérrez (Yalitza Aparicio). Of course, these are not mutually exclusive, but for clarity and to keep things manageable (and to align it with the approach used so far), the following will focus on Cleo and projected intimacy.

One scene that illustrates this is the rescue of the children by Cleo, and her "confessional" utterance that she never wanted her baby to be born, which takes place at the end of the film. This can be compared to the street protest scene which has different attributes of projected intimacy. Both these scenes are interesting in their similar structuration of cinematography (the long, sweeping, and continuous shots), the sense of real-time and screen time aligning, and the use of camera angles to position people within complex motions in spaces. This technical aspect is noteworthy here because it acts on *res materialis*, devising an affective turn between the body and its environment. How this plays into the projected familiar can be read through Dufrenne's (1966) reimagining (beyond Kant) of the *a priori* as having objectness as well as being a type of knowledge of these objects. Cleo's projected familiar intimacy is demonstrated more overtly in the beach scene, in part because of the (sacrificial) care she expresses, but mainly because of the confessions of her pregnancy. The two of course are closely entwined. Cleo has shown various sacrificial acts of care throughout the narrative; these are projected intimacy that permits the film to show class relations, emotional bonds, and the dual lives of citizens. However, Cleo's admission of her feelings about her baby carries even more intimate signification, and therefore shapes the spatiality of the world order in a more affective manner. This is how we can read Cleo's body in terms of the *a priori* and its projected intimacies. Dufrenne, in devising the idea of the *a priori* as corporeal, states: "here again the subjective *a priori* finds its correlate in an objective *a priori*: in what could be called the vital value of the object—e.g., the desirable, the reposeful, the provoking. These are authentic *a priori* forms that could be compared to affective qualities; but instead of soliciting feelings in the subject, they call forth the body itself and its vital forces: the living, not the thinking, body. . . . Therefore, we can speak of the *a priori* of presence: such are the vital *a priori* by which the body expresses its living being" (Dufrenne 1966: 161).

Part of the way Dufrenne negotiates the complexities of designating the corporeal as *a priori*, and therefore (from a Kantian perspective) attributing to it transcendental functions, is to propose a double transcendence derived from the body as "center of reference and center of indetermination" (1966: 162). This aligns with the modality of projected familiarity[22]; in the example

IMAGE 16 *From* Roma.

---

[22]It indeed aligns with all of these modalities, but in different fashions.

at hand, Cleo's rescuing body (center of reference) manifests its indeterminacy through the acts of sacrificial care (and here we move somewhat toward Kristeva's reading of *Cura*) and confessional cries. That these two processes (physical and emotional) take place at the same time (a phenomenological now-point it needs to be stressed) and in a cinematic spatiality defined by powerful motion (the sea's impositional waves that threaten the body) works in this double transcendence. Similarly, when Dufrenne reminds us that "the body itself can be understood as transcendental only in reference to consciousness" (1966: 162) we can note the projected familiarity of intimacy within this. Cleo's body at this moment becomes the affective manifestation of consciousness (which aligns with the psychoanalytic reading of the body as psychical conversion). Within this scene, various bodies are called forth (Cleo's, the drowning children, the siblings and mother watching), with Cleo's body becoming the focus as a vital (*a priori*) force and set of values (care, love, and confessional) that are presentified as the maternal. This maternal value is complex, resonating with the care for the child and the painful confession of loss.

The street protest scene works in similar ways, with contrasting affective turns. Here the sequence (reinforced both narratively and formally through the camera work and *mise-en-scène*) constructs the body called forth in terms of violence. The body in crisis "out there/over there from the Ego" (through the window, on the street, away, removed from the intimacy of the acts within the space of the baby furniture, and seemingly anonymous) becomes the crisis "in here/near here, the Ego" when gunmen enter the shop where Cleo is looking for a baby's cot. The vital value of the object and the *a priori* calling forth of the body is played out in fear and anxiety. Here we see the projected familiar incorporate Cleo's intimacies of her pregnancy; one that is filled with anxious and insecure feelings. The intensity of these feelings is magnified through the choice of a love object within the maternal

IMAGE 17 *From* Roma.

(which is replicated in the beach scene). This is a cinematic example of Freud's *Einschränkung*, the restrictions and limitations placed on object choice; Lacan subsequently links this to the libidinal object and the mother (see *Seminar X*, notably the section "Not Without Having It"). Of all the possible object choices for the ego, these limitations are defined and enacted through the libidinally charged. In *Roma* it is Cleo that becomes the recurring and central figure for this. The imposing waves in the beach scene are replicated here in the waves of bodies and the waves of violence as the men enter the shop, shoot people and threaten others.[23] This movement of the outside bodies coming into the space of the shop (i.e., Cleo's intimate space) is the *a priori* of presence determined by the corporeal. This is read here as cinematic flesh; the corporealization of the *a priori* is also the producing of cinematic (aestheticized) flesh. We read it this way because the corporeal *a priori* stands outside of the dualism of subject-body/object and allows for the affective to be experienced in a context more akin to the transcendental.

The External as Intimacy Introjected into the Internal, Producing Intimacy (Introjected Familiarity); And the Inversion (External Intimacy Producing Anxiety) (Introjected Defamiliarization)

The first two modalities are primarily concerned with projective acts; these next two will consider the equivalent introjection acts in more detail. Because both introjection modes have a parallel inversion, there is some expediency to be had by discussing the two iterations simultaneously. In this first case this means introjected familiarity and introjected defamiliarization are read through notions of intimacy, even though the affective objects produced are distinguished by their relationship to intimacy and anxiety. The example to be used here to elaborate further on introjection and the *a priori* as corporeal and the *Umwelt* (the outside world/environment) and *Innenwelt* (the inner world) is *Persona* (Ingmar Bergman 1966).

Two of the contexts in which Lacan speaks of the *Umwelt* are: anxiety, space, and the production of traces, that is, a form of language; and the relational constructions of narcissism. Within the first of these, we observe Lacan's idea of the truth and the trace: "One part of animal behavior consists in structuring a certain field of its *Umwelt*, its surroundings, by way

---

[23]This is done at the formal level as well with the camera's motion and long takes.

of traces . . . Animals, I tell you, efface their traces and lay false traces. . . . There is one thing that animals don't do—they don't lay false traces to make us believe they are false, that is, traces that are taken for false. Laying falsely false traces is a behavior that is, I won't say quintessentially human, but quintessentially signifying" (Lacan 2017: 63). The "falsely false" that Lacan speaks of is part of what can be called an epistemological pathology; that is, no matter what the outside environment (*Umwelt*) tells us, embedded and often blindly held beliefs can and do continue regardless of the evidence.[24] That Lacan describes this as signifying is important; if we are removed from the environment, and if part of this removal has taken place because we can no longer "speak" of it, a falsely false signifying practice can only increase the caesura. This is the rupturing anxiety of our relationship to the *Umwelt*, which does not necessarily lead to some venture of escape, but rather can lead to a self-confirming epistemological pathology. It is also why the falsely false is not the truth, but the doubled falseness of the act: the act itself (erasure as the false trail) and the language system around that falsehood (the falsely done/spoken).

This is what we see in *Persona* where the external (*Umwelt*) is introjected, creating a self-confirming internal (*Innenwelt*) epistemological pathology—the falsely false. *Persona*, and the other films discussed here, are examples of the inversion actions taking place synchronically; that is, the introjected familiarity (the external introjected to form intimacy) which becomes (perhaps even induces) introjected defamiliarization (the external introjected to form anxiety). In both cases this is played out through the female body as corporeal *a priori*, where the called forth body is a manifestly split one, and consciousness operates as "the sign of subjectivity" (Dufrenne 1966: 163). This also aligns with Lacan's (and even more foundationally, Freud's) *Ichspaltung*—the split subject.

Persona plays out the falsely false (the epistemological pathology) through the process of introjection. This takes place in at least three manifestations: Elizabet Volger's (Liv Ullmann) silence is introjected defamiliarization at the commencement of the film, presenting the withdrawn body as one of anxiety and closure. As the narrative progresses the introjection alters to become one of familiarity (intimacy) as she manifests a version of control over the external. This takes place at the beach-house and its environs where she is more powerfully located in the spaces, becomes the quasi-therapist figure, and her silence is a determining one played out through the gaze. This presentification (phenomenologically speaking) is the reworking of

---

[24]This relates to Gregory Bateson's ideas about epistemological error and epistemological habit—that is, how we think "knowing" and how we fall into repeated errors in doing so. As Bateson puts it: "Epistemological error is often reinforced and therefore self-validating. You can get along all right in spite of the fact that you entertain at rather deep levels of the mind premises which are simply false" (Bateson 1969: 456).

Elizabet's intentionality of consciousness from the powerlessly solitary to the analytically invitational. The falsely false of this signifying practice is most readily apparent in the unsealed letter where she writes of her analysis of Alma (Bibi Andersson), demonstrating an active engagement as opposed to the presented absent, withdrawn subjectivity. It is significant that both examples, which are crucial elements in the diegetic processes, are *eidetically* formed. The re-presentational attributes are cinematic *epoché*, bracketing off the natural attitude through a distancing effect (memory and the past, the absent author). The second manifestation is Alma's recounting of her sexual activities, and subsequent abortion. This is the falsely false of Alma as the dutiful nurse, the faithful fiancée, the reliable carer. This is not to say that Alma's previous sexual activities are overdeterminations of her current subjectivity (which is an altogether different temporal now-point construction); rather, the trails that the narrative has laid down need to be retentionally revised once Alma tells the concupiscent story and its hovering before us (herself, Elizabet, and each spectator) to produce current implications. In this way, Alma's sexual story is a version of the projected familiar (in the telling it creates a spatial intimacy) and forfeiture (once revealed control is lost). It is introjection here because of the narrative's play on narcissism and the double; and the introjection is manifested in both iterations, creating intimacy, a conflation of the self and other, and anxiety at different points in the narrative. The third falsely false takes place within the post-revelatory scenes (the sexual memory and the letter), when the blurring of the distinction between the two women is more directly articulated. This process aligns with the idea that has underpinned the relationship between intimacy and anxiety—where one is, the other must follow.

Narcissistic identification shapes the introjections in *Persona*, creating intimacy and anxiety in parallel and mirroring fashion, devised from the double introjections of familiarization and defamiliarization of the external and internal. Lacan (1988a) speaks of two narcissisms: one originating from, and devised through, the corporeal image and shaping the individual's *Umwelt* through an assertion of unity; and one constructed out of reflection and forming a relationship to and with the Other. In this seminar, Lacan further discusses the schema with two mirrors and its developments of the mirror stage. This is a recurring theme in the Seminars and operates as a type of unifying concept for Lacanian theory. (The implications of the two narcissisms are discussed further in Chapter 1, particularly in relation to Husserl and the double ego.) It is in Lacan's presentation on the mirror stage that he indicates the reflexive relationship of the *Innenwelt* and *Umwelt*: "The function of the mirror stage . . . is to establish a relationship between an organism and its reality—or, as they say, between the *Innenwelt* and the *Umwelt*" (2006: 78). In *Persona* we witness a key variation (although probably far more common than is spoken of, and certainly a recurring cinematic theme) which is the relationship of the self to another's reality.

However, even if these two narcissisms are not posed as progressions or sequences, it is possible to read *Persona* as the movement from the initially corporeally derived, into a relationship of self to Other, and then an oscillation which emphasizes the instability of identity. It is this oscillation that determines the shifts between the intimate and anxious, blurring in much the same ways as the two women do. The first of these narcissisms is quite literally articulated by the similar physicality of the two women—but this is not enough to satisfy us here. The first order of narcissism is not derived from the corporeal mirroring, rather it emerges from the interplay between realities. This is the vital value of the body as objective *a priori*— the "value," its purposeful force, is a multiplicity, including the desirable, the reflexive, and the remembered. The value, as intentionality (hence valueness as determinant), is a corporeal driven attachment (of self to other) so that the self becomes enmeshed in the objective other. Each woman's body (and this is a corporeality that carries with it the past as a resonating subjectivity) does not simply mirror the other's; it sets up a relationship based on a narcissism of the real which necessarily interplays between the subject's consciousness and the objective. Hence when Lacan speaks of "the relation between the constitution of reality and the relation of the form of the body" (1988a: 124) we can witness this as the first narcissism between Elizabet and Alma. Each constructs a reality from their own body and the body of the other, and it is that reality that is introjected (from the familiar to the defamiliar) to form an intimacy (with the self, the other woman, and the construction of reality). We see this most readily in two signifying moments—Alma's sexual recounting, and the complex maternal (the vital value of the body for both women) based on absence.

We can take this notion of "value" and its intentionality further. Recalling some of Husserl's key qualifiers of intentionality, we can note the following: that intentionality is "an inclusive term for a number of pervasive phenomenological structures;" that it may not always be readily apparent, but is always present in acts of consciousness; that it is an orientation of the Ego, and as such determines not just interpretation but also actual perception (without directed intentionality things can remain in the fringe-experience or invisible); intentionality "characterizes consciousness" and in doing so provides a unary "perspective"; it produces and sustains experienceability; and it is a "unique peculiarity of experience" (1931: §31). Within such a context, consider Lacan's interpretative gesture on anxiety and the mirror (i.e., the reflexive stance "forced" upon us): "Even in the experience of the mirror, a moment can come about when the image we believe we abide by undergoes modification. If this specular image we have facing us . . . allows the dimensions of our gaze to emerge, the value of the image starts to change. . . . There's an *initium*, and aura, a dawning sense of uncanniness which leaves the door open to anxiety" (Lacan 2017: 88). Lacan's interest here is anxiety, and its capacity to emerge when we least expect it, that is, unaware; Husserl's interests are the interstitial moments between intentionality and awareness (as well as the lack of). Both allow us to think through the idea of anxiety as intentionality as a determining awareness which comes into being. The intimate spectator, and their emerging awareness of anxieties, operates within this structuration precisely because (as both Husserl and Lacan address) this is a merging of frames and acts of consciousness into a reflexive modality. The proposal here is that this is a fundamental process in the act of spectating; it is somewhat of a gift that *Persona* is a cinematic playing out of this, that is, a representation of two women's experientiality of this uncanny anxiety in its beginnings (its *initium*). Husserl's notion of intentionality helps to foreground the ways in which the two women "blend into the unity of a single intuition, that of a consciously grasped field of objects" (1931: §84)—which is a requirement (cinema's desire) for the spectator. For the two women, and cinema's intimate spectator, this is the adoption of the "potential field of perception in the sense that a special perceiving (an awareness of the type *cogito*) can be directed toward everything that thus appears" (1931: §84). However, when we add Lacan to this, the "special perceiving" is one determined by and through anxiety. Anxiety, as intimacy, becomes its valuing value.

The second narcissism is described by Lacan as follows: "For a person the other has a captivating value, on account of the anticipation that is represented by the unitary image that is perceived either in the mirror or in the entire reality of the fellow being" (Lacan 1988a: 125 translation modified). Elizabet and Alma certainly have this "captivating value," a notion that aligns with the vital value of the body, in this case the *a priori* of the unitary as objective. This is the reflected other seen as whole and complete. Of course, a counter to this is that both women are presented precisely as not whole, not the unitary image, as fragmented and detached from the real world (the *Umwelt*). However, this is the quality of the second narcissism that requires the other (person, self, image, object) to hold up—to presentify in effect—that which is absent from the self. This is, in part, why this narcissism " . . . enables a person to locate precisely his/her imaginary and libidinal relation to the world in general" (Lacan 1988a: 125 translation modified). Alma and Elizabet locate the imaginary and libidinal first within a specific series of *Umwelt*, including the hospital, the beach-house, the beach itself, and the spaces in-between. The libidinal beingness is important here because it ultimately defines Lacan's concept of the second narcissism, and it operates at a cinematic spatiality in the film. This is the libidinous spatiality manifested in Alma's story, reasserted in the sexual act when Elizabet's husband mistakes Alma for her, and in the parergonal frame that begins *Persona* with near-subliminal images of sexuality and violence. Read in this fashion, the vital value of the body shifts to the libidinal to (re)establish relationships with the individual's *Umwelt* and even act as a determination of the world in general. This is a further oscillation, for now the world is made sense of through narcissism and all objectivities and subjectivities are bracketed in this manner. Simply put, Elizabet and Alma, through the two orders of narcissism construct a world that requires an initial removal from the world (the natural attitude as it were) because of these imaginary (in Lacan's sense, i.e., *imago*, image, and ego) and libidinal reflections. The subsequently built relationships are all tied to this negotiation of the real and the illusion in and as the body. In these terms we can circle back to Husserl when he defines the corporeal as follows: "Let that which is given bodily in any perception be, as is taught there, "mere appearance," in principle "merely subjective," and yet no empty illusion" (1931: §40).[25] The wider context here is the distinction between the bodily given thing as "mere appearance" and the "true thing" derived from phenomenological processes. Husserl wants to distinguish what he calls true Being from corporeal reality (1931: §40; §41), which lies in recognizing primary qualities. The green of a tree is not, for Husserl, part of its essence, but rather belongs to signs of appearances. Colors, textures, smells, and even memories are not of the tree but do seem to adhere to the thing itself. Lacan's narcissistic illusions of the body, like Husserl's "no empty illusion," are formed through this adherence of the primary qualities to the body. In the two narcissisms this is reflection/mirroring itself. This idea of the empty illusion provides a good opportunity to turn to the next modality.

The External as Anxiety Introjected into the Internal, Producing Anxiety (Introjected Crisis); And Its Inversion, External Anxiety Producing Intimacy (Introjected Masochism)

The first iteration of this modality is that of the external world as one of such anxious anarchy that when it manages to bypass all defense mechanisms, it is introjected as anxiety. With the previous example of *Persona,* we witnessed a variation on this, only the introjection was based around intimacy's mirroring of anxiety; here only crisis ensues. However, in keeping with the overall argument here, there is a need to recognize the role of intimacy within this introjected crisis. The example to be employed here is *Dogtooth* (Yorgos Lanthimos 2009)[26] and introjected masochism.

---

[25]As noted elsewhere here, "mere" and "merely" are read not in a negating manner, but as belonging to a defined conceptual order.
[26]*Dogtooth* constructs a bizarre world constructed within a house cut off from the rest of the world and controlled by a father and mother. Two sisters and a brother are raised with no

Introjected crisis and its anxious variations of spectatorship critically resonates in its companion other, external anxiety producing intimacy referred to here as introjected masochism. As noted earlier, this issue of the spectator will be discussed in a later chapter, so for the moment it is possible to return to a textual example.[27] The spatial domain of *Dogtooth*, the suburban house where the controlling, sadistic father (Christos Stergioglou) isolates and controls his three teenage children, provides a *mise-en-abyme* effect, laying spaces within spaces of intimacy and anxiety. Here we witness a series of sub-sets, each constructing and removing the *Umwelt*. The outside world (what lies beyond the walls) is one of fantastical terrors of the abandoned fictitious brother and murderous cats, rendered invisible to the three siblings, which is subsequently replicated so that each space (bedrooms, the pool, the living room, dining room, and so on) is an external anxiety to the other intimately constructed spaces.

Let us return to some of the ideas which opened this chapter, notably the freeing aspect of *epoché*, the Thing and *das Ding*, and work through them in terms of cinematic thingness in *Dogtooth*. The aim here is to relate phenomenology's space to objects via psychoanalysis. To do so there is a need to grasp space in its intuitable, affective, and ego-based context; that is, the devising of space as an "extension" of the conscious world order through the *epoché* and anxious ego. This is an appropriate moment to recall Freud's assertion that anxiety can only exist for the ego: "Anxiety is an affective state and as such can, of course, only be felt by the ego" (*SE XX*: 71). He does provide the addition that the source of some anxieties for the ego is the id, hence the ego's organizing, mediating role. For the purposes here, this id-induced anxiety is part of *das Ding*.

At one level the most literal manifestation of *das Ding* in *Dogtooth* is the father, who metes out cruelty on all levels with impassive disdain. The mother (Michele Valley), as the willing collaborator, forms part of this paternal *das Ding*. As such, both parents exchange the phallic function, which is the crucial marker in Lacanian psychoanalysis. (See *Seminar III The Psychoses* for a discussion of the psychotic father, and *Seminar VIII Transference* where Lacan, somewhat tongue in cheek, states "At the beginning of psychoanalytic thought was the father" (2015: 293); this is followed by an examination of the origin of the law.) Such a reading also accounts for qualities such as dislocated signifying practices (*das Ding* lies

---

outside contact, given nonsensical renderings of words and a perversion of sexuality (including incest). They are told that they can only enter the outside world once they lose their "dogtooth." The elder daughter, as the final act of resistance, knocks her tooth out and attempts to escape in the boot of her father's car.

[27]It is possible, for example, to see the experience of watching certain films, and even their cultural production, as a type of introjected masochism. Does this offer some explanation as to why horror films are so popular and produced in such high numbers?

beyond language; the siblings ascribe disjunctive words to things outside the wall), primordial sensations, and an existence beyond the Symbolic because it cannot be held by the socializing order. There is a need to account for the variant here, which is *das Ding* and introjected masochism, and Husserl's ideas on space can prove insightful. To do so let us consider further Husserl's Thing in order to frame *das Ding* within the introjected masochistic. This, it will be argued here, is the subsuming of an externalized *das Ding* so that it becomes an internalized one.

Recall that for Husserl the Thing, as spatial concern and the objects therein, is an interplay between a "wandering" glance and a unifying stream of experience. He describes this as a very open-ended process, fluid, and requiring fixity until the intuition brings focus and direction. Space, thus constituted, is a "infinite series of possible modifications" when composed by "free intuitions" (1931: §150). Of course, where Husserl is going with this is the focused, phenomenological method and its capacity to enable understanding of consciousness through bracketing, reduction, and reflection. It is possible to re-read Husserl's account of what he terms the "Idea of regional Thing" as cinematic spatiality. Consider the description of the intuitably graspable Thing and its appearances and how it aligns with the cinematic text: "The regional Idea prescribes series of appearances that are fully determinate, definitely ordered, progressing ad infinitum, and taken in their ideal totality, precisely limited and fixed, a definite inner organization of their modes of development" (1931: §150; 1998: §19, §24). These are objects that have a certain notion of value attached to them, that is, are presented as such.[28] It is noteworthy that prior to this Husserl has aligned the "determining content of meaning" of the regional Idea of the Thing as prescribing "rules for the manifolds of experience" (1931: §150). In terms of cinematic spatiality and its things this is important. The spectator's capacity to "wander," to allow the infinite possibilities of what transpires on the screen, becomes intuitable because of a double function of the Thing: cinema's determination through its rules of manifold experiences; the spectator's own self-same rules. Each of these, in turn (either in complicity or in contradiction), becomes the intuitable experience of the film.

We can burrow even further down with this and note how *Dogtooth* is a type of phenomenological exercise of the regional Idea of the Thing. The father creates the "fully determinate, definitely ordered" world, to the point where transgressions (incest, violence, rape, and captivity) align meaning with these perversely normalized appearances. The intervention comes,

---

[28] At a far broader level, cinema can be read in this manner following Husserl's own methodological qualification of objects and their value: "Such are all types of *objects bearing a value*, all *practical* objects, all concrete cultural organizations which as hard realities determine our actual life, *the State, for instance, the Church, custom, the law*, and so forth" (Husserl 1931: §152).

somewhat appropriately for this reading, through the contraband movies on video tapes watched by the older daughter (Angeliki Papoulia). The Thing that was "precisely limited and fixed" is challenged by her corporeal replication of signifiers from the external world (her mimicry dancing is one such example). The "unity of experience" of space, as Husserl puts it, is how we arrive at the intuitable regional Thing; which is precisely where the resistance and challenge take place as intimate spaces of anxiety are revealed. This becomes the conflictual interplay between father and daughter, a challenge to the phallocentric *das Ding* which is contested in no less than the signifier of the dogtooth. In this manner, the dogtooth is the overarching *das Ding*, notably as it moves from the invisible to the visible, the uncontested to contestation, and a usurping of the unitary field of experience to one of fragmentation and multiplicity.

When the older daughter removes her dogtooth, she reveals a version of *das Ding* that exposes all of its ethical complexities. For as long as the dogtooth remains hidden, that is outside of the controlling, meaning-determining, and intuiting gaze, the fearful *das Ding* is infused within all objects of the cinematic space; essentially, it "wanders" through all the cinematic things. This is why we need to avoid a direct alignment of the father with this. The unrepresentable nature of *das Ding* means that in as much as the father can act as a personification, the real affective force rests in all objects (which must also include people as well as the phantasms of the external world beyond the walls, false brothers, and murderous cats). As such, *das Ding* becomes the determination of spatiality and therefore defines its objects and their constitution. To reappropriate Husserl when he states: "the essential nature of all the noematic (and noetic) phenomena, wherein space exhibits itself intuitionally and as the unity of appearances, and of the descriptive modes of such exhibiting 'constitutes' the spatial" (1931: §150) is to read the noematic as shaped (Husserl's sense of shaded is perhaps more appropriate) by *das Ding*.

When the daughter stands before the mirror (as stage, in Lacanian terms, and as a space of rebellious performativity) and violently removes the semblance of the dogtooth, wrestling with *das Ding*, she evokes the challenge to the phallocentric order through one of the greatest fears (Freudianly speaking), that of castration.[29] (It is noted in passing that Lacan configures the castration complex as the negotiation of the Symbolic order and as such is aligned to the mirror stage). Here we see the introjected anxieties in all their difficulties; for as the daughter demonstrates with bloody effect, once introjected at the masochistic level such anxieties are extremely difficult to see and even more to remove. The unitary of appearances means that all objects have been aligned, attached, and embedded within each other so

---

[29]Lacan states: "At the level of castration, anxiety represents the Other" (2017: 332).

IMAGE 18 *From* Dogtooth.

that fringe-experiences are rendered to the nearly invisible. Catch the light in the right way, at the right angle, and what appears are the flickerings of *das Ding*, or if that is too extreme, the notations of anxiety. The desire to know, to gain the knowledge that seems to be denied, is what is pursued. The daughter, bloodied before the mirror, dogtooth revealed and excised, reveals to us Lacan's version of anxiety: "Anxiety is sufficiently staved off and misrecognized in the mere capture of the specular image . . . The best one may wish for is for it to be reflected in the eyes of the Other—but there is no need for this since we have the mirror" (2017: 332). Thus, *Dogtooth*'s resistant daughter becomes the spectator's mirror, revealing and reflecting anxiety. If cinema existed for no other reason than this, it would be more than enough.

If we were to pass back through the examples utilized in this chapter, we would witness the common ground of object, anxiety, and power. These objects—debris, the child, waves, letters, confessions, memories, the dogtooth, and so on,—share this thingness of anxiety and desire played out before the intuiting gaze. That desire has this connection to anxiety (and vice versa) reveals intimacy as a uniting but uneasy bond. In this way there is somewhat agreement with Lacan's idea of the reciprocal relationship between desire and anxiety (2017: 254), but some divergence when we add this idea of intimacy. What this common ground holds in terms of cinematic spatiality demonstrates the exchange of the intimate spectator with the cinematic spaces and what has been described here as modalities. The following chapter takes up these aspects from an altogether different perspective, particularly in terms of margins and their fluidity.

4

Shading the Real

Cinema's Sensual Phantasms

This chapter examines in-betweenness and (transgressive) margins, which includes the phenomenological and psychoanalytic self-reflexive explorations, their own revelatory statements, regarding their own approaches and methodologies. This further involves the difficulties revealed when such a mirroring takes place, and the ways in which cinema can pry open crevasses for potential ways forward. At various moments each of these systemic processes, individually and compositely, will occupy the role and space of marginalia, that is, the province between the materiality (the "text," be it analytic or cinematic) and the edge of all that lies outside (as noted in the previous chapter, the fringe to experienceability). This "whitespace" is both of and exterior to the body of the text; it is, via Kant and Derrida, parergonal—supplementary, an embellishment, an addition to. Underlying this is the recurring issue at hand here, a reflection on the performance of analysis and the potential of the analytic experience. The demarcating aspects here will be to focus on the "real" as it is figured in phenomenology (notably in *Husserliana* Volume XI *Phantasy, Image Consciousness and Memory* (1898–1925),[1] and throughout a number of Lacan's seminars. In turn, the discussion will take up possible cinematically derived solutions to the conceptual and methodological tensions which exist in the bringing to bear on the issue of the real between phenomenology and psychoanalysis. The aim here is to explore the idea/exemplar of the intimacy of the cinematic "real." Underpinning this is the question: Is phantasy an

---

[1] This is a translation of Husserliana *Volume XXIII Phantasie, Bildbewusstsein, Erinnerung: Zur Phänomenologie der anschaulichen Vergegenwärtigungen* (1898–1925).

analytic performativity (essentially, what we do to film or film does to us) that changes it to image re-presentation/presentification?

The layout of this chapter is as follows: some orientating remarks on the notion of the "real" in Husserl and Lacan; from this we can extract a number of key ideas which will be explored through cinematic examples. Despite this straightforward sounding direction, we confront one of the most complex problems in this critical approach—that of the question, as well as positionality, of the unconscious for psychoanalysis and phenomenology. Herein lies the issue: psychoanalysis presupposes the unconscious, setting its course to explore it, rather than questioning if it indeed exists; phenomenology is, at best, somewhat interested, somewhat agnostic, and at worst dismissive, regarding its existence. Eugen Fink's *Beilage XXI* in *The Crisis* is a good example of this problematized position: "Only after an explicit analysis of consciousness can the problem of the unconscious be posed at all" (Fink in Husserl 1997: 387). Throughout this short piece, Fink's thinly veiled antagonism underscores his attitude toward Freudian theory, and yet even here there are moments where the idea of the unconscious is not dismissed outright. Certainly, he describes the current (i.e., most likely, Freud) theories of the unconscious as "philosophically naïve," but at no point does he argue for its dismissal. Husserl's position is somewhat more invitational. Leading up to comments on the idea of the unconscious he speaks of *Geltungsfundierungen*—the processes around the founding, or statements, of validity (1997: §55). (Noteworthy for the concerns here, he raises the issues of how such validity-foundings operate in terms of madness and children, and the mediating role of "normal human beings," which psychoanalytically aligns with the super-ego and Lacan's Symbolic.) This discussion feeds back to Husserl's investigation of value and consciousness in *Ideas*. Crucially, Husserl speaks of value formations and the frames of consciousness devised, not as fixed and stable, but as a dynamic interplay that may aim for synthesis but necessarily involves transition and difference. So, for example, there are the "tensions" between formative values of consciousness and their relationship to belief as well as noematic characterizations (1931: §116). Hence, and this is of deep significance here, the validity formations will need to accommodate and modify depending on the consciousness. "Value" (or pleasure, the good, anxiety, and so on) becomes uncertain at times, and what was held to be "as such" shifts in the modalities of consciousness. The valuing consciousness/Ego can become uncertain, shifts in its modality (from, e.g., belief ("this object is of value") to the noetic ("this object proposes that it is of value to me"), and what was given as "of value" becomes less certain (see 1931: §117)). Husserl's return to this in *The Crisis* takes the form of configuring what he calls transcendental problems of constitution, of which he cites the unconscious as a specific issue, describing it as "existing in the world common to all [with] ontic verification" and so all forms of analysis of the concept of the unconscious "naturally come under the transcendental problem of constitution" (1997: §55). The unconscious is, therefore, not at all dismissed by Husserl, but seen as something that needs to be explored and explained as part of a wider set of phenomena. More than this, phenomenology's positioning of the constitutional problem of the unconscious can actually be seen as an acknowledgment of its existence. The difficulties lie in exactly what it is, how we determine its manifestations, and how it is accounted for—but these are precisely the same issues that psychoanalysis has!

The position taken here is that in phenomenology there is not an antagonistic dismissal or denial of the concept of the unconscious, rather a prioritization of method. Put another way, Husserl's compulsion is to develop and put into practice a phenomenological method, articulating how to be a phenomenologist, reordering philosophy under its (ideally for him) unifying principles, and showing how it works analytically. Determining the constitutional realities of the unconscious' existence is not part of this methodological development. It is for this reason that this issue is tackled here not through a direct "reading" of the unconscious, but through Lacan's reimaging of things through the Real, and Husserl's exploration of *irreal*. As we progress it will become necessary to distinguish between different types or constructions of "real." Hereafter, Real (capitalized) will refer to Lacan's concept, and *irreal* will refer to Husserl's concept. Both are employed to distinguish them from the concept of real (i.e., reality—whatever form that may take, but mostly in the sense of external reality). Finally, later the term ir-Real is proposed to represent a combining of elements from Husserl and Lacan. The perverse irony here is that both the Real and *irreal* are precisely located outside (as marginalia) of reality, and yet—and this is the crucial, unifying idea—both are positioned as more real than reality, both phenomenologically and psychoanalytically speaking. Indeed, both these analytic systems are somewhat premised on this distinction.

Lacan's Real

Lacan articulates the Real within that deeply significant triangle of the Symbolic, Imaginary, and Real. It recurs throughout his work, appearing at least as early as 1936 with the presentation on the mirror stage, more formally announced in the 1950s, determining and structuring much of Lacan's thoughts in the 1970s. The following will discuss various iterations of these recurring manifestations. What is noteworthy, from a broad perspective, is the shift we see from the address *Le Symbolique, L'imaginaire et le Réel* ("The Symbolic, the Imaginary, and the Real") (1953), to the revisions in the 1974–5 *Seminar XXII RSI: Real, Symbolic, Imaginary* (note the shift of Real to a position of primacy in the title), via the disjunctive and somewhat uneven *Seminar XIX . . . Ou Pire* (1971–2), . . . *Or Worse*,[2] and on to Seminar *XXIII Le Sinthome* (1975–6) which aligns the Real with the symptom, until Seminar *XXV Le Moment de Conclure* (1977–8) where we witness a "revision" of Freud's Oedipus Complex in terms of the Imaginary, Symbolic, and Real. The early seminars and addresses see Lacan articulating what he calls the "essential registers of human reality," the Symbolic, Imaginary, and Real, required because "reality (*réel*) . . . escapes us" (Lacan 2013: 4; 5); but by the time we get to *Seminar XIX*, the Real has undergone some curious and complex transformations;[3] these transformations are completed when Lacan adds the symptom to become the fourth component of the Real, Symbolic, and Imaginary. So, there is development and divergence in Lacan's theorizing of the Real, but there is also consistency; it is this constancy that allows us to speak of the Real as a (relatively) stable concept in his theory. To that end, following is a summary of the Real as it pertains to the issues at hand.

Given that the Real is most often located in relation to the Symbolic and Imaginary, this is a good place to begin. Simply put, the Symbolic (via Lévi-Strauss's influence on the early Lacan) is the exchange of "symbols." This is the social domain, invested with language, containment, curtailing, ritual, and laws. It is what allows, and is demanded of, the subject to become part of the social order. This is why Lacan states that the signifier exists prior to the subject; we enter the Symbolic with a language structure and system of exchange already in existence and functioning. Thus, we might speak of a cinematic Symbolic as the shared and predetermined language of the system and within each film iteration. Each film exists at the level of exchange, each moment within the film exchanged with other moments, other films, other "texts," other spectators internally and externally. It is through the preexistence of limitations and bindings that the Symbolic approaches a state of sharedness; in this way the Symbolic can seem most like what is usually thought of as reality, or at least a social reality. More than this, at one point Lacan describes the Symbolic as creating reality (Lacan 2013: 45). (It is very likely that part of the reason we find resistance to the Symbolic in

---

[2] It probably did not help that Lacan was presenting the material, during the same period, to two different audiences in different locations. The seminar is marked with audience protests of Lacan whispering, his long pauses, and his irritated outbursts. (At one point he says he hopes he has not damaged his ring from banging his hand on the table so often.) This is also an aging Lacan, eccentric and distracted.

[3] It is beyond our direct concerns here, but it is noteworthy that in *Seminar XIX*, Lacan refers consistently to Plato's *Parmenides*, a text focused on logic, form and Oneness, which are the defining aspects of the Seminar's engagement with the Real and reality. Oneness is at the core of the Seminar and Lacan clearly has Plato in mind as he articulates the themes of the presentations; at one point he even declares "Plato is a Lacanian!" The idea of form, especially how it is devised in the *Parmenides* text and its relationship to reality, existence, and consistency, is an important, but digressive, issue here.

Lacan's style, with its convolutions, self-confessed baroque flows, incessant puns, and neologisms, is a reflexive methodology flowing against such constructions of "reality.") However, the Symbolic is processional as well as deterministic. By this I mean that the Symbolic must be invitational and accommodating as well as what precedes us and requires adoption.[4] The Symbolic is primarily negotiated through the ego and super-ego.

The Imaginary, from the *imago*, comes from Lacan's concept of the mirror stage and is the egocentric positioning of the self. If the Symbolic is the "socialized" exchange, the Imaginary is the exchange of the self by and to the self as it passes through these other orders. This is the negotiations of the self in, for example, alienation and *aphanisis* (*Seminar XI The Four Fundamental Concepts of Psychoanalysis*), the analytic situation (the ego in/as the Imaginary), and even the relationship between knowledge and truth; see, for example, *Seminar XX Encore* where he locates the "true" between the Symbolic and Imaginary because in the analytic situation the analyst must listen to the speech of the Imaginary through the formalizing processes of the Symbolic. This is why, by way of illustration, Lacan argues that we think about the Symbolic in terms of reality and our position in it, because we are caught up in our being, and it is through the Imaginary relationship that we enter the Symbolic "as a subject" (Lacan 2006: 40). In cinematic terms we can see this in a number of interconnected ways, but at the very least this is the cinematic "truth" (for the spectator, the film itself, the cultural situation, and so on) as it binds the Symbolic to the Imaginary.

The Real is part of this nexus of the Imaginary and Symbolic, and yet an altogether different prospect. Much of the remainder of this chapter will be devoted to exploring the Real, so for the moment I would like to offer the parameters and determining attributes; this is slippery material indeed. The Real is most closely aligned with the unconscious, and as such shares many of the qualities that psychoanalysis attributes to its most originary of ideas. As such, it is part of the (Lacanian) Other and its manifestations in the *objet petit a*, and subsequently, desire.[5] This is precisely why we find in Schema L, in "*Seminar on 'The Purloined Letter'*," (see what follows) the relational "lines" formed between the subject (S, although also note that Lacan includes "Es," the Id, here) and the Other (A) in terms of the unconscious; and the ego (a) and *objet petit a* in terms of the Imaginary

---

[4]Julia Kristeva's *Revolution in Poetic Language* is an exploration of the Lacanian Symbolic and the disruptive force of what she terms 'poetic' language—the *sémiotique*. The relative stability of language in the Symbolic is constantly challenged and disturbed by these other languages invested with polysemy, innovation, disruption, and difference.
[5]Other, *Autre*, is the 'big' other—otherness itself; the *objet petit a* (a stands for *autre*) are the objects of little otherness—the manifestations of the Other; Lacan asserts, often, that the "true aim of desire is the Other." The Other is not simply the unconscious, but we are not too astray in seeing them as entwined and embedded.

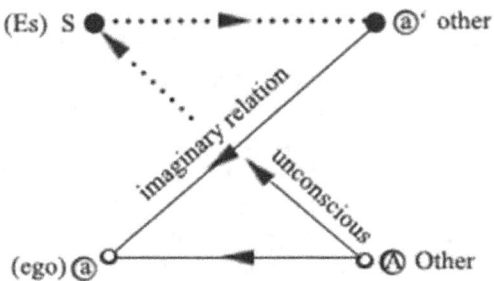

DIAGRAM 6 *From* "Seminar on 'The Purloined Letter.'"

(which, in turn, becomes a crucial factor in transference). Typical of Lacan's diagrams, this one also includes a vertical relationship (subject and ego on the left, versions of otherness on the right) which represents a dynamic exchange in the formation of the subject's desires in and for the Other and its manifestations. This also provides the relational context of ego to Id (Es) in the subject.

Further, because it is aligned with the Other and the unconscious, the Real becomes the source of many tributaries. In *Ou Pire*, for example, it is described as the resistance to logic; defined as both being the impossible and indicated by the impossible (e.g., "the Real . . . may be defined as the impossible," and as "signaled precisely by the impossible, the impossibility of reaching it . . . "); as the absent thing for the analyst (Lacan 2018: 30; 60–1; 134), and as something the subject experiences as an absence in the analyst's silence (Lacan 2013: 42). Lacan calls it the Real because, for psychoanalysis, this is the material it needs to deal with; it is also the material each of us deals with constantly in the relationship of the unconscious to the conscious. It is the interplay between this Real of the subject—your "youness" as it shapes how you engage with the world as a subject. Your Real is part of the Symbolic and Imaginary, fashioned by them, articulated through them (of sorts), and managed because of them. This is psychoanalysis' primacy of psychic reality, distinguishing it through (as Freud does) *Wirklichkeit* (reality, truth, actuality) and *Realität* (reality, but in Freud's sense of the psychical).

Another key aspect of the Lacanian Real is derived from the encounter with it. Given the intimate and hidden placement of the Real (our unconscious and all the attendant desires) it is not surprising that Lacan describes this encounter as invested in and with trauma. This encounter with the Real, what he calls, via Aristotle, the *tuché* (see *Seminar XI*) emerges through all the material at psychoanalysis' core: the dream, chance, slips, seeming errors, as well as this traumatic moment. This is why Lacan, with such deftness and insight, shows how reality is conceived as laying underneath and as transferential (working with Freud's *unterlegt, untertragen* to the French translation of *en souffrance*, in suspense as well as the play on *souffrance* as suffering. See *Seminar XI*: 52–7). We can thus speak of cinema as a version of *tuché* in the following terms: the intimacy of spectating is, through anxiety, a mode of trauma; our encounter with the cinematic Real is premised on the suspension of knowledge (as a version of suffering as we look for meanings and resolutions), with meaning always lying underneath; psychoanalysis locates creative work as part of the unconscious, hence the Real; the very ambiguities, of slips, chance, and missed material, that constitute a film exist in the domain of the cinematic *tuché*; cinema, like dreams, represents the interplay between reality and phantasy—an interplay located in this encounter. This is the material that will need to be developed further, notably in articulating a sense of the cinematic Real, but for the moment let us turn to Husserl.

Husserl's Irreal

It is telling that Husserl's examinations of reality are complex, interconnected, revised over time, and enfolding on themselves. After all, the deliberations, the real work, of phenomenology is the reflexive turn toward understanding "reality" and our relationship to it via the experiencing: "Its [phenomenology] sole task and service is to clarify the meaning of this world, the precise sense in which everyone accepts it, and with undeniable right, as really existing (*wirklich seiende*)" (Husserl 1931: 21). Incidentally, this "precise sense in which everyone accepts it" is not so far from Lacan's Symbolic domain. The acceptance aspect is a requirement for both models, and of course for a shared sense of reality and/as the world. When Lacan articulates the Symbolic as "essential reality" through symbols "organized as a language and which thus function on the basis of the link between the signifier and signified" (Lacan 2013: 16) it is done so on the basis of a shared sense, understanding, and exchange. Here we witness Husserl's "phenomenological clarification of the meaning of the manner of existence of the real world (and, eidetically, of a real world generally)" (1931: 21). Given such a task there is little wonder that the processes and definitions will carry weight. The task at hand is to establish a sense of the real and/as reality within itself, unique to phenomenology's reflexive mode, and located in the marginalia so that it can be connected to the psychoanalytic and cinematic models. One complication we have is with Husserl's multitude of terms for this issue; when speaking about real/reality at various times he employs *Wirklich, Wirklichkeit, Realität, Reales, Realen, wirklichkeit Welt* (real world), *Lebenswelt* (lifeworld), as well as the term to be explored here, *irreal*. There are distinctions as well as blurring in these uses, but the way through this relates to a specificity correlated to consciousness. Herein lies our potential bridge to psychoanalysis.

Irreal, as a qualifying sense, depends on Husserl's interpretation of noema and noesis, as well as the *hyle*; it is the noetic and hyletic attributes that establishes the *irreal* because in many ways they are phenomenological processes to arrive at this version of the real. A brief recap may be of some use here. Husserl wants/requires us to move from the natural attitude to the phenomenological; this is the intentional correlate of the method. That is, we take up intentionality in our eidetic reduction to bracket the natural attitude (world). Here is a useful summary that Husserl provides:

> ... *pure or transcendental phenomenology will be established not as a science of facts, but as a science of essential Being* (as "*eidetic*" Science); a science which aims exclusively at establishing "knowledge of essences" (*Wesenserkenntnisse*) and *absolutely no "facts"*. The corresponding Reduction which leads from the psychological phenomenon to the pure "essence", or . . . from factual ("empirical") to "essential" universality, is the *eidetic Reduction*. (Husserl 1931: 44)[6]

From this Husserl emphasizes, indeed emphatically reiterates, that phenomenology's pure essence provides knowledge of the essential nature of the real, as well as "an essential knowledge of the non-real (*irreal*); and from these two orders of knowledge will reveal that "transcendentally purified 'experiences' are non-realities, and excluded from every connexion within the 'real world'" (Husserl 1931: 45). This is phenomenology's defining aspect, this method to take up the transcendental interrogative position in order to examine the non-real (*irreal*).[7] It is the *irreal* that is the fundamental material of phenomenological investigation. The motivation for the move to the irreal, which has been broadly applauded in philosophy, was Husserl's aim to escape the charges of psychologism and subjectivism. The eidetic reduction achieves this goal by transforming what is merely individual into a general principle, Husserl's notion of essence.

The noematic content (the noema) is what "gives" meaning and in this we come to recognize and understand experiences, including the cinematic through the intimate spectator. This is in keeping with Husserl's examples of perception, judging, pleasure, and remembering (*Ideas* §88)—the noematic

---

[6] See also Husserl *Cartesian Meditations* and *The Crisis* for extensive discussions on *epoché* and phenomenological reduction. For example, §71 in *The Crisis* offers a fruitful, albeit incomplete, series of comments on phenomenology and psychology in terms of method, ego, the other, the world.

[7] " . . . the phenomena of transcendental phenomenology will be characterized as non-real (irreal)" (Husserl 1931: 44)

content yields up the "meaning" of perceiving, judging, pleasing, and remembering. Similarly, we can direct consciousness to the thing perceived (judged . . .) or the act of perceiving (judging . . .) (see also Husserl *Modes of Reproduction and Phantasy Image Consciousness* for the distinction between reproduction and impressional processes in this regard). Aligned to this is *Geltungsfundierungen* as validating formations are required in a stabilizing (and synthesizing) function for these acts of consciousness. This is the *irreal* attribute we derive from the noema. It is not what is being perceived/judged, etc., or even that action as such; the relationship between perception and what is perceived is suspended (*epoché*). It is the pure immanence, born out of what Husserl describes as the "left over" material (1931: §88) of the experience that phenomenology deals with. Here we move closer to at least one key attribute of the Lacanian Real (as well as the cinematic variant, which will be taken up in a moment). This left-over material, this noematic produced "meaning" that is outside of both object and experience (yet involves both initially and explicitly), is the Real's impossibility. Both the *irreal* and the Real require a reflexive moment to understand them (the analytic situation and experience, phenomenological transcendental consciousness), both stand outside of reality, are experienced (noumenally), and are gained through this analytic "experience." The Symbolic, the world of things as Lacan once called it,[8] cannot be the *irreal* because it is so invested in the natural attitude and this world of "facts" (as validating formations); the Imaginary is excluded because its investments lie in the positioning of the alienated self.[9] Yet, just as Husserl devises the *irreal* within the self and the "real" world, so the Real is determined through the resonating "negotiations" of these other orders. Or, put another way, the interpretative differences of experience/experiencing are fundamental to the formations of the Real and *irreal* and their consequential influences. This is the attribute of intentionality in which Husserl locates this reflexive investigation called phenomenology. It is "the clear-cut separation between the real (*reeller*) portions of one's whole experience which belong to the experiencing itself, and those which belong to the noema" (Husserl 1931: §96). This is the core aspect of the *irreal* and why it is not reality; it is only after the noetic processes, as distinct from the hyletic phenomenology (concerned with the material stuff of and in perception), that we can experience the *irreal*. Just as it is crucial, for Lacan, to see the Real as experienced (noumenally speaking)

---

[8] See "The Function and Field of Speech and Language in Psychoanalysis."
[9] " . . . we must absolutely define the ego's imaginary function as the unity of the subject who is alienated from himself" (Lacan 2013: 24). In *Ideas* (§80) we note that the ego is alienated from the *epoché*; in *The Crisis* Husserl argues that when the subject (i.e., the person in subjectivity) becomes phenomena it is "a peculiar new sense—and this reorientation is called, here, the phenomenological-psychological reduction" (§70). Such a reduction is arrived at through *epoché*.

as the unrepresentable, impossible absence, the silence emerging from the unconscious.

This is a timely moment to remind ourselves of Husserl's intriguing *Abschattung ist Erlebenis*—shading (adumbration) is an experience, comparing it to the shading of the Real and the cinematic turn. In *The Crisis* Husserl distinguishes between the experienceable subjectivity of the lifeworld and the not perceivable, not experienceable objective, "true" world. This appears contradictory, and only makes sense by reason of the qualifier "in its own proper being" (Husserl 1997: §34d). To understand this more fully we can consider this idea of shading. Our experience of the world, its objects, things, people, indeed all that the real contains, is not perceived as a whole and complete. Instead, Husserl argues, we experience the world through adumbrations, filling in details (correctly or incorrectly) in the stream of experiences. We appresent to fill out and contain the absences. Husserl acknowledges that no matter how complete this process may be, there is always more of the missing than what presents itself or what becomes known as the present. Colors, shapes, tones, gradients, and shades are all adumbrations, aligned with the thing but never actually of it. They are laid onto it, sometimes with such fierce adherence that they seem to become fixed, unremovable from our sense of it. One can see the complexity of something like "truth" within such a model; similarly, this has rich implications in cinematic terms. This layering is potentially endless, each shading within itself adding further levels. This is not just a process of perception; for memories and recollections, feelings of pleasure or pain, sensations and affects, and so on, are all made up of and through this shading. How we take up these adumbrations (and indeed which ones we take up) determines how meaning is located, established, exchanged, and even challenged.[10] Husserl's example of the apple tree touches on this. We see the tree, note its colors, surroundings, perhaps sounds of leaves, dapples of light, height, signs of age . . . each of these is not of the tree, but shadings that become part of our perception. If the tree is being remembered, then there is the presentification of the tree and the remembering of the tree— each most likely involving different and further shadings. The tree in a film shows even further adumbrations taking place in the iterations of cinematic techniques, narrativization, and the formations of the intimate spectator. In Malick's *The Thin Red Line*, for example, we experience the cinematic

---

[10]"Take up" is misdirection because it implies a voluntary, conscious even, act. Not all shading is done in this way, just as what adumbrations are experienced are not necessarily "chosen." It is left to stand here, acknowledging the problems inherent in it, defending it partly through Husserl's sense of the "gift" in meaning—something given and taken, sometimes without awareness of capacity but always with obligation, as Derrida reminds us. A less complicated explanation would be that a good many adumbrations are simply part of Husserl's passive syntheses.

construction of angles, light, camera positioning, the words of Whitt speaking of nature vying with itself so that the tree is shaded in a range of interpretations. To call on another Malick example, *Badlands*, after we hear Holly's voice-over declaring that she and Kit were slowly falling in love, there is a scene of them playing cards beside a river. Holly says how nice the place is, Kit declares "Yeah, the tree makes it nice." Holly's romanticized world order (her shading) contrasts with Kit's disinterested version. For Holly the scene is genuinely "nice," full of potential memories, and worthy of preserving (she says to not pick the flowers); for Kit the shading of the tree as "nice" reveals his incapacity to engage emotionally, which indicates the dispassionate attitude toward the killings he later commits. Meaning is being produced through all these shading experiences; but it is far from stable and far from uniform. Shading can be seen as a much larger part of the phenomenological project, for it is echoed in the issues of how consciousness devises positionality when it is required to engage in multiple and heterogeneous materials. Husserl terms this synthetic consciousness (its "synthetically unitary consciousness"), having to actively construct (synthesizing) positions from polythetic experiences; it is a consolidating and determining construction (Husserl's *Fundierung* which we see as part of *Geltungsfundierungen*) (1931: §118; §119). For the issues at hand, this synthetically unitary consciousness is reality constructing and testing which carries with it the (polythetic and disguised) unconscious. Lacan's Real, in these terms, becomes a validating foundation that challenges the consciousness positionalities produced through the ego and super-ego. That there is conflict and alterations to the positionality is consistent with both analytic models. In the *Badlands* scene, and indeed throughout the entire film, there is no synthetically unitary consciousness; precisely the opposite is at play. *Badlands* continually produces polythetic experiences to undermine constructions of reality and challenge its testing.[11] Thus shadings in this film are themselves foregrounded and made to question their role.

To shade the Real or *irreal* is to appresent that which is impossible, the leftover, the residuum, the absent, and unknowable. The idea of the shading of the Real and *irreal* presents us with some unique potential. If this is possible, it cannot be seen to happen in the same way that it takes place in the stream of experience of, say, perception. One way of thinking through this would be a two-flow model: the flow of the phenomenological *epoché* to arrive at the *irreal* (Husserl's "pure consciousness") as Real; the flow from the *irreal* and Real to appresent it within the Symbolic, thus rendering it as "language." I do not think this is viable as it would require conflation, side-stepping and,

---

[11] This is certainly a recurring aspect of Malick's cinema. We witness this aporiastic "tension" in, for example, *Tree of Life* and *Days of Heaven* in terms of the voice-over and the visual playing out of the narrative.

honestly, some chicanery. Instead, and in keeping with the tenets of this overall project, the idea here is to think through this Borromean knot with intimacy and its Real/*irreal* capacities. Hereafter this combination is to be termed "*ir-Real*" to suggest not conflation and certainly not sameness but a critical entwining. This, in turn, allows a reading of cinema as a version of phantasy[12] (as positioned in phenomenology and psychoanalysis). The aim is to explore how cinema as phantasy, and as marginalia, devises and promulgates the intimate *ir-Real*.

Before turning directly to the concept of phantasy and the *ir-Real* an example of what has been discussed so far will help illustrate the cinematic possibilities as well as set up the ensuing issues. As an instance of textual phantasy/fantasy, *The Wicker Man* (Hardy 1973)[13] would appear to work most overtly in terms of genre. The fantastical setting, threatening and terrifying themes, and adherence to the horror form's conventions, all contribute to such positioning. However, such an approach limits the investigation here and aligns it too closely with an almost literal use of the concepts. In these terms, the *ir-Real* in this film is not affiliated with any of the fantastical material and its rendering; indeed, this is precisely what it is not. Rather it is the almost understated, almost missed through misdirection, recurring phenomenon of the Nothing.[14]

The film sets up its narrative motivation through the theme of the investigation of a missing schoolgirl, Rowan Morrison, allowing for the arrival of Sgt. Howie (Edward Woodward) on the island. An example of the *ir-Real* of the narrative is not derived from the sinister and threatening behavior of the inhabitants, nor even from the contrasting belief systems (paganism and Christianity), nor from the disturbances of typologies (merging of the human and animal, law/authority and its enforcements and resistances), nor even the representation of sexuality as carnivalesque. Rather, the *ir-Real* is "found" in the negotiation of the Nothing. At one level this is the use of absences to mark the distances that are the intercessional (e.g., Howie's adherence to Christianity, law, and his moral perspective of being right); at another level, it is the *ir-Real's* capacity to exist "outside" of

---

[12]By way of clarification, there is a distinction here between "phantasy," in this phenomenological and psychoanalytic context, and "fantasy"—a form/genre-based positioning. Thus, phantasy stands in here as the material of consciousness (and unconscious in the psychoanalytic context), whereas fantasy refers to the textual forms, manifestations, and iterations.

[13]Sgt Howie arrives at the remote island of Summerisle to investigate the disappearance of a young girl, Rowan. His investigations are passively and then more actively resisted by the population, governed by Lord Summerisle. This is a film heavily invested with a style and narrative elements of folk horror, including references to the Green Man myth, pagan rituals of fertility (notably the May Queen), and the carnivalesque. The sinister aspects are invariably woven into the narrative, antithetically positioning religion and morality from different sources (Christianity and folk traditions).

[14]The concept of the Nothing is discussed further in Chapter 1.

language (Lacanian Symbolic, Husserl's distinction of *irreal* from facts, and so on). Rowan's status of missing (the defining aspect of her beingness[15]) appears, cinematically speaking, generically typical. This is the well-devised narrative trope of the missing person and ensuing police/detective/investigator narrative. However, the *ir-Real* aspects here illustrate, and can be used to analytically explore, another type of absence. This special category of absences operates outside of facts (phenomenal to noumenal) and beyond, or at least resistant to, Symbolic laws. In *The Wicker Man* we see the *ir-Real*, in these terms, through the signifiers of Rowan's nothingness. These "manifestations" of *ir-Reals* include: her empty school desk (Figure 1); the vacant space on the wall holding harvest festival photographs; the barren harvest (revealed in the hidden photograph in Figure 2); the lack of a birth certificate; the absent body in the grave (replaced by a hare). This is a type of Kierkegaardian version of the negative as a momentum-inducing force: " . . . *the negative* is used as the quickening power that brings movement into everything . . . The negative, then, is the immanence of movement, it is the vanishing factor, what is annulled" (Kierkegaard 2015: 17; 18). This sense of the negative is Kierkegaard's engagement with the Hegelian dialectic and so annulment needs to be read within the context of *Aufhebung*.[16] In this sense, the negative, these nothings, are the movement of cinema itself, as every film builds itself not around the presence but this cinematic vanishing factor. The instillation of movement takes place in terms of *Gewahren*, as the spectator's "becoming aware of" is formulated through intimacy. The cinematic *ir-Real* has a particular relationship to this movement, for it is in these that we most often discover the work of intimacy. In *The Wicker Man* these *ir-Reals* are further confirmed in their status when Rowan appears, alive and acknowledging her part in the conspiracy, at the end of the film. What has changed is the shading (*Abschattung*) of them, altering their meaning, but sanctioning their status.

As a parallel reading to this, we can note Klein's work on the psycho-sexual symbolism in objects and structures of schools. She describes the recurring appearances of the teacher as father/authority figure and school desks as mother as psychoanalytically typical, that is, to be considered as a widespread symbolism (see Klein "The School in Libidinal Development," 1988). Furthermore, the child's negotiations of his/her entry into the world

---

[15]It is too far from the central discussion here, but there is an intriguing analysis to be had with this status of the missing in terms of Michel Foucault's concept of the "disappeared" and madness. See in particular *History of Madness*. The intrigue of such an approach is aided by Louis Althusser's confessional autobiography (after he murdered his wife and was found to be mad) *The Future Lasts a Long Time*. Althusser refers to himself as one of Foucault's disappeared.

[16]See Chapter 1 for a more detailed discussion of this concept of the Nothing and its Kierkegaardian resonances.

of the school, for Klein, are based on a destabilizing of gender, with the feminine identity of the child (boy or girl) being relinquished and regained at various points. The absented desk, the trans-gendered figure in the carnivalesque parade, and the symbolic castration of Howie as a symbol of (Christian) law, and the disappearance/reappearance of the child all fit within this Kleinian reading.

The *ir-Real* signifiers (most often located within the registrar of nothings, absences, silences, denials, refutations, negations, but also within

IMAGE 19 *From* The Wicker Man.

IMAGE 20 *From* The Wicker Man.

iterations such as distortion, contradiction, and embellishment) confirm the shading process determining the stream(s) of experience within the film. For phenomenology, this is an essential aspect of consciousness; it is a continuous, unending networked action that is defined as fluid. Husserl is speaking of the larger order of pure consciousness, yet his description fits well with this reading of cinema and its *ir-Real* aspects: "We can draw from our reflexions the eidetically valid and self-evident proposition, that *no concrete experience* can pass *as independent in the full sense of the term.* Each "stands in need of completion" in respect to some connected whole, which in form and in kind is not something we are free to choose, but are rather bound to accept" (Husserl 1931: §83). This is the cinematic text as it is experienced by the spectator; what we are foregrounding here is the *ir-Real's* capacity to underscore and draw attention to this process. In other words, because the *ir-Real* is a "product" of the Real's and the *irreal's* outsideness (its marginality and parergonality) and sites of resistance to stabilized meanings (including the "fixing," determination of, and establishing a sense of, resolved "truths"), when encountered there are noumenal resonances which, at the very least, demonstrate the continuing work of interpretation/ analysis, and in potentia reveal the very acts of hermeneutics.[17] In this manner, the relationship between the *ir-Real* and the composing Nothing is brought into sharp relief. Hence, when Husserl delivers the idea that not only are these processes on-going, but also unifying as an attempt to produce understanding, we are reminded of Lacan's edict that the Real and truth "*se confound apparemment du vrai et du reel*" (Lacan 1975: 84) (*se confound*— to get confused or to overlap, so "the confusion/overlapping of truth and the Real"): "Advancing continuously from one apprehension to another, we apprehend in a certain way . . . *the stream of experience as a unity also.* We do not apprehend it as a single experience" (Husserl 1931: §83). The key here is the on-going roll of apprehension as a pluralism, a continuous process of producing the "truth" only for it to be qualified, revised, and shaded with differences; that is, the *Geltungsfundierungen* as a process in the synthetizing unary consciousness positionality.

In the examples from *The Wicker Man* we see a cinematic version of this continuous process, incited by the film itself. Each signifier of nothingness, invested with interpretative force and potential, carries further internal overlappings and lacks (of meaning, veracity, destabilized authority): the school desk, when opened, reveals a trapped beetle, which reveals a sense of cruelty in the act; the missing photograph is reproduced/revealed by Howie from

---

[17]Wahl, in dialogue with Lacan, makes the point: "The Real is, in a way, an experience of resistance" (Lacan 1986: 89). This is a crucial aspect for psychoanalysis, for in resistance we discover meaning(s) as they are inverted, disguised, misleading, and declared through their nothingness. This is why we observe the cinematic *ir-Real* most often (but certainly not exclusively) in the polysemic and ambiguous.

a hidden negative, revealing the missing Rowan, and then further revealing the failed harvest; the coffin holds not a body of a child, but a hare, which is then used to reveal the confrontation of the two phallocentric law-makers of Howie and Lord Summerfield. Both men are constructed as sites of "truth" and "reality," which is a status challenged in the *ir-Real*. This is particularly the case with Howie as he rendered as the other within the carnivalesque acts. Each of these layered "reveals" suggests a further set of nothings; the cycle insists on a lack of ending, a denial of sensible meaning and interpretation.

These are *ir-Real* moments because they show the contesting of facts/truth and the acts of knowledge formation. The *ir-Real* stands in for, perhaps mimics, truths even though it is not facts or facticity (for phenomenology) and not the Symbolic (for psychoanalysis). This standing in for truth is how we, to draw on Husserl, "advance continuously" in a film, from one apprehension to another; that is, from one (contestable) "truth" to another. In doing so the very status of textual truth is challenged and can be seen as a version of polythetic positionality of experiencing. Herein lies the heart of the phenomenological method, concerned not with facts but perception and experiencings. The *ir-Real* moments in cinema reveal this in their status of the Nothing, the impossible, and silences. There is some fortuitous terminology here as Husserl's concept of apprehension, *Auffassungsform*, (the phenomenological process of apprehending, so a something more that "perception"), aligns with the anxious iteration of being apprehensive.[18] This is the interplay of seizing (understanding) and being seized (by fear, usually of something in the future, so in anticipation). The advancing continuous apprehension is enjoyed in the film as a type of anxiety as the spectator, seeking the meaning, shades and fills the *lacunae*, and allows him/herself to be located in a destabilized site of composing Nothing(s). This is the pleasurable anxiety of apprehension.

Phantasy of the Intimate ir-Real

To work through the idea of the intimate *ir-Real* and how phantasy can be reimagined in the marginalia of psychoanalysis and phenomenology, I wish to put to one side the copious and interesting material that film studies has

---

[18]It is noteworthy that Husserl, in later revisions, emphasizes this aspect of apprehension as a continuous and unending process. It is not contradictory to the producing of the *irreal*. Indeed, it confirms the status being explored here. From the sense of apprehension, we obtain "to understand" and "to fear"; this meaning of fear comes about through the shared sense of to grasp with the mind. Thus, etymologically, it is the internal, mental grasping that enables apprehension to be both understanding and anxiety. Already in the *Logical Investigations*, Husserl views this process as an "increasing trajectory (*Steigerungsreihe*) of "proximate commonalties" of "inexact essences," (2000: 450) a qualification of his idea of meaning identity that is increasingly explored in his *Nachlass* volumes. (Hua XX/1; XX/2; XXXIX; XLI).

engaged in when it considered phantasy. Instead, the following will focus on a somewhat concealed concept to shape the potential links between the two analytic approaches. This is the idea of *semblance*—a term that both Lacan and Husserl employ at various times in their works. By looking at semblance as a unifying concept, the *ir-Real* should become clearer in both the cinematic and analytic contexts. To begin, let us consider some of the issues of phantasy, hallucination, and perception.

In different ways, and for different reasons, both Lacan and Husserl arrive at a point that has been articulated here as the *ir-Real*—that the objects and streams of experience such as phantasy, and hallucinations need to be positioned as different from reality, but not in some binarism of "real" (and therefore significant) and "not real" (and therefore less valued), nor as something excluded from reality. A key part of this includes the analytic shift away from "facts" as the focus to arrive at. Instead, this is an analytic setting that needs to recognize there is more at work than trying to divide the real from its others. For phenomenology, this is because the act of consciousness, in its apprehensions, encounters a real object, a memory of that object, a phantasy of that object, a filmed version of that object, and so on, distinguishing them not primarily on their ontology, but their presentation and reference to consciousness. For psychoanalysis, the need to treat memories, phantasies, hallucinations, and dreams as if they are absolutely filled with meanings (perhaps more real than reality for the person) is crucial to the analytic situation. This is not to imply that either approach somehow avoids or denies distinctions; but what is at hand is the development of innovative ways of examining such distinctions as critical, thinking processes.

Husserl's investigations into phantasy fall within the larger arena of consciousness, presentations, and re-presentations (*Vergegenwärtigungen*). As such this includes our relationship with (experience of) the perceived object as a layered process—our consciousness of the object, and how that shifts if it is, for example, a remembered object. This is the layering that we witnessed in time consciousness (see Chapter 2) as an interwoven process. Indeed, time is precisely one of the primary issues in this nuancing of consciousness, often playing a part in distinctions between what is real and what is remembered, and therefore re-presented. Husserl utilizes this presented/re-presented differencing to make further distinctions on phantasy:

> Phantasying is set in opposition to perceiving and to the intuitive positing of past and future as true; in short, to all acts that posit something concrete and individual as existing. Perception makes a present reality appear to us as present and as a reality; memory places an absent reality before our eyes, not indeed as present itself but certainly as a reality. *Phantasy*, on the other hand, lacks the consciousness of reality in relation to what is phantasised. (Husserl 2005: §1)

In passing we note here that *Volume XXIII Phantasie, Bildbewusstsein, Erinnerung: Zur Phänomenologie der anschaulichen Vergegenwärtigungen* is an important text of Husserl's in terms of developing a phenomenological theory of aesthetics, given his efforts to clarify what "works" and "texts" of arts are, notably within this context of phantasy. The examples given include literature, painting, photography, wax works, music (less so here), as well as a few, limited mentions of cinema, which suggests that Husserl's interests are not formulated through aesthetics (of high art), but are designed to act across disciplines. These transdisciplinary aspects are important because Husserl is laying down a foundational direction which orientates phenomenology as less formally engaged.

Husserl articulates the issues of what it is to phantasize as distinct from seeing or reading a phantasy; he also distinguishes dreams as a different version of this phenomenon (which we will return to shortly). That said, Husserl explicitly excludes or at least curtails the creative acts of producing phantasy as an area of interest; his separation is between the work of phantasy (i.e., creative) and the products of phantasy as they may be presented to us. He makes these distinctions by introducing what he calls objectivating experiences: "What interests us are phenomenological data understood as the foundations of an eidetic analysis that we are going to undertake. What specifically interests us here, therefore, are intentional, or better, so-called objectivating experiences—so-called 'phantasy presentations'" (Husserl 2005: §1). Husserl's clarification here is to delimit his analysis through a phenomenological bracketing of phantasy as a presentification rather than an aesthetic act. This is the strategy Husserl adopts in articulating phantasy experience as what he calls phenomenological data; that is, the re-presentation (*Vergegenwärtigung*) which takes place when we encounter phantasy. In this way we witness here an aspect considered in Chapter 2 (Freud's notion of things and words in the dream-work)—that the object is presented, in its experience, the same way regardless of whether it is an actual object or one of phantasy (by way of context, Husserl's example is centaurs). Crucial to this re-presentation and how phantasy experience comes to hold this status is *vorschweben*, that which hovers before us internally, as opposed to things presented to us externally (see, e.g., Husserl 2005: §1). This idea that what "hovers before us" to distinguish phantasy as internal is the non-object "given in consciousness" that is different from objects and given in "reproductive acts in a way different from the impressional" (Husserl 2005: 439). Let us tease this out some more for it has significant cinematic implications.

Husserl wants to distinguish the experience of phantasy as an internal re-presentation (the given in consciousness); however, even though he acknowledges that the objects of phantasy are not real, they still need to be phenomenological positioned as (re)presented to our consciousness; this is why they hover before us, seeming real to the point where we can act as if they are real;[19] "impressional" is a term Husserl uses to distinguish between experiencing (impressional is the experiencing in internal consciousness), the acts of reproduction, which is the modification, and the re-presentation of the experience. The impressed belongs to individual consciousness, so is part of the experiencing of the object; but because it is experiential, the actual status of the object (phantasy or real) is encountered (re-presented/reproduced) as an act of consciousness and not as an actual object, hence it hovers before us. They are reproductively conscious rather than presentational experiences (see, e.g., Husserl 2005: 439). This crucial distinction between reproductively conscious and presentational experience is precisely *vorschweben*, what hovers before us, within us, and even our own self.

Cinema, as a phantasy, hovers before us in a temptingly literal manner, however, to be true to the phenomenological project, we need to read cinema's phantasy as internal, impressionally driven, and reproductively conscious. A specific example will enable the discussion to turn back to Lacan. *The Favourite* (Yorgos Lanthimos, 2018)[20] employs a technical device which produces an *ir-Real* moment that locates the re-presentational aspect of phantasy in a sense that illustrates the hovering before us, the spectator, and the hovering before all elements within the film itself. Once more, we put to one side all the "usual" aspects of phantasy/fantasy within the film (it plays out as a comedy of manners and so has all of the generic conventions associated with that style and hence semi-fantastical elements), and rather select an example which seems to hover within (i.e., a version of Husserlian "internal") the film itself. The historical setting (early eighteenth-century England) of *The Favourite* lends itself to a visual style recognizable within cinema language, and as such sets up a textual representational system; in short, we come to expect certain images and styles of dress, hair, settings, language, and so on. It should be noted that only some, perhaps none, of these are necessarily historically accurate, but this is because they need only to be textually/cinematically "accurate." As long as they adhere to a cinematic semiotic convention the spectator is likely to accept them as representationally sound. This is our acceptance, as spectators, of the

---

[19]Husserl gives the example of wax models and their life-like features. He sounds mildly irritated that this blurring can be so disturbing to him; the testing of phenomenological analytic powers it would seem. This anticipates the "uncanny valley" response and could provide fruitful in analyzing something like the television show *West World* and its phenomenological hovering before us of affect and the human *contra* AI.
[20]*The Favourite* maps the sexual politics of three women, Queen Anne, Lady Sarah, and Abigail. The black comedy articulates a version of power and manipulation as the women vie for favor, notably Sarah and Abigail to be the queen's favourite. As with Yorgos Lanthimos's other film discussed here, *Dogtooth*, this is a film that aligns power with a near Foucauldian sensibility of the hidden rather than the obvious manifest.

IMAGE 21 *From* The Favourite.

textual order, its cinemaness, so that we can engage with a film.[21] However, intermittently we encounter shots composed through fish-eye lens (see Images 21–23 as examples) which act as modifications of the impressional so we experience the re-presentation of the experience. It is, as Husserl might put it, reproductive acts given differently from the impressional. This issue is made more complex because we are attempting to distinguish between phantasy (cinema), a specific film as phantasy (*The Favourite*), and an element of phantasy (the fish-eye lens effect), all within the context of re-representation and phantasy. To achieve this we will need to evoke the eidetic analytic method, arguing that the fish-eye lens is bracketed off and within the film *The Favourite*, which in turn has to be bracketed off from all cinema, which is bracketed off from all textual forms, which are bracketed off from the natural attitude. There are two (compatible) ways through this: the first, a scrappy side note in Husserl's "Modes of Reproduction and Phantasy Image Consciousness (1912)" (1980); the second, an idea from Lacan to be employed in a complimentary fashion.

Husserl introduces *vorschweben*, this hovering before us, to distinguish between phantasy and other objects, the internal/external qualifications standing. He consistently avoids the trap of real and not real, precisely because this is about how we experience such objects. He wants, instead, to differentiate between the "reproductively conscious" and "presentational experiences." Herein lies the idea of hovering before us: "Perhaps it is best

---

[21]This is another way of understanding the contestable nature of "real" in cinema. Cinematic conventions are more likely to seem real and accurate than any version of actual historical veracity.

IMAGE 22 *From* The Favourite.

IMAGE 23 *From* The Favourite.

to use the expression "to hover before us" (*vorschweben*) here. This is then suitable for every intentional content that we can find in reproductive acts; for example, the correlates that are certainly not objects and yet are given in consciousness (*bewusst*) in a manner different from objects. And given in reproductive acts in a way different from the impressional" (Husserl 2005: 439). This "certainly not objects and yet given in consciousness" is phantasy as an objectivating apprehension. It is different from objects, and re-produces (in a phenomenological sense) objects that are different from the real but are still given in consciousness.[22] Let us return to the example of the fisheye lens in *The Favourite*. This is given to the spectator, but not as an object that aligns with the reproductive system devised by the rest of the film. It holds itself up, disturbing our perception and experience beyond the larger order of phantasy that is *The Favourite*. These fisheye shots are reflexive perceptual moments, adding additional layers of experience. As we experience them, our apprehensive processes (meaning-making as a qualifier within acts of perceiving and experiencing) have a further hovering that needs to be located within the phantasy experience. It is the reproductive act yielding up another layer, modifying these acts within themselves as well as what it is to be a film spectator. In one way this can be seen as the object (both the fish-eye technique and the film *The Favourite* itself) as performing a phenomenological analysis of what cinema is.[23] To link this back to the *ir-Real* we can turn to Lacan.

Lacan's famous analysis of Holbein's painting *The Ambassadors* lends itself to a reading of his interpretation of the anamorphic stain in terms of objectivating apprehension; this skull, which floats at the feet of the two imperious figures, undercutting their phallocentric surety, the self-celebration of European power and conquest, and false idea of immortality with the memento mori. To summarize, Lacan anticipates the talk on anamorphosis by working through parts of Merleau-Ponty's posthumous *The Visible and the Invisible*. The fact that he lays down the groundwork for theories on subjectivity, desire, and the gaze through a phenomenological reference is significant.[24] For in doing so, Lacan positions his ideas within this context of experience as consciousness, perception, and the unconscious. The anamorphic floating skull in the painting is, for Lacan, the annihilated subject; it is "the imaged embodiment of the *minus-phi* of castration which . . . centers the whole organization of the desires through the fundamental drives" (Lacan 1986: 89). The floating skull becomes the referent for

---

[22]By way of example, consider the following: When we look at an object in a film—an empty desk, for example—there is the perception of the desk, which is a re-produced object (there is no desk actually there). Our consciousness is perceiving a desk, but one made in re-production. This in turn changes our consciousness so that we are conscious of our re-producing perception of the desk. Should we remember this desk after the film has finished, we have entered into yet another level of experiencing the desk; another level of re-producing it, this time through memory. Each of these are distinctive, and possibly interconnected, hoverings before us, even if we are not aware of such differences in status.

[23]The same can be said of this device in painting as a larger order. The *Arnolfini Portrait* by Jan Van Eyck is a further example. The convex mirror hovers before us in the background, qualifying the subject matter between it and the spectator.

[24]A certain precautionary note is necessary; Lacan's attitude toward Merleau-Ponty's ideas shifts from what is largely an agreement and even congratulatory, to one that becomes more antagonistic in later seminars and addresses. However, Lacan does continue to demonstrate phenomenological interests outside of Merleau-Ponty's works.

all other significations within the image. (In this sense it is a composing Nothing, poised on the precipice of being absent from being experienced.)

One of the more straightforward approaches to all of this is to read the anamorphic stain of *The Ambassadors* and the fisheye shots in *The Favourite* as performing similar, perhaps even the same, functions. And there is certainly something to be gained in such an approach. Lacan's stressing of the imaged embodiment of castration (i.e., power as invested in the phallic order) aligns with the politics (sexual and otherwise) of the three women in *The Favourite*. Such an approach also allows us to consider the *minus-phi* of castration as a motivating and organizing principle in the film. There is even the capacity to see how shifts in power (negotiations of this *minus-phi*) take place within the film, centering desires through the drives (sexual and death). This has the potential to work as a psychoanalytic reading, but how to bring in the phenomenological sense of phantasy here? For this reason, I would propose a slightly different tack, that of the gaze and its *ir-Real* capacities, which will also engage with the analytic experience and the cinematic processes.

Lacan insists that to understand the anamorphic stain we need to grasp the dialectic of desire—which essentially brings to bear the gaze of the other(s). Once he does this the register of the unconscious also comes into play. Lacan's theorizing of the gaze of the other(s) (which is derived at least in part from Sartre's phenomenological sensibility, notably in *Being and Nothingness*) performs a key function, and one that we can align with the hovering before us. Lacan argues that this gaze of others disturbs and disrupts perception (Lacan 1986: 89); with perception standing in here for the larger context of the formation of the subject, thus becoming a variant of experiencing. Lacan goes on to say this is the subject not "of reflexive consciousness, but that of desire" (1986: 89). Does this create an issue, particularly because of Lacan's phenomenological backdrop here? How are we to negotiate this seeming difference between a phenomenological subject of reflexive consciousness and a psychoanalytic subject of desire? The answer lies in the way that Lacan himself manages to incorporate the two. The anamorphic stain compels us to recognize the dialectic between self and other, in doing so Lacan's apparent distinction melts somewhat: the subject of desire becomes the subject of reflexive consciousness by moving through this process. The disturbance of the gaze (yielded from this subject position of desire and producing a reflexive consciousness) in the field of perception is what we witness in the fish-eye lens in *The Favourite*; that it operates not within the film, but hovers over/before it confirms this *ir-Real* attribute. Once the *ir-Real* is recognized in its experiencing, the result is a reflexive desire, including a reflexive desiring site. Here we witness a transition from an intimacy-led desire to an anxious-based reflexivity; both formed out of the experiencing of the *ir-Real*. All that is contained within these fisheye lens shots are removed from the film, bracketed from it through this disturbance of the perceptual field. This is completely different from, for example, dream sequences or the recalling of past events by a character, because of this hovering, disruptive attribute.[25]

The *ir-Real* aspect of these shots works in another way. By arresting our gaze, these compositional constructs foreground the objectivating apprehensions of phantasy. Lacan's discussion of mimicry, deception, and intimidation (once more, framed by Merleau-Ponty, this time from *The Phenomenology of Perception*) concentrates on what he calls the sexual aim. The section on "The Line and the Light" in *Seminar XI* works exceedingly well for a reading of *The Favourite*—a film filled with Lacanian lures and deceptions (see, e.g., 98–101). Further to this psychoanalytic reading of the film, note Lacan's comments on the competitive function of the gaze and desire: "At the scopic level, we are no longer at the level of demand, but of desire, of the desire of the Other" (Lacan 1986: 104). The narrative plays out the intercessional actions of demand and desire as Abigail (Emma Stone) and Lady Sarah (Rachel Weisz) compete for the desiring gaze of the Other, Queen Anne (Olivia Colman). This Other becomes the "imaged embodiment" of "annihilation." Consider Queen Anne in terms of Lacan's description of vision as such: "We shall see emerging on the basis of vision, not the phallic symbol, the anamorphic ghost, but the gaze as such, in its pulsatile, dazzling and spread out function" (Lacan 1986: 89). This is what Abigail and Sarah seek recognition from. This is also the return to the idea of the object, in this context the object of desire, as a site of anxiety and intimacy. However, the objectivating apprehensions that take place in terms of the *ir-Real* are revealed through what Lacan describes as *dompte-regard*—the laying down of the gaze by the spectator to "become" part of the image; which is Lacan's articulation of being in the realm of desire (i.e., the dissymmetry of the Cartesian *cogito* with the Freudian "I desire"). Thus, objectivating apprehensions—the manner in which phenomenology locates phantasy—participates in this *dompte-regard* process, not as a laying down of the (phenomenological) gaze, but as the site where the *ir-Real* is to be found. Is this a contradiction? Should not the objectivating apprehensions be seen as an active provocation of the determining gaze, and therefore counter to the *dompte-regard*? No, precisely because of something like the fisheye shots in *The Favourite* or the active nothingness in *The Wicker Man*. Throughout the experiencing of the film, as with all films, the spectator lays down the gaze to be inserted into the picture; when the spectator encounters the *ir-Real* this laying down is arrested, meaning (both as interpretation and as a mode of

---

[25]Space does not permit, however such a line of thinking invites comparisons between what Hitchcock does with dreams and memories, what Lynch does with menace (Frank in *Blue Velvet*, Alice in *Lost Highway*, particularly in the final desert scenes), or what Malick does with contradictory voice-overs (in, e.g., *Days of Heaven*) in terms of the *ir-Real*, desire, and reflexivity.

interpretative production) contested, and phantasy becomes the motivating (in Husserl's sense) apprehension. Yet this is only possible because of the interplay between the *dompte-regard* position and the phenomenological action of apprehension and shading. This is the modification aspect that Husserl speaks of in the encounter with phantasy, particularly as it aligns with his two factors of the phantasy object: "appearing objectivity is always taken not for itself but for another nonappearing objectivity appearing in the image . . . the mental image is an appearing objectivity" (Husserl 2005: §14, 96).[26] The nonappearing objectivity is the layering that forms in the foregrounding effect of the fisheye lens shots in *The Favourite*, only in this cinematic context it is the appearing objectivity (the elements contained within the fisheye shot image) sets up the nonappearing objectivity, which is the disruptive (anamorphized) gaze.

On Semblance

There is one further connection to be explored here in terms of phantasy and the *ir-Real*, which is the idea of semblance. In different ways, this is a term that both Lacan and Husserl use in the analysis of truth and knowledge. Semblance sets up relational contexts between phantasy and reality, experiencing consciousness (in this context, being/subject), and representational systems. Let us begin with Lacan, who locates semblance within the domain of knowledge and truth, as well as the negotiation between the Symbolic and Real. Here is his schema from *Seminar XX, On Feminine Sexuality, the Limits of Love and Knowledge: Encore* (hereafter *Encore*).

What is immediately apparent here is the way semblance is located between the Symbolic and Real. Only passing reference can be made here to the other relationships (reality between the Real and Imaginary[27]; true between Symbolic and Imaginary), but what should be noted is that much of the material of this Seminar was laid down in *Seminar XIX, . . . or Worse*, and prior to that, *Seminar XVIII: D'un discours qui ne serait pas du semblant* (Of a Discourse that would not be on Semblance), in particular this idea of semblance. Throughout these seminars Lacan locates it within a

---

[26]Which reminds us of Lacan's comment that "a phenomenon is analyzable only if it represents something other than itself" (Lacan 2013: 15). This is also how Lacan describes the object that is here (*l'objet là*) which becomes "incarnated in its duration" (2013: 31) when absent. This is the operation of the symbol in the Symbolic.
[27]A version of this will be returned to later in this chapter, however it is worth noting that Φ (capital phi), for Lacan, is the "symbolic phallus that cannot be negativized, the signifier of *jouissance*" (2006: 697), and so positions the masculine in a different relationship to perversion. This is a core idea that underpins much of Lacan's later work on sexuality—for better or worse.

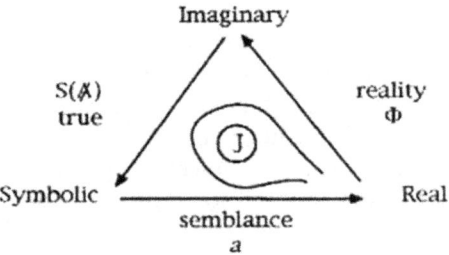

DIAGRAM 7 *From* Seminar XX, On Feminine Sexuality, the Limits of Love and Knowledge: Encore.

string including truth, *jouissance* and *surplus jouissance* (which is discussed further in Chapter 6 in terms of the nightmare). However, the key aspect of semblance that we see in all of these seminars is its qualifying and qualified status to these other terms. This is because semblance is the discourse of the analytic experience and is linked to the *sujet supposé savoir*, the analyst as the subject who is supposed to know. Such is this relationship of knowledge to truth in the analytic experience that Lacan goes so far to say that the analyst occupies the position of semblance (Lacan 2018: 151) precisely because of *jouissance*. This is why semblance must be located "between" the Real and Symbolic; the analyst is engaged in the negotiations of the Real and how they shape the discourse(s) of the Symbolic. This can be extended to the focus here, so that analytic experience is the domain of semblance. From this assertion Lacan continues to place the analyst and his/her analytic knowledge within a context of the wearing of the mask. It is telling that the section from . . . *or Worse* that deals with this is entitled "Knowledge about Truth," whereas the companion lecture in *Encore* is entitled "Knowledge and Truth." The slight alteration is important, for semblance as the analytic discourse produces something outside of truth, something that is a semblance of truth in the shadow of *jouissance* and its surpluses.[28] This is also the reason why, in the schema (shown earlier) we see the *objet petit a*, carrying and connecting desire and its otherness between the Symbolic and Real; this is, according to Lacan, the site of the analyst who "occupies this position of semblance as *a*" (2018: 154). This has considerable potential for the concerns at hand. The semblance as *a* acknowledges the construction

---

[28]This would have been a disturbing moment for Lacan's audience; to be told that one's knowledge is a mask, and that you, as analyst, occupy the site of semblance cannot be easy to hear. Lacan's strategy, beyond our direct concerns, lies in the larger issues of psychoanalytic knowledge holding a unique status and the impossible truth(s) within its discipline. This is the knowledge *about* truth rather than the joining of knowledge *and* truth. Yet another inflection/interpretation of this is to be found in Joan Riviere's conceptualization of "Womanliness as Masquerade."

of knowledge and truth in a very phenomenological manner. This is very close to the phenomenological reduction, bracketing off the natural attitude to go beyond facts, as Husserl might put it. The semblance as *a* is also where we locate the intimate spectator and their anxious configurations. The Symbolic domain of cinema (where we find not just its textualities but also its cinemaness) exists because of the intimate spectator of the Real. In these terms we align the analyst's occupation of semblance as *a* with that of the spectator. The "not-real" (or *irreal* to use Husserl's term) of semblance is part of this otherness. The intimate spectator's anxieties are thus based on this semblance, this alliance of desire, between the (Symbolic) film and our (Real) relationship to it. For the intimate spectator in these terms, anxiety comes from a multitude of relationships, the two primary ones being the anxieties of the film in its othered state and the anxieties from our Real. These relationships are also formulated in the Imaginary, that is, the spectator's insertion of the ego into the experience. It is in these combinatory flows (particularly in the drivers of *a*, reality, and true) that participate in the function of the cinematic *ir-Real*.

Of interest here, Lacan speaks about the value of cinema in these terms of making manifest the mask of semblance (2018: 151). His almost off-handed mention of cinema provides us with a path back to Husserl's devising of semblance. Lacan says: "This [masks and the act of masking] is indeed what constitutes the value of cinema. There, the mask is something else. It is the unreal aspect of the projection" (Lacan 2018: 151). Cinema as that which has the mask of something else, the unreal, is part of the *ir-Real*. It is for these reasons that we can argue that cinema positions us, the spectator, in the semblance of *a*, requiring the transference of cinema's other to enable us to produce knowledge about truth (including cinematic truth and truth through cinema). More simply put, in the analytic discourse the analyst requires the analysand's "reality," their truth, to perform comprehension; in the cinematic discourse the spectator requires the film's "reality," its truth, to perform comprehension; and in even greater specificity, in *The Favourite* the spectator requires the film's "reality," its truth, to comprehend the unreal. Thus, the fisheye shots, the monstrous feminine, the overt semblances of truth in the sexual politics of Abigail and Lady Sarah, and so on, are part of the supplementary *jouissance* which "forces" the spectator to take up the site of semblance. The analyst and spectator are sited in the semblance *a* precisely because they are othered from knowledge, *jouissance*, and its supplements. That *Encore* is the somewhat troubled seminar on feminine sexuality, complete with Lacan's famous "there are no sexual relations" lends itself well to a psychoanalytic reading of *The Favourite*. The minus-phi of castration, found in different guises in Lacan's seminars (e.g., *The Four Fundamental Concepts of Psychoanalysis*, *Transference*, particularly section XVI "Psyche and the Castration Complex," and *Anxiety*) could be utilized to analyze much of the sexual politics of the film. If, for example,

Queen Anne is to be read as the minus-phi for Abigail and Sarah, she is necessarily located as what Lacan describes as the *a* as the intervening signal of anxiety (2017: 86, see also 47). She is the site of anxiety, signaled as and by desire, which becomes the object of anxiety—the object *a*. The insightful cleverness of Lacan's argument is subtle, for the *a* is not simply a signal that can be interpreted and recognized as if a signifier designated in a language. Rather, the *a* as it is found in anxiety is "like a thread designed to enable us to recognize the identity of the object behind the various incidences in which it appears to us" (2017: 86). In *The Favourite* we witness each of the characters attempting to recognize this identity as it shifts in its variety of incidences. Here this is anxiety determined through power, becoming the "final irreducible reserve of libido" (2017: 107) and the true motivating force for the women's actions, and, as noted earlier, the location of the relationship to perversion. Lacan's locating of The Woman *sous rature*—which is really a form of phenomenological bracketing—is exactly what the three principal characters play out. Further, this is a film that moves through a comic anxiety (a common feature of comedy of manners) interplayed with politically driven intimacies and their mimicry.

Returning to Husserl, we can ask if it is possible to locate the semblance *a* phenomenologically speaking. Before turning to the more substantive discussion that we witness in *Husserliana XI*, where Husserl looks at phantasy and semblance, it is conceivable to secure a further link in the way Lacan and Husserl wrestle with truth and reality as they are prescribing within their specific disciplinary practices, and how this leads into the cinematic variant. As noted earlier, Lacan's seminars are primarily about truth and reality in the analysts' discourse and setting; the equivalent for Husserl is how phenomenologists work through these issues within the problematizing of the *cogito*. This is the crux of phenomenological reduction—to move from the "real" to the phenomenologically analytic (which necessarily distinguishes the *irreal*) via bracketing. Here is Husserl explicating further on noema and noesis: "But we allow no judgement that makes any use of the affirmation that posits a 'real' thing . . . As phenomenologists we avoid all such affirmations. But if we 'do not place ourselves on their ground', do not cooperate with them, we do not for that reason cast them away . . . Rather, we contemplate them ourselves; instead of working with them we make them into objects" (Husserl 1931: §90). Both Husserl and Lacan are trying to bracket off the sense of the "real" and true, not to discard them, but to recognize the complicity of their status. This is why Lacan's seemingly problematic stance is actually quite phenomenological in its attempt to locate the site and production of knowledge. Just as Husserl, in devising his method on noesis and noema, urges us to not cast away the "real thing," instead bracket it off and allow it to stand in a different status, so Lacan urges the bracketing of the real thing of psychical material. The words of the hysteric must be taken as "true" and meaningful, but in a bracketed fashion;

just as when Husserl talks about the blossoming tree[29] as having the reality of being out there but bracketed off. This is its noematic meaning in the analytic process. Similarly, the noematic meaning of the hysteric's utterance shifts the perception and holds it as real (i.e., does not cast it away) for both the hysteric and the analyst, but in the phenomenological reduction to its essences of hysterianess. This is the alignment with cinema in terms of the "real," for it allows us to reconfigure cinema's capacity to act as if it is real. This is the spectator's refusal of the affirmation of the real in a film and precisely why analytic intimacy forms.

In this way it is possible to align how psychoanalysis and phenomenology in their critical approaches to "true" and "real" construct the *ir-Real* (recalling Husserl's qualification that phenomenology doesn't deal with facts) and the Real. Formations of noematic meanings are crucial to both systems. This is why semblance, as concept and performance, helps resolve a difficulty, that is: how are we to negotiate the ways in which psychoanalysis holds the material of the analytic situation (conversion hysteria and the corporeal signifiers of psychical issues; our dreams; the forgetting of names, and so on) as apprehensions of the true and real; and how phenomenology requires differentiation between real and phantasy as consequential; and how cinema performs through the semblance of masks with this same version of phenomenological consequentiality. For example, when Husserl talks about the discrediting qualities of phantasy (e.g., that a phantasy judgment requires no choices) it would appear counter to the way psychoanalysis treats such material. When we wake from a dream, perhaps in terror, believing the events to be real, or react to a film as if what is on screen is a genuine threat, it would seem that we have momentarily lost the discrediting aspect; the phantasy is apprehended as if real.[30] However, both systems allow for this because there is the mediating "zone" of "truth" and "real." This aligns with Lacan's model (earlier) where we see semblance between the Symbolic (real-making acts of language and social constructions) and the Real, and why apprehending judgments (in his case the role of the psychoanalyst) is a semblance of knowledge. Further to this is the idea of a semblance of cinematic knowledge as it becomes possible through intimacy and is enacted in anxiety.

Husserl leads into the phenomenological enacting version of semblance by first distinguishing between reality (i.e., something perceived as having a presence, of being present in temporality (its formation in and through now-points) and having reality), memory (something perceived as present

---

[29]In *Ideas* §90 it is the blossoming tree out there, perceived with the qualifier "as such."
[30]Roman Ingarden (1973a, b), Husserl's student and intellectual follower, speaks of quasi-judgments in the literary work to address some of these issues. These same quasi-judgments are essential in cinema.

but with an absent reality, including this construction of now-points), and phantasy, in which the consciousness of reality is absent. Husserl differentiates these further though *Schein*, translated as semblance.[31] Semblance is part of Husserl's drive to establish phantasy as a unitary phenomenon (i.e., excluding a wider range of acts that might fall under this umbrella), which are phantasy presentations and their apprehensions. This enables him to isolate the two aspects of phantasy as a distinctive experience: the content of the apprehensions (which is relatively self-evident—what the phantasy is) and, perhaps more significantly, the distinctiveness of the apprehensions themselves. It is not just the status of the phantasy, but how we are sensorially connected to it, and this is Husserl's wonderfully conceived notion of sensuous phantasms: "exclusive of any apprehension, such as the phantasy of a centaur, a house, and so on, the phantasm, too, is a sensuous content that is something *totally* different from the phantasy" (Husserl 2005: 78).[32] These sensuous phantasms are the distinctive apprehensions of phantasy—it is what enables a phantasy to be experienced as such, and not as the perception of something "real." In other words, they do not exist as such in the phantasy but are part of the apprehension of that phantasy as a phantasy. In this sense, they have the "hover before us" attribute (*Vorschweben*), delivering aspects of the phantasy in this sensorial fashion, as well as the action of phenomenological shading. This is certainly part of the objectivating apprehensions, distinguishing what the phantasy is (how it is formed and presented) and how it is experienced. The other quality that Husserl ascribes to phantasms is their instability. "Real" objects are perceived as stable, whereas phantasms shift and change constantly. This is in part why the hovering phantasms are unique, for it is in how their instability is played out that the apprehension of the phantasy is made more fluid and perhaps transitory in terms of experience, shading, meaning constructions, attachments (to veracity, purpose, affect), and so on.

---

[31]Husserl speaks of "mere semblance" (e.g., 2005: 71), but *bloss* (mere/merely) is a complex word in this context. I refer the reader to Rodolphe Gasché's analysis of Kant's use of *bloss* in *The Idea of Form: Rethinking Kant's Aesthetics*. Gasché makes a compelling argument that *bloss* in Kant should not be read in a dismissive tone, but rather as a concept: "It could thus well be that rather than occurring incidentally in Kant's text, *merely* is used for systematic reasons, and that its status is that of a philosophical concept comparable, say, to that of the pure" (Gasché 2003: 16). I would suggest that Husserl employs the term in a similar fashion. Thus, we read 'mere semblance' as having a discriminating inflection; and when we encounter a statement such as: "what is phantasied is something merely imagined, that is merely semblance" (Husserl 2005: 71) it is read as clarifying the status of phantasy as somehow distinct. Similarly, in *Husserliana XI* there are numerous discussions of "mere" phantasy as a demarcation category, including: "The Relationship of Mere Phantasy and Memory"; and in Appendix XXXIX "On the Distinction between Memory and Mere Phantasy."
[32]This idea of phantasms is taken up in Chapter 6 on breathlessness and nightmares.

This link between the real object/thing and its phantasy variants is part of perception and semblance. Our apprehension of phantasy presents complexity because of this link "back" to the object (which, as Husserl points out, may not exist, such as with dragons and centaurs). Thus, Husserl's comments on cinema and photography are focused on how and why such links take place in the apprehending moments (see e.g., 2005: 146; 171; 181). How and why do we trace back to the empirically existing object in a film; how do such objects exist in the Lacanian notion of masks and semblance? Recall that this issue is central to Husserl's distinguishing features between real, memory, and phantasy—the absence or presence of the real in the perceiving of it. This is why the semblance judgment (Husserl uses the example of theatre, but cinema works just as well) usually matches with the semblance perception—"usually" because there are disturbances where this alignment shudders. This is also why the fish-eye shots in *The Favourite* hover in difference from the rest of the film; judgment and perception have to be realigned or read in a different register because in a domain of semblances established as coherent (the created world order of the film), the fish-eye shots are an uncoupling of semblance judgment to semblance perception. In this sense, there can be different phantasy objectivating apprehensions within a film, each requiring an adjustment according to their status. Further to this, what is being posited throughout here is that intimacy and anxiety (and their "production" of flesh) are part of this disturbance of the semblance judgment. Furthermore, as noted earlier, intimacy and anxiety are crucial to the semblance *a* position for the spectator.

We encounter here an overlap between Husserl and Lacan's interpretation of semblance as two orders: apprehension and object. Significantly, both critical approaches distinguish and conflate these at various times, with a similar analytic intent. We noted earlier Lacan's positioning of the analyst as the semblance *a*, which is the articulation of knowledge as the desired object, not as truth but rather as the holder of interpretative knowledge, as the one who is "supposed to know." This aligns with Husserl's apprehension semblance—the phantasy which may or may not link back to reality but requires this judgment from us. On another level, the *objet petit a* is the (phenomenological) semblance object, which is presented in phantasy. The first is, thus, semblance as a type of judgment "performed" on phantasy (how we recognize and read phantasy), the second is a type of object created as and from the sensuous phantasms of phantasy (what objects we perceive in our encounter with phantasy). For Husserl this is the semblance consciousness, a "unitary complex of intentions harmonious in themselves" (2005: 361–2). When we watch a film, enter a world of the semblance object, as Husserl puts it (2005: 295),[33] we take up the semblance *a*, positioning and

---

[33] He was speaking of the total immersion of a stereoscope in a darkened room, completely removed from the world.

being positioned by the sensuous as one who is supposed to know (or will acquire such a status as we watch the film), which is our unitary semblance consciousness as spectator; and what we encounter are those semblance objects of phantasy. The fisheye shots in *The Favourite* are semblance objects, held as such precisely because of this semblance consciousness we adopt as spectators. More than this, it is only possible to adopt and sustain such a position, and hold these phantasy objects as such, because of intimacy. It is intimacy that invests us in this unitary complex, places us in the semblance *a*, allows the phantasms to hover between us and the layer of the film and its mechanisms. This intimacy is so powerful that we seek out the status of semblance rather than authenticity; as such we perhaps begin to recognize the power of cinema itself.

5

Passionate Abnormalities and the Disturbances of Wildness

Wild flesh is perhaps the most disturbing version of cinema's representational field. This is anxiety at its most overwhelming combined with the compelling nature of, and connection with, intimacy. These are the things we wish we could turn from and yet are bound to them by cinema's affective, emotional constructions. This is the aching gaze, fixed by an impulse and made complicit in all that follows. The "flesh" is concupiscence—here taken to mean the transformative aspect of desire rendered as anxiety. This is the moment when flesh is given and judged in a different manner than we have previously spoken of here, for it is the body revealed as a distinct version of fleshification. In other words, how desire, via intimacy, comes to produce cinematic flesh that is a causality, and yet a potential working through, of cultural anxieties. This is the too beautiful, the too sensual, the too provocative, for a culture, as well as the individual, to hold and comprehend. A further version of this is how wildness (in and beyond flesh) produces anxiety as a version of the sublime.[1] *Wildness* is used here as a dualism: the overcoming, disruptive, beyondness of wildness, particularly in terms of the generation of meaning and meaningfulness; and wilderness as the repressed and negated primordial forces beyond civility and the urban.

To proceed, then, two versions of wildness that interweave at the level of disturbance. One is sublime flesh arresting proper behavior (which includes

---

[1] The ensuing discussion remains true to the overall focus of this book—that is, interweaving and combining Husserlian phenomenology and Freudian/Lacanian psychoanalysis. This distinguishes the approach to, and exploration of, the work in film philosophy which has been dominated by on the one hand Merleau-Ponty (see Sobchack 1992, 2004), and on the other a distinctly psychoanalytic approach without phenomenology. The approach to the sublime here is very much based on the issues of anxiety and intimacy.

the body[2]); the other is Nature resisting the proper cultural order. This configuration positions "wildness" against "proper," with its etymology from L. *propius* to the French *propre*—both containing the ideas found in English of own and individual, and correct and appropriate. We will begin with the idea of wildness as disruption and resistance.

Merleau-Ponty's final work, *The Visible and the Invisible* (hereafter *The Invisible*), comprises of an unfinished manuscript and working notes. As with Husserl's *The Crisis*, we are left with sets of intriguing and tantalizing thought-threads often more evocative than defined or resolved. Key to this work are the conceptual frames and the agitational interpretative possibilities of flesh and the wild.[3] It is somewhat of a stretch to say that *The Invisible* is Merleau-Ponty's return to the Husserlian homeland, but there is certainly enough to suggest that if the book had been completed it would have demonstrated an engagement of considerable depth with Husserl's key ideas. It is telling, for example, that the final words of the manuscript (*The Intertwining—the Chiasm*) include the following: "In a sense the whole of philosophy, as Husserl says, consists in restoring a power to signify, a birth of meaning, or a wild meaning, an expression of experience by experience . . . " (1998: 155).[4] Even with the evocation of Husserl, we are not so far from "classic" Merleau-Ponty, however, and much of *The Invisible* is concerned with the issues of the body in the world, the critical inflection given at this point, in the work, is the intertwining, the chiasm. Because Merleau-Ponty is so careful to deconstruct binary relations, we should not hasten to see the chiasm as the moment where the binary modes are resolved. The intertwining, the moment where the two lines of the X intersect, is not the reduction to permutations of duality such as the visible-invisible, or world-body, or even meaning-non-meaning. What, then, is to be made of the use of *flesh* and *wild* in these nascent ideas of the chiasm? And what use is to be made of them within this discussion of cinema?

Let us begin by articulating wild meaning, this "birth of meaning" and the "expression of experience as experience" as a way to explore the wild and its resistance to the proper Being in meaning. In other words, and true to Merleau-Ponty's project, the wild's problematizing ontology. There is something reminiscent of a line from Husserl in wild meaning: "Between the meanings of consciousness and reality yawns a veritable abyss" (1931: §49). Is this Husserl's chiastic structuring that leads to the birth of meaning?

---

[2]There is resonance here with Kristeva's *corps propre*—one's clean and proper body—which is discussed as follows.
[3]We should be under no illusion as to the ambiguity of these terms given the incomplete status of the text and ideas. The strategy here is not to attempt to define them in any concrete fashion, but to utilize their potential.
[4]It is striking just how much Merleau-Ponty constructs metaphors of birth and pregnancy throughout *The Invisible*. What is to be done with this is a discussion to be had elsewhere.

A phenomenological recognition of the abyss and the subsequent efforts to understand it? It would certainly seem that the Husserlian abyss sets up the analytic requirements for meaning through an iteration of wildness. Merleau-Ponty draws heavily on Husserl's notion of the horizon of things to work through the idea of flesh and its interplays of primary and secondary visibilities and their hidden counterparts. This leads him to "the most difficult point, that is, the bond between the flesh and the idea" (Merleau-Ponty 1968: 149). This is the visible as flesh (and the inversion of flesh as determining and determined in the visible) and the idea as invisible (which becomes the invisible as the space for the idea). Now compare this to his interpretations of perceptual experience and the synthesis of horizons, in *Phenomenology of Perception*, and the relational contexts of body and world: "I detach myself from my experience and pass to the *idea*. Like the object, the idea purports to be the same for everyone, valid in all times and places" (Merleau-Ponty 1962: 71). This act of detachment is crucial to Merleau-Ponty's conceptualization of the visible and invisible, body and world because it involves the engagement with the "idea." It is possible to see this detachment process as being the negation (rendering invisible) of the abyss between consciousness and reality. And if there appears to be a slippage here, a misrecognition of the meta-positioning of Merleau-Ponty and Husserl within the devising of the phenomenological project, well, this is only an appearance. The issue of Husserl's attention to essences and return to phenomena that Merleau-Ponty argues is a methodological shift is not a contradistinction to these points (1962: 49). Wild meaning (the incitement to engage with meaning), it is suggested here, is against the detachment of body to idea, a seeking of the return to reflexively resist such a process. *The Phenomenology of Perception* extensively engages with the problems involved with a non-positing consciousness,[5] with its lack of reflexive positioning and the body in the world.

There is a difficulty here, reading wild meaning in this incitement to the reflexive; a difficulty embedded in Merleau-Ponty's incomplete, dangling, imperfect note on wild perception: "perception *qua* wild perception is of itself ignorance of itself, imperception, tends of itself to see itself as an *act* and to forget itself as latent intentionality, as being at—" (1968: 213). This indicates not the reflexive, but something altogether different, something that seems to be antithetical to an awareness. However, there are three aspects that allow wild meaning (or wild perception, wild judgment, wild phantasy, wild intimacy, wild anxiety, and so on) to be articulated in this

---

[5]Merleau-Ponty's interpretation of the non-positing consciousness is to be found in *The Phenomenology of Perception*—" . . . that is, a consciousness not in possession of fully determinate objects, that of a logic lived through which cannot account for itself . . . " (Merleau-Ponty 1962: 49).

sense of incitement to reflexivity. The first is to locate *wild* within the abyss between consciousness and reality; the second is to acknowledge that the implicit detachment (from flesh to idea) is to hold the perception or experience *sous rature*, an absented presence that is never truly negated (i.e., the latent intentionality as well as the "an expression of experience by experience"); the third is to catch the reflexive potential in Merleau-Ponty's next fragmentary sentence, and reread the wild accordingly: "Same problem: how every philosophy is a language and nonetheless consists in rediscovering silence" (1968: 213). If these three conditionals are accepted, then it is possible to read this aspect of wild as a disturbance to meaning and, in turn, a challenge to the proper Being (in the world).[6] To unpick this challenging idea further we can turn first to a case study of Freud's, which should pave the way for an engagement with the cinematic.

Wild Meaning and the Wolves

The point of drawing on Freud's Wolf Man case study is to test how these terms—chiasm, abyss, and the reflexive turn—can be utilized in a scenario where the disturbance of proper Being in the world is invigilated as wild. This in turn shapes how we might consider cinematic thinking as wildness. The temptation to ascribe the reflexive turn to the Wolf Man's own memoirs will be resisted here precisely because of the inherent issues of imperception and latent intentionality.[7] That said, there will be moments when these documents are worthy of reference. Merleau-Ponty was, of course, acutely aware of psychoanalysis' somatic investigations; a significant example is Chapter 5, "The Body in its Sexual Being," in *The Phenomenology of Perception*. This Freudianly infused section acknowledges the "relationship of reciprocal *expression*" (1968: 160) between body and psyche, proposing

---

[6] Note Merleau-Ponty's comment that "learning is *In der Welt Sein* [to be in the world], and not at all that *In der Welt Sein* is learning" (1968: 212). A tangential point to this: in dealing with abductive thought, Bateson gives the following example in an analysis of the social systems of an Indigenous tribe in Australia: Their [the tribe's] ideas about nature, however fantastic, are supported by their social system; conversely, their social system is supported by their ideas of nature. It thus becomes very difficult for the people, so doubly guided, to change their view either of nature or of the social system. For the benefits of stability, they pay the price of rigidity, living, as all human beings must, in an enormously complex network of mutually supporting presuppositions (Bateson 1980: 158). These "mutually supporting presuppositions," a version of *learning*, locates Being in the world within a binding (cultural and psychical) situation.
[7] This would be a project worth pursuing. The Wolf Man, and Judge Schreber, wrote from positions external to the psychoanalytic moment; the Wolf Man through temporal distance, Schreber through his deep psychosis. In doing so they present a pursuit of the language out of silence. Dora's silence remains.

that the body exists (is "brought to life" 167) through desire's inflection of consciousness.

There is no need to engage with all the material of the case study, instead we can focus on the specific event of the dream that Freud notes as causal to the onset of anxiety. The focus here must be on how this event, as an exemplar of anxiety-hysteria transforming into obsessional neurosis (see Freud *SE XVII*), allows us to consider the challenge to the proper Being in the world, and how the abyss between consciousness and reality is foregrounded in such cases.[8] Of significance to the issues at hand, and adding another layer of complexity, is that the Wolf Man's event crisis takes place not because of an external trauma, but because of a dream-induced anxiety. This ontological slippage relates to further discussions here on phantasy (Chapter 4) as well as the nightmare (Chapter 6). As Freud points out, the source material for the dream comes from fairy tales, notably a picture from a book that his sister (who Freud describes as "vastly superior" *SE XVII*: 30) teased him with. The recollection of the dream, including a drawing by the Wolf Man (as shown in the following), contains a number of key aspects which become the focus of Freud's dream analysis. These include: the color of the wolves (white), their number (six or seven, although only five appear in the drawing—a number that becomes increasingly important in the analysis and the traumatic origins), why they are in the tree, and their origins in fairy tales (the Wolf Man says it is most likely "Little Red Riding Hood" to which Freud proposes the story of "The Wolf and the Seven Little Goats" as a further possibility). These details are significant to the issues at hand, the wild's disturbance of proper Being in the world.

The chiasmic nature of this disturbance stems from the attributes of the dream, and the anxiety produced from the dream (leading to the Wolf Man's subsequent traumas). This is a psychoanalytic rendering of a disturbance of the proper, disallowing a Being in the world, a demonstrated split between consciousness and reality that widens the abyss. The wild is doubly located; in the dream, and in the anxieties which follow. The first of these is the wildness of dreams and their capacity to disturb; the second is the wildness of meanings that are produced through (and in themselves produce) anxieties. These white wolves, bizarrely positioned in a tree and immobile, refuse the Wolf Man's place in the world, just as they disturb the (Freudian) psychoanalytic techniques. This is where their wild meaning lies; in the Wolf Man and in Freud. To reiterate, wild meaning is the incitement to engage with meaning because of a disturbance, which in turn has a reflexive modality. Wild meaning is not simply the anxious life of the Wolf Man, for it is also the consequences of, and for, psychoanalysis as an analytic process. Freud describes how the

---

[8] For an exemplar reading of Freud's case study in terms of visuality and the word see Whitney Davis *Drawing the Dream of the Wolves: Homosexuality, Interpretation, and Freud's "Wolf Man."*

FIGURE 2 *The Wolf Man's drawing of the wolves.*

Wolf Man emphasized three crucial factors in the dream: "first, the perfect stillness and immobility of the wolves, and secondly, the strained attention with which they looked at him. The lasting sense of reality, too, which the dream left behind it" (*SE XVII*: 33). Freud's subsequent analysis (e.g., he reads the immobility of the wolves as an illustration of dream inversion, so their stillness is actually a manifestation of violent and sudden motion) tracks the dream material within psychoanalytic theory. However, and this does not negate the analysis proposed in the case study, this description of perfect stillness, attentive focus, and lasting reality is precisely what we would expect to work as a description of the psychoanalyst at work; and at the same time, the uncomfortable stillness, piercing (attentive) gaze, and lingering sensory material bleeding into reality are what someone will feel in the analytic situation. Wild judgments necessarily carry with them this beyond to the analytic situation; in this example, the wolf works as an embodied version of the wild. To reshape Merleau-Ponty in this regard: "It is this wild or brute being that intervenes at all levels to overcome the problems of the classical ontology," (1968: 211) which is a bold, seductive idea.

There is a further famous wolf case in psychoanalytic literature that can be utilized to explore this idea of wildness and its disturbances. This is the analysis presented by Rosine Lefort during Lacan's seminar on technique (1953–4).[9] Once more, we do not need to recount the extensive details of

---

[9]Lefort wrote more extensively on this case study (with Robert Lefort) in *Les Structures de la psychose: L'Enfant au loup et le Président*. Significantly, in this work Lefort makes comparisons between the wolf-child and the psychoses of Schreber.

the case, suffice to say that this is a disturbing story of a boy, Robert, (aged three and a half when the treatment began)[10] who, through neglect and mistreatment, was unsocialized and lacked language. His vocalizations consisted entirely of animal-type sounds (growls, screams) and the only two words he knew, "Miss" and "wolf." As Lefort describes: "This word, 'wolf!' he repeated throughout the day, so I nicknamed him the *wolf-child*, because that really was the image he had of himself" (Lefort in Lacan 1988a: 92). In terms of our developing concept of wild meaning (and "judgment" is also apposite here), the key moment occurs at the end of Lefort's presentation when she discusses the child's relationship to reality and its connection to an event in her own life. The following is her description, which is preceded with some analysis of Robert's trauma from his abusive mother and the withholding of food: "His fantasies had become reality. Lately I have had to confront him with something real. I was away for a year, and I returned eight months pregnant. He saw me pregnant. He started playing with fantasies of the destruction of this child. I disappeared for the birth. While I was away, my husband took him into treatment, and he acted out the destruction of this child. When I returned, he saw me thin, and childless. So he was convinced that his fantasies had become reality, that he had killed the child and hence I was going to kill him" (Lefort in Lacan 1988a: 100). Lefort eventually brings her baby daughter to Robert; subsequently, he becomes less agitated because "he was becoming attached to something living and not to death" (100). In the ensuing discussion, Lefort was asked where the word "wolf" came from for Robert. She offers the explanation that it is something commonly used by nurses in children's homes (and was also used in a punitive fashion where he was lodged); more significantly, when asked by Hyppolite "Do you think that the wolf is always the devouring mother?," she replies, "In children's stories, the wolf is always about to eat. At the oral-sadistic stage, the child wishes to eat its mother, and thinks that its mother is going to eat it" (1988a: 101). Lefort, Lacan, and the members of the seminar would of course be acutely aware of the iterations of Beingness that took place between Lefort, the psychoanalyst, and Lefort, the mother, within this context of a child abandoned by an abusive, paranoiac mother. She even notes her transitional roles, in Robert's eyes, between the good (protective, nurturing) and bad (devouring) mother object. Just as the reading here of the wolves in the Wolf Man case led to the positing of a disturbance in meaning, so Lefort's own analysis of her (maternal)

---

[10]This is an important issue for psychoanalysis in these cases. Freud's Wolf Man case study is a significant analysis in part because it is detailing repressed childhood issues and their subsequent manifestations in adult life. This is the case study where Freud details his theory of the primal scene, and much of the material is drawn from this very early period of his life. Lacanians will note the formations of the mirror stage, although in this case study there is an impediment to development.

body in relation to the wolf-child reveals a range of corporeally driven significations. The fact that he meets her first as a woman, then pregnant, and then as a mother, shapes the analysis (and his rehabilitation) in a way that would be impossible for a man. Yet nothing is really made of this in Lacan's seminar; Hyppolite asks about the devouring mother and Lacan focuses on the access to the psychical collapse through the word "wolf," but there is no dialogue or analytic investigation indicated regarding her corporeal situations and shifts. For the issues here however, Lefort's body (and the maternal body in itself) is crucial to wild meaning. Let us consider this from a phenomenological perspective.

One of Merleau-Ponty's investigative lines is the relationship of the body to spatiality and motility. In these terms, body image thus becomes the state of the body in the world, determined by movement rather than space because "movement is not limited to submitting passively to space and time, it actively assumes them . . . we must therefore avoid saying that our body is *in* space, or *in* time. It *inhabits* space and time" (1962: 101; 102; 139). The two wolf cases can be read in terms of this structured phenomenological body in movement, with meanings and ontologies determined through motion (and immobility) as sites of control and power. The body images of the Wolf Man, Freud, the wolf-child, and Lefort are chiastic in this underpinning of the motile body in the world. The wolf (devised here in the three iterations of Man, child, and dream symbol; a fourth is possible if we read Lefort, via Robert, as the devouring wolf-mother) is a body fixed and lacking motility, in doing so it inhabits (in this phenomenological sense) a space and time determined as a disturbance. It is this disturbance that precisely shifts the inhabiting body so that it, perversely, is fixed and full of violent motions. This happens on a number of levels, including:

a. The psychoanalytic version of negation, *Verneinung*, (where meaning is posited in its opposite—the immobile dream wolves are thus full of motion, psychically speaking), producing in turn converted alienation (see Lacan 1993: 43) and beyond socialized somatic acts (the wolf-child is described as being in constant hyperagitation: " . . . he was hyperactive, continually prey to jerky and disorderly movements, without aim. Unorganized prehensive activity—he would throw his arm out to take hold of an object . . . " (Lefort in Lacan 1988a: 92). This is the challenge to Merleau-Ponty's inhabitation of the world when the body has yet to relate to that world. In this sense it is of a different order of abyss.).

b. The body in stasis while the psychical is in turbulent action and disorder.

c. The presence-absence/remaining-leaving intertwinings (Lefort leaves and returns with a child; Freud ends (leaves) the analysis, declaring it complete, but the Wolf Man pursues (returns to) analysis for the rest of his life.

d. The phenomenological body's inhabiting of the world in its active processes. Lefort's maternal body comes to represent the corporeal as transitional inhabitation (a type of movement of the body from one status to another, which in some ways positions it in the phenomenological hyle), which works in contradistinction to the wolf-child's body cast away from inhabitation. This is the wild meaning of disturbance, played out in the body-made flesh. Let us turn to some cinematic examples for further explication.

The body in film problematizes the inhabitation of, and movement through, space, and in doing so works as an example of Merleau-Ponty's "expression of experience by experience," however it is also correct to state that certain bodies in certain films foreground these processes and experiences. We can even go so far as to assert that there is a cinematic "type" of such films. A recurring motif of this is in terms of disturbance and movement as one bodily iteration, and stasis and entrapment as the contrasting other. In both cases we witness an interplay between the corporeal and psychical. It is precisely this interchange and mirroring of disturbance and movement that determines the relationship of self to Other, and flesh to wildness. It is possible to read this as a version of what Lefort, in *The Birth of the Other*, describes as the traumatic subject's recognition of the other/Other and its "menacing *jouissance*" (1991: 236). Iterations of this are the basis of terror in cinema, formulated through the self's composing Nothings of the menacing *jouissance*: the policeman, Howie, and the island community in *The Wicker Man*; Marion and Norman (as well as the Bates motel, the illicit affair) in *Psycho*; the family and Jack in *The Shining* (Kubrick 1980), and Carla Jean Moss (Kelly Macdonald) in *No Country for Old Men* (Coen Bros 2007)[11] are versions of anxious flesh as it is caught in this reflexive otherness of menace. In all these examples there is a wild meaning generated from the inhabiting of space, tracking how each of them negotiates (successfully or otherwise) this inhabitation. As we proceed it is important to not conflate wild meaning with the representation of wildness in films. Tempting as

---

[11]This Coen Brothers film will form a substantive part of the following discussion. The film is both stylistically and thematically a "typical" neo-noir Coen Bros. film, weaving acts of violence with an almost empty despair of ordinary lives. Escaped killer Anton Chigurh (Javier Bardem) dispassionately threatens and kills people, displaying a total lack of empathy. The coin toss scene in the gas station reveals an almost randomness to his acts, yet there is also a compulsive and methodical process involved. Contrasting to his carnivalesque psychopathy are the other main characters, including husband and wife Llewelyn Moss (Josh Brolin) and Carla Jean (Kelly Macdonald), representing moral acts and vulnerability, and Ed Tom Bell (Tommy Lee Jones) an aged Sheriff who pursues Chigurh.

this is, and clearly there are moments when they do align, wild meaning is outside such representational fields. Wild flesh, through corporeality and its movements, foreground what Merleau-Ponty describes as our access to the world: "Our bodily experience of movement is not a particular case of knowledge; it provides us with a way of access to the world and its object, with a *praktognosia*, which has to be recognized as original and perhaps as primary" (1962: 140). *Praktognosia*, "practical knowledge" is the body's capacity to perform tasks in movement. At a more abstract level, this is how anxious bodies are separated in the inability to inhabit different spaces. These fleshified characters take on a Kierkegaardian sensibility when we consider them in terms of escape: "Freedom's possibility announces itself in anxiety" (Kierkegaard 2015: 91). These anxieties, lacks and desires, of motility and its loss, are the psychical embedded in the corporeal, which is how Merleau-Ponty articulates the body in the world. Note how complex the versions of entrapment are in these examples. Marion and Carla Jean seem caught in the menace of the other through chance; Carla Jean's relationship to this is foregrounded in her refusal to partake in the toss of the coin offered by Anton Chigurh (Javier Bardem). In both *Psycho* and *No Country for Old Men* we witness versions of the wild as personified, masculine menace, as spaces of otherness/othered (the dream-like landscape of the desert, the nightmarish Bates's Motel, and Norman's bird-filled room). This is a different version of the body-as-flesh in space, interjected into wildness, that is discussed in the four modalities of anxiety, intimacy, and space in Chapter 3. All these "exchanges" of flesh and space are versions of freedom (and its lack), a corporeal politic of control, and the flesh's capacity to reconfigure wild and/or socially responsible spaces. Cinema has these relational contexts and shifts as a core aspect of its existence; cinema has its existence because of this wild flesh. Central to this is the interplay between flesh in and of spaces, and the in-mixing of motion and stillness. Cinema's existence in these terms renders it as a core version of our experiencing the world, and hence our engagement in the analytic experience.

Wild meaning, its attributes of disturbance and reflexivity, is played out in this inhabiting of space(s) in these film examples. Indeed, it is a recurring component of how we can read this concept in its cinematic versions. Carla Jean's coin toss refusal, stating that ethical acts cannot be laid on chance, and Ed Tom Bell's (Tommy Lee Jones) recounting of his dream at the close of the film can function as exemplars here. At both the denotative and connotative levels, the coin toss and the dream are acknowledgments of the different inhabitations required for both to survive. The coin and dream are, narratively speaking, simultaneously a marker of traumatic inhabitations and acceptance of the intimate anxieties. The coin toss refusal is a distinctive example of the menacing *jouissance* as the self confronts the other. However, to read these signifiers in terms of a wild meaning, the coin/dream can be aligned with the word "wolf" in Lefort's case study, for each is suspended (in the tree, in the air-tossed coin, and in the "air" of non-closure for the dream) as prescient, immobile, and overdetermined as the wolves in the Wolf Man's drawing. The point here is not to try and conflate Lefort and Lacan's reading of the (overdetermined) signifier *wolf* with the coin/dream; rather it is (to rework Merleau-Ponty's words) to take up the "expression [*wolf*/coin/dream] of an experience [inhabitation] by experience [analytic experience and the sensory]" and how they function as wild meanings in the disturbance of proper Being in the world.

Lacan takes *wolf* and reads it within the context of the super-ego and law. This is a relationship based on the preservation and adherence to the law, or, in the case of neurosis, the law and its destruction held simultaneously. It is important to recall two key aspects of the super-ego in psychoanalysis: first, as Freud points out (e.g., *SE XIX*), the super-ego is formed when a component of the external world is internalized; second, as Lacan consistently reiterates, the super-ego is fundamental to the relationship of the subject to the external world through language. Hence, the proper Being in the world, the phenomenological inhabiting of space and time, has successfully negotiated the harmonious integration of ego and super-ego, and the status of the speaking subject. In the specific examples, proper Being in the world is in abeyance because the signifiers are so invested with disturbing, unresolvable meanings. Wild meaning is the disturbance of this, and so most readily takes place in these domains of the proper and "language." More broadly, cinema, it is posited here, occupies the site where wild meanings can be generated. Within this larger order of wildness (i.e., in the current context, cinema's disturbing potential realized), the focus here is on the specificity within the language.

The cry of "*wolf*," in Lefort's case study, becomes the signifier to unlock the troubled world of Robert, form a relationship, and help him through the hallucinatory disturbances (a specific diagnosis is not resolved). Lefort describes Robert as existing entirely in the Real (and therefore cut off from the Symbolic and its performance of language and consequential socialization), with the singular articulation of *wolf* providing the capacity to establish relationships. This is the *wolf* cry as wild meaning, disturbing both internal world orders and their external interplays. That Lefort is positioned as the devouring wolf-mother and Robert is known as the wolf-child, confirms the reflexivity of the processes. In this way, *wolf* is wild meaning not because it allows for deciphering, but because it reflexively disturbs. This is how the coin/dream in *No Country for Old Men* can be read in these terms of wild meaning. To recall, Merleau-Ponty's provocative lines on wild meaning: "a birth of meaning, or a wild meaning, and expression of an experience by experience, which in particular clarifies the special domain of language" (1968: 155). The coin/dream, like the white wolves and the cry of *wolf*, occupies this special domain of language not simply as a mode of communication, but a phenomenological positing of the sensorial body inhabiting worlds which have become unstable. This instability is a key marker of flesh here. This plurality is noteworthy. Carla Jean and Bell, like Robert and Lefort, inhabit at least two external worlds (the Husserlian version of the *Umwelt*) as well as their inner worlds (the *Innenwelt*). These are the external worlds of complete alienation and the negotiated world of a subject bound to inexplicable forces (fate and the unconscious). Between these external worlds and the intimate inner world lies the utterance of *wolf* and the coin/dream. These complex signifiers do not inhabit either world order, liminally positioned as neither one nor the other, they force confrontation with existence, but not resolution. In this way even though they are ostensibly played out in the Symbolic, their true capacity is in the Imaginary and its connection to the self. The proper Being of each character and Robert has collapsed, with these signifiers allowing for a disturbed space within the Symbolic. Yet because they are incapable of absorption, they always retain a disruptive capacity. (A disruption, it should be noted, made forceful through its intimacy and invested in anxiety.) *Wolf* and the coin/dream are located in a space of transition and are inextricably tied to flesh and its experience as it "breaks forth into things and transcends itself in them" (Merleau-Ponty 1962: 303). This is in part due to their overdetermined nature; simply put, they are invested with meaning to a degree where they test the limits of language, and language's desire to hold and have fixed and even shared meaning.[12]

Owness, Nature, and the Sensually Seen Body

Such a statement is self-evident with the *wolf* cry, but can the same be said of the fate invested coin and the closing dream? It is certainly true that, in terms of the narrative, *wolf*, coin, and dream are deeply complex, open-ended signifiers. The coin and dream are relation-formation aspects, bridging the external to the internal, which is also how Lefort speaks of her (transferential) relations with Robert, and, in another case history, Nadia. Nadia and Lefort's relationship forms through exchange gifts of food (see Lefort 1994 "Nadia or the Mirror."[13] The coin and dream work as a epistemic extension of this trope, marking relationships (the unasked for dream and the unwanted coin toss). As wild meaning, however, the coin and

---

[12] Note Kristeva's devising of the *sémiotique* as the disruptive force of language.

[13] Lefort's work with Nadia is interesting in this regard because it works from what she calls the initial transitive relations with the Other to a psychical version of exchange, manifested in these objects (mostly of food). Lefort postulates that Nadia's psychical breakdowns have to be negotiated through connections with the Real and the body of the Other (in this analytic moment it is Lefort's body as Other). See Lefort, particularly section 6, "The Pre-Specular: Ambivalence," where she also talks about anxiety, the body, and otherness.

dream's existence is not a resolving point of connection and bonding; rather it is the impossibility of their coexistence, opening up differences rather than confirming and establishing meanings. Hence, the cry of *wolf* and the coin/dream are sensuous (in a phenomenological manner), foregrounding resistance over resolution, while at the same time proffering access to a closed-off inner world. The capacity to create these signifiers, their *praktognostic* performance, originates in wild meaning. At least part of our fascination with such signifiers is their capacity to reveal, or remind us of, that all too often hidden world of otherness, the "canvas [that] underlies the picture and makes it appear unsubstantial" as Merleau-Ponty put it (1962: 293). This is to reconfigure the "unnatural" Chigurh as part of the dreamscape of the desert and the threatening game of chance, and to remind us of the dream's capacity to exist as natural and unnatural at the same time. This underlying, perhaps quasi-noumenal, existence of the natural world speaks to a Western frame of consciousness. (Kant's writings of the non-European world in terms of wildness is an issue that will be returned to shortly.) But first let us address one more aspect of flesh in and of wild meaning, this time from an issue raised by Husserl.

Husserl, in speaking of intertwining regions, declares: "the phenomenology of material nature holds a pre-eminent position" (1931: §152), this is the "commonness of Nature" as he puts it in the *Cartesian Meditations* (1950: §55). It is important to recall Husserl's continually working through of the concept of the natural attitude, the issue of phenomenology and the natural sciences, and Nature as and in the world, and as a construct. We should not rest too easy, or read too quickly, when the word "Nature" appears in such contexts. However, rather than this being some sort of *originaliter* (to employ Husserl's term) or "base" reference point from which to extend a sense of certainty and consistency, Husserl goes on to posit that all types of realities "brings with it its own constitutive phenomenology" (§152) and that the task of phenomenology is to examine conscious formations as they alter and function in these varying "realities." (This is somewhat taken up in the discussions on phantasy, notably cinema here, and space in Chapters 3 and 4.) This, in turn, links back to a much earlier discussion on reality, where he notes that "no domain of reality is isolated" (1931: §51). This is clearly a complex issue for phenomenology, with its requirements of reduction and bracketing (how does one form a bracket around regions that are so necessarily and fundamentally intertwined?) particularly in terms of the negotiations of the natural attitude. Similarly, the pre-eminent region of material nature would seem to suggest that all regions somehow track back to this—an issue Husserl was acutely aware of. Husserl's answer lies in the idea of phenomenologically directed consciousness: "The existence of what is natural *cannot* condition the existence of consciousness since it arises as the correlate of consciousness" (1931: §152). Bell's return to the dream suggests as close as possible a return to an isolated (i.e., bracketed) reality, a region if not beyond then at least removed from the social order and correlated by and through his consciousness. This correlate of consciousness is what is denied to Bell in the dream's resistance to meaning. Similarly, the commonness of Nature is revealed in its separated regionalities through Carla Jean's threatened flesh. That is, her motility of flesh (in its movements in and out of sensuousness) becomes the site where Nature's regions are distinguished (as haven, retreat, falsehood, crisis, death, and loss). This is how the flesh of the coin and the dream mark these regions as impossible to collapse into one, for it remains forever in transition between the dividing worlds of the internal and external. Similarly, Robert's corporeal manifestation through the *wolf* utterances and Lefort's maternal body show these states of Nature as correlates of consciousness and transitivity.

Let us note one further aspect on the phenomenology of the body before taking up the issue of wildness and the sublime. The "sensuously seen body" as Husserl puts it (1950: §55) is determined through apperception. That is, we do not just see the body of the other, we also enact appresentations of it. Through this we come to form identifications with the other's body. These identification-forming appresentations, Husserl argues, operate as co-perceptions, that is, the fusion between actual perceptions and appresentations so that they function simultaneously. There is something of psychoanalysis' concepts of (Kleinian) identification and (Freudian) transference, not simply because of the processes toward the formation of ego-identification, but because of the *intentionality* involved. This is a complex alignment, in part because there is neither commonality nor resolution in psychoanalysis regarding these terms. However, the issue of a psychoanalytic version of appresentation in terms of identification and transference holds intrigue. Similarly, a phenomenological intentionality read in terms of say Klein's projective identification has considerable potential. This would be the intentionality of intense aggression and intent to harm,[14] and as such would be the appresentation of the other body accordingly. Cinema invites such projective identificatory appresentations, for it is an integral part of the spectator's engagement with the narrative and its characters. However, this is not some version of character identification by the spectator; the directed consciousness of the spectator "crosses" regions (from perception to re-presentation, i.e., phantasy and its cinematic variants) and appresents/identifies on at least two levels. First, there are the co-perceptions of perception and appresentation in its simultaneous moments (how we "see" the body in a film and how we appresent it); second, how these appresentations form a relational

---

[14]Klein argues that projective identification "establishes a prototype of an aggressive object-relation" (Klein 1975: 8). The capacity for good object relations, and therefore "positive" identification, lies elsewhere; see her discussion in "The Emotional Life of the Infant" (1975).

context of intentionality and identification. In other words, how we move from the other's sensuously seen body to what Husserl describes as "one psychophysical reality" (1950: §55; §43)[15] where the body and psyche of the other become accessible. In a film such as *No Country for Old Men* the sensuously seen body performs at this level of originally inaccessible, that is, as flesh. This body-as-flesh, almost categorical in its cinematic manifestations, is seen as isolated and removed, located in the interstitial spaces of "in between," its otherness as well as its very existence (as Being) bound up to anxiety and trauma.

This is cinema's capacity to grasp and link, both phenomenologically and psychoanalytically speaking, the other's body and establish a relational context for the psychophysical. This is also how cinema can, even as phantasy constructed through and within intentionality, facilitate the experiential devising of the Objective (i.e., actual and external) world of people and culture. This is also why the appresentation of the sensuously seen body of cinema can participate in what Husserl describes as "the Objective world [that] has existence by virtue of a harmonious confirmation of the apperceptive constitution" (1950: §55; see also §43 for comments on syntheses and "harmonious verification"). Thus, the harmonious confirmation of the re-presented world of a film (or dream, and other versions of phantasy), no matter how disturbing, is formed and held in a single psychophysical reality by the spectator's (and this must also include a wider cultural sense of the spectating position) appresentations.[16] That we first encounter the body of the other and are excluded from the psychical is part of the negotiated processes of appresentation. This is the *ego's* (in both the phenomenological and psychoanalytic versions, even with the differing conceptual frames withstanding) identification of the self's own environment (one's own corporeality, fleshness, surroundings of objects, and thingness) as distinct from all others.[17] The encounter with the other's sensuously seen body, with its attendant owness of environment, is where the appresentational processes take place. Cinema's power resides in its capacity

---

[15]The Fifth Meditation in *Cartesian Meditations* commences with a critique of phenomenology as solipsism and of the distinction between *solus ipse* and the transcendental ego. Husserl is laying down the issues of "monadological intersubjectivity" (§42) which is why so much of this section focuses on the self and Other, and social interrelations. The idea of the psychophysical, then, relates to this issue of "in the world" and our connections to others. I refer the reader to the excellent ten-point summary of Husserl's arguments in favour of monadic intersubjectivity in the *Nachlass* volumes of Hua XIII, XIV, XV in Ruthrof (2021: 73ff.).

[16]Thus, when I watch the opening scene of *LaLa Land* this "sphere transcends my owness" (Husserl 1950: §55) and I appresent these bodies (and cinematography, for this is very much the "camera" as flesh as well) with their exuberant and joyous flow, even though it directly contradicts all my experiences of driving on a highway into Los Angeles.

[17]In this sense of *owness* we can find Merleau-Ponty's inhabitations of space as well as Husserl's regionalization of space and the acts of consciousness in their transgressions.

to re-present the sensuously seen body and the owness of environments in ways that would not normally be possible. This owness of environments is perceived through different versions of the body, for example: the owness of a New York neighborhood, divided by racial tensions displayed on the ethnicity of the body (*Do the Right Thing*); the (White, female) mediated owness of a desert (*Walkabout* Nicholas Roeg, 1971); the disputed owness of parallel worlds, merging reality and the dream-like (perhaps all cinema, but one example to suffice *Celine and Julie Go Boating* Jacques Rivette, 1974). What is also revealed through all these examples is cinema's capacity to show contested owness of environments. The neighborhood in *Do the Right Thing* is demarcated into spaces which become the contested owness of race, none so more powerful constructed as the picture-covered wall in Sal's pizzeria[18]; the Australian desert landscape in *Walkabout* is a contested environment of alienation (white), home as reinscribed *aphanisis* (Indigenous), devolving to death. In these we see a cinematic inflection of the superimposed secondary stratum of the experiential phenomenon (see Husserl 1950: §55), which is laid onto the primary stratum (Objective Nature) in our experiencing of the other. Cinema, as re-presentation, must offer a tertiary stratum of the experiential in this regard, and a version of this can now be taken up.

Wildness and the Corporeal Sublime

There is another side to Husserl's "harmonious confirmation of the apperceptive constitution," where disturbances are so forceful that the apperceptive processes are challenged and perhaps even negated. This is wildness as a version of the sublime, which necessarily contains a compulsive desire that is contradicted by the (equally powerful) wish to turn away. These are the moments where composed (i.e., in all senses of such a word—constructed, made up of, unified, and in control) intentionality collides with a certain resistance to that stance. One of the ways this takes place is through the intimacy of intentionality merging with the anxious moment. This is the divergent wildness, compelling in its essence, disturbing the harmonious confirmation. This can be worked through with some cinematic examples, beginning with the idea of passionate abnormalities.

Husserl of course anticipates the impossibility that all appresentations, all appresented strata of one's experience being layered onto the other (beginning with the body) to form a shared givenness, can perform in this sense of harmony. His answer rests on a number of qualifying (but not negating

---

[18]This is the wall populated with images of Italian-Americans, of which Buggin Out (Giancarlo Esposito) asks Sal why there "ain't no brothers on the wall."

or even necessarily conditional) propositions, notably: (1) That there are "abnormalities" which can problematize owness, and its relational contexts, with the other; (2) however, such abnormalities need to be recognized as such, and this takes place by their position outside of the determining, apperceptive order (this is the "intrinsically antecedent normality" (1950: §55)); (3) the externality of such abnormalities is necessarily recognized through phenomenological processes, and as such allows for a preservation of the Objective world (which exists in its representational modes precisely because of these harmonious confirmations); (4) this situation allows for consistency and continuation, and deals with the abnormalities through "corrections"; (5) abnormalities are also accommodated through the "recasting of apperceptions" and/or the "constitution of new unities" (1950: §55). It is important to recall that this whole notion of harmonious apperceptions and abnormalities is derived from Husserl's need to address the issue of self and other, notably commencing with the corporeal. Therefore, the processes involved, for Husserl, move from a position of centrality and certainty, to the need to adjust through the experiential. One of the positions we are working toward here is the ways in which cinema is located as an abnormality.

This section began with the idea that there is a tertiary stratum at the level of the cinematic (i.e., re-presentational), which is distinguished from the secondary stratum (the experiential phenomenon). How such a distinction might occur needs further elaboration, and this can emerge within these qualifying conditions and contexts. Husserl does offer a further condition when he states that " . . . appearance-systems are by no means always absolutely identical and that whole strata (although not all strata) can differ" (1950: §55; see also 1998: §24 for Husserl's discussion on space and perception). The significance here is that because not all strata can differ, apperception must be attached, in some ways, to a relatively stable environment.[19] This makes sense; cinema as an appearance-system continually negates, denies, as well as constructs and preserves apperceptive processes. The spectator adjusts accordingly (quasi-judgements are a perfect example of this), preserving the strata that contain the apperceptive continuity and disregarding the others. The re-presentational (image-consciousness) qualifiers of cinemaness means that the spectator necessarily enters into the

---

[19]In comparison, the psychoanalytic situation is unique in this regard, but the principle remains. The utterance of the psychotic (Judge Schreber is an excellent example because his memoirs are so detailed and internally consistent; Lefort's (1988) comparative analysis with the wolf-child, Robert, is a further demonstration of this complex language system) represents an extreme version of an appearance-system on the verge of collapse because of the multiple layers of strata differentials. In a manner, these differences in the apperceptive strata form the core business of psychoanalysis. The issue thus becomes the apperceptive reconceived through, for example, the hysteric, neurotic, psychotic, as well as the everyday pathologies.

film with such caveats and a preexisting proclivity for abandoning certain strata. This is the domain of cinema as a tertiary stratum, requiring specific and somewhat unique positions for its appresentational processes. This commitment to apperceptive continuity is another of the components of intimacy. Indeed, as with all relationships of intimacy, there is a commitment, a sense that this is something to be meaningful toward.

Passionate Abnormalities

When Husserl states that abnormalities need to be "constituted as such," he is tacitly articulating a phenomenological strategy for the recognition of such an attribute; however, he does not actually elaborate to any great extent how this is supposed to take place. It can be deduced that an abnormality is revealed precisely through this difference (and even abandonment) of strata in the appearance-systems. This suggests that we might become aware of this *during* the apperceptive processes or that we enter into a relational context with the other Ego *already aware* that this might take place and adjust in anticipation. In this way the very concept/status of the abnormal must be regarded as of crucial significance. Herein lies the issue, for Husserl seems at ease with the very notion of the abnormal standing as a given, how the determining and *originaliter* Ego establishes its abnormalness. However, how do we proceed when the determining and *originaliter* Ego must be an idealized form, far from "normal" in itself? Positions of gender, sexual orientation, ethnicity, and so on, thus become either the determining and *originaliter* Ego or the abnormal, depending on the harmonious appresentational starting point that is taken up. In cinematic terms this operates in at least three ways: the film's re-presentational world order and its construction of determining and *originaliter* Ego(s); the spectator's determining and *originaliter* Ego; the vast, perhaps immeasurable, number of heterogeneous otherness of spectating positions that lie in potential as determining and *originaliter* Ego(s). Husserl does note a further variant on such apperceptive differences when he speaks of the appresented other Ego as not actually being the same as the owness Ego because it perceives from another space and time; he/she appresents from "over-there." (In passing, this concept of the "over-there" status is something that underpins much of Merleau-Ponty's *Phenomenology of Perception*). For psychoanalysis, there is an additional complexity because the over-thereness can also be internal. The unconscious is an over-there positionality for the conscious, for example. Similarly, the ego and id have a relationship of over-thereness, and in this case over-thereness necessarily includes a temporality. Freud argues that the ego acquires time from the perceptual system, organizing, categorizing, and synthesizing material accordingly and subsequently creating a unified version (of the self, the external world, events, and so on);

the id lacks all such conceptualizations of time (see, e.g., *SE XXII*, "The Dissection of the Psychical Personality"). The id's lack of temporality and the ego's determinations through it, means that each is an over-there for the other.

This over-there positionality is a fundamental aspect of cinema for it is where we find both intimacy, that is, a film's capacity to enable us to see from over-there, and anxiety, that is, the disruptive potential of seeing from over-there. Over-thereness is part of the apperceptive continuity, linked as they are through formations of intimacy. We, as spectators, can only achieve such acts of continuity by engaging in the gaps (another version of the abyss) that emerge in over-thereness. Furthermore, cinema creates methods to reduce or emphasize over-thereness, embedding anxiety (as distance) and intimacy (as closeness) accordingly. Once this over-there positionality is recognized and/or adopted the apperceptive processes (how we perceive objects, spaces, times, events, things in their thingness) are no longer seen as the presumptive sameness. Of course, this does not always take place, and quite often a film's confirming apperceptive (harmonious) processes operate as if they are not over-there. Propaganda, for example, relies on closing the over-thereness of its ideological base. In this regard, the abnormal becomes the site of extraordinary potential to allow the appresented other *ego* to disrupt our determining and *originaliter* Ego and challenge interpretative systems.

This disruptive potential can be seen as the "corrections" to the apperceptions and their assumptive values. Similarly, this is also the "recasting of apperceptions" and/or the "constitution of new unities." This is complex material, so let us rework the ideas through the cinematic. As has been noted earlier, at one level the phenomenological concepts being discussed can be utilized to interpret the large-scale operations of spectatorship, cinema's capacity to disrupt, and the positionalities of self and other. The cinematic variants of the recasting of apperceptions caused through the differing strata of apperceptive processes takes place when our intimate relationship(s) with the film forms. As a spectator, we are necessarily placed in the over-there position (willingly or otherwise, adoptive or adaptive, compliant or resistant, knowingly or in innocence, demanded of or seduced). This is a dynamic system and so the film and/or spectator can, and often do, formulate new unities that emerge from the appresented other (cinematic) *ego*.

The crucial and recurring dynamic in all these processes is, of course, apperception. Recall that Husserl commences his discussion at this position of a sense of denied or restricted access to the other (initially as the body). This is fundamentally about connectivity and "communalization," about how "same" and "other" can be understood within and for each other; it is the question of "how I can constitute in myself another Ego or, more radically, how I can constitute in my monad another monad, and can experience what is constituted in me as nevertheless other than me" (1950: §55).[20] The inflection here is that cinema provides this capacity of the constitution of the other monad and the experience of the other than me. For this is the formation and actualization of our intimate relationship with a film. Read in this way, cinema becomes nothing less than a phenomenological apparatus, allowing the connections to formulate and configure in continually evolving fashions.

The radical constitution of one's monad accommodating the monad of the Other is itself a phenomenological process; it is also seen here as the intimate work of cinema. From such intimacies flows the anxieties of the monad's "unity." Whenever we watch a film, we willingly give in to such (adaptive) anxieties, some with their oh-so-faint shudderings, others with their bracing invigilating crises. Even in the near impossible moments when the appresented other *ego* has such sensuous sameness to our *ego's* owness, there will be anxiety. Even in those rarest of moments when a film establishes (within itself or within a larger context of culture, history, ideology, biopolitics) an appresentational system of such normalizing propensity, the spectator is required to work to keep the unity as harmonious as possible. For any slippage in this regard leads invariably to the over-there, so well hidden in these cases, being revealed. It is in these extreme versions (think Leni Riefenstahl *Triumph of the Will* (1935) or D.W. Griffith *Birth of a Nation* (1915)) that the forceful nature of appresentations can be at its darkest. Or what of certain films that meticulously devise multiple positionalities which harbor an over-thereness that is problematic (e.g., prioritized scopophilia) outside the level of its own resistances? One such example is *La Belle Noiseuse* (Jacques Rivette 1991), with the sensuously seen body positioned in its over-thereness as the artistic act/struggle (the constant workings of the (male) hand in sketching) and the other sensuously seen body as pure form (the naked (female) body-as-flesh under constant examination).

Beyond the more overt cases, how might this operation and function of intimacy in and through appresentation be simultaneously invited and challenged? Here we have the passionate abnormalities that demand recastings of apperceptions and the constitution of new unities precisely because they are foregrounded in the film. It is possible to think of this as a cinematic category, internally defined by this intimate invite and anxious-laden challenges. Let us begin with an example that illustrates a key idea of sublime flesh, Claire Denis's *Trouble Every Day* (2001).[21] This is a film

---

[20]Husserl explicates the idea of separation and unity in terms of temporality, notably *omnitemporality*. For the issues at hand, this links to the discussions on time in Chapter 2.
[21]*Trouble Every Day* explores a number of Denis's recurring motifs, particularly the intersection of sex, violence, and gender politics. Shane Brown (Vincent Gallo) pursues his obsessive desire for Coré (Béatrice Dalle) and returns to Paris to look for her. Coré, now married to neuroscientist Léo Semenau (Alex Descas), is locked in a house by Semenau, escaping to have

that lends itself perhaps far too easily to a conversation about the anxious body's sublimity, so it will be necessary to offer some divergent possibilities to test the critical issues. The primary concern is how sublime flesh evokes the recasting of apperceptions, of how the sensuously extreme seen body simultaneously provides an attraction and radical challenge to an accommodation of the Other's monad. This is why the body in a film such as *Trouble Every Day* produces sublime flesh, whereas the hyper-sexualized body in, for example, pornography, is not always capable of doing so. The pornographic requires its appresented objects be met as unending, unrequited, but of momentary, satisfaction; it is resolutely clear on its constructions of phenomenological psychophysical realities, even within its sub-cultural and sub-textual domains (fetishisms e.g., particularly in Lacan's sense of fetish as the conditioning situation where desire sustains itself (e.g., 2017: 103)). It invests its entirety in the superimposed second strata (the experiencing of someone else) without extending beyond that. Indeed, this body, this fleshification that overdetermines all relations, cannot extend beyond, for in doing so it becomes something else. The pornographic body's impossibility (its insatiability, vociferous corporeality that can perform immediately, and absolute concupiscence) is accepted, and in being as such exists in opposition to the body as-is. Finally, it agitates to collapse the over-thereness of the other's body, because to work as a form of textual desire it must create false intimacies, and knowingly (i.e., self-reflexively) does so. Somewhat ironically, the reflexive hyper-sexualized body does have the capacity to devise a different order of intimacy, one that might be termed a quasi-intimacy, based entirely on mimicry and simulacra. What the hyper-sexualized pornographic body and other versions of sublime bodies share is a foregrounding of anxiety in its corporeal Beingness as form(s). How such anxieties develop and are sustained (at the level of the individual, through the systemic controlling super-ego, to the institutionalized codes of morality) is of less relevance here than it is to note such anxious states of being. When the body-as-flesh finds itself in such states it reveals what Lacan describes as the site of anxiety and desire: "Anxiety is thus an intermediary term between *jouissance* and desire in so far as desire is constituted and founded upon the anxiety phase" (2017: 175). Thus, Lacan asserts, anxiety is located in the space between desire and *jouissance*; which is also where sublime flesh is formulated. Such a situation raises the vexatious question of what constitutes sublime flesh.

---

sex, and then murder men. These murders are performed as her bites become increasingly violent; we witness the transition from the sexual, erotic bite to the disturbingly savage. This is paralleled in the relationships between the main characters (particularly as Brown comes to perform these same acts of hyper-sexualized wildness after Coré's death).

Coré (Béatrice Dalle) provides one such example of sublime flesh, but not at the literal level as first may appear. The excess of libidinal anxieties, manifested through ravenous violence and destructive sexuality, provides the apparent, overt versions of sublime flesh. Examples of this include: fluid's abandonment of, or exceeding, its "containers" (the body, skin, medical containers, purity against contamination); re-ascribed orality from sexuality to violence (cannibalism); aggressiveness aligned with projective identification (thus corporeally dismantling the distinction between self and other). However, let us recall some of Edmund Burke and Kant's definitional aspects of the sublime to collocate the idea of sublime flesh in a different sensibility.

It is worth recalling two of Burke's fundamental aspects of the sublime, its differences from the beautiful, and how the body can be read in such terms. The first relates to the terror and overpowering emotion: "Whatever is fitted in any sort to excite the ideas of pain and danger, that is to say, whatever is in any sort terrible, or is conversant about terrible objects, or operates in a manner analogous to terror, is a source of the sublime; that is, it is productive of the strongest emotion which the mind is capable of feeling. I say the strongest emotion, because I am satisfied the ideas of pain are much more powerful than those which enter on the part of pleasure" (Burke 1991: 29). The second aspect is his ideas on smooth and rough bodies as beautiful and sublime respectively:

> If it appears that smoothness is a principal cause of pleasure to the touch, taste, smell, and hearing, it will be easily admitted a constituent of visual beauty; especially as we have before shown, that this quality is found almost without exception in all bodies that are by general consent held beautiful. There can be no doubt that bodies which are rough and angular, rouse and vellicate the organs of feeling, causing a sense of pain, which consists in the violent tension or contraction of the muscular fibres. (Burke 1991: 36)

Once more, this is in keeping with Coré and her corporeal presence in the film. Denis is a filmmaker who understands that the body on screen will have a propensity toward both these aspects of eliciting strong emotions and rousing and vellicating feeling; it is a core function of flesh in her cinema. The body is foregrounded and configured in such a manner that it announces itself as a version of "thereness-for-me," Husserl's transcendental theory of experiencing someone else and, consequently, of the Objective world (1950: §43). The crucial shift here is from this thereness-for-me to a community of participants (a thereness-for-everyone who exists in that cultural order). Cinema, as a cultural object, is particularly invested in such a duality of thereness-for-me/for-everyone, even if the thereness-for-everyone is very much an artifice peddling an impossible political mimicry of sameness and unity. Let us be clear: there can be no thereness-for-everyone, but social institutions (such as cinema) can operate as if they are precisely that—a shared relevancy that "speaks" for, and interpolates, all; thereness-for-everyone and thereness-for-me are political constructions. What is at hand here, then, is how sublime flesh functions at the level of performative intimacy as a cultural object (thereness-for-everyone) while "simultaneously" appearing as a thereness-for-me. The sublimity of this intimacy emerges from the terror of the overpowering emotions (notably a form of extreme anxiety) and the vellicating body.

The merging of cinema, phenomenology, and psychoanalysis that presents itself here rests in this interchange between thereness-for-me at the level of internalized intimacy, and how it is played out in the cultural object(s) of thereness-for-everyone. In other words, sublime flesh relies on a double layering of the external (the cinematic and the community of cultural objects) and internal (the affective and *ego* formations and confirmations) which is an experiencing of someone else intimately, as well as someone else's intimacy. It can be noted here that Stein's understanding of empathy aligns with certain aspects of intimacy as it is being explored here. Two aspects will serve as examples of this. The first is when Stein argues that what she terms the "foreign living body" comes into an empathetic relationship with us in a "primordial givenness in bodily perception of our own fields of sensation" (1989: 57), leading to a distinction between this foreign living body and all others. Effectively, this empathetic relationship produces the "seen" other body as living, giving it what Stein calls "con-primordiality" (57). Simply put, Stein sees all of our own feelings as primordial—they exist as our fundamental, present experiences. Others (as bodies) acquire a similar status, the con-primordiality, through the empathetic relations. When we watch a film, the screen is filled with bodies, of which we may acquire a version of empathy; the vast otherness of bodies is reduced to a few with this con-primordiality. For Stein this is empathy, for the issues here it is one of the aspects of intimacy. The second aspect addresses the issue of the screened body as distinct from the living body before us. Stein distinguishes between the feelings for the other (body, person) and feelings experienced in representations. Her example is reading, specifically "the enamored schoolboy [who] thinks he feels Romeo's passion" (32). This passion, these feelings, for Stein, are ephemeral and lack what she calls "primordial value" and are therefore absent of genuineness. For this reason, we can locate empathy as only a component or inflection of intimacy; intimacy is substantively more than the experienced feelings (of passion, disgust, fear, love . . .) and yet are integral to this Steinian con-primordiality and the formations of relations with the foreign living body. For this reason, a key defining attribute of sublime flesh is that it tends (but is not universally bound) to the transformation of this intimacy into a version of extimacy. Psychoanalysis can help us think through this issue from a different perspective.

The first, classical psychoanalytic, reading of Coré is her regressive behavior to the first stage of sexuality, that is the oral or cannibalistic. Just as with the Wolf Man, Coré has returned to the oral stage because of disturbances: "In this phase the sexual aim could only be cannibalism—devouring . . . It appears, moreover, that there is an anxiety belonging to this phase . . . which manifests itself as a fear of death" (Freud *SE XVII*: 147–8). Coré sexual acts of devouring are a sublime terror as she positions all other bodies as there-for-me to be consumed; whereas her acts produce these anxieties of death not within herself (she is presented as ecstatic in her acts, roused and filled with intense vellications), but within the other characters, and presumably the spectator. Within these devouring formations of subjectivity, we can note two comments from Lacan on sexuality and the unconscious. Lacan articulates the relationship as follows: "the unconscious as a remanence of that archaic junction between thought and sexual reality" and "sexuality is the reality of the unconscious" (Lacan 1986: 152). These two conceptualizations are embodied in the excessive abnormalities of Coré's acts. As such her devouring body becomes sublime flesh in the externalizing (thereness-for-everyone) of unconscious realities (thereness-for-herself). That the representational field of Coré's body is dominated by carnality, including fluids of blood, saliva, and mucus, locates it at the archaic junction of the unconscious' remanence. The levels of excess are, subsequently, the reality of the unconscious rendered in the sexual; Coré's "kiss" becomes the cannibalistic as the sexual (in its corporeal performativity) which becomes the unrestrained devouring of the other's flesh. Her libidinalized flesh is inscribed with a version of destructive desire, becoming an extreme version of Merleau-Ponty's erotic perception which is "not a *cogitation* aimed at a *cogitatum*," located in the actions of an "erotic comprehension not of the order of understanding" (1962: 157).

Such a reading reaches a certain point of analysis, yielding some satisfaction, and yet to push forward we can consider phenomenology's idea of owness as a "peculiar kind of *epoché*" (Husserl 1950: §44) within the context of seeing oneself and the *objet petit a*. Coré's devouring acts, now located within the archaic junction, are sublime in their compelling attractiveness (i.e., they attract the spectator's gaze in an inescapable manner, the look almost too much to bear). The spectator should turn away, recoil in horror, after all this is corporeal roughness (its vellicating urgencies) at its most anarchic, and yet as with all such sublime images/representations we continue to gaze. The challenge is how the sublime can sustain this attraction of the gaze within the thereness-for-me and thereness-for-everyone; the fact that it can must be seen as part of the definitional aspect of the sublime, and hence sublime flesh. As such it acquires the con-primordiality that binds us, the spectator, to the image in intimacy. One possibility is to see this attraction as a quasi-

IMAGE 24 *From* Trouble Every Day.

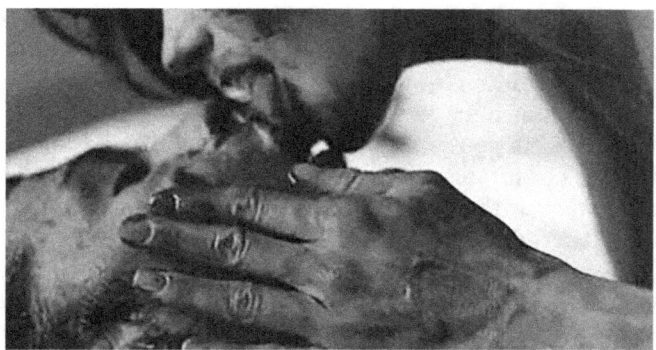

IMAGE 25 *From* Trouble Every Day.

regression, a version of cinema's phantasy image-consciousness allowing the spectator (and cultural community) to revisit the archaic junction and the earliest sexual stage of orality. However, a more compelling reading may lay in the function of the *objet petit a* and the owness formed through the peculiar *epoché*. This requires further locating of these terms.

Lacan, in positioning the *objet petit a* in terms of transference, states: "I love you, but, because inexplicably I love in you something more than you—the *objet petit a*—I mutilate you" (1986: 268). Lacan explicates further, aligning this psychical act with orality and mutilation, which is all quite Kleinian in a way. (Lefort's case notes on Nadia, referred to earlier, demonstrate this same relationship of transference to and through orality.) At the representational level, this is Coré's oral drive. The men she consumes (sexually and cannibalistically) are "loved" (i.e., occupy what Lacan terms the nodal points of desire and what is termed here as the sexualized composing Nothing) but what is really wanted by her, and consequently the intimate spectator, is the *objet petit a*—the something that is more than you/them, leading inevitably to "mutilation." It is located deep within these others, which is why Coré quite literally digs into their flesh in the attempts to find it; it is also formed within the unrestricted unconscious (no repression here!), allowing for sexuality to be seen as her "reality."[22] Thus, "mutilation" here is not the represented, but the conditional for intimacy and anxiety in the spectator. How might we read this *objet petit a* in terms of the peculiar owness? Clearly, the *a* (otherness) posits it within the phenomenologically determined other, and therefore outside the transcendental Ego. Similarly, it cannot be seen as part of Husserl's Objective Nature or the external world, because it is derived from, and originate in, the self/ego. For psychoanalysis, it is an otherness constructed out of the most intimate part of the self, that is, the unconscious. Perhaps an answer lies in a marginal note made by Husserl (mostly to himself, but then passes into the domain of the reader) in *Cartesian Meditations*: "The question after all concerns, not others, but the manner in which the Ego . . . constitutes within itself the distinction between Ego and Other Ego—a difference, however, that presents itself first of all in the phenomenon, 'world' . . . " (1950: §44 note 1) (translation modified). Lacan's "in you, something more than you" is of this same order of how the ego "constitutes within itself" distinctions. This is an absolutely fundamental issue for the analytic experience, for it engages with how self and other are determined.

Lacan's utterance (made within the context of transference, so for psychoanalysis one of the foregrounded positions of subject relations and formations) begins with "I love you," hence self and other acknowledged in the most compelling of psychical (intimate) connections. However, this "I love you" can be read as a parallel to Husserl's footnote when he speaks of the peculiar *epoché* related to owness because even though it appears to be about others, it is really about the constitution of distinctions *within* the self. These objects of the little otherness are the negotiating objects of the distinctions within the self; hence their foreignness, like *extimacy*, is a contrivance, a peculiar owness. Transference begins with the self, and all determining aspects, no matter how far they stretch out from this point of origin, are linked back to the self. The objects of otherness found in this process (and countertransference must also be included here), for all their alterity, are really about the self and its relationships to the external world.

---

[22]Another film that explores the idea of the devouring female, within a similar fairy tale structure of *Trouble Every Day*, is *La Bête* (Walerian Borowczyk 1975).

Before continuing with this line, a brief returning note should be made of sublime flesh, intimacy, and empathy. As has been noted elsewhere here, intimacy and empathy have a deeply complex relationship; for all their common points, there are a multiplicity of differences. Flesh, intimacy, and empathy find their common points in the sensuous body, for this is the starting point of apperception, the shaping of intentionalities, the connecting materiality of *Abschattung* (shading) as experiential, and the attending to a considerable portion of psychoanalysis' material. When the sublime is introduced into this mix, we find a certain barrier, a foregrounding of relationships that may in other conditions and circumstances be hidden or repressed. For the sublime does not work in any easy way with empathy and can sometimes be resistant to its formation. We may wish to go so far as to suggest that sublime's resistance to empathy is part of its challenge to being represented. These are vellications that are not simply antithetical to empathy, for the sublime, by definition, must always contain within it the "compulsion to look" aspect. Instead what we witness in such moments is the Lacanian "mutilation" of the self through the desire to be connected to the material of the sublime.[23] The otherness of the body, positioned in and even as the sublime, forms in the peculiar owness, producing a pathological version of empathy. As noted earlier, Stein's version of empathy recognizes the external, foreign, otherness which we initially experience through that body (which, incidentally, anticipates much of Merleau-Ponty's later work on the body): "We have a primordial givenness in "bodily perception" of our own fields of sensation. Moreover, they are "co-given" in the outer perception of our physical body in that very peculiar way where what is not perceived can be there itself together with what is perceived. The other's fields of sensation are there for me in the same way. Thus, the foreign living body is "seen" as a living body. This kind of givenness, that we want to call "con-primordiality," confronts us in the perception of the thing" (Stein 1989: 57). Con-primordiality (the other's scope and range of sensations as they are given to us) must take on unique attributes when the seen living body of the other is rendered as sublime flesh. The holding of the "not perceived" with the perceived means that the appresentations of sublime flesh are experienced in a complex, internally conflictual, fashion, where the elements of con-primordiality are filled with terror and yet not rejected, are fearsome and yet all the more compelling for being such.[24] The sublimity, in all its terror, of the other's body-as-flesh comes to form its desirable nature

---

[23] This may seem contradictory to Kant's insistence that the sublime is unrepresentable. However, even given this there must always be a materiality of the sublime. See Kant *Critique of Judgement* and further discussion as follows.

[24] A further idea that could be devised here is to compare this resistance to resistance to Stein's assertion that empathy is essentially not a feeling of oneness. See, for example Stein 1989: 16. Similar struggles are contained within psychoanalysis' *Verneinung*, negation/denial.

in the con-primordial, a pathological empathy which is confronted within the self. This is different from, for example, the repulsive, the terrifying, and the abject, because they can be located "outside" the self/Ego. The body transformed into sublime flesh means that the "something more than you" (the *objet petit a*) actually becomes the "something more in me." The other key aspect to note here is that the sublime is not simply terror; there is a sensuousness to the sublime which necessarily transforms the terrifying to the desirable, the seductive, the wanted. The origins for this lie in the primordiality of our experiencing; that is, we sensuously experience from our own owness (which takes us full circle back to wild thinking).

Coré's body as a version of sublime flesh (very much in that gap between desire and *jouissance*) demonstrates how this con-primordiality is replicated at the level of cinema. There is nothing contradictory here, for even though the re-presentational (phantasy) aspect of the body in cinema adds the qualifier of "quasi" (i.e., the quasi-body producing, and operating within, quasi-con-primordiality, along with the earlier noted quasi-intimacy) it is still possible to speak of it in these terms. The idea of cinema's quasi-empathy has been discussed in an earlier chapter, so we can limit comments to function as an additional note here. When a film constructs the quasi-con-primordiality of its characters it does so within its own created world order (the Objective world of the film), drawing on other films (in an inter-textual fashion[25]) as well as other cultural objects and fields. Similarly, the spectator's appresentations of a character (as the other inscribed initially through the sensuously seen body) takes place within the world of the film and as an experience shaded (Husserl's *Abschattung ist Erlebenis*) through other cinematic, cultural, personal, and psychical experiences. These two forces of text and spectator can align, disagree, diverge, or complement one another. Thus, the "site" of all quasi-con-primordialities may or may not be a shared and uniform one (harmonious in a Husserlian sense). Our satisfaction may or may not be achieved through alignment of dissent, our pleasures gained through compliance or resistance, and so on. When either film or spectator constructs the quasi-con-primordiality as a version of sublime flesh these positionalities (these phenomenological presentifications or, as a variant, psychoanalytic considerations of representability) become all the more fraught and destabilizing. Their state is a far more anxious one. The nature of cinema is premised somewhat on these affective

---

[25]Inter-textuality is used here in the sense of Bakhtin's dialogism and transposition, and then Kristeva's interpretation and so beyond the mere referencing of other texts, and instead within a vast modality of textualities. As Kristeva puts it: "The term *inter-textual* denotes this transposition of one (or several) sign systems into another; but since this term has often been understood in the banal sense of 'study of sources,' we prefer the term *transposition* because it specifies that the new passage from one signifying system to another demands a new articulation of the thetic" (1984: 59–60).

negotiations and its history is constituted of such experiences. Our capacity or otherwise to experience quasi-con-primordialities of the other depends on the interplay between our own peculiar owness and the field(s) of the sensuously seen other, how receptive we are to the otherness (these *objet petit a*), including the cinematic techniques to encourage or discourage what amounts to transferentiality between spectator, culture, and texts. This is an important aspect in the construction of the space of spectatorship as a site of intentionality. We witness a willingness to bear the quasi-con-primordiality in films where our alliance with the character has been affirmed, but what of Coré's field of the devouring, anarchic sensuous? Is this too much to bear? Does it require a displacement "into" the sublime flesh that is a mutilating of the self?[26] This goes beyond the sense that an empathetic response requires context and explication; do we, for example, engage the quasi-con-primordiality of Travis Bickle in *Taxi Driver* (Martin Scorsese 1976) because there are intentional markers and textual urges toward certain forms of appresentation? We are not so far here from aligning the sublime with the space of the Real (see also Chapter 4), notably in these terms of the archaic junction; a junction where the sublime is to be located and the properness of the body will be challenged as a version of flesh.

The concept of pathological empathy as a product of the sublime (see earlier) returns us to some of Kant's principle distinctions between the beautiful and sublime. These include the following: (1) the sublime has boundlessness and is "lacking" in form ("The sublime, on the other hand, is to be found in the formless object, in so far as in it or by occasion of it *boundlessness* is represented") which in turn leads Kant to say that the beautiful produces satisfaction through quality, but the sublime's satisfaction is derived from quantifying (Kant 1951: 82). These interrelated qualities of boundlessness and formlessness are the basis of Kant's qualifier of the sublime as experience and leads him to speak of the quality of the mathematical sublime. Quantity forms the limitlessness of the sublime, being beyond the comprehension of the mind; (2) the sublime has "negative pleasure" ("the mind is not merely attracted by the object but is ever being alternately repelled, the satisfaction in the sublime does not so much involve a positive pleasure . . . which deserves to be called a negative pleasure" (1951: 83)); (3) the sublime has a unique position in terms of purpose. This is not a lack of purpose, but rather a resistance to purpose, a challenge to it: "that which excites in us, without any reasoning about it, but in the mere apprehension of it, the feeling of the sublime may appear, as regards its form, to violate purpose in respect to judgment, to be unsuited to our

---

[26]Further examples abound: Lars Von Trier's *Antichrist* (2009) and *Nymphomaniac* (2013); Catherine Breillat's *Anatomy of Hell* (2004); Pier Paolo Pasolini's *Salo* (1975) all demonstrate this vellicating site of text and spectator.

presentative faculty, and as it were to do violence to the imagination; and yet it is judged to be only the more sublime" (1951: 83).

Before continuing with this particular issue, this is an appropriate moment to note Kant's sublime as part of wild nature and some of the ways in which phenomenology has explored nature as an issue. There is a certain amount of fortuitousness in this for the discussion at hand, however it should be noted that there is no intent to conflate Kant's sublime with the (diverse) ways in which phenomenology positions nature; rather, the rendering of the body of Coré as sublime flesh will act as exemplars.[27] To recall, Kant states: "nature excites the idea of the sublime in its chaos or in its wildest and most irregular disorder and desolation" (1951: 84).[28] It is important to note that Kant does not separate nor merge "nature" and the "sublime," but under certain conditions we experience the sublime in and through nature. The examples at hand locate both Coré, and in quite different ways Chigurh, as wild flesh. Here is the flesh returned to wildness, Coré as the embodiment of chaos, and the wildest in its most "irregular disorder." Beyond this more literal reading, however, it is possible to interpret these bodies as flesh in other phenomenological and psychoanalytic ways. One such iteration is Husserl's assertion that nature needs to be bracketed off from the transcendental standpoint (see, e.g., *Ideas* "The Region of Pure Consciousness"[29]). This is, of course, part of the bracketing of the "natural attitude"; but perhaps more can be made of this if cinematic flesh is seen

---

[27]It is entirely for the sake of expediency and limitations of space that these bodies are used as examples. There is no reason why cinematic examples discussed elsewhere here, such as the bodies of the daughters in *Dogtooth*, the women in *The Favorite*, O'Brien in *The Tree of Life*, and so on, could not be included. As noted as follows, cinema's fleshification of the body creates a particular type of re-presentational domain.

[28]Kant, like Burke, seemed quite at ease producing highly specific comparisons and distinctions between the sublime and the beautiful, even when asserting that this takes place at the level of feeling. For example, "Tall oaks and lonely shadows in a sacred grove are sublime; flower beds, low hedges and trees trimmed in figures are beautiful. Night is sublime, day is beautiful . . . The sublime moves, the beautiful charms" (1960: 47). What sense, then, do we make of the highly tamed and formalized gardens, in all their evocations of disturbance and threat, in Resnais's *Last Year in Marienbad* or the constructed maze in *The Shining*? In this case we witness a version of sublime time, where memory and truth are contested. The concept of sublime time is beyond our direct concerns; the cinema of Christopher Nolan, David Lynch, and Malick would work within such a framing.

[29]Husserl elsewhere in *Ideas* notes a distinction between the "real (*realen*) world and of Nature" (1931: 21); the phenomenological bracketing off is somehow different for Nature than the real world. At another point, Husserl locates Nature as a condition of eidetical propositions that condition our understanding of them. See, for example, *Ideas* §6. Perhaps even more compelling, yet alas incomplete in its theorizing, is Appendix II of *The Crisis* "Idealization and the Science of Reality—the Mathematization of Nature" where we find notes on an ontology of nature "in itself," and the experiencing of nature as what Husserl terms a pure idea. Similarly, in Appendix III "The Attitude of Natural Science and the Attitude of Humanistic Science. Naturalism, Dualism, and Psychophysical Psychology," Husserl positions nature as "the realm of pure *res extensae*" (1997: 315). See Chapter 3 on space for further discussion of *res extensae*.

as the production of the determining bracketings, and sublime flesh (wild in this case) is simultaneously a recognition of this action, and a further requirement for its performance and performativity. Read in this manner, the body of Coré is subjected to a further bracketing because it is an iteration of wild, sublime, flesh. This is the phenomenological method of reduction, as consciousness brackets the real world (see the note earlier on the issue of empathy and oneness, via Stein), and nature, and elements within them, and further elements within them, and so on. In these terms, wild flesh, like wild meaning, operates differently and is appercepted and bracketed in different ways. For this reason alone, I find myself in disagreement with Dufrenne's humanistic assertions regarding nature.[30] Nature requires a unique attitude of the *epoché*. It is also worth recalling at this point Husserl's concept of consciousness as *Sinngebende*, literally "meaning-giving" (see *Ideas* §55); "nature" in these terms is highly mediated and occupies a unique position of meaning-giving and yet in itself is mediated as giving-meaning. Although it should be clarified that "unique" is used in this instance not to suggest this takes place only for "nature" and variants such as "natural"; the unique aspect to nature is tied directly to the notion of wild as it has been discussed. This suggests cinema's wildness, and something like its representational fields of nature, locate this *Sinngebende* in the analytic experience.

These three aspects of the sublime (i.e., boundlessness/formlessness, negative pleasure, and the violation of purpose) are found in pathological empathy. The question can rightly be posed as to whether such a constitution can be described as empathy at all. Does not the pathological nature delimit or disqualify the sensation, the experience, as empathy? It certainly would seem to challenge a Husserlian harmonious system of experience and the "constitution of the world [as] essentially involving a harmony of the monads" (1950: §49). But of course, Husserl does not intend this to be understood as a synthesizing process leading to a compliant and necessarily unifying situation. This is precisely why he speaks of "abnormalities" and the experience of the other as a "pseudo-organism, especially if there is something discordant about its behavior" (1950: §52) (translation modified). This is certainly in keeping with other conceptual frames mentioned here, notably Lacan's "in you, more than you" *objet petit a*, and Stein's con-primordiality of the foreign living body.

The actual questions that confront us here are not derived from the issues of the harmoniousness of experiencing the other, rather that cinema is in fact experienced not occasionally as a version of pathological empathy, but *entirely*

---

[30]For example: "Even before we control it, that is, before our industry creates a technological environment, the natural environment is in a certain sense human" (1966: 236); "man is not added to nature: it is nature which is human" (1966: 235). Within the crisis of climate change happening over the course of the twentieth and into the twenty-first centuries, the disjunctive relationship that "man" has to nature needs to be re-evaluated outside of Dufrenne's terms.

experienced as such. This is what is proposed here: that cinema requires of the spectator, and the spectator willingly (i.e., with intentionality) engages in, pathological empathy, which becomes the relational ground of intimacy. Furthermore, it is through a combined phenomenological and psychoanalytic methodology that such a positionality (i.e., positing, appresentations, intentionalities, the "in you something more than you," and, yes, even the unconscious) can be understood. The sublime, in these terms, becomes the foregrounded version of the travails and complications of being a spectator. For, mostly, cinema's seeming invitational stance (it ultimately can only invite within a range of positions) will negate (in the psychoanalytic sense of denial) sites of resistance to becoming a spectator. This transferential spectator is the required inclusion of monad formations, including the spectator's own(ness). As such, it requires something like pathological empathy or the sublime (or, by way of a further example, alienation along a Brechtian line) to elicit awareness of these processes. Read in this way, Coré's acts are foregrounded as the abnormal, provoking (possibly) pathological empathy, sustaining the sublime; and yet they are not of another order or type, but a variation on all acts, all versions of the other in the film, and indeed all films. The extimacy of the sublime is heightened in such re-representations, just as the qualities of the sublime heighten the sensations of extimacy.

What is being proposed here is that cinema itself is formed through iterations of con-primordialities which are necessarily bound up with the "abnormal," the discordant, and otherness. Depending on the critical framework adopted, different reasons are yielded to explain why there is such sophisticated disguising, negation, and subterfuge involved. Here we find Lacan's version of anxiety's signal and its relationship to the ego. (This interpretation runs against the "willing suspension of disbelief," for there is no capacity for "willingness" to take place, there is no choice or option, no moment for such a declaration. The agency of willingness does not exist, or at least very rarely.) For psychoanalysis, via Lacan, this is the extimacy of the hidden, the lure of transference (and the need for it to be denied); for Husserl it is the negotiation of the abnormal, once it has been acknowledged and apprehended; for Kierkegaard it is bound up with guilt and anxiety ("the individual gazes at guilt with something close to desire and yet fears it. Like the glance of the serpent, guilt has the power to fascinate" (2015: 126),[31] and so on. This indeed returns us to the issues and concepts that commenced this chapter—of wild ideas and non-positing consciousness (as a version of the spectating position), and wild perception as an act which has forgotten its status of intentionality.

---

[31]In a typical Kierkegaardian statement, he later goes on to say: "Guilt is a power that spreads itself everywhere and which, nevertheless, no one can understand in a deeper sense while it broods over human existence" (2015: 126). In some ways, guilt is Kierkegaard's sublime—a stance that does, covertly, find a place in later existentialist thought. This is taken up in the context of innocence elsewhere here, including the discussion of *Dogtooth* in Chapter 4.

6

The Desire to Not Be Protected

Breathless Desires of the Nightmare

There is a need to find some common analytic ground between phenomenology and psychoanalysis on the nature of the nightmare. First, this arrives with all the attendant problems of origins and explanatory functions (where does a nightmare come from?), intentionality (why does it exist? what purpose and function does it have?), and analysis (how do we make sense of the phenomena of the nightmare? how do we create an analytic approach to investigate it, particularly within the context of these other issues?). Second, the status of the nightmare presents complexity for the analytic issues at hand; at the very least this raises the issues of where the nightmare resides and what forms its materiality. Third, how do we map the nightmare and cinema (including cinema as part of the larger cultural manifestations of nightmare) as phenomenological and psychoanalytic texts and processes? What are their commonalities and differences, and why should we attempt to discuss them together? Finally, the nightmare is epistemically resistant, formulated at the level of the subject as well as the wider cultural domain, and divergent in its diachronics. Simply put, we all have our own unique and particular nightmares, just as different cultures have versions of shared nightmares; and these nightmares (and how they are manifested and understood) are unstable in time and across time.

The first question that presents itself, then, is "what is a nightmare?" and this immediately raises the issue of materiality/manifestation as distinct from experience. For we need to foreground the proposition that the nightmare has a duality, in that it is its materiality (phantasy, images, narratives) which is different from the experience (affect, acts of consciousness). The nightmare is the anxious state of rest; it is the psychical playing out of fears and terrors, and film's relational processes are the cultural manifestation of such affects. How these are represented will vary, and even if it seems there is a representational repository of the nightmare (a version of a lexicon of fears and disturbances), solidified over time and performing as a "shared" cultural usage/exchange, it is important to note that there is an inherent and necessary instability. Nightmares, as an experience, are universal, but what is manifested, and what is retrospectively defined (for there is always the combination of regression and review in these phenomena) to be a nightmare, is not. In this regard we can engage in a revisiting of Merleau-Ponty's "expression of experience by experience" in and as the nightmare.

To proceed then, we can lay the groundwork for an approach that combines psychoanalysis and phenomenology in terms of the experience and materiality of the nightmare. By commencing with the "how" of the nightmare (i.e., how do we experience the nightmare? How do we have nightmares and know them as such?) some of the key issues can be explored, even if resolution proves an elusive dream. Once this is done, the "what" of the nightmare can be investigated, notably within its cinematic iterations. Between these two lies the function of the nightmare (why do we have them and why do we culturally construct them?) If we permit a rather sweeping division by suggesting that psychoanalysis provides us with the capacity to address the "why" and phenomenology the "how," it is the combination of the two that may present us with answers to this functionality question and its cinematic possibilities. One final note, the concept of desire is introduced here to provide a link between psychoanalysis and phenomenology. The underlying strategy for this is to read desire as an egocentric positionality that can incorporate a psychoanalytic hermeneutic (i.e., desire as interpretative) and phenomenological intentionality (i.e., desire as a determining consciousness as well as a consciousness determination), but of course, this is invertible, and psychoanalysis' hermeneutics engages with consciousness determinations just as phenomenology provides interpretative gestures toward all intentional acts. Thus, desire will also provide the link between anxiety, intimacy, and the formations of cinematic flesh as they are played out in the nightmare and through the experiencing of it.

Nightmares' Aporiastic Howness

It is clearly shown through the numerous corrections (within the texts and those addressed to the self), questions raised, amendments, exasperated tones and expressions, and marginalia found in *Vol. XI* that Husserl openly engaged, and struggled, with the aporia of phantasy. There is far too much of this material to deal with here, suffice to say that one of the most exciting aspects of this collection of material is watching Husserl's mind at work, and not always in resolve. His attempts to categorize and separate, types of phantasy within themselves and within the larger context of perception/presentation serve as constant reminders that this is a near impossible task. I wish to take this infused aporia and link it to the nightmare, notably in its howness. This is to propose that the nightmare has an aporiastic nature, akin to Husserlian phantasy, but also somewhat unique. For unlike these other forms of phantasy, the aporiastic in the nightmare directly flows to, and stems from, desire, and the compulsive and compelling representational field(s) that have been produced to evoke it, including cinema. Similarly, cinema is seen as the evocation of the aporiastic. By aligning this aporiastic attribute as a unique aspect with how the nightmare comes to be (particularly in its cinematic materiality and experience), the investigation aims to address some of the issues of the "why."

We can commence by tracing the nightmare onto Husserl's ideas on phantasy, even though this will take us only so far.[1] To recall and collocate, here are some of the key issues that Husserl develops in his discussions of phantasy (indeed, uneasy discussions—he stated late in life that "determining the essence of phantasy is a great problem" (2005: 671)). Our path here must be how the nightmare is a unique variation on (phenomenologically ascribed) phantasy; thus, we add a problem to this great problem! Husserl distinguishes, with considerable consistency throughout his works, the two orders of *Gegenwärtigung* (presentation/perception) and *Vergegenwärtigung* (re-presentation). The first of these is what we experience in our encounter with the actual thing before us; it has what Husserl calls *leibhaft* (2005: 405), "real" and actual, or *leibhaftig* incarnate, of having the presence of, or being present through/as, "flesh"; and as having *Wirklichkeit* (2005: 601), actuality. This is also described as a "positing perception" which is taken as true (2005: 558–9). In short, Husserl reiterates, insists even, on the attributes of presence, reality, and actuality in the act of perception/presentation. The significance of this is that re-presentation is defined exactly as *not* having the thing in presence, in reality, and in actuality. (Later it will be necessary to ask if there can be a unique type of flesh that lies between presentation and re-presentation, or perhaps even if this fleshification renders it between the two.) Re-presentation presents itself through acts of consciousness which lack the actuality. For example, a memory is a re-presentation because what is being recalled (the loved one's face, the feeling of the wind across the water as you stand beside the lake) are real in as much as they once existed (or might exist again), but lack this *leibhaft*, this incarnate presence. Along with memories, phantasy, and what Husserl calls image consciousness (looking at a photograph or a painting, and for our concerns, watching a film) share this lack of actuality. A dream adds an extra layer in this

---

[1] See also Chapter 4 which deals with phantasy and the "real."

process. The dream is a re-presentation as we dream it, and the telling of the dream is a re-represented re-presentation, which, for Freud is at least in part determined in the considerations of representability (*SE* V) and is somewhat hermeneutically connected to *Vorstellungsrepräsentanz* (as discussed in this chapter). That psychoanalysis employs the dream work in analysis suggests that, phenomenologically speaking, there is a distinct analytic frame in operation that will shift this definitional sense of presence in the world. Let us also recall that the dream is the encounter with the Real (Lacan's interpretation of *tuché*), which explains, in part, why the nightmare can be of such affective substance and perhaps even offer up a reason for the seductive nature of its traumatic material.

For the act of consciousness, these re-presentations can have as much force and affect as presentations; indeed, because of what they are they can be all the more affectively powerful, more real than actuality/reality in their stirring potency. Further to this, we can note Husserl's defining of consciousness as *Sinngebende*, "meaning-giving," which is reimagined here as the meaningfulness of the nightmare. Part of the reason why this is so is because of what Husserl describes, variously, as "as it were," "as if" and the attributes of the quasi (which includes quasi-presenting, quasi-meant/meaning, quasi-consciousness, and so on).[2] This leads to a "modified consciousness" (2005: 459) where the distinction between the experiencing of something and its lack of actuality is forgotten, or psychoanalytically speaking, repressed. That is, we experience the thing as if it is actual, as if it were actually there before us; this is the act of quasi-experiencing (2005: 660) that is common in phantasy. It is noteworthy that Husserl attributes to quasi-experiencing something that goes against the unifying consciousness act found in perception/presentation. This is the capacity for contradictory processes to take place (his example is in a phantasy someone can begin as blond-haired but changes to brown). It is only if there is an attempt to hold both positions that conflict arises, otherwise the re-presentational allows for fluidity and constant change. In a memory a childhood room can be re-presented with such vivid clarity, and then reproduced with equal clarity, but with quite different objects or dimensions. The only time that becomes conflictual is if we try to reconcile the memories, or they are compared to the

---

[2]Husserl's use of "quasi" mostly reads as a qualifying or conditional variant on the "real"; hence, for example, a quasi-judgment is a variant on a judgment determined through this idea of *limited within* or *directed towards* in a particular way. However, he does sometimes attribute a more forceful distinction which reveals a different relationship of the quasi to the real. For example, at one point he states: "mere phantasy is not simply an intention but the antithesis [*Gegenstück*] of intention, quasi-intention . . . " (2005: 472). *Gegenstück*, *opposite* or *counterpart* are other possible translations, seems to position "quasi" in a different manner here, much more what the real is exactly not, rather than a variant.

actual room (in say a photograph or video).³ Cinema's processional system of continuity, in these terms, becomes less about a technicality for avoiding breaking the illusion through consistencies in space and time, and more about quasi-experiencing. This is also why the encounter with the Real is located in the space between experiencing and quasi-experiencing. As Lacan puts it in terms of the primary process (of dreams): [they] are apprehended in its experiencing of rupture, between perception and consciousness, in that non-temporal locus" (1986: 56). It is proposed here that cinema is located in this same place, and it is through quasi-experiencing (the state of in-betweenness of actual and re-presentationality) that cinema is formed.

Cinema, like dreams, is formed in this in-betweenness in other ways. Like the dream, cinema can sustain multiple contradictory events and representations within its own internal logic. It is only in the considerations of representability (as a unifying consciousness act) as narrativization, or in the recounting of the material can this become a conflicting issue. In this regard both condensation and displacement function as representational processes for both negotiating and resolving the contradictory constructions in both forms. Such a comparison, it must be noted, can only be made within the larger context of the encounter of the Real and the phenomenological distinction of re-presentation and its quasi attribute. If, as is being proposed here, it is in the in-between region of the Real, in all its otherness, that we encounter cinema (between perception and consciousness, of a different temporal order, spatially distinct and distinctive, and so on), then cinema can be aligned with Lacan's idea of the Real as "a prisoner in the toils of the pleasure principle" (1986: 55).⁴ Cinema's enduring capacity to render the nightmare is exemplary of this entrapment; how the spectator is (willingly) trapped is part of phantasy's materiality. Finding ourselves in such a position can be seen as part of phenomenology's "as-if," to which we can now turn.⁵

Phantasies are active processes, constructed and reconstructed through the "as if" process. In Husserl's example this is the phantasy of a house, gazing at different parts of it as if it were actually being looked at: "I live in quasi-perceptions and quasi-perceptual judgments" (2005: 221). (In this point of the analysis we also find Husserl evoking the idea of *vorschweben*,

---

³Husserl distinguishes between "real memories" (or what he calls primary memories) and one derived from re-presentations such as phantasy, which he terms re-presentational memories (2005: 214).
⁴By way of further illustration, another iteration of this in-between state is when we are located between a dream and reality. Lacan refers to the burning child dream in *The Interpretation of Dreams* as an example of when the two different orders of perception and consciousness are lived simultaneously and outside of time. This is being extended here to suggest that cinema creates its own in-between state.
⁵The main source of Husserl's accent on the "as if" appears to be Part II of the third *Critique* where Kant describes the reflective-teleological judgment as an artistically inspired "as if" approach to the not of "truth" but *intelligibility*.

"hovers before me," which has been discussed elsewhere here, notably Chapter 4.) Even though Husserl doesn't deal with it directly, these processes of "as it were," "as if," and the quasi- . . . (judgments, actuality, feelings, and so on) all form key aspects of what will later become a vibrant strand of phenomenology's aesthetics and (in literary studies in particular) reception theory.[6] This proactive and dynamic aspect represents a complex side to the issues at hand, because it requires us to address the "as it were" and "as if" in the experience and experiencing of the nightmare. It is in this aspect that psychoanalysis will prove of particular significance. There is some more phenomenological work to be done here before turning to that, however.

At the heart of all nightmares is conflict, but this is not a homogeneous or unitary conflict. Psychoanalysis requires itself to provide analytic reasonings for a nightmare's existence. When we wake from a terrifying dream we ask (oneself, as well as the person beside us who has also been awoken, or indeed anyone who will listen the following morning) "why did I dream that? Why would I want to dream that?"; when genuinely disturbing films are made, we need to ask both how they are so troubling and why do people wish to see them? Such films are distinct from, say the politically incisive ones that address disturbing issues and histories; these disturbing films are of that order of "pleasure" or are attached to pleasure without question. These disturbances are the aporiastics of the nightmare at the levels of the definitional (conflict is what makes a nightmare), the material (the agitational material in itself or as it is read), and the affective (as it emerges with the encounter with the Real and the traumatic origins). In all such modalities and processes it is important to note Lacan's ongoing engagement with Freud's idea of *Vorstellungsrepräsentanz*—a struggling, binding term combining ideational and representational. The word itself comes from Freud's piece on repression (*SE XIV*) where he states repression "turns representations away and maintains them at a distance from consciousness" (147). Lacan at one point articulates this in terms of the displacement, rather than repression, of affects (see 2006: 598[7]); this links with the aporiatic aspects of the nightmare and goes some way in explaining why it can exist. For without

---

[6]By way of example, Roman Ingarden and Wolfgang Iser are key figures in these developments. It is also possible to add the semiotic turn of Roland Barthes and Umberto Eco, as well as Derrida's phenomenologically based approaches to the text. More recently we see interesting, divergent interpretations in Horst Ruthrof's work.

[7]It is somewhat appropriate that this point comes from Lacan's "In Memory of Ernest Jones: On His Theory of Symbolism" given his admiration for Jones' work on the nightmare—which is discussed as follows.

Elsewhere Lacan points out that this term is mistranslated as representative representative, to which he offers the alternative of that which takes the place of representation (see 1986: 60). Curiously, in this offering he does not engage in the issues of representation and ideation, that is *Vorstellung* as "idea" as well as imagination. Perhaps this is because he is so deeply engaged with this issue of the underlyingness of the Real.

the repression of affect the nightmare's true disturbing qualities will always be made manifest. This, it is suggested here, is a model that helps us work through cinema's relationship to repression and the nightmare.

Such conflicts exist at the internal as well as the external, cultural levels. At the core of the nightmare's aporiastics is the contesting of the quasi, the as if, and as it were; and this contesting originates from the positing of consciousness and its modifications. The contestation, thus, operates in two interconnected ways: first, there is the disputation of the quasi-reality of the nightmare because of an exaggerated affective force (the qualifying status of "this is a phantasy" is lost to overwhelming belief so that the nightmare is experienced as "real" and "actual"); second, the experiencing (which necessarily includes the revelatory moment of terror) of the nightmare is a possessive phantasy. "Possessiveness," it is proposed, is a type of intimacy—which shall be returned to in a moment. That is, just as the nightmare possesses us (to make itself of greater reality), we possess our nightmares so that they are one's own, particular and ego-centric in design and intent. This is a variant on con-primordiality. Once the possessive takes place, the nightmare becomes a configuration of perverse desire and embraces the conflict of unpleasurable wants; its anxiety is found in that gap between desire and *jouissance* as it slides between the deeply personal and the culturally inscribed. Part of the motivation for this is what is termed here as the "desire to not be protected," for in this state we pursue, and even embrace, our nightmares.

When ascribing nightmares to this (required) aporiastic-defining quality we encounter a methodological issue common to both phenomenology and psychoanalysis. They both devise analytic conditions for revealing such internal conflicts, often acknowledging their unsolvable, contradictory nature. Thus, for example, when Husserl speaks of unity and consciousness, he invariably is concerned with the acts that shore up a unitary position: "every act, no matter how complex, is an act unity. Thus, for example, an act as judgement is one belief that, as a complete act, has a unitary object. And then this underlying presentation would have to include in itself all the differences between being and non-being, and not only all modalities but all modalities: which, as modalities actually accomplished, are surely matters for the judicative performance itself. Examined closely, this presentation as underlying act is an invention" (2005: 693). An equivalent in Freud is the famous navel of the dream (*SE IV, V*), the unresolvable, unthinkable material of the dream that resists all analysis (description even); in Lacan it is the Borromean knot, where every subject in analysis is "always given over . . . [to] an ambiguity" (2016: 20); in Merleau-Ponty (1968) it is the wild as well as the invisible; in Kristeva (1984) the *sémiotique* and so on.[8]

---

[8]Of course, even though Freud acknowledges the unplumbable depths of a dream and the resistances found therein, his theories are premised on being able to both recognize and

For this reason, the nightmare, as phantasy and as desire, unpicks and resists aspects of the methodologies in its push-pull qualities of desired and repulsive, to possess and to be possessed by, in simultaneity. Two aspects of phantasy will allow us to look further at how the nightmare is an affect-process that challenges, via the intimate possessive, the analytic conditions (of psychoanalysis and phenomenology) and cultural apparatus such as cinema. The first of these, nullity, is the space that nightmares are experienced in; the second, belief, is the collapse of the capacity to distinguish.

Nullity: Nightmare As the Deceptive Object

In re-presentation the status of absence (of the object, person, place) is not experienced, that is, it acquires nullity: "it is nowhere at all, not in any space, not in any time" (Husserl 2005: 302). In our phantasy we do not distinguish between the real and the imagined, remembered object, and the fact that there is no presence is unrecognized and ignored. For as long as we are in the phantasy this is not necessary (or even possible), and so our position of intentionality is of phantasy. It is only when phantasy and reality confront each other, or there are attempts to merge them and their ontological status is confronted, that conflict happens as the status of objects (present or absent, real or phantasy, remembered or incarnate) cannot be reconciled. This delivers up, sometimes, what Husserl describes as the *deceptive object*, where there is doubt as to the "realness" of the object. Husserl gives the example of the human body and a mannequin that appears to be a real body and our incapacity to initially distinguish the two and then reconcile the presence of the re-presented body: "In spite of the nullified intention, the appearance nevertheless continues to exist. The belief, the intention belonging to actual experience, is annulled but the appearance is preserved. Now, indeed, we do have precisely a deceptive object. A nullity." (2005: 301). The nightmare, read within such a context, would appear to be this deceptive object, a nullity which challenges the status of, and distinctions between, real and imagined. However, it is suggested here that the aporiastic basis means that before the nightmare becomes the deceptive object, this

---

interpret them. Freud overall tends to refer to nightmares as anxiety dreams, which in turn he defines as an issue of anxiety rather than one of dreams (see *SE IV, V*). So, for example, when he speaks of an anxiety dream he had as a child of his mother dying and being carried away by bird-like creatures, he asserts: "I was not anxious because I had dreamt that my mother was dying" (*SE V*: 582); rather the anxiety came from sexual repression. The point here is that Freud aligns anxiety dreams with the nightmare, but in doing so shifts the issue to one of anxiety itself. Hence, to interpret the dream really requires an understanding and interpretation of the underlying issues of anxiety. In this regard, the whyness of these dreams lies elsewhere.

nullity process is particularly powerful, binding it through possessiveness; and cinema has developed an elaborate system of such possessiveness. It is as if we require the nightmare to be real, and as such this becomes an integral component of its nature. The nightmare's deceptive objects (i.e., the recognition of them as deceiving) only become such as they pass through a type of psychoanalytic afterwardness (Freud's *Nachträglichkeit*). In this way, nullity operates twice fold in the nightmare: there is a nullity in the experiencing of the nightmare (i.e., the howness of it) as our consciousness takes up the intimate possessive position; from this the nightmare is preserved in its conflict between "reality"(notably as an external mode), the *ir-Real*, and phantasy. Let us turn to psychoanalysis to consider the possible reasons why this possessive preservation takes place.

Ernest Jones's *On the Nightmare* presents a Freudianly conceived study of the nightmare, working through the historical, linguistic, and psychical aspects of the phenomenon. The structure of the book is telling: an opening section entitled "Pathology of the Nightmare"; the substantive second section which links the nightmare to Medieval superstitions; and the extensive analysis of "Mare" and "Mara," described as a psychoanalytic etymology. This is how Jones concludes: "It was Freud who first demonstrated the inherent connection between intrapsychic dread and repressed sexual impulses, and we can now understand the Nightmare as an event in which such impulses have been overwhelmed, and shrouded, by extreme fear" (Jones 1971: 343). Such an "inherent connection" is read here as phenomenological "experiencing" (*Erlebenis*) and *Sinngebende* as meaning determined through terror, tied as it is to the (deeply) internal made manifest, and a shading invested in possessiveness. It is this work of intentionality that further produces the intimacy of the nightmare; just as the entwining of intrapsychic dread with profoundly held sexual impulses produces anxiety. This internality is bound to phenomenology's concept of being positioned (by intentionality): "The experience of being delighted, of perceiving and so on, is something posited in internal consciousness. If it is delight in something merely phantasied then it is positionless (better: nonpositing) " (Husserl 2005: 559). This is the nonpositing of the nightmare through the repressed material of sexual impulses, as well as the nonpositing (i.e., intentionality) of the nightmare (as phantasy) relating to nullity and conflict. Simply put, the nightmare's nonpositing "allows" for the conflictual, aporiastic, status of neither internal or external, real or imagined—but both and all at the same time.[9] What is being added as a motivational, or driving,

---

[9]This may appear to go against Husserl's comments on the combinatory processes of actuality and phantasy. See, for example Appendix XLV "Mixture of Phantasy and Actually Perceived Reality" and Appendix XLIII "Mixture of Imagination and Reality in the Cases of Immediate and Iconic Phantasy" (*HUA XI*). Husserl discusses the mixing of the reality and phantasy (fiction, memories, light shows, and daydreaming) and the complexity of sustaining them

force here is the repressed sexual material and its impulses. This is a force that from a psychoanalytic perspective is part of the economic model (psychical energy and its release or otherwise), while from a phenomenological one it is about moving from what Husserl calls the purposeless realm of phantasy (2005: 695) which then becomes something of purpose once it gains a modification, such as is the case with the aesthetic, the philosophical, and so on. Thus, purposelessness (the free-ranging acts of phantasy) comes from the nullity (the "lack" of the object before us). This should not be seen as a binarism, and so to move from purposelessness to having purpose is not an either/or. A film before us has both aspects for the freedom given to the spectator is tempered by the cinematic devices (narrative, characterization, verisimilitude or otherwise, social references, temporal and spatial organizations, and so on) but not entirely controlled by them either. The free-ranging phantasy is part of the spectator's active construction of the film. Once consciousness is modified (e.g., Husserl 2005: 169; 459; 706) so it becomes, for example, a contemplation of the aesthetic, delight, memory, the phantasy can be said to have gained purpose. When we regard a picture, have a memory, or watch a film, they occupy the realm of purposelessness until our intentionality is modified; the film is looked at as aesthetic, the memory as pleasure, and so on. Herein lies the complexity of the nightmare as intimacy and anxiety. The purposelessness of phantasy is based on the intrapsychic disturbances and from there the shading that takes place (the giving of purpose (Husserl), the concretization (Ingarden) of the phantasy, and the considerations of its representability (Freud)), which all come to determine how it forms in our experience, to allow the repressed sexual material to be presentified.

So, why a nightmare? Why not allow the purposelessness to be pleasurable or the concretization to be contented? Why cannot the *Abschattung* (the shading) as experience be performed as positive and being in enjoyment? And why throughout this book has there been such an alignment between anxiety and intimacy? This would seem to suggest that the analytic sticking point rests in resistance and the unconscious, via repression. As Freud states, in *The Ego and the Id*, "we obtain our concept of the unconscious from the theory of repression. The repressed is the prototype of the unconscious for us" (*SE XIX*: 5).[10] For phenomenology's emphasis on intentionality, the apodictic, the capacity for the *epoché* to operate, and so on, would suggest

---

equally. Ultimately, he tends toward the domination of one over the other through three processes: temporal slippage (we move between phantasy and reality in time, one moment lost in a daydream the next back to reality); determining orders (phantasy determines reality and vice versa); enthymemic constructions. These are taken up in various sections throughout this work.

[10]This is one of many moments when Freud stresses that the unconscious is not to be thought of as some region inside of us, but as effects of mental processes.

that the nightmare has no reason to exist; psychoanalysis, on the other hand, sees it as an anxious functioning dynamic of repression linked directly as such to the unconscious.

Belief (At the Point of Collapse)

One possible way out of this conundrum is to see the repressed sexual impulses as crossing between presentation and re-presentation (*Gegenwärtigung* and *Vergegenwärtigung*), which is a further variant on the encounter with the Real/*ir-Real*. When this takes place, these sexual impulses are in nullity, but consciousness modifying. They are the ultimate deceiving object, producing semblances that stand in on the one hand for the repressed material, and on the other hand the shading and representable signifiers. As such they become both a part of the individual's (possessive), as well as wider cultural signifying repository, of signs. This is the repository where cinema emerges from. Such a configuration allows us to think of the nightmare as having a reshaped intentionality. Its material source is not (necessarily) nightmarish, but conscious modification shifts it to become this. This is significant because the nightmare cannot be singularly something given to us or confronted by us. The complexity is that there seems to be a double intentionality: the experience of the nightmare, which brings with it the intentionality of the nightmare itself (which is phenomenological difficult to accommodate, but certainly not impossible;[11] psychoanalytically sound in reasoning). This is our confrontation with the nightmare as something intimate yet foreign to us, the *extimacy* of it. There is also the other intentionality, where we intuit the material as nightmarish. This is the possessive anxiety because it can be highly specific (the wolves of the Wolf Man e.g.,—this has been discussed in Chapter 5) and idiosyncratic. The comparison here might be something like the aesthetic position. We do not have to take up this position when gazing at an object or watching a film. There may well be elements within the film that hover before us (such as the *auteurisms* in a film by a certain director, the reputation of the historical accuracy of the film, camera shots or montage performed in certain aesthetic ways, and the status of veracity, notably in a documentary), but we are not obliged (although sometimes we are "corralled") to perceive it as such.[12] There is also the collective force

---

[11]Not precisely of this order but note Husserl's comment: "Here to the 'positing', the 'believing' in something, is 'missing'. The terms 'phantasy' and 'fiction' therefore have two significational directions: 1) One is directed towards reproduction (and re-presentation of whatever kind), and in that case every memory is called a phantasy . . . 2) The other is directed towards the mode of performing, in which case one can speak of perceptual fiction, and then the memory is not a fiction, not a phantasy" (2005: 693).
[12]See Appendix XL in *HUA XI* on the idea of abstaining from taking up a position.

of cultural objects that may cajole us into this position, but again there is nothing that can actually compel us to see it in this way. Even the most adamantly expressed interpretations, developed over time and consensus, at some point must be met in agreement by the spectator, only to stand tenuously at that moment as legitimate. A nightmare, on the other hand, is psychically "designed" to disturb us (in a dream, in a phantasy, in a film) and there does not appear to be a capacity to abstain, although there is the capacity to reimagine the experience as one of pleasure. This returns us to another facet of the aporiastic nature of the nightmare and its possessive nature. Neutrality (of consciousness) would seem to be excluded, but as Husserl puts it: "Phenomenological, therefore, there are many different forms of neutrality consciousness" (2005: 695), so it is possible to imagine such a form that is unique to the nightmare. This aligns with the psychoanalytic causes of the nightmare, and why they are repeated. The repressed sexual impulses bind us to the very fears and anxieties that we should be seeking to avoid; they deny an abstaining option for consciousness. However, this all has to be reinforced within the textual system (the dream, the film, the image) itself and the attendant image consciousness.

The possessive attribute of the nightmare, derived from its intimacy as well as *extimacy*, holds on to us during and after the experience. This is more than the recalling and remembering that can take place (both part of the image consciousness), for it involves a return to the affective material that may not be wanted or wished for but cannot be repressed. It can be no coincidence that of all film forms, horror carries with it, defines as part of its core value, the recurring motif of the return, the never-ending ending, and the physical clutching to drag the body back into the nightmare. In as much as this is akin to Freud's "unfinished business of childhood," what we witness in the nightmare's return is the internally derived possessive. That is, a consequential intimacy that returns the body (as fleshified subjectivity and thus consciousness) back to the anxious state of rest. This entire process is fundamental to the nightmare's capacity to exist and exert affective force, and it does so through the blurring of what is real and what is imagined/phantasy. Husserl allows for the phantasm to be taken to be real, to be supposed as actual: "Belief is nothing more than actually experiencing intention" (2005: 469). Does this mean that the difference between the rational, the mad, and the film spectator hinges on the capacity or incapacity to move between the realms at will, or at least be cognizant of such moves?[13] That within the phantasy belief must take place just as it does in the real world? Husserl's answer seems to be yes, for he proposes the idea of the double Ego: "If . . . I live simultaneously in phantasy and in

---

[13]I have discussed some of these issues from a largely psychoanalytic perspective elsewhere. See Fuery (2004).

actuality, then, speaking abstractly, a double Ego is there, the actual Ego and the reproductional Ego: both, of course, posited in a certain manner as united" (2005: 422). The phantasy Ego, lives in phantasy and performs acts of consciousness within that realm as if they are real. It will judge, perceive, enjoy with an intentionality that these are felt as actually taking place. In this way, belief, as an experiencing intentionality, shapes what is perceived as real. Here we see comparisons of Lacan's two narcissisms, except "identification" (read as possessive here) is added to connect the double Ego to the phantasy/imaginary. Recall that for Lacan the second of the two narcissisms is about the libidinal relationship to the world (1988a: 125); which is how we can join this material together. The reproductional Ego, in phantasy, coopts the narcissistic position and devises the phantasy as intimacy through these libidinal relations to the world (phantasy and/ or real). In the case of the nightmare, these libidinal relations are sexual relations enmeshed in intrapsychic dread. It is the union of the double Ego and the two narcissisms that makes the nightmare inescapable, just as it makes the desire to escape a weakened force, more derivative of desire than an actuality. In the nightmare, desire drags us into anxiety because in it we see our own Imaginary. Hence, the desire is the desire to not be cared for, not be protected. In this way we, our nightmared self (which can be seen as a doubled *ego* of terror) in all its troubled shudderings, approach the status of neurosis; as Lacan tells us "the neurotic won't give up his anxiety" (2017: 52), just as the film spectator won't give up her delights in the nightmare. This is made all the more powerful (at the individual and cultural levels) because it is shrouded in the Husserlian version of belief.

Let us turn to some examples to see how these issues can be furthered in the context of cinema. The central tenet in this regard stems from the earlier posed question of the aporiastics of the nightmare and their role in the intimate relationship formed through the experiencing (which necessarily includes processes such as appresentation and shading) of it. This question, to recall, indicates the possibility of a phenomenological approach to the "howness," and a psychoanalytic approach to the "whyness," of the nightmare. Three variants will be considered: first, phallocentric and racist nightmares at the level of the repressed (*Get Out* Jordan Peele 2017 and *BlacKkKlansman* Spike Lee 2018); second, liquefication of flesh at the level of the double Ego *The Lure* Agnieszka Smoczyńska 2015); third, the mirroring effect of the nightmare at the level of desire (*The VVitch: A New England Folktale* (hereafter *The VVitch* Robert Eggers 2015).[14] Each of these

---

[14]Most of these films are well-known, with the exception of *The Lure*. Smoczyńska's film is a somewhat bizarre retelling of Hans Christian Anderson's story of *The Little Mermaid*. Set in 1980s Poland, the film reimagines the fairytale in terms of the fate of the mermaid sisters Golden and Silver, who come ashore after hearing a rock band playing on the beach. Transformed into human shape, the mermaids become backing singers and strippers, before forming their own

is described as "at the level," which here indicates the confluence of real, phantasy, and cinema as their distinctions are tested through the intimate nature of the nightmare. It is also important to acknowledge the differences, no matter how interconnected they are, between the individual's nightmare, a projected version of that, and culturally shared/compelled iterations. Each of these have their cinematic basis of spectator, the film itself, and cinema's cultural domain. Within all of the following discussions lies the contestation of the body in terms of the way Lacan describes the othered body: "What has a body and does not exist? Answer—the big Other" (Lacan 2017: 66). It is also important to note that at the meta-discursive level, a number of the following discussions are directed toward a very specific iteration, that of the nightmare as feminine sexuality. The intent here is to explore how one system (in this example phallocentricism) positions alternatives to itself (feminine sexuality) as the nightmare. In these terms there is a sense that the desire to not be protected emerges from a system that actually configures what it desires through intimacy and anxiety.

Phallocentric and Racist Nightmares at the Level of the Repressed

I do not wish to spend any considerable amount of time revisiting the well-known work by Freud on the uncanny. There will be moments when points will be drawn on from *The Uncanny*, but for the most part it will be assumed that this important work frames both the tenor of the discussion as well as a number of the key ideas here. One such framing resonance that can be seen in Jones's thesis will serve as a starting point: "the malady known as Nightmare is always an expression of intense mental conflict centering about some form of 'repressed' sexual desire" (1971: 44). That Jones insists on the centrality of conflict aligns with the ideas explored so far, in that phantasy's aporiastic nature accommodates this variant (the psychical). The proposal here is that the long-standing and pervasive mental conflict is derived from a cultural order—phallocentricism—and the repressed sexual desire originates from a set of fearful *lacunae* that this order harbors. This is not the more obvious castration complex (although this is not entirely excluded), but a variant based on the female body, childbirth, and the maternal. What this immediately sets up is a deeply complex idea of "masculine" and "feminine" mental conflicts and their

---

act (The Lure). Golden murders and devours a man, becoming more insatiable for blood; Silver falls in love with a man, who refuses her. In desperation she has her tail removed to gain legs (in doing so loses her singing voice), but this disgusts the man even more. Silver dies, refusing to eat him and save herself; Golden kills him in revenge and returns to the sea.

nightmare renderings. Some of this, and other variants, will underpin the following but there will also be some aspects that are simply left unresolved or frustratingly underdeveloped. This is a consequence of keeping within the direct concerns here, all the while acknowledging there is much work to be done. It should be noted, in terms of these unresolved issues, that Lacan, in *Seminar XXIII The Sinthome*, offers us a potential path for such discussions when he asserts that "the uncanny incontestably pertains to the Imaginary" (2016: 36).[15] By tying the uncanny to the Imaginary, this issue of phallocentric and/or culturally specific nightmares can be seen as a reflexive modality. That is, the nightmares produced (culturally speaking) will always result from a reflection, no matter how unconsciously formed this is. To work through this, we can commence with a broad sweep of an idea, a more nuanced manifestation, and then a specific film example. First, the expansive idea.

The fairytale is a long-standing phantasy structure. It is well-known that the earlier European versions are more ghastly, cruel, and macabre than what appears from the early part of the twentieth century onward (notably in their cinematic renditions). The Brothers Grimm and E.T.A. Hoffmann (the story of the Sandman being Freud's choice for the paper on the uncanny) provide excellent examples of the fairytale's nightmarish forms transformed into "safer" versions in their cinematic renderings. There are a multiplicity of arguments and reasonings why this process has taken place,[16] and the one offered here is not intended to supplant or deny any of these specifically; instead, the interpretative gesture is to explicate the operation of the fairytale as nightmare as phantasy in terms of the encounter with the Real rather than suggest this is in any way complete or thorough theorizing of the form. In this sense, this reading of the fairytale is less about the fairytale and more about phallocentric anxiety and its nightmares.[17]

The anxiety invested in certain (continually reimagined) fairytales stems from the repressed psychical conflict regarding menstruation as singularly feminine. (The more obvious castration anxiety is held in abeyance here.) Positioned thusly, the recurring signifiers of red include the (poisoned) red apple given to Snow White by the old witch, Red Riding Hood's attire, the blood-filled shoes (as the stepsisters slice their feet to try and fit the glass slipper) in Grimm's *Cinderella* are read as phallocentric anxiety of menstrual blood (which is also linked to the repressed sexualization of these characters). In these terms, the white rabbit's cry of "don't be late" signifies

---

[15]Somewhat appropriately for the discussion at hand, Lacan goes on to speak about the exorcizing of the uncanny—another level of possession it would seem.
[16]Vladimir Propp's *Morphology of the Folktale* is one of the more famous examples.
[17]The example taken up as follows focuses on a specific interpretative gesture, there are, of course many other approaches that can be adopted to position the fairytale within the analytic scene.

the fear of a missed period for Alice, just as the Queen of Hearts (red) and the Red Queen are located as figures of anxiety and challenge. In all these examples, the central characters are girls/young women transitioning to adulthood, their sexuality becoming bound to the maternal as well as the libidinal. The managing of these apprehensions translates to the anxious-laden signifiers being more heavily disguised as the repression is asserted at the cultural level.[18] (Is it any coincidence that Cinderella and Alice become recurrently dressed in blue, the socially contrived, textual representational color antithetical to menstrual red, as these stories were cinematically redesigned, particularly in the hegemonic acts of Disney, in the twentieth century?)

The issue at hand is not to defend such an interpretative gesture, but rather to consider how such a reading explains a type of nightmare originating from a phallocentric anxiety. Because it is designated as phallocentric, the initial (phenomenologically speaking) purposelessness of the phantasy act (its unregarded positioning) is constructed through a non-feminine determination. The "non-feminine" is employed here to acknowledge that the phallocentric is not simply masculine, but a much more complex investment in psychical, cultural, and historico-political agendas.[19] Here we witness the nullity process at work. Phallocentricism is a version of intentionality that shapes perception through modification. Just as Husserl asserts that neutralization and nullity are achieved through modifiers of consciousness, and thus reality ("phantasy and Imagination are intentional modifications of perception" 2005: 432–6), so phallocentricism is seen as a phantasy with all the attendant phenomenological and psychoanalytic implications of a (political) intentionality of modifications of perception. Nullity in these fairytales is made more complex because of the phallocentric bias and the forces of repression.[20] Here we witness a type of nullity based on denial, which reveals the deceptive object. Teased out, this reads as: the menstrual anxiety fairytale creates the nullity, and so deceptive object, because of the intrapsychic (sexual) conflict, thus producing denial, negation, and repression (these tales are socially positioned to not to be read as being about menstruation). This allows, at one level, the anxiety to function within the phallocentric order, adapting to textual systems, formal censorships, historical and political specificities, and so on. The anxiety is played out in this disguised form and so is diffused or sublimated, to use

---

[18]There is of course considerable work, notably in psychoanalysis and anthropology, on menstruation, and anxiety. As Klein put it: "Menstruation has always been looked upon by men as a dangerous event against which they react with fear, anxiety, and disdain" (Klein 1975: 318); Freud speaks of the sexual connection to menstruation in, for example, *Totem and Taboo*; Emile Durkheim (1963) links it to prohibition and incest.
[19]The work of Cixous, Kristeva, and Irigarary immediately springs to mind here.
[20]This aligns with the discussion of *The Favourite* discussed in an earlier chapter.

the psychoanalytic term. At a further level, and because this operates as repression, the sense of (male) exclusion (from the feminine/maternal) is negotiated so that control is asserted. In this way, these fairytales' nullity can be coopted into phallocentricism's power structures; the disruptive feminine body (from the masculine perspective) is both present and not present. Furthermore, the double Ego produced within the phallocentric intentionality of these phantasies can only *perform* a sense of unity, rather than have one, because the reproductional Ego holds the fairytale as real, in nullity, whereas the actual Ego confronts them as mere (in that Kantian sense of *bloss*) phantasy, and in doing so exists in (psychoanalytically speaking) negation. This is the symptom of phallocentric anxiety of menstruation specifically, and the feminine body more generally.

What is missing here, of course, is the feminine as she engages in these phantasies (the fairytales and their cinematic versions, phallocentricism, and so on). This is deliberate, because these fairytales are read as a phallocentric nightmare, which is not to say that there cannot be feminine anxiety at play in these fairytales. The difference, and it is a profoundly significant one, is that feminine anxiety about the female body can serve as resistance to the dominating phallocentric order, and so is located outside the nightmare. This is precisely what we see in certain films on race, indicatively White and Black relations. *Birth of a Nation* is a white anxiety about the black body as nightmare; *Get Out* (Peele 2017), *Us* (Peele 2019), and *BlacKkKlansman* (Lee 2018) variously show counter positions of the black body as resistance to white culture (acknowledging that neither of these are homogeneous groups or identities). This is the subtle cleverness of *Get Out* as it presents itself as a horror film, but the cultural anxiety it deals with is equally resistant to the generic positioning. This also returns us to the issue raised earlier, that of the unique type of flesh that lies between presentation and re-presentation. These films by Peele and Lee are (phenomenologically speaking) re-presentations, perceived through image consciousness. However, the bodies for so long under dominant white ideological systems, evoke a resistant presentational modality. The body moves from the nullity, and its quasi-corporeality, to the actual because of the political agitation involved in the spectatorship. In both these cases we witness two sites of resistance (the feminine and the non-White) as they seek representational space which is an alternative to the phallocentric and White-centric system(s). This suggests that the political and ideological issues at their heart are contestations of distinctions between the actual and phantasy, the presentational and re-presentational, the represented and the repressed, and perhaps even the *Vorstellung* and *repräsentanz*. It is significant that this is played out within the context of phantasy because the shifts (in, e.g., intentionality or meaning constructions) can only be addressed and understood if we acknowledge the underpinning anxieties. *Get Out* is far more than a horror-comedy, and its treatment of anxieties in and through race is done in a manner that tests the phenomenological distinctions of intentionality. The nightmare lies closer to the surface (it does, after all, form the story), so the double Ego (the spectator of the film and the re-presentational spectator *in* the phantasy) can only be unified if the issue of racism is seen within the film (the re-presentation of image consciousness) and the wider social and historical situation (the presentational consciousness in the world). The menstrual anxiety reading of the fairytale is more buried and therefore more repressed than we find in these examples. This is because there is a directed intentionality to race issues in Lee and Peele, while the fairytales lack this directed perspective.

Such interpretative efforts are measured not by the "complexity" of the film text, but rather by the stitching of the double Ego to the act of spectating unify the double Ego, allowing what is taking place in the phantasy to also be seen as part of the "actual" world (which in this sense can be seen as something along the lines of the *Umwelt*). Herein lies one of the most compelling aspects of cinema and its capacity to shift the spectator "between" consciousness positions. This aligns with Husserl's assertion that phantasy can act as a modifier of subjectivity (2005: 683). What is being argued here is that this requires participatory effort to bring the repressed to the surface and see the underlying anxieties in terms of their ideological functions. This dislocating of the double Ego, so what is taken as phantasy is also seen as being of consequence in the actual, forms a resistance to the idea of neutrality. This suggests that the double Ego is more than a doubling in certain instances. Each spectator occupies the site of the doubled Ego because of the distinction between actuality and the quasi in phantasy and its cinematic versions. However, there must also be a multiplicity of Egos determined ideologically, sexually, racially, through biases and similarity, and so on. We can even go so far to say that each element of a film, realizing its qualities of the phantasy, hovers before each spectator in different ways. Some are so apparent they seem obvious to certain spectators, and yet entirely invisible to others. This is precisely at the heart of Husserl's work on phantasy and aligns equally (perhaps even surprisingly) well with both Freud's and Lacan's engagement with that same concept, its materiality, and its psychical consequences.

As with nullity, neutrality is Husserl's idea that consciousness in phantasy means that all that is perceived is read as phantasy, that is, neutrality. Husserl acknowledges that as we shift between conscious modifiers (in the actual, in phantasy, watching a film, having a memory or a dream) we take up a different positional Ego (e.g., 2005: 690). Appropriate to the issues at hand, when Husserl engages with the idea of positional Ego and the *epoché* he uses cinema, or as he describes it "a stereoscopic, cinematographic semblance" as an example. He describes the shifts that take place between being lost in the phantasy of the film as we watch, and then the recognition of connections with the actual world. (2005: 692). Our psychoanalytic and cinematic inflections mean that this positional Ego has to come to terms with repressed or denied/negated (*Verneinung*) material and a film's ideological resistances. Thus, the positional Ego is actually constructed through what is given to it as well as what it takes up itself. In the anxious nightmares discussed here, this can require a positionality entirely foreign, or even oppositional to the known or believed, which must also be seen as part of the anxieties. In turn, this requirement to take up the nightmare (its possessiveness) forms the intimacy between consciousness/Ego and the exogenous.

In these terms it is important to remember Lacan's insistence, via Freud, that anxiety has a rather particular stance as a signal. As Lacan puts it: "I dared to formulate for you that anxiety, of all signals, is the one that does not deceive" (2017: 160). At this point is worth recalling that anxiety as a signal is not a negation of Freud's theory of anxiety as libidinally based. Lacan reveals to us the potential to reread both anxiety and the libidinal drives as a particular type of signal; this is one of the core issues at hand. How are we to read this in terms of the deceptive object in phantasy and the positional Ego? In one sense the veracity of the anxious signal is precisely what we have seen in cinema's requirement to take up a spectating position which may not be a "usual" or comfortable one. Phantasy's modifier of subjectivity is particularly powerful in the intimacy of anxieties. This can only take place if the repressed anxiety's signals are perceived as such; the other's body (in the earlier example of the non-White body in a White-centric normalizing and privileging environment) is not just othered, but the othering of it is seen as creating anxiety or being derived from such a creation. The counter position to this is that the anxiety is missed entirely (the othered body remains othered and racism, gender, or biases are sustained). In this sense, anxiety's signal may not be deceptive, but that does not mean that it will be read and understood as such. The "truth" of the anxious signal will insist on a modified consciousness; if it takes place in phantasy (such as a film), then this can lead to the modification of subjectivity. Here we see the complication of "whose anxiety?" The menstrual fairytale has been read here as a consequence of phallocentric anxiety (the masculine situation of intrapsychic dread) about the feminine body. It is still a signal (of anxiety) but the repression (due to the sexual impulses phallocentrically ascribed to it) means that it is a heavily disguised one.

Get Out embeds the anxiety signal as part of its narrative, critiquing racism (specifically White appropriation of Blackness and the problematics of White-Black relations in the United States, particularly as they are enacted in the twenty-first century) and the attendant anxieties it produces at the same time. In doing so it efficiently foregrounds the nightmare of racism and the anxious signals that continue to circulate. Spike Lee's *Do the Right Thing* and *BlacKkKlansman* engage with racism in a similar manner, with the endings of both films being particularly important in their critique of socio-historical normalizing of racism and the violent consequences. *BlacKkKlansman* adopts positional strategies for moving the spectator's image consciousness into collapsing distinctions; that is, the transition from the film's narrative to news footage is a remarkable demonstration of phantasy's capacity to modify subjectivity and confirm the veracity of anxious signals. By further aligning the events from the past to contemporary events (right-wing political extremes, complicit mainstream political support, and the continued rise of racial violence) the film adds a further layer to this intentionality and subject positioning. This is the film's capacity to shift the spectator's (and even a wider cultural order's) positionality. Yet *Birth of a Nation* demonstrates no such anxiety of this type because it excludes those signals, and the associated positioning processes, to enable them in its celebratory narrative of racism and bigotry. (An inverse example would be Oscar Micheaux's *Within Our Gates* (1920) which directly addresses anxious race relations.) The textual signals here are of the othered black body, but the sense of anxiety is appropriated through the racist ideologies of the film. However, this is not to suggest that there is no anxiety in *Birth of a Nation*—indeed, quite the opposite is the case. There are two, conflictual signals of anxiety in this film: the film's own racist anxieties about the black body; the anxieties which are oppositional to this internal politics, which reads the film as racist. It is only by reading against the film, by adopting a positional Ego that constructs anxiety, that such a signal can be devised. In this way we distinguish between: anxious films that require work to read the signals (the menstrual fairytale and its contemporary cinematic iterations); films that overtly construct positions of phantasy modifying subjectivity so that the spectator is required to see the anxious signals (Spike Lee's films are good examples of this); and films that deny anxiety and so this modification (i.e., anxiety), as intentionality, is developed external to the text.

Liquification of Flesh at the Level of the Double Ego

The previous section raised the issue of nightmares and politically defined anxieties manifested corporeally (whose anxiety is it and why should it be viewed as such?) allowing a consideration of the ambiguity of status and the contesting of the signal which does not deceive. This is the contesting of anxiety as a political process, showing the role of intimacy in formations, acceptances, and denials. The contestation of anxiety is significant because it foregrounds the idea that what is anxious is fluid and unfixed. This is in part why there is an insistence here of the relationship to intimacy; that is, where intimacy is, there anxiety will follow. This section will take up a different version of this, considering Agnieszka Smoczyńska film *The Lure*. We can begin by recalling Lacan's alignment of anxiety to surplus *jouissance* and then seek to read this in terms of how cinema constructs such objects.²¹ Invariably these cinematic objects of anxiety and a particular type of *jouissance* are found within a nightmarish environment; in keeping with the previous discussion, the focus here will be on the gender politics of subversion and disturbance.

Lacan employs the term *plus-de-jouir* (surplus *jouissance*)²² within a number of conceptual frames, including: (1) language (" . . . we are beings born of surplus *jouissance*, as a result of the use of language" (2017: 66) which, at this level, aligns it with the Symbolic and the exchange processes); (2) related to this social inflection, as value in a Marxist sense ("this [Marx's] surplus value is a memorial to surplus *jouissance*" (2017: 80) and "Marx would have realized that surplus value is surplus *jouissance*" (2017: 107–8)); (3) the emergent child libidinal impulses as an accumulative process (2017: 99–101 in the discussion of the Dora case study); and (4) that it is the Other's *jouissance* (2017: 53). There does not seem to be a lot of overt connections within all these conditions, and to this we must add perhaps the most significant meaning Lacan ascribes to it, the discourse of the hysteric and its relation to the "master." Let us be transparent before proceeding; the material in these seminars (*XVI D'un Autre a L'autre, XVII The Other Side of Psychoanalysis*, and *XX On Feminine Sexuality, the Limits of Love and Knowledge*) presents some deeply problematic work by Lacan in his travails to explicate feminine sexuality and locate it within a longer psychoanalytic tradition (principally Freudian). There are limited achievements here. This is a Lacan attempting, in some ways, to respond to the political climate of the time (primarily the rise of women's challenge to certain psychoanalytic concepts and readings); notably, *Seminar XVI, D'un Autre a L'autre* was delivered in 1968 and *XVII, The Other Side of Psychoanalysis* in 1969.

---

²¹There is another line of analysis that could be explored here but would take us too far from the central discussion. In *Seminar XI The Four Fundamental Concepts of Psychoanalysis*, Lacan develops one of his recurring themes of desire, the subject, and the gaze. A core idea within this is that of the lure: "the relation between the gaze and what one wishes to see involves a lure" (1986: 104). Just as the film's title of the lure introduces a level of ambiguity (what is the lure? Who is being lured? How is the allurement being played out and disguised? And so on), so the lure holds the false recognitions of both the mermaids and Lacan's concept. It is worth recalling that for Lacan the lure is contained within his idea of *méconnaissance* (misrecognition and the ambiguous). Similarly, the lure and desire are defining aspects of phantasy: "But the objects of desire, in the usual sense, is either a phantasy that is in reality the *support* of desire, or a lure" (1986: 186). This is a near perfect description of the sexual politics of *The Lure*.
²²*Plus-de-jouir* both "beyond" and "more" pleasure/desire. Lacan introduces the idea in *Seminar XVI D'un Autre a L'autre* where he states that it is perversion that shows this in its most fundamental of forms. The play on "beyond" and "more" becomes a key aspect when Lacan speaks of women's desire as *plus-de-jouir*; the beyondness of this desire, being beyond desire, more than desire, more than that which can be contained or considered desire, and so on. This raises the complexity of the issue in a different manner. Lacan could be seen as aligning "perversion" as that which is located outside phallocentricism (a descriptive approach); or, more worryingly, he could be seen as adopting a prescriptive line, and any desire outside the dominant order must be positioned as perversion.

It was during the 1960s that Luce Irigaray attended Lacan's seminars, challenging a number of his positions on the feminine. On a more positive note, within this context of the intellectual struggle, these seminars introduce the four discourses that shape a great deal of his later work. The strategy here is to locate the concept of surplus *jouissance* somewhat "outside" its methodology and to see it as a meta-critical and reflexive moment. In this way it is possible to utilize the concept to read cinema all the while locating the concept as a type of critical performativity. Thus, the task before us is to locate the nightmare, its cinematic versions (here explicated through *The Lure*), and the concept of surplus *jouissance* as different variants on the surplus developed through and with *jouissance*. Further to all of this is the compelling idea that cinema itself may function as surplus *jouissance* within the psycho-social climates of its production and reception.

That Lacan reads surplus *jouissance* within the context of Marx's *Mehrwert* (surplus value) is important to note. *Jouissance*, a signifier of excess and extreme (pleasure), is repositioned as an excess to itself, a beyond to what is already a beyond. However, this is where Lacan's use of *plus* takes a different turn; the "surplus" is not an excess of *jouissance*, rather it is a different type that cannot be held within the discourses of *jouissance*. We are used to thinking of *jouissance* in purely sexual, ecstatic terms, but the surplus that Lacan introduces pushes it in different directions. This is why, for example, he can declare that "the path toward death is nothing other than what is called *jouissance*" (Lacan 2017: 18). This allows us to consider constructions such as: the nightmare's surplus as *jouissance*; a cinematic surplus configured through and as *jouissance*; and even, surplus anxiety and intimacy as *jouissance*.

Recalling that the nightmare has (phenomenologically speaking) an aporiastic component, "surplus" is the space where the contradiction between the phantasy (nightmare, film, memory) experienced as needed/required and desired, and the fears and anxieties played out. The interplay between having the dream or watching a film (as an experience of desire) and the affective processes that happen when these terrify and haunt is the surplus—the something more that comes to (re)define the experience. The nightmare's aporia is located within the surplus as well as the subsequent shapings of that surplus. Seen in this way, "surplus" is a qualifier of how we experience the phantasy and aligns with phenomenology's conscious modifier; the surplus is where intentionality becomes determined. Just as Lacan speaks of surplus *jouissance* as the other's *jouissance* (2017: 53), so we might speak of the nightmare's surplus being the other's dream or film; or cinema's surplus (*jouissance*) being the cinema of the other.

What all of this yields, and it is certainly an issue that haunted some of Lacan's later ideas, is that being located as "surplus" is to suggest an outsider, a less-than, a not whole, an addition to. However, this is Lacan and therefore the idea that we can speak with any degree of comfort that these are binary positions is not viable in the least. Lacan's declaration "*woman* does not exist" (1975: 7) can only really make sense if it is read as "woman" as an eidetic form, that is, at the generalized conceptual level. The (political as well as ontological) difficulty really stems from him not making a parallel statement that "*man* does not exist either." The non-existence of a woman is to recognize the pervasive and normalizing power of phallocentrism. When Lacan speaks of the "barred Woman" (*Il n'y a ici de la que barré*) he is effectively constructing "Woman" as *sous rature*—under erasure, present and yet absent and barred from full subjectivity, existence, and in this case, pleasure.[23] However, key to this is that Woman is barred for specific reasons and in different ways, thus yielding feminine *jouissance* which exists outside of phallocentrism; the excluding apparatus of phallocentrism operates differently for "Man" (Man). One only has to note Lacan's examples (Kierkegaard is one) to see that although "Woman" is othered through her *jouissance*, so "Man" is through castration. Perhaps the larger issue is not to have one's alternative being, through *jouissance*, recognized by the dominant, homogenizing order (phallocentricism, whiteness, heteronormativity, and so on), but to change the order itself. In this regard we witness another version of cinematic surplus *jouissance*, that is, the capacity to locate/be located outside normative positions. (Of course, the opposite is also true, which is cinema's capacity to institutionally resist the spectator's surplus sites of being.)

Let us return to the notion of the nightmare as surplus, existing as and through the other's dream or film. Dream or film, as phantasy, are devised around image consciousness, which here is being aligned to this particular interpretation of surplus, which is the position "outside" and othered. This may sound somewhat similar to Husserl's double Ego, and there are connections; however, the surplus (of *jouissance*, of the nightmare, of the film) can be seen to operate in terms of a double *epoché* for it is here that aporias take hold. What is a cornerstone of the aporiastic definition of the nightmare is its capacity to challenge the division between the presentational (actual) and re-presentational (phantasy); and this is what encourages or even demands this doubling. This same attribute is found in concupiscent texts and their affect, which certainly resonates within a psychoanalytic interpretation.[24]

Jouissance, as the sensual, be it sexual or fearsome, is surplus because it goes beyond the limits and cannot be contained by the determining structures. If it does not do so then it cannot be sensual and passes unnoticed

---

[23]*Sous rature* is explored at length by Jacques Derrida, who critiques Heidegger's use. For Derrida, via Heidegger, this is done in terms of Being, S̶e̶i̶n̶. See Derrida, *Of Grammatology*.
[24]This surplus erotics was discussed in detail in Chapter 5. Recall Lacan's comment referenced earlier on *jouissance* and death.

within the determining consciousness.²⁵ However, it would be wrong to assume that this quality rests within the "text," for this is where the larger order of possessiveness operates. One distinction that needs to be made, and this relates directly to the double *epoché*, is that the nightmare may well only gain that status afterward and through deferral, hence *Nachtäglichkeit*. When we watch a film, our consciousness attends to all its elements as such (in Husserl's sense of the "as if")—that is, all acts of consciousness perceive the elements in the unitary fashion. The death on the screen is seen in the context of the framing "as if," the threat in the woods as one imbued with the quasi, the sensually seen body "is such" because of these attentive acts, and so on. However, the psychoanalytic motivation behind the nightmare (at the least as proposed here as intrapsychic dread and repressed sexual impulses) means that the unconscious requires us to hold off for as long as possible perceiving it to be something unpleasant. Deferral and delaying are psychical "strategies" to allow the affect to last as long as possible. This is another aspect of the aporiastic in action; our directed consciousness is required to accommodate two completely different experiences—pleasure and unpleasure. (Along with this is the issue/question of "whose nightmare?" i.e., the inherent instability of the status of the nightmare. As observed earlier, one person's nightmare may well be another's dream.) This is the surplus *jouissance* of the nightmare. The nightmare as a dream or as a film (in both cases as a doubled phantasy structure) performs this process, albeit in differing fashions. We choose to watch a film that disturbs, frightens, or horrifies us, experiencing its terrors within a bounded, elected context, but we do not choose to have a nightmare, at least not at the conscious level. That the experiencing of a film is a deliberate act, one consciously decided, means that what is experienced is framed within the acknowledged re-presentational. That is, we choose this disturbance and often have a pre-given sense of the shapes it might take. The disturbing, nightmarish qualities stem from a conscious decision; this is more significant than what first seems to be an obvious distinction between watching a terrifying film and having a nightmare. What makes the film nightmarish stems from consciousness (even if it feeds into unconscious motivations of pleasure and release). More than this, the disturbing nature of the film is derived precisely from an attribute of consciousness which Lacan describes as its only homogeneous function, namely: "the ego's imaginary capture by its specular reflection, and in the function of misrecognition that remains tied to it" (2006: 705). For all the cultural sharedness of horror films, the insatiable production and consumption, the real compulsion operates at the level of this capturing of the ego and its Imaginary relations. The shared surplus takes place in

---

²⁵Here we are very close to the sensual as configured by Merleau-Ponty (1962, 1968) and Dufrenne (1973). This version of the sensual will be turned to shortly.

the sense of pleasures (distorted *jouissance* or variants of masochism) that are formed in the experience, which originates (and returns to) a unique process of self-reflexivity. The fear-inducing film's defense, just like that of the nightmare, is bound up with this Lacanian version of misrecognition; that is, the disguising of the ego's true aims. Yet again, this is the aporia of the nightmare, for the anxiety that is produced and then read as pleasurable would seem to go against both phenomenological (with intentionality) and psychoanalytic (at the very least the seeking of pleasure and avoiding of unpleasure) interpretations. This is why it must be seen as a surplus (*jouissance*) and functioning as the double *epoché*—this latter term requires some additional clarification.

For phenomenology, the double *epoché* is a necessary part of contemplation (of the phantasy, film, dream ...) and reflexive understanding. It is formed precisely because of the intentionality of consciousness as it operates in the image consciousness as well as in the actual. We watch a film, and in doing so our consciousness (this positional Ego) enters the domain of "as is" and the companion idea of "as if," perceiving everything within that context. We then take up a second position, reflexive and shaped through an intentionality that recognizes the quasi-status of objects, events, and people in the film. As Husserl puts it: "At first I lose myself in as if contemplation; I contemplate the events as if they are actually happening ... I posit the semblance image as reality, as 'what is seen' in this quasi-seeing. I establish a second Ego which does not take part in the quasi-*believing* ... but contemplates it and the 'noema', the 'image' in it, reflexively" (2005: 692). To arrive at this reflexive position, Husserl argues, we need to enact the two levels of *epoché*—the first to situate one's self in contemplation, that is for the concerns here, in the film; the second to recognize the quasi-believing and all the attendant aspects (of the film) that allow it to take place. In passing, Husserl's qualifier of reflexivity can be seen as of the same order as Lacan's Imaginary capture, with both concepts contextualized within versions of misrecognition. Of course, there can be—and often is—more than a doubling of the *epoché*.

This is the double *epoché* within the "normal" sense of cinema; what is being put forward here is that in cases such as the nightmare the relationship between the formation of the two has a number of unique aspects to it. The internal tension (the aporiastic) means that holding the two positional frames is different than, for example, a romantic comedy. In the nightmare, the second *epoché* as distinct is tested and is less "secure" in itself (as with the materiality of the nightmare itself, it follows into the second positionality, problematizing its status as "outside" the film). Similarly, the reflexive stance of the second *epoché* is challenged through the affective, sensual force embedded in the first position. There is a decidedly adhesive, fastening (possessive) nature to the nightmare which makes the shoring up the *epoché* often take place at a tertiary level; the phantasy of as if; the reflexive determining of the quasi-seeing and believing; the struggle with the sensual as it questions this secondary separation. This third *epoché* is the surplus *jouissance* because the nightmare necessarily undermines and challenges the spectator's capacity to distinguish affect and the sensual as being actual or quasi. As seen in the Husserl quotation earlier, the qualifier of "quasi" is crucial; for a theorizing of cinema in these terms it offers a rich critical reward. This is why the spectator can engage the film as happening (and react accordingly), "saved" by the emergence of the second Ego which does not have to, nor should, embrace the act of believing. In some ways the resulting reflexive modality that results is cinema's (affective) force and the work of analysis that psychoanalysis extracts.

In one sense this suggests an ideal form of the nightmare, something that in the experiential is so affective that the spectator is rendered incapable of distinguishing the Ego positionalities. In this version the reflexive second Ego position does not escape the nightmare and instead binds us ever more tightly to it. From another perspective, it suggests a closer alignment with neurosis and psychosis and the struggle to maintain a connection with reality. It is possible, however, to recognize these attributes in less extreme forms of (aesthetic) idealism or psychical collapse. As tempting as it is to offer a definition of the nightmare as based on the absolute breakdown of the *epoché*, there is a great deal to be gained by instead seeing elements of this within all nightmares. To explore this at the textual level let us turn to the specific film examples of *The Lure* and *The VVitch*.

One only has to recall the (bizarre and divergent) narrative of *The Lure* to see a surplus *jouissance* at work: two vampiric mermaid sisters come to shore (having fallen in love with a human) in 1980s Poland and are exploitatively employed as singers at a garish dream-like nightclub. There is little in this film that could be described as "ordinary," including the texture of the images (colors, shapes), the representations of gender politics, sound (which sets up a parallel between the near cacophonic sounds of the band and the siren songs of the mermaids), and the multiple narrative trajectories. Men come across as predatory, exploitative, unsafe, and immoral, and the two mermaids (Gold (Michalina Olszanska) and Silver (Marta Mazurek)) as simultaneously innocent and threatening, exploited, and powerful. All of this to say that the film in both narrative and style operates at a certain level of cinematic surplus *jouissance*. The mermaids' expressions and actions, indeed their very existence, are akin to Lacan's descriptions of mystics, notably St. Teresa in Bernini's statue, and *jouissance*. To the question he poses (about St. Teresa's orgasmic expression) of what has excited her, he replies: "It is clear that the essential testimony of the mystics consists in saying that they experience it, but know nothing about it" (1975: 76). The mermaids exist almost entirely within this experiencing of the human world, but epistemologically removed from it. From here, Lacan goes on to speak of women's *jouissance* as *en plus*. Again, this beyond, this something more, can only make analytic sense if it is seen as a type of idealized position of Woman, located outside the phallocentric order; in *The Lure* we witness the *en plus* in and through the fleshification of the mermaids. Their womaness is an example of flesh as surplus *jouissance*.

The mermaids are at least doubled in this regard; women as phantasmagorical creatures (outside the human) that are simultaneously exploited and challenge the male order. Their expressions often rest within this space of the surplus *jouissance*. They experience the world of humans, but their knowledge and seeming understanding, are outside of it. This renders them as having childlike innocence and simultaneously being menacing, other-worldly powerful in equal measure. Recalling Lacan's psychoanalytic reconceptualization of Marx's *Mehrwert* (surplus value) as playing out through language (and its lack, or perhaps more accurately, lack of access) and social inflection as value ("surplus value is surplus *jouissance*"), it is possible to articulate the mermaids as a disturbance to the surplus value of economic exchange, as well as women's surplus *jouissance*. This is played out precisely in these terms of masculine exploitation (both in terms of capital and sexually) and denial of language (human and sea creature). As such, these liminally placed mermaids come to occupy a status that is more excessive than is usually seen in cinema, and yet also an almost universalizing sense of the representation of women.

This is why the mermaids are described here as the liquefaction of the body at the level of the double. There are two narrative strands that can be drawn on to illustrate this idea of the liquified body as surplus *jouissance* and the nightmare's adhesions in the double *epoché*. The first is the anatomical. The mermaids have tails in water, which become legs on land, but they still lack human genitalia. Gold becomes murderous, killing and eating men, while Silver has her tail surgically removed so she can have legs and genitalia, hoping that she will be loved by the human. These parallel acts are inverted orders of castration anxieties; Gold as the threat to masculine power (an orally derived *vagina dentata*), and Silver as a physical manifestation of the masculine anxieties of othered, feminine sexuality. The second narrative strand is the fate of Silver. Rejected by the human, she must kill him if he marries or be turned into sea foam. At his subsequent wedding she refuses, only for Gold to kill him once Silver liquifies. Thus, the fluidity of their status becomes Silver's literal fate. The surplus *jouissance* which they embody and enact (simply in their otherness, but also through their resistances to normative sexuality and acts of passion) extends to the questioning of "value" in its Marxist and Lacanian iterations.

This is a crucial aspect for this reading. For *The Lure* does not position the mermaids as nightmare creatures, rather it is the male dominated, loveless world of humans that contains and propagates the terrors. The nightmares are what takes place in the liquification of the mermaids' bodies: mutilation, loss (Silver loses her singing voice when her tail is removed), exploitation (voyeurism as well as all versions of capitalism's corruption of the body), and violence (toward the mermaids as well as Gold's murderous acts in self-defense), and imprisonment. In this sense, the surplus *jouissance* acts as a resistance to the phallocentric and its castration anxieties (which in many ways parallels the earlier reading of menstrual anxieties for phallocentricism). Similarly, the film's critique of power and feminine sexuality acts *in potentia* as a positionality derived from the double *epoché* of the feminine. What is at hand is cinema's capacity to reposition (i.e., conscious modification) the spectator to take up another's/the other's perceptual site. This would mean that the film has the capacity to "enforce" a different type of *Abschattung* (shading) (and thus Ego positionality) from the spectator. It is highly unlikely that any single film could achieve this revolutionary surplus in totality, but such awareness can and should take place. The feminine *epoché*, in this regard, actively challenges the phallocentric order, bringing into both perspective and question the formations and iterations of as-if and quasi. The nightmare in *The Lure* is not the threat of the mermaid, as feminine posited in phallocentricism, but the threats to them in that system. As observed in the examples on race, the status of the nightmare is the of liquidification of values.

The Mirroring Effect of the Nightmare at the Level of Desire

To continue this idea of the inversion of nightmare and its capacity to foreground, and even challenge, dominant modes of positioning (with the attendant acts of conscious modification), we can now turn to another film, *The VVitch*. The strategy here is to work through some psychoanalytic concepts on anxiety and how these might be read in terms of the phenomenological *leibhaftlig* ("in person"). The cultural conceptualization and historical documentation and representations of the witch are extensive and represent far too large a collection of material to be dealt with here. Hence, the focus must remain within the film itself with some reference to additional material when necessary. Suffice to say, a study on witches from a combined psychoanalytic and phenomenological approach would yield rich rewards.

Let us commence with Jones's core psychoanalytic thesis on the phenomenon of witches: " . . . the Witch belief represents in the main as exteriorization of the repressed sexual conflicts of women, especially those relating to the feminine counterpart of the infantile Oedipus situation" (Jones 1971: 190).[26] In these terms *The VVitch*'s claustrophobic family setting (the

---

[26]Jones also cites Riklin's (1906) *Wunscherfüllung und Symbolik im Märchen* on witches as a girl's sexual competitive development with the mother. For the issues at hand here, see in

isolation of the barred and abandoned family, sent into the woods and without any form of contact with others) foregrounds the fraught relations. Katherine, the mother (Kate Dickie), and William, the father (Ralph Ineson), demonstrate a marriage on the border of collapse, with past infidelity and mistrust defining their feelings. Similarly, the five children—Thomasin (Anya Taylor-Joy), Caleb (Harvey Scrimshaw), the twins Mercy (Ellie Grainger) and Jonas (Lucas Dawson), and the baby, Samuel (Axtun Henry Dube)—develop relationships based on suspicion, paranoia, incest, and threat. The film efficiently sustains the cultural nightmare of the witch through this familial dynamic of insinuation and fear. Rather than the family unit being one of nurture and protection, the *eidos* of the nightmare is found deep within its structure and operations. It is precisely the underpinning of the sinister, the side glance of menace, that defines the family and allows for the presence of abnormality. It should be noted that this does not simply take place at the narrative level, for the film's diegetic compositions, its cinematography (shot in a 1:66:1 aspect ratio), disturbing, conflicting sounds, and bleeding, dull colors contrasted with harsh daylight are all components that create an uneasy perception.

As noted earlier, the exteriorization of repressed sexual conflicts is at the heart of this threat, taking place at the signifying level of the threat of feminine sexuality to men, but also playing out masculine fears and anxieties. The aspect of exteriorization is important here, for psychoanalysis returns to this idea often, indeed, it is one of its fundamental analytic tenets. The witch, in these terms, is the manifestation of sexual anxiety; but there is a pluralism here. Such anxieties stem from: the conflict of repressed urges becoming manifested, causing self-disgust (at the level of the Symbolic) for both men and women; the conflicts between the child and mother, and child and father because of these manifestations; fear of sexual threat, which includes the loss of sexual performance and fertility (witch narratives are dominated by the souring of milk, ruining of crops, and blighting of the land—all symbolic of sexual threat); and the threatening power of sexuality which exists outside of the power structures (in this case, the feminine to phallocentricism, beliefs outside the Church that are translated into a sexual nature, sexuality outside of heteronormativity, and so on). The exteriorization, which leads to self-loathing, demonstrates *extimacy*, and the compulsion of the return, for it is the intimate anxiety that coerces such cultural narratives, their cinematic versions, and the spectating site of pleasure. Three examples should prove insightful on these matters.

---

particular chapters VI "*Die Verlegung nach oben. Infantilismus*" and VII "*Einige besondere sexuelle Märchen-motive*" which engage with an analysis of the mother-daughter-witch dynamic via a theory of dreams.

Feminine Sexuality and Daughter-Mother Conflict

The mother-daughter conflict is manifested in *The VVitch* at numerous levels, and far beyond the literal playing out seen between Katherine and Thomasin. However, it is worth noting two scenes where we witness examples of exteriorization and the feminine Oedipal[27] conflict in their relationship: the accusation of the stolen cups; and the killing of Katherine by Thomasin. The stolen cups are exchange signifiers, standing in as a (classical) psychoanalytic trope for the vagina (just as Freud reads Dora's dream of the jewelry box). The exchange value (as well as their surplus value) is played out as Oedipal conflict, first as we learn in William's confession to Caleb that he stole the cups and traded them for supplies, and then as the contested feminine site. Katherine's questioning of Thomasin about the cups takes place in the same scene that she lays blame on the daughter for the loss of Samuel (the baby). The theft of the cups (the symbol of the mother's sexuality) becomes linked to the theft of the baby, which in turn links the daughter with the father as she "replaces" the mother. This relates to Klein's comments, in examining the interrelationships of envy and gratitude, on anxiety and fear of sexual parts of the body: "envy plays a part in the desire to take away the attributes of the other sex [this is particularly true of the relationships between all the children—Thomasin takes from Caleb, the twins take from Thomasin, Samuel is taken by the witch and so on] as well as to possess or spoil those of the parents of the same sex" (1975: 201). In these terms, the act of taking becomes a version of the possessive in the nightmare, forming the contesting sites of terror. The surplus value as surplus *jouissance* is invested in the act of taking/possessing. Similarly, the true theft of the cups by the father is confessed to the son, and so this knowledge binds the brother and sister in the Oedipal situation.[28] These Oedipal and incestuous relations are developed further when, the following day, Thomasin and Caleb go into the woods where he

---

[27] I have retained this phrase of the "feminine Oedipal" (rather than the so-called "Electra complex") in keeping with the founding principle of the complex, that is, the transitional phase as the individual, male or female, moves from the ego-centric domain to the socialized world of the Symbolic order. This eschews the more literal interpretation of the killing of the father to marry the mother.

[28] Jones deals at length on the relationship of the theft of symbolic objects as sexual processes. A key example is the horseshoe; he offers a detailed and well documented argument on the link between the horse (the "mare" of the nightmare), infantile sexuality, and mythologies. He points out, for example, that the horseshoe is the symbol of sexuality, castration, and female genitalia. Cups, like the horseshoe, are commonly given these attributes. Their shape and function (hollowed and holding fluids) are apposite symbols in these terms. In this way, the cups, and their theft, are over-determined signifiers of sexuality and power.

is taken by the witch, seduced and possessed. The repetition of the son's abduction, while in the company of Thomasin, is narratively neat in its symmetry, but its psychical dimensions are complex. Thomasin becomes the mother figure who loses her "children," which is the playing out of the feminine Oedipal conflict of the mother and daughter. This is further reinforced, psychoanalytically speaking, in reading this as a version of *fort/da*, notably as this aligns with negotiations of pleasure and anxiety, power, and refusal. Even though Freud attributes such negotiations particularly to our childhood, there is a sense that we retain this playing out and its attachment to pleasure and power: "children repeat unpleasurable experiences . . . [so] they can master a powerful impression far more thoroughly by being active than they could by merely experiencing it passively" (*SE XVIII*: 33). This is what we witness in the children's acts and inter-familial manipulations.

The second example of the mother-daughter conflict is the killing of the mother by Thomasin which takes place toward the end of the film. This act becomes the culminating moment in the Oedipal conflict, for it is after this that Thomasin "speaks" with the devil figure of Black Phillip and enters the woods. However, this seems too literal a reading of the scene and more might be extracted if we note Jones's comment on the mother in witch narratives: "The Witch idea is an exteriorization of a woman's unconscious thoughts about herself and her mother, and this is one of the reasons why Witches were for the most part either very old and ugly or very young and beautiful. As was pointed out . . . fornication with the Devil represents an unconscious incestuous phantasy" (1971: 232). In these terms we note the following: the witch in the woods appears to Caleb as young and beautiful and then old and wizened; Katherine appears maternal and nurturing and then corporeally disturbed and disturbing (e.g., the crows at her breast); the killing of the family (proceeding through the males and finally the mother until only Thomasin is left), allows for the reiterated incestuous phantasies, including Caleb's attraction to his sister and then the witch in the woods, which becomes a condensation of both his mother and sister (which further aligns the mother-sister psychical position); and Thomasin's removal of the mother (initially symbolically through the taking of her cups and then quite literally in her death) to free herself for the father figure of Black Phillip. In Kleinian terms, this must also include persecutory anxiety. Here we read the process as follows: the bad object of breast/witch, which lacks gratification, is "negotiated" through the persecutory anxiety played out by the infant; because "the fear of the object's greed, owing to projection, is an essential element in persecutory anxiety" (1975: 64), the good object of breast/mother requires gratification to alleviate anxiety and fear. In *The VVitch* (and this is a common trope throughout many cultural narratives), the feared "greedy object" is the witch, and Thomasin is a liquification of the flesh (i.e., transitional, fluid, and subject to alteration and instability) of the Kleinian good/bad object, splitting and holding at the same time.[29] Klein continues this line when she analyzes the splitting off of terrifying (often persecutory) and idealized figures in the unconscious (see, e.g., Klein's "The Development of Mental Functions" and "Some Reflections on *The Oresteia*").

Hysteria as Resistance; Flight as Sexual Act and Surplus Jouissance

This exteriorization (of the mother-daughter conflict, and of sexual phantasy often at the incestual level) align with the extensively developed interpretations of the witch and hysteria; this, in turn, links to masculine anxieties of the female body, notably menstruation in this case. What can also be noted in passing is how this interweaving of anxieties and the othered (for men) body is a playing out of different orders of intimacy. That is, a version of intimacy which is premised on a double *epoché* which is intimate for the feminine and othered for the masculine. In these terms we can propose a related, yet alternative, reading of the earlier discussion on menstrual anxieties and masculinity can be found in the history of women's nightmare and the recurring, deeply embedded, connection to menstruation,[30]

---

[29]Beyond the scope of the present discussion, consider how Thomasin presents the site of hallucination and persecution in these terms: " . . . in hallucination the persecuting breast is kept widely apart from the ideal breast, and the experience of being frustrated from the experience of being gratified. It seems that such a cleavage, which amounts to a splitting of the object and the feelings towards it, is linked with the process of denial" (Klein 1975:65). The annihilation that Klein goes on to speak of as a result of this denial is literally manifested in the film's conclusion. The liquification of the witch's body can be related to the sexual fluidity. Klein, in one dream analysis, defines the fear of the witch on a broomstick as representing the "dread of the mother with the penis" (1975: 316). Such a reading of the broomstick certainly aligns with the historical records cited and analyzed by Jones.

[30]This is a rich history, in which we see details of long histories of linking nightmares to menstruation and seminal discharges, but two examples will serve here. John Bond *An Essay on the Incubus, or Nightmare* 1753, is based entirely on the primal relationship of blood to the nightmare. He speaks of the restrictive flow of blood to the brain as one such cause. He devotes an entire section to the relationship of menstruation to nightmares, citing case studies as "evidence." We should not be too surprised how he is oblivious to the self-evident sexual nature of the first case study, which describes a fifteen-year-old girl who has a nightmare about "some great heavy Man came to her bedside, and, without farther ceremony, stretched himself upon her" (Bond 1753: 46); her groaning woke her father. (Or perhaps Bond was aware and allowed analytic repression to take hold?)

J. Dalassus *Les incubes et les succubes* (1897) reflects closer attitudes to the emerging psychoanalytic interpretations, although his work is somewhat of a pretense to prove the existence of witches and the supernatural, given that he was convinced that the supernatural exists, "proven" by "men of immense scientific talent." In terms of sexual acts and menstruation, he speaks of sexual ecstasy and religious mysticism (a line evident in *The Witch*): "L'extase religieuse présente, en effet, de très grands rapports avec les jouissances physiques de l'amour.

just as has witchcraft and hysteria. The conflictual Oedipal drama played out in *The VVitch* is foreshadowed in Thomasin's physical transition: as we are told in the film "She hath begat the sign of her womanhood." For psychoanalysis, the larger cultural narratives of the witch, as with so much of the phenomenon of the nightmare, is a psychical playing out of internalized anxiety in an attempt to alleviate self-disgust embedded in repressed wishes and desires. The further tension, as has been noted earlier, is the surplus *jouissance* of the feminine within phallocentric societies. There is no space for alternative desires and wants, and so they are condemned to a double anxiety and a double *extimacy*. This doubling is the originary anxieties and intimacies (of the internalized self), followed by a secondary order when they are exteriorized as (often disguised) anxieties and *extimacies*.

This crucial (psychoanalytically speaking) attribute of the nightmare, the aporiastic nature of repulsion and desire, the internal-made manifest, and inciting *extimacy*, this crisis in the subject who confronts their troubled and troubling inner thoughts and passions through the nightmare, is also where resistance takes place. In *The VVitch* we watch these conflictual positions resolve into the final scene of the naked and smiling Thomasin joins a group of flying witches in the woods, ostensibly liberated from the aporiastic moralities of the family drama. It is an ending that at least one level runs counter to the usual nightmarish quality of tortuous returns, invested in vengeful acts and retribution. It would seem that Thomasin's *extimacy* has been reimagined as intimacy, anxiety has been absolved, and the extremes of attraction and repulsion (of repressed desires manifested in signifiers of the same order) successfully negotiated. Thomasin becomes her own surplus *jouissance* and hysteria converted to a resistance not toward the self, but the (feminine) Oedipal conflict. Does this mean that Thomasin's negotiations of the nightmare's aporia necessarily include familicide? And if this is the case, then does this present us with a different order of the nightmare? Jones's summation of the nightmare is relevant here: " . . . an *Angst* attack, that is essentially due to an intense mental conflict centering around a repressed component of the psycho-sexual instinct, essentially concerned with incest" (1971: 54). In these terms, Thomasin and the Older Daughter (played by Angeliki Papoulia), in *Dogtooth* share similar trajectories of escape through (the hysteric's) resistance, anxiety, and incestuous family entrapments. Similarly, the three women in *The*

A l'époque de la puberté, au moment de l'éveil sexuel, très souvent se produisent des extases religieuses accompagnées de délires érotico-mystiques." For Dalassus, the link between menstrual blood and witches produces strange semi-fluid creatures that exist entirely for sexual acts; "En effet, le sang menstruel, de même que le sperme et tous les liquides sécrétés par les organes générateurs, abonde en forces vitales non employées qui s'extériorisent et cherchent à se fixer, à s'utiliser. Ce sont de véritables larves dont les forces astrales s'emparent, s'enveloppent comme d'un corps dont elles sont l'esprit. Ce qui produit des entités étranges, semi-matérielles, semi-fluidiques, qui n'ont d'autre but que la satisfaction des désirs sexuels épars dans toute la nature."

Favourite play out a version of these incestuous entrapments, imprisoning themselves and one another precisely through the politics of sexual surplus. In all these cases we witness different iterations of flesh as surplus *jouissance*, and so it is perhaps no coincidence that they are all female.

So far this has been a psychoanalytically driven reading of *The VVitch*; let us now attempt to read this final scene, and the idea of resistance, in terms of a phenomenological interpretation—one which is based on rather than distinctive from the readings so far. As has been done throughout, this is an interpretative gesture toward the film as well as a reflection on the analytic interplays between psychoanalysis and phenomenology, drawing cinema into the analytic experience. The phenomenological approach comes from the idea of *leibhaft/ig*, literally "bodily" or "personified," but for Husserl carrying the sense of actually being there, presented in person (see, e.g., "On the Theory of Intuitions and their Modes," 1918), and "actuality."[31]

As has been noted earlier (see Chapters 1 and 2), the strategy posited throughout is that there is an othered (at least) layering of consciousness when we watch a film. There is the intentionality of consciousness as we, the spectator, intuit the phantasy that is a film; there is also the intentionality of consciousness *within* the film itself. That is, the spectator, often and usually without awareness, observes the (phenomenologically defined) acts of intuition, *cogitationes* (acts of consciousness), intentionality, and so on, within the film. This is akin to Husserl's notion of the double Ego, but different inasmuch as the film spectator's doubled Ego (the Ego in phantasy consciousness) is not the same as the filmic constructions of it. As also noted earlier (particularly in terms of empathy and primordiality), it is best to avoid seeing the film's Ego positing as directly aligning with a character or even group of characters. This is the platform which enables a link between a psychoanalytic and a phenomenological reading of the nightmare.

Thomasin ascends with the other witches, symbolizing her resolution of the *extimacies* of the feminine Oedipal conflict, the persecutory splitting of good and bad objects, and the aporiastic tensions. Her Real has trampled laws underfoot, to paraphrase Lacan; and in doing so she has apparently somehow managed the impossibility of squaring the surplus value of *jouissance* and paying the debt (as Lacan puts it, all *jouissance* incurs a debt to the Law—see *Seminar VII The Ethics of Psychoanalysis*, particularly the section "The Death of God"). How this is achieved is through Thomasin's enacting her surplus *jouissance* as counter to the Law, and in doing so she escapes the demands of the superego which, in the submission to the moral

---

[31] Also see Husserl's increasing emphasis in the *Nachlass* volumes on language (Hua XX/1 and Hua XX/2) where *anschaulich, Anschaulichkeit* (vivid picturability) and *lebendige Vorstellbarkeit* (vivid imaginability) loom large. (XX/1: 3, 4n3, 31, 38f., 41, 44, 105, 231f.; XX/2: 2f., 7, 143, 151, 191, 298). I am grateful to Horst Ruthrof's suggestion on this point.

law "grows increasingly meticulous and increasingly cruel" (Lacan 1992: 176). This is the psychoanalytic reading of her transformation. Consider now how Husserl explicates actuality as a presence and as a marginality. Our conscious experience has an apprehension directed by explicit awareness (*Gewahren*), to become aware of, (1931: §35), as distinct from all that lies on the periphery, on the margins. Hence, "every perception of a thing has such a zone of *background intuitions* (or background awarenesses), if 'intuiting' already includes the state of being turned towards" (1931: §35). During the phantasy (image consciousness) experience of the film our judgments, sense-making processes, and intuitions have been directed accordingly. These are the qualifiers of "as if" and "quasi" that enable us to experience the film as phantasy without conflict with the actual.

However, how might we interpret this phenomenological experience with the psychoanalytic reading of the film's ending? One of the ways this takes place, as has been articulated throughout this exploration, is to see the film-world itself as a field of intuition, with directed and redirected (and even misdirected as misrecognition) acts of consciousness operating within the film. In this way the spectator observes and engages with the acts of consciousness (and their intentionalities) given up to them. This "given up" (see Husserl 2005: notably 599–625) relates to *leibhaft*, for the construction of the field of intuition is derived from this positionality. In phantasy this is a quasi-*leibhaft* for there is "no person/body" there. As Thomasin rises and flies with the witches it is her airborne body, the fleshed (surplus) version of subjectivity, that becomes the directed perception, that is, the intuiting, sense-making intentionality. Throughout the film the *cogitatum*—the "something perceived" (Husserl 2005: §35))—has placed Thomasin's status in a conflictual place of background intuitions and what Husserl calls marginal actualities. The soaring, floating body of Thomasin is a redirection of the movement from marginal actualities to directed ones. In such a context it is noteworthy that Husserl distinguishes between the two modes as wakeful actuality (*Aktualität*) and dormant actuality (*Inaktualität*); which can be read as Thomasin's sense-making intentionalities as she exists between (wakeful) daughter and (dormant) witch. This is also what we witness with the mermaids in *The Lure* and the daughter in *Dogtooth*. It is perhaps no coincidence that all three films present women requiring sense-making intentionalities to recognize and disrupt their marginal actualities. Combining this with the psychoanalytic reading reveals a synergistic potential; the "what lies beneath" of the sexual conflicts and repressed wishes and desires can be seen to occupy the dormant (sleeping) actuality, whereas the processes of the family and its struggles, confusions, and internal tensions have occupied the wakeful (denial or negation) actualities. This capacity for a (phenomenologically defined) directed consciousness (actuality) to be one of (psychoanalytically defined) denial/negation is one of the most complex issues we face in bringing the analytic experience to some sort of common point.

BIBLIOGRAPHY

Bakhtin, Mikhail. *Rabelais and His World*. Bloomington: Indiana University Press, 1984 (trans. Hélène Iswolsky).
Bateson, Gregory. *Steps to an Ecology of Mind*. Chicago: University of Chicago Press, 1969.
Bateson, Gregory. *Steps to an Ecology of Mind: Collected Essays in Anthropology, Psychiatry, Evolution, and Epistemology*. Chicago: University of Chicago Press, 1980.
Bollas, Christopher. *Catch Them Before They Fall: The Psychoanalysis of Breakdown*. London: Routledge, 2013.
Bond, John. *An Essay on the Incubus Nightmare*. London: Plato's Head, 1753.
Burke, Edmund. *A Philosophical Enquiry Into the Origin of Our Ideas of the Sublime and Beautiful*. Oxford: Oxford University Press, 1991.
Cixous, Hélène. "The Laugh of the Medusa." *Signs*, 1 (1976): 845–93.
Davis, Whitney. *Drawing the Dream of the Wolves: Homosexuality, Interpretation, and Freud's "Wolf Man"*. Bloomington: Indiana University Press, 1996.
Derrida, Jacques. *Of Grammatology*. Baltimore: Johns Hopkins University Press, 1976 (trans. G. C. Spivak).
Dostoevsky, Fyodor. *The Brothers Karamazov*. London: Penguin 2009 (trans. Richard Pevear and Larissa Volokhonsky).
Douglas, Mary. *Purity and Danger: An Analysis of the Concepts of Pollution and Taboo*. London: Routledge, 1966.
Du Bois, W. E. B. *The Souls of Black Folk*. New York: Penguin, 1903.
Dufrenne, Mikel. *Notion of the A Priori, The*. Evanston: Northwestern University Press, 1966 (trans. Edward S. Casey).
Dufrenne, Mikel. *The Phenomenology of the Aesthetic Experience*. Evanston: Northwestern University Press, 1973 (trans. Edward S. Casey).
Foucault, Michel. *History of Madness*. London: Routledge, 2009 (trans. Jean Khalfa).
Freud, Sigmund. *An Autobiographical Study, Inhibitions, Symptoms, and Anxiety, Lay Analysis, and Other Works SE Vol. XX*. London: Hogarth Press, 2001 (trans. James Strachey).
Freud, Sigmund. *An Infantile Neurosis and Other Works SE Vol. XVII*. London: Hogarth Press, 2001 (trans. James Strachey).
Freud, Sigmund. *Beyond the Pleasure Principle, Group Psychology and Other Works SE Vol. XVIII*. London: Hogarth Press, 2001 (trans. James Strachey).
Freud, Sigmund. *Case of Hysteria, Three Essays on Sexuality and Other Works SE Vol. VII*. London: Hogarth Press, 2001 (trans. James Strachey).

Freud, Sigmund. *Case History of Schreber, Papers on Technique and Other Works SE Vol. XII.* London: Hogarth Press, 2001 (trans. James Strachey).
Freud, Sigmund. *Ego and the Id and Other Works SE Vol. XIX.* London: Hogarth Press, 2001 (trans. James Strachey).
Freud, Sigmund. *Interpretation of Dreams, The SE Vol. IV, V.* London: Hogarth Press, 2001 (trans. James Strachey).
Freud, Sigmund. *New Introductory Lectures SE Vol. XXII.* London: Hogarth Press, 2001 (trans. James Strachey).
Freud, Sigmund. *Pre-Psychoanalytic Publications and Unpublished Drafts SE Vol. I.* London: Hogarth Press, 2001 (trans. James Strachey).
Freud, Sigmund. *Two Case Histories: 'Little Hans' and the 'Rat Man' SE Vol. X.* London: Hogarth Press, 2001 (trans. James Strachey).
Fuery, Patrick. *Madness and Cinema: Psychoanalysis, Spectatorship, and Culture.* London: Macmillan, 2004.
Gasché, Rudolphe. *The Idea of Form: Rethinking Kant's Aesthetics.* Stanford: Stanford University Press, 2002.
Husserl, Edmund. *Cartesian Meditations: An Introduction to Phenomenology.* The Hague: Martinus Nijhoff, 1970 (trans. Dorion Cairns).
Husserl, Edmund. *Crisis of European Sciences and Transcendental Phenomenology.* Evanston: Northwestern University Press, 1997 (trans. David Carr).
Husserl, Edmund. *Die Idee der Phänomenologie: Fünf Vorlesungen.* Den Haag: Martinus Nijhoff, 1950.
Husserl, Edmund. *Ideas: General Introduction to Pure Phenomenology.* London and New York: Allen and Unwin, 1931 (trans. W. R. Boyce Gibson).
Husserl, Edmund. *Ideen zu einer reinen Phänomenologie und phänomenologischen Philosophie I: Allgemeine Einführung in die reine Phänomenologie,* 2nd ed. Den Haag: Martinus Nijhoff, 1950.
Husserl, Edmund. *Die Lebenswelt: Auslegungen der vorgegebenen Welt und ihre Konstitution,* ed. R. Sowa, Dordrecht: Springer, 2008.
Husserl, Edmund. *Logical Investigations vol. 1.* New York: Routledge, 2000 (trans. J. N. Findlay).
Husserl, Edmund. *Logische Untersuchungen Ergänzungsband Erster Teil: Entwürfe zur Umarbeitung der VI. Untersuchung der 'Logischen Untersuchungen',* ed. U. Melle. Dordrecht: Kluwer, 2002.
Husserl, Edmund. *Phantasie, Bildbewusstsein, Erinnerung: Zur Phänomenologie der anschaulichen Vergegenwärtigungen.* Den Haag: Martinus Nijhoff, 1980.
Husserl, Edmund. *Phantasy, Image Consciousness, and Memory (1898-1925).* Dordrecht: Springer, 2005 (trans. John Brough).
Husserl, Edmund. *Phenomenology of Internal Time Consciousness, The.* Bloomington: Indiana University Press, 1973 (trans. James Churchill).
Husserl, Edmund. *Thing and Space (Dingsvorlesung): Lectures of 1907.* Dordrecht: Kluwer, 1998 (trans. Richard Rojcewicz).
Ingarden, Roman. *Cognition of the Literary Work of Art.* Evanston: Northwestern University Press, 1973b (trans. David Carr).
Ingarden, Roman. *The Literary Work of Art.* Evanston: Northwestern University Press, 1973a (trans. David Carr).
Jones, Ernst. *On the Nightmare.* New York: Liveright, 1971.
Kant. *Critique of Judgement.* New York: Hafner, 1951 (trans. J. H. Bernard).

Kant. *Observations on the Feeling of the Beautiful and Sublime*. Berkeley: University of California Press, 1960 (trans. John Goldthwait).
Kierkegaard, Søren. *The Concept of Anxiety: A Simple Psychologically Orientated Deliberation in View of the Dogmatic Problem of Hereditary Sin*. New York: Liveright, 2015 (trans. Alistair Hannay).
Kierkegaard, Søren. *Fear and Trembling; Repetition*. Princeton: Princeton University Press, 1983 (trans. Howard V. Hong and Edna H. Hong).
Klein, Melanie. *Envy and Gratitude, and Other Works, 1946–1963*. London: Vintage, 1975.
Klein, Melanie. *Love, Guilt and Reparation and Other Essays*. London: Vintage, 1988.
Kristeva, Julia. *Powers of Horror: An Essay in Abjection*. New York: Columbia University Press, 1982 (trans. L. Roudiez).
Kristeva, Julia. *Revolution in Poetic Language*. New York: Columbia University Press, 1984 (trans. M. Waller).
Lacan, Jacques. *Anxiety*. Cambridge: Polity, 2017 (trans. A. R. Price).
Lacan, Jacques. *Écrits*. New York: W.W. Norton, 2006 (trans. Bruce Fink).
Lacan, Jacques. *Ego in Freud's Theory and in the Technique of Psychoanalysis, The*. Cambridge: Cambridge University Press, 1988b (trans. S. Tomaselli).
Lacan, Jacques. *Encore*. Paris: Seuil, 1975.
Lacan, Jacques. *Ethics of Psychoanalysis, The*. London: Routledge/Tavistock, 1992 (trans. Dennis Porter).
Lacan, Jacques. *Freud's Papers on Technique*. Cambridge: Cambridge University Press, 1988a (trans. J. Forrester).
Lacan, Jacques. *Formations of the Unconscious*. Cambridge: Polity, 2017 (trans. Russell Grigg).
Lacan, Jacques. *Four Fundamental Concepts of Psychoanalysis, The*. Middlesex: Penguin, 1986 (trans. A Sheridan).
Lacan, Jacques. *Le Séminaire. Livre XVIII D'un discours qui ne serait pas du semblant*. Paris: Seuil, 2009.
Lacan, Jacques. *L'envers de la psychanalyse*. Paris: Seuil, 1991.
Lacan, Jacques. *On Feminine Sexuality: The Limits of Love and Knowledge*. New York: W.W. Norton, 1988 (trans. Bruce Fink).
Lacan, Jacques. *On the Names -of-the-Father*. Cambridge: Polity, 2013 (trans. Bruce Fink).
Lacan, Jacques. *Other Side of Psychoanalysis, The*. New York: W.W. Norton, 2017 (trans. Bruce Fink).
Lacan, Jacques. *... Or Worse*. Cambridge: Polity, 2018 (trans. A. R. Price).
Lacan, Jacques. *Psychoses, The*. London: Routledge,1993 (trans. R. Grigg).
Lacan, Jacques. *Quatre Concepts Fondamentaux De La Psychanalyse*. Paris: Seuil, 1973.
Lacan, Jacques. *Sinthome, The*. Cambridge: Polity, 2016 (trans. A. R. Price).
Lacan, Jacques. *Transference*. Cambridge: Polity, 2015 (trans. Bruce Fink).
Lefort, Rosine *Birth of the Other*. Urbana: University of Illinois Press, 1994 (trans. Marc du Ry, Lindsay Watson, and Leonardo Rodríguez).
Lefort, Rosine and Robert Lefort. *Les Structures de la psychose: L'Enfant au loup et le Président* Paris: Seuil, 1988.
Malcolm, Norman. *Dreaming*. London: Routledge, 1962.

Merleau-Ponty, Maurice. *Phenomenology of Perception*. London: Routledge,1962 (trans. Colin Smith).

Merleau-Ponty, Maurice. *Visible and the Invisible*. Evanston: Northwestern University Press, 1968 (trans. Alphonso Lingis).

Rank, Otto. *The Trauma of Birth*. Abingdon: Routledge, Trench and Trubner, 1929.

Riviere, Joan. "Womanliness as Masquerade." In *Female Sexuality: The Early Psychoanalytic Controversies*, edited by Russell Grigg, Dominique Hecq, and Craig Smith, 172–82. London: Routledge, 1999.

Ruthrof, Horst. *Husserl's Phenomenology of Natural Language: Intersubjectivity and Communality in the Nachlass*. London: Bloomsbury, 2021.

Ruthrof, Horst. "A Translation Problem: The Thing-at-Itself in Light of Kant's Pragmatism." *Analysis and Metaphysics*, 12 (2013): 47–67.

Sobchack, Vivian. *Carnal Thoughts: Embodiment and Moving Image Culture*. Berkeley: University of California Press, 2004.

Sobchack, Vivian. *The Address of the Eye: A Phenomenology of Film Experience*. Princeton: Princeton University Press, 1992.

Stein, Edith. *On the Problem of Empathy*. Washington, DC: ICS Publications, 1989 (trans. Waltraut Stein).

INDEX

ablaufenden 96, 96 n.32
Ablaufsphänomene 79, 96–8
abnormalities 14–15, 183–98
Abschattung ist Erlebenis 106, 144
abyss 168–71, 174, 185
Achtsamkeit 38, 44
afterwardness (*Nachträglichkeit*)
  model 72–3, 99–100
Ambassadors, The (Holbein's
  painting) 156–7
analytic experience 5–7, 20–1; *see
  also* experiences
  ego 6–7, 30–45
  psychoanalysis (*see* psychoanalysis)
  unconscious in 12–13, 26
anamorphic stain 13
Antonioni, Michelangelo 119–20
anxieties 205–33, 205 n.8
  cinematic 2–18 (*see also* cinemas)
  cinematic ego and 5, 7, 30–45
  desire and 16–17, 41, 53, 134,
    140, 156–7, 199–233
  epoché and 10, 20, 26, 104–6,
    112–13
  film spectator and 5–7
  flesh with 3–4
  innocence and 5, 19–22, 24, 27–8,
    33, 121, 185
  intimate 3–5
  nightmares as dreams 205–33,
    205 n.8
  Nothing to 5–6, 19–24
  of/as past and future 75–93
  othered consciousness and 5–6,
    20–30
  of reflexivity 24
  spaces of 103–34
  temporal 8, 69–71

wild flesh and 13–15, 167–78
apperceptions 14–15, 31–2, 35,
  38, 66, 103, 180, 183, 185–7,
  193
apprehension 150, 150 n.18
appresentations 180–3
a priori 123, 125–6
Arnolfini Portrait 156 n.23
associations 82
Auffassungsform 150
Aufhebung 147
auteurism 76
Autre 139, 139 n.5

Badlands 145
Barthes, Roland 204, 204 n.6
Bates, Norman 119
belief 206, 209–12
Bergman, Ingmar 125–6
Bickle, Travis 195
Binoche, Juliette 120 n.19, 121
Birth of a Nation (Griffith) 17, 186
Birth of the Other, The (Lefort) 175
BlacKkKlansman (Lee) 17, 211, 215,
  217–18
bloss (mere/merely) 164 n.31
Blow-Up (Antonioni) 119–20
body 4
  Coré's 190, 194
  ego and 34–5, 37–8
  as erotic object-choice 35–45
  and motility, relationship of 174–5
  sensual 178–82
  to spatiality, relationship of 174–5
  and world 169–70
body-as-flesh 176, 181, 186, 193–4

Cartesian ego 30, 32

Cartesian Meditations (Husserl)   14, 26, 42, 76, 179, 181 n.15, 192
Casebier, Alan   3
case studies   14, 21–2, 122, 170–3, 176–8, 219
Celine and Julie Go Boating   182
chiasm   14, 168, 170–1
cinemas   1–2, 5
   as cultural object   15
   enduring objects of   8, 73–93
   fluidity of time and   8
   identificatory appresentations   14
   now-point in   8–9, 67–91, 96–9, 163–4
   and over-thereness   14–15
   phantasms, sensual   135–66
   positionality   14–15
   presentifications   9–10, 93–101
   spaces   103–34
   spatiality   10–11, 103–34
   things   10–12, 107
cinematic manifestations   15–16
cinematic spectators   5–7; *see also* spectators
cogitare   30
cogitatio   32–4, 40–2, 104–6, 117, 190, 232
cogitationes   10–11, 104–5, 117, 232
coherency   31–4
coin   177–9
composing Nothings   6–7, 9–10, 28, 62, 74, 83, 91, 104, 149–50, 157, 175
condensation   93–101
con-primordiality   15, 193
consciousness   105, 110, 137, 151–2
   modifications, enthymematic   47–8, 54–6
   phenomenology's analysis of   49
   re-presentations   202
   reproductive   69, 95
   as *Sinngebende*   197, 202
   and time   58–60
   value   137–8
continuity   69, 72–6, 78, 183–5, 203
corporeal image   51

corps propre   168, 168 n.2
Crisis of European Sciences and Transcendental Phenomenology, The (Husserl)   26, 34, 136, 143–4, 143 n.9, 168
Cuarón, Alfonso   11, 120

das Ding   10–11, 107–11, 114–19, 131–4
Denis, Claire   11, 15, 120–1, 186–7
desire   16–17, 41, 53, 140, 156–7
   and anxiety   15, 134
   internal *vs.* external   61–2
   as interpretative   16
   for intimacy   90–1
   to know   134
   nightmare as form of   16, 199–233
   psychoanalysis *vs.* phenomenology   16
   to reality   73
dinglichkeit (thinghood)   106 n.6
Dingvorlesung (Husserl)   25
disturbance   13–14, 167–84
Dogtooth (Lanthimos)   12, 130–4, 130 n.26, 153 n.20, 233
Don't Look Now (Roeg)   9, 59, 93–101, 93 n.28
Do the Right Thing   182
double ego   7, 17, 28, 44, 44 n.25, 55–6, 218–26
double *intentio*   39–40
double Nothing   22
Douglas, Mary   104–5
"Dream of the Botanical Monograph"   94
dreams   6, 24, 68, 94, 151–2, 177–80, 203
Dufrenne, Mikel   2, 123–4

Eco, Umberto   204, 204 n.6
Ego and the Id, The (Freud)   30–1, 208–9
ego-consciousness   37, 53, 53 n.32
ego/egocentrism   5, 7, 21
   as apodictic   31–4
   and body/flesh   34–5, 37–8
   Cartesian   30, 32
   as coherency   31–4

INDEX

dependent/independent, relationship to 43
double 7, 17, 28, 44, 44 n.25, 55–6, 218–26
  as doxic positions 48
  Freudian/psychoanalytic version 30–45
  Husserlian/phenomenological sense 30–45
  in-difference 46–7
  internal and external, relationship to 41
  and intimacy 32–3
  libido 38
  memory's status and 46
  modifications 42–4
  and narcissism 47–8
  originaliter 184
  picture 55–6
  position 55–6
  reflexivity 41
  self and other, relationship to 41
  series of 43–7
  spectator and 30–45
  splitting of 27
empathy 15, 32–3, 195
enduring objects of cinemas 8, 73–93
enthymemes 45–56
  cinema's "system" of 47–56
  Husserl on 45–56
  lacunae and/as consciousness modifications 47–8, 54–6
  phantasy and reality, relationship between 45–56
epoché 10, 20, 26, 104–6, 112–13, 143, 145, 190–1
etymology 168, 207
experience-fringes 109–10
experiences 27, 41–2, 74, 168, 170, 175, 177, 200
externality of things 10
extimacy 192, 210

falsely false 125–7
fantasy 146 n.12
Favourite, The (Lanthimos) 153–9, 153 n.20, 161–2
feminine sexuality 228–30

film 2–4, 3 n.5; *see also* cinemas
  phenomenology 2–3
  psychoanalysis 2–3
Film and Phenomenology (Casebier) 3
film-to-concept approach 5
Fink, Eugen 136
flesh/fleshification, cinematic 2–4, 3 n.4
  ego and 34–5, 37–8
  liquification of 218–26
  and spaces 104
  in spatiality 10, 103–34
  thingness-*das Ding* and 10–11, 107–11, 114–19, 131–4
  in time 93–101
  wildness and 13–15, 167–78
flight as sexual act 230–3
flowing *vs.* fixing 80
Ford, John 120
forfeiture 11
Four Fundamental Concepts of Psychoanalysis, The (Lacan) 34
Freud, Sigmund 2, 5, 7–8, 23 n.7, 64 n.6, 205
  on cinematic ego 30–45
  das Ding 10–11, 107–11, 114–19, 131–4
  dream, model of 6, 9
  Ego and the Id, The 30–1, 208–9
  Einschränkung 125
  Inhibitions, Symptoms and Anxiety 22–3, 31–2
  Interpretation of Dreams, The 9, 59–60, 62–4, 71, 81–2, 93–4
  narcissism, conceptualization of 50, 50 n.29, 53
  now, model of 59–73
  psychoanalysis 2, 21–4
  regression 65–6, 71, 191, 200
  time, model of 59–73
  Wolf Man case study 14, 170–8
fringe-experiences 109–10

Gegenwärtigung (presentation/perception) *vs.* *Vergegenwärtigung* (re-presentation) 16, 201, 209

Geltungsfundierungen 12, 136, 143
Get Out (Peele) 17, 211, 215, 217
Gewahren 6–7, 26, 28, 41, 63, 146
givenness 15
Gravity (Cuarón) 11, 114–17
Griffith, D. W. 17, 186

hallucinations 24 n.24, 53, 61–2, 151
High Life (Denis) 11, 120–2
High Noon (Zinnemann) 75–6
Hitchcock, Alfred 59, 75–6, 119–20
Husserl, Edmund 2, 5, 7–8, 85 n.25, 136, 196 n.29
  Abschattung ist Erlebenis, sense of 106
  on apprehension 150, 150 n.18
  Cartesian Meditations 14, 26, 42, 76, 179, 181 n.15, 192
  on cinematic ego 30–45
  on cinematic spaces 103–34
  cogitationes, digressive path of 10–11, 104–5, 117, 232
  Crisis of European Sciences and Transcendental Phenomenology, The 26, 34, 136, 143–4, 143 n.9, 168
  Dingvorlesung 25
  double ego, notion of 28, 44, 44 n.25
  double *intentio* 39–40
  on enthymemes 45–56
  Geltungsfundierungen, concept of 12
  identification-forming appresentations 14
  on *irreal* 12–13, 141–50
  knowledge, analytic versions of 13, 159–66
  körperlich/körper as physical vs. *Leiblich/Leib* as living body 35–7
  leibhaftigen 43
  nature, ideas on 14
  on Nothingness 24–8
  now, model of 59–73
  on perception 25–6, 25 n.9
  on phantasy 17, 45–56
  phenomenology 2, 93–101
  Phenomenology of Internal Time Consciousness, The 9
  presentifications, idea of 9
  quasi, use of 202–3, 202 n.6
  on reality 17, 111–12
  theories of representation/ representational processes 9
  Thing analysis 111–12
  Thing and Space 106 n.6
  time, model of 59–73
  truth, analytic versions of 13, 159–66
hysteria 120–2, 230–3

ideas 5
identification 180, 211
  appresentations 14, 180–1
  ego 180
  Klein's projective 14, 180, 188
  narcissistic 127
Ingarden, Roman 2, 47, 204, 204 n.6
Inhibitions, Symptoms and Anxiety (Freud) 22–3, 31–2
Innenwelt 125–7
innocence 5, 19–22, 24, 27–8, 33, 121, 185
intentionality 6, 9, 17, 37 n.22, 68–73, 112–13, 115, 117, 142–3, 169–70, 180, 193, 195, 198–200, 205–11, 214–16, 218, 220
  of aggression 180
  anxiety as 129
  vs. apprehension 39
  of consciousness 12, 27–8, 36–7, 69, 110–12, 117, 127
  das Ding and 117
  of debris 115
  ego and 39
  of flesh 113
  intimacies of 14, 29, 120
  of memory 99
  nothingness of 26
  phantasy through/within 181
  phenomenological 16, 65, 68–9, 120, 180
  quasi-judgements 71
  repression 112

INDEX

temporality within 68–71
value and 128–9
internal-as-self 10
Interpretation of Dreams, The 9, 59–60, 62–4, 71, 81–2, 93–4
inter-textuality 194, 194 n.25
intimacies 2–3
 anxieties and 2–5 (*see also* anxieties)
 anxious 3, 57
 body and 4, 93–101
 cinema 8 (*see also* cinemas)
 crisis, introjected 130–4
 defamiliarization, introjected 125–30
 familiar, projected 119–25
 familiarity, introjected 125–30
 flesh with 3–4, 93–101
 masochism, introjected 130–4
 of/as past and future 75–93
 othered consciousness and 5–6, 20–30
 othered conscious spectator 6–7, 20–30
 possessiveness as 16–17
 projected forfeiture 113–19
 (re)producing intimacy within external space 119–25
 spaces of 103–34
 struggle with 86–91
 temporal 8–9, 69–71
 and time 8–9, 57
introjection 105–6, 105 n.4
 crisis 130–4
 defamiliarization 125–30
 familiarity 125–30
 masochism 130–4
inversion 125–30
ir-real 12–13, 137, 141–50
 and composing Nothing 149
 manifestations of 147
 phantasy and 150–66
 in *Wicker Man, The* 146–50
Iser, Wolfgang 204, 204 n.6

Jones, Ernest 2, 207
jouissance 160, 175–6; *see also* surplus *jouissance*

Kessler Syndrome 114
Kierkegaard, Søren 5, 19–20, 49, 115, 117, 119, 121, 147, 176, 198
Klein, Melanie 2, 117–19
 persecutory anxiety 117
 primal process 117–18
 projective identification 180, 180 n.14
 on psycho-sexual symbolism in objects/structures of schools 147–9
 theory of good and bad object 105 n.4
knowledge 159–66
körperlich/körper vs. *eiblich/Leib* 35–7
Kowalski, Matt 116
Kristeva, Julia 2, 104–5

La Belle Noiseuse (Rivette) 186
Lacan, Jacques 2, 4 n.6, 5–6, 82–3, 96, 125–30
 anamorphic stain, idea of 13
 aphanisis, notion of 116
 on *das Ding* 10–11, 107–11, 114–19, 131–4
 extimacy, version of 38, 41
 Four Fundamental Concepts of Psychoanalysis, The 34
 Holbein's painting (*The Ambassadors*), analysis of 156–7
 knowledge, analytic versions of 13, 159–66
 on mimicry 13
 narcissism, analysis of 50–6, 127–8
 psychoanalytic secret 111–12
 real, concept of 12–13, 32, 137–41
 truth, analytic versions of 13, 159–66
Lanthimos, Yorgos 12, 130–4, 153
La où était ça, le je doit être 4
Lee, Spike 17
Lefort, Rosine 2, 173
leibhaft 201

leibhaftig 201
leibhaftigen 43
Leiblich 37–8
libido 38
Lure, The (Smoczyńska) 18, 211, 218, 220, 224–6, 233

Malcolm's theories 27 n.12
Malick, Terrence 9, 59, 74–93
masochism, introjected 130–4
mediated materiality 106
melody 81
memories 59, 71, 99, 151
Merleau-Ponty, Maurice 2–3, 14, 168–9, 170 n.6
 body to spatiality and motility, relationship of 174–5
 on *cogito* 31, 34
 experience by experience 168, 170, 175, 177, 200
 Phenomenology of Perception, The 31, 158, 169–70, 169 n.5, 184
 praktognosia (practical knowledge) 14
 Visible and the Invisible, The 14, 156, 168–9
mirror stage 139
mise-en-abyme effect 131
mother-daughter conflict 228–30

narcissism 47–8, 127–8
 double 51–3
 and ego 47–8
 Freud's conceptualization of 50, 50 n.29, 53
 Husserl's on 50–6
 Lacan analysis of 50–6
natural attitude 24–7
nature 14, 90, 168, 170 n.6, 171, 178–82
 of anxiety 19
 aporiastic 16
 in *Cartesian Meditations* 179–82
 of cinema 15, 80
 consciousness and 180
 of *das Ding* 133
 material 179–82

 of noematic (and noetic) phenomena 133
 now-point 83
 polysemic 55
 of real 142
 speculator 91
 surreptitious 19
 of things 107
 transitivity and 180
negation, things of 111–12
neutrality 210
nightmare 15–16
 as anxiety 208–9
 aporiastics 16, 200–6
 belief 209–12
 capacity 16
 as deceptive object 206–9
 definition/description 199–200
 of desires 16, 199–233
 as experience 200
 feminine sexuality and 228–30
 as intimacy 208–9
 materiality 199–200
 mirroring effect of 226–7
 mother-daughter conflict 228–30
 phallocentric 212–18
 possessiveness of 16–17
 racist 212–18
 representational repository of 200
No Country for Old Men (Coen Bros.) 14, 175, 175 n.11, 176, 181
noema 142
noesis 142
Nothing/Nothingness 5–6, 19, 146
 to anxieties 5–6, 19–24
 composing 6–7, 9–10, 28, 62, 74, 83, 91, 104, 149–50, 157, 175
 double 22
 dream as 24
 of innocence 24
 interpretative 24–6
 manifestations 21–3
 second order of 25–6
 and something 20–1
 in terms of psychoanalysis 6, 21–4
nowness 9, 57, 59–60, 66, 70–3, 86, 100

now-points 8–9, 67–91, 96–9, 163–4
nullity 206–9

objet petit a 139, 139 n.5, 160–1, 165–6, 190–2
On the Nightmare (Jones) 2, 207
originaliter Ego 184
othered consciousness 5–7, 20–30
othered conscious spectators 5–7, 20–30
over-thereness 14–15, 185
owness 178–82
    abnormalities and 183
    Ego of self as 31, 184, 186
    of environment 181–2
    as *epoché* 190–5
    objet petit a 190–5
    of race 182

paradox, phenomenological 112–13
pathological empathy 195
Patterson, Robert 120 n.19, 121
Pcpt system 65
Peele, Jordan 17
perception 25–6, 25 n.9, 61–2, 68, 71–2
Persona (Bergman) 12, 125–30
phantasies 13, 16–17, 71, 93, 93 n.29, 151, 202–3
    cinematic 153–9
    ego 211
    vs. fantasy 146 n.12
    Husserl on 17, 45–56, 200–1, 208
    and *ir-real* 150–66
    presentifications 68, 152
    purposelessness realm of 208
    and reality, relationship between 44–56, 45 n.25, 165–6
    semblance and 159–66
phenomenology 1–18
    cinemaness 86
    of consciousness 49
    on ego 5, 7, 30–45
    epoché 10, 20, 26, 104–6, 112–13
    film theory 2–3
    Freudian/Lacanian 2, 21–4 (*see also* Freud, Sigmund; Lacan, Jacques)
    Husserlian 2, 24–8, 79–80, 93–101 (*see also* Husserl, Edmund)
    nightmare of desires 15–16, 199–233
    othered consciousness 5–7, 20–30
    paradox 112–13
    and psychoanalysis 1–2, 5–7, 20–30, 199–233
    of reality 49
    things 10–11 (*see also* things/thingnes)
    time and 57–9
Phenomenology of Internal Time-Consciousness, The (PITC) 9, 58, 58 n.2, 80
Phenomenology of Perception, The (Merleau-Ponty) 31, 158, 169–70, 184
Plato's *Parmenides* 138 n.3
positionality 44–5 n.25
possessiveness 16–17
postulates 2
Powers of Horror (Kristeva) 104–5
praktognosia (practical knowledge) 14, 176
preconscious 71
presentifications 9–10, 46, 150–1
    cinemas 9–10, 71, 93–101
    condensing 93–101
    idea of 9
    imaginary 73
    memory and 71
    for *Now Don't Look Now* 93–101
    perception and 71–2
    phantasy and 68, 152
    real 73
    reflexive 71
    and representation 68
    symbolic 73
    temporal 69–71
    time-consciousness and 70
Project for a Scientific Psychology (1895) 59–65
projection 105–6, 105 n.4
    familiar 119–25
    forfeiture 113–19
Psycho 175–6

Psycho (Hitchcock) 119–20
psychoanalysis 1–18, 79–80, 190
   afterwardness (*Nachträglichkeit*),
      model of 72–3
   on anxiety (*see* anxieties)
   of association 82
   of ego 5, 7, 30–45
   etymology 207
   film theory 2–3
   Freudian/Lacanian 2, 21–4 (*see also* Freud, Sigmund; Lacan, Jacques)
   Husserlian (*see* Husserl, Edmund)
   materiality of 21
   nightmare of desires 16, 199–233
   Nothing in terms of 6–7, 21–4
   othered consciousness 5–7, 20–30
   and phenomenology 1–2, 5–7, 20–30, 199–233
   pre-analytic status in 20
   secret 111–12
   with things 10–11
   unconscious 12, 32–4, 136–7

quasi, attributes of 202–3, 202 n.6
quasi-doxic *ego* 48
quasi-experiencing 202–3, 202 n.6
quasi-intimacy 187, 194
quasi-judgements 71, 203–4
quasi-perceptions 203–4

real 12–13, 17, 32, 45–56, 203
   encounter with 140–1
   and Imaginary 137–9
   Lacan's 137–41
   in *Ou Pire* 140
   shading of 144–5
   and Symbolic 137–9
   and truth 149
reality
   of object 206
   phenomenology's analysis of 49
   principle 111–12
   Symbolic as 137–9, 141
Rear Window (Hitchcock) 59, 75–9
reflexive turn 73, 141, 170
regression 65–6, 71, 191, 200
repetition automatism 70

re-presentations (*Vergegenwärtigungen*) 16, 151–2, 201, 206
repression 21, 24, 33, 59, 72–3, 111–12, 204–6, 208–9, 214–15
reproduction 69, 95, 95 n.30
reproductive consciousness 69
res extensa 11, 113–14, 117
res materialis 11, 103–4, 113–14
retention 68
Revolution in Poetic Language (Kristeva) 139 n.4
Riefenstahl, Leni 186
Rivette, Jacques 182, 186
Roeg, Nicolas 9, 93–101
Roma (Cuarón) 11, 120, 120 n.19, 122–3, 125

satisfaction 61–2
Schein 164
Schreber, Judge 22
Searchers, The (Ford) 120
secret 111–12
self-reflection 63
semblance 151
   apprehension and 165
   consciousness and 159–66
   irreal of 161–2
   object 165
   objet petit a 160–1, 165–6
   phantasy and reality, relational contexts between 13, 159–66
   and real 159–61
   representational systems and 159–66
   sujet supposé savoir and 160
sensuous phantasms 13
sexual impulses 206–10
sexuality 120–1, 125–30
Shining, The (Kubrick) 175
sin-consciousness 117
Sinngebende 197, 202, 207
Smoczyńska, Agnieszka 18
spaces, cinematic 103–34
   crisis, introjected 130–4
   defamiliarization, introjected 125–30
   external 105–6, 111–34

familiar, projected   119–25
familiarity, introjected   125–30
and flesh   104
internal   105–6, 111–34
inversion   125–30
of marginalia   135
masochism, introjected   130–4
projected forfeiture   113–19
(re)producing intimacy within external space   119–25
unity of experience of   133
spatiality, cinematic   10–11, 104–34
spectators   3; *see also* cinemas
and cinematic ego   30–45
othered consciousness   6–7, 20–30
Stein, Edith   2, 15, 32–3
stimuli in external world   60
perception-sensation-memory, movement of   61–2
quality *vs.* quantity   60–1
relational movement of   60–1
Stone, Rosetta   1–2
Stone, Ryan   115–18
subjectivism   30, 142
sublime flesh   167, 186–97
super-ego   37–43, 52, 136, 139, 145, 177, 187; *see also* ego/ egocentrism
surplus *jouissance*   18, 160, 218–28, 230–3
syllogisms   7
synchronism   68

Taxi Driver (Scorsese)   195
temporality   8, 46, 70–1
terza rima   79–80, 79 n.16, 83, 85–7
textual systems   5
Thing and Space (Husserl)   106 n.6
thing-in-itself, Kant's   10, 106, 106 n.5
thingness-*das Ding*   10–11, 107–11, 114–19, 131–4
things/thingness   10–11
as/in space (*res materialis*)   11, 103–4, 113–14
as/in time   11, 113
cinematic modalities of   11–12, 106–7

as enduring (*res extensa*)   11, 113–14, 117
of negation   111–12
and perception   25–6, 25 n.9
phantasms of   104
Thin Red Line, The (Malick)   144–5
time   8–9, 57–9
and anxiety   8–9, 57
consciousness in relation to   58–60, 81
flesh in   93–101
Freud model of   59–73
Husserl model of   59–73
and intimacies   8–9, 57
phenomenology and   57–9
as state of consciousness   57
things as/in   11, 113
transference   180, 192–3
Tree of Life (Malick)   9, 59, 74–93, 79 n.15
Trieb   59
Triumph of the Will (Riefenstahl)   186
Trouble Every Day (Denis)   15, 120–1, 186–7, 186 n.21
truth   149, 159–66
tuché, cinematic   141

Ullmann, Liv   126
Umwelt   51, 125–30
unawareness   33–4
unconscious   12, 32–4, 136–7
union/unity   68–73, 75–6, 80, 127, 129, 211
of appearances   133
of experience   133
and relationship   51
of subject   51, 143 n.9
of time-consciousness   58

value   137–8
vergegenwärtigen (to recall)   68–9
vergegenwärtigenden (to visualize)   9, 68–9
Verneinung   174
violence   125–30
Visible and the Invisible, The (Merleau-Ponty)   14, 156, 168–9
vorschweben   152–5

Vorstellungsrepräsentanz 202, 204
VVitch: A New England Folktale, The (Eggers) 18, 211, 224, 226, 228–32

Walkabout 182
white-space 135
Wicker Man, The (Hardy) 146–50, 175
wild flesh 13–15
wildness 13–14
   and corporeal sublime 182–4
   disturbances of 13–14, 167–84
dualism 167–8
Freud's Wolf Man case
   study 170–8
   meaning 168–78
Wirklichkeit 201
Wo Es war, soll Ich werden 4
wolf cry 177–9
Wolf Man case study (Freud) 14, 170–8, 170 n.7, 173 n.10

Zinnemann, Fred 75

www.ingramcontent.com/pod-product-compliance
Lightning Source LLC
Chambersburg PA
CBHW062131300426
44115CB00012BA/1884